A Modern Guide to the Economics of Happiness

ELGAR MODERN GUIDES

Elgar Modern Guides offer a carefully curated review of a selected topic, edited or authored by a leading scholar in the field. They survey the significant trends and issues of contemporary research for both advanced students and academic researchers.

The books provide an invaluable appraisal and stimulating guide to the current research landscape, offering state-of-the-art discussions and selective overviews covering the critical matters of interest alongside recent developments. Combining incisive insight with a rigorous and thoughtful perspective on the essential issues, the books are designed to offer an inspiring introduction and unique guide to the diversity of modern debates.

Elgar Modern Guides will become an essential go-to companion for researchers and graduate students but will also prove stimulating for a wider academic audience interested in the subject matter. They will be invaluable to anyone who wants to understand as well as simply learn.

Titles in the series include:

A Modern Guide to State Intervention
Economic Policies for Growth and Sustainability
Edited by Nikolaos Karagiannis and John E. King

A Modern Guide to Citizen's Basic Income
A Multidisciplinary Approach
Malcolm Torry

A Modern Guide to Public Policy
Edited by Michael Howlett and Giliberto Capano

A Modern Guide to the Economics of Happiness
Edited by Luigino Bruni, Alessandra Smerilli and Dalila De Rosa

A Modern Guide to the Economics of Happiness

Edited by

Luigino Bruni

Professor of Political Economy, Department of Law, Economics, Politics and Modern languages, LUMSA University, Italy

Alessandra Smerilli

Professor of Economics, PFSE-Axilium University, Italy

Dalila De Rosa

Research Officer, Department of Finance, Ministry of Economics and Finance, Italy

ELGAR MODERN GUIDES

Edward Elgar
PUBLISHING

Cheltenham, UK • Northampton, MA, USA

Published by
Edward Elgar Publishing Limited
The Lypiatts
15 Lansdown Road
Cheltenham
Glos GL50 2JA
UK

Edward Elgar Publishing, Inc.
William Pratt House
9 Dewey Court
Northampton
Massachusetts 01060
USA

Paperback edition 2022

A catalogue record for this book
is available from the British Library

Library of Congress Control Number: 2020950864

This book is available electronically in the **Elgar**online
Economics subject collection
http://dx.doi.org/10.4337/9781788978767

ISBN 978 1 78897 875 0 (cased)
ISBN 978 1 78897 876 7 (eBook)
ISBN 978 1 0353 0025 9 (paperback)

Typeset by Servis Filmsetting Ltd, Stockport, Cheshire
Printed and bound by CPI Group (UK) Ltd, Croydon, CR0 4YY

Contents

v

Figures

Tables

Contributors

Leonardo Salvatore Alaimo, University of Rome La Sapienza, Italy.

Luigino Bruni, Department of Law, Economics, Politics and Modern languages, LUMSA University, Italy.

Luca Crivelli, Department of Business Economics, Health and Social Care, University of Applied Sciences and Arts of Southern Switzerland and Swiss School of Public Health, Switzerland.

Dalila De Rosa, Ministry of Economics and Finance Italy, Department of Finance, Italy.

Richard A. Easterlin, University of Southern California, United States.

Neli Esipova, Gallup, United States.

Giovanni Ferri, Department of Law, Economics, Politics and Modern languages, LUMSA University, Italy.

Bruno S. Frey, University of Basel and CREW – Center for Research in Economics and Well-Being, Switzerland.

Mario Lucchini, Department of Sociology and Social Research, University of Milan Bicocca and Department of Business Economics, Health and Social Care, University of Applied Sciences and Arts of Southern Switzerland, Italy.

Filomena Maggino, University of Rome La Sapienza, Italy.

Kelsey J. O'Connor, Luxembourg National Institute of Statistics, Luxembourg.

Anita Pugliese, Gallup, United States.

Maurizio Pugno, University of Cassino, Department of Economics and Law, Italy.

Julie Ray, Gallup, United States.

Egidio Riva, Department of Sociology and Social Research, University of Milan Bicocca, Italy.

Matteo Rizzolli, Department of Law, Economics, Politics and Modern languages, LUMSA University, Italy.

Jeffrey Sachs, Columbia University, Center for Sustainable Development, United States.

Paolo Santori, LUMSA University, Italy.

Francesco Sarracino, Luxembourg National Institute of Statistics, Luxembourg.

Alessandra Smerilli, Auxilium University and LUMSA University, Italy.

Fei Wang, School of Labor and Human Resources, Renmin University of China, China.

Shun Wang, KDI School of Public Policy and Management (Korea), Korea.

Abbreviations

ACC	anterior cingulate cortex
BES	Equitable and Sustainable Wellbeing
CA	Capabilities Approach
CAS	Complex Adaptive System
CFPS	China Family Planning Studies
CGSS	Chinese General Social Survey
CHFS	China Household Finance Survey
CHIP	China Household Income Project
CIS	Commonwealth of Independent States
EB	Eurobarometer
EFT	episodic future thinking
EQLS	European Quality of Life Survey
EVS	European Values Survey
FE	Fixed effects
GCC	Gulf Cooperation Council
GDP	Gross Domestic Product
GNI	Gross National Income
GWP	Gallup World Poll
HA	Happiness Approach
HDI	Human Development Index
ICA	International Co-operative Alliance
MAI	Migrant Acceptance Index
MDD	massive depressive disorders
NBER	National Bureau of Economic Research (United States)
NBS	National Bureau of Statistics of China
NE	Nichomachean ethics
OECD	Organisation for Economic Co-operation and Development
OLS	ordinary least squared
PAG	periaqueductal grey
PERMA	Positive emotions, Engagement, Relationships, Meaning, and Achievement
PFC	prefrontal cortex
PTSD	Post-traumatic stress disorder
PWT	Penn World Table

QoL	Quality of life
RE	Random effects
SES	Socio-economic status
SOEs	state-owned enterprises
SWB	Subjective wellbeing
TMS	*Theory of Moral Sentiments*
WB	World Bank
WDI	World Development Indicators
WVS	World Values Survey

1. Happiness and wellbeing: past foundations, modern evidence and future paths

Luigino Bruni, Dalila De Rosa and Alessandra Smerilli

The modern approach to the economics of happiness can be reconduced to the impressive work known as the 'Easterlin paradox'. At the beginning of the seventies the economist Richard Easterlin observed that, even though within each country higher incomes were associated with higher levels of happiness, in a country over time average levels of happiness do not increase as the average income increases. In other words, the very rich are happier than the very poor, but as the country gets richer happiness remains almost constant. The evidence was first proposed in his original work for the US during the period 1946–70 (Easterlin 1974) and then during the period 1972 to 2002 (Easterlin 2005) when the gross domestic product (GDP) in the United States almost doubled while happiness remained constant. In a more recent paper (Easterlin 2015) the author confirmed the validity of the paradox using US data in the period 1972–2014.

This evidence suggests that, beyond a certain income level required to meet basic needs, the so-called *subsistence level*, additional income doesn't lead to additional happiness. Individual wellbeing is made of a broader set of factors (health, relations, life sense), other than pure income, which need to be accounted for in order to define a worthwhile life. Indeed, it is worth remarking that, in a modern sense, the economics of happiness can no longer be confined to the evaluation of subjective or psychological wellbeing, but also has to encompass the whole intellectual and political movement known as going *beyond GDP* and its implications in terms of the measurement and analysis of quality of life (QoL).

In this sense, the last decades have seen growing attention to measuring what makes life worthwhile both from a subjective and an objective point of view. The awareness of the limits of GDP as a measure for wellbeing has risen, and since 2007 the debate on going beyond GDP has been placed at the frontiers of both the academic and political agenda. The Easterlin paradox, the capability approach (CA) and the Stiglitz–Sen–Fitoussi Commission, opened the door to a new perspective centered on the pursuit of people's wellbeing. Notably it implied effort on the methodological side, namely the design of appropriate and robust measures and the analysis of the determinants of wellbeing, but also effort on the philosophical side, that is the inquiry into the real meaning and the ethical borders of happiness, wellbeing and quality of life. Not least, political effort to embed such novel discussion in the political debate. Indeed, after the Stiglitz–Sen–Fitoussi Report (2009) numerous attempts and initiatives to depict quality of life arose at the national and international level: the OECD Better Life Index, Eurostat Quality of Life Indicators, Canadian Index of Well Being, Measuring Australia's Progress, measuring national wellbeing in the UK, the Italian BES (Equitable and Sustainable Wellbeing), just to mention a few. And also the current experience of the Sustainable Development Goals goes in this direction.

This is to say, despite the enormous progress this stream of research has made, the debate is still modern and the aim of this book is to guide the reader over the historical roots of the economics of happiness, the measurement issues, the political implications and the empirical applications, which have led the debate over the years and opened room for further and future improvements.

1.1 HISTORICAL AND PHILOSOPHICAL PERSPECTIVES OF THE ECONOMICS OF HAPPINESS

Economics has taken two long centuries to rid itself of the 'dismal science' label and to gain a legitimate standing in society. Finally, today, not even the most critical observers can convince us that economic variables such as income, wealth or employment are not important objectives for a good life. Who can deny the evidence that wealthier people usually enjoy better health, longer life spans, lower infant mortality rates and greater access to goods, services and education? From the enjoyment of such benefits it should take just one short step to affirm that, on average, those who possess more are happier than those who possess less.

Moreover, it is not difficult to agree with the thesis that it is very hard to be happy and live a good life under extreme poverty. On the basis of these ethical justifications, political economy, along its journey, began to investigate the means for living well. It became known as the 'science of wealth', with the 'hope that poverty and ignorance may gradually be extinguished' and 'that all should start in the world with a fair chance of leading a cultured life, free from the pains of poverty and stagnating influences of excessive mechanical toil' (Marshall 1890: 3–4).

There is no need to start our history of happiness in this introduction from Aristotle or from ancient philosophy. Modernity has a rich enough history of the concept of happiness in relation to economics. In Chapter 5, written by Luigino Bruni, one can see Malthus's ideas about happiness and his criticism to Smith. The young Malthus felt the need to analyze directly how and under which conditions riches could be transformed into happiness. This was the path followed by the Italian tradition of public happiness (Genovesi, Filangieri, Bianchini, etc.) (see Bruni and Porta 2003). For this reason, those economists devoted their intellectual efforts to analyze the dimensions of social life that directly affect happiness or wellbeing, such as trust, civic virtues and reciprocity. The 'transformation problem', wealth into welfare, was therefore their main concern as social scientists. The mainstream political economy left aside this transformation question. In the Cambridge tradition after Malthus (1798) we find both a special attention to the relation between means (wealth) and end (happiness), and the same ambiguity of Malthus due to the gap between the methodological claims and the real content of economic theory.

But it is impossible to reconstruct the evolution of the idea of happiness in economics without taking into account Utilitarianism, built around the golden rule: 'the greatest happiness for the greatest number'. In Bentham's idea of happiness we immediately see that in his system happiness is equal to 'pleasure', as it comes straight from the very first lines of *An Introduction to the Principles of Morals and Legislation*: 'Nature has placed mankind under the governance of two sovereign masters, pain and pleasure' (Bentham 1789: 11).

The Benthamite vision of happiness can therefore rightly be called psychological hedonism, having an individualistic nature; people are depicted as seekers of happiness/pleasure. This psychological feature is essential to the Utilitarian programme in which social happiness is seen only as an aggregation, a sum of individual pleasures.

J.S. Mill, who on happiness diverges deeply from Bentham and from his father, James, in his Utilitarianism explicitly states that in early Utilitarianism there was an identification between pleasure and happiness: 'By happiness is intended pleasure' (Mill 1861: 210).

The other key word of Bentham is 'utility' (from which the term 'Utilitarianism' came), and the 'principle of utility' (inherited from Beccaria's *Dei delitti e delle pene*) is stated appropriately, in the first page of his Introduction, as the 'foundation of the present work' (Bentham 1789: 11). In all his works the words happiness, pleasure and utility are used interchangeably as different ways of expressing the same basic concept of

Utilitarianism. In Chapter 1 of *An Introduction to the Principles of Morals and Legislation* he wrote that by utility he meant 'that property in any object, whereby it tends to produce benefit, advantage, pleasure, good or happiness' (Bentham 1789: 12).

With Bentham the distinction between end (happiness) and means (wealth) disappeared, and happiness/pleasure also became the direct end of economic actions. Bentham's approach to happiness, therefore, is far from either the classical vision of happiness (from Aristotle to Genovesi) and the Cambridge tradition that kept the distinction between happiness (the final end) and wealth.

Bentham's methodological project, as is well known, nurtured economics, thanks mainly to the works of Jevons and Edgeworth. Most of the leaders of the new economics based their subjectivist approach to economics on a hedonistic philosophy. In Edgeworth's early works up to *Mathematical Psychics* (Edgeworth 1881), the Utilitarian and hedonist philosophy had a great impact. To him happiness means pleasure, and maximizing happiness means maximizing pleasure (Edgeworth 1881: 7, 16).

Jevons (1871) defined economics as the science of utility, explicitly stating his acceptance of the Utilitarian philosophy of Bentham (Robbins 1998: 262). Happiness entered neoclassical economics fully identified with utility, the new subject of the new economics. Jevons not only states the old Utilitarian thesis that happiness is related to utility, but also that economics is the 'calculus of pleasures and pain' (Jevons 1871: 'Introduction'). To Jevons pleasures are different 'only in degree, not in kind' (Schabas 1990: 39). Economics deals with the 'lowest' ones and he does not exclude the fact that men can renounce pleasures coming from the economic domain for the sake of ethical or superior pleasures, but, as Bentham's, his ethical rule is to maximize the sum of pleasures, both individually and socially. In the theory he states:

> The theory which follows is entirely based on a calculus of pleasure and pain and the object of economics is to maximize happiness by purchasing pleasure as it were, at the lowest cost of pain. (Jevons 1871: 91)

For British marginalist economists, economics became the science of the direct analysis of happiness/pleasure. The domain of economics was no longer 'wealth' but happiness/pleasure directly. While the classical economists were dealing with objective, external aspects ('material prerequisites'), with Jevons or Edgeworth economics came back to a 'subjective' approach, the domain of economics is inside man's mind.

Contemporary rational choice theory (based on the preference-satisfaction approach) is, from a methodological point of view, a continuation of the Benthamite approach: 'The analysis assumes that individuals maximize welfare as they conceive it' (Becker 1996: 139). Contemporary rational choice theory is far from the classical/neoclassical economists and very close to Bentham or Jevons (more than they thought: if we consider Hicks' and Samuelson's battle against hedonism in economics in the 1930s). Why? First, like Jevons the domain of economics is 'maximizing' pleasure (preferences); second, the place of pleasure has been taken by preferences-satisfaction, but the core elements of the Utilitarian approach are still there:

1. The domain of economics is no more wealth or economic welfare (the material prerequisites) but to directly bring about happiness, which can be translated into concepts such as pleasure (old marginalists), ordinal utility or preferences (Hicks), or choices (Samuelson).
2. The tools utilized for studying the 'means' (maximization, quantitative calculus, instrumental rationality) are now used for specifically studying 'happiness'.

After Bentham happiness/pleasure became the object of economics: therefore, it is not true that happiness is not central in neoclassical economics. The reductionism of happiness/eudaimonia to utility/pleasure is the real break point in the history of happiness in economics: the distinction between material prerequisites and happiness, Cambridge's and classical political economy's cornerstone, has been lost.

Recently, however, other economists, psychologists or philosophers, such as Sen, Kahneman or Nussbaum, criticize a 'subjective' approach to the relationship of income/happiness, claiming that happiness cannot be measured on the basis of subjective evaluations. Sen and Nussbaum, in an Aristotelian approach, remind us that happiness must be translatable into the 'good life'. Then happiness has to be measured in terms of capabilities and functionings, human rights and freedom. As Sen notes:

> As Aristotle noted at the very beginning of the Nicomachean Ethics (resonating well with the conversation between Maitreyee and Yajnavalkya three thousand miles away), 'wealth is evidently not the good we are seeking; for it is merely useful and for the sake of something else'. If we have reasons to want more wealth, we have to ask: What precisely are these reasons, how do they work, on what are they contingent and what are the things we can 'do' with more wealth? In fact, we generally have excellent reasons for wanting more income or wealth. This is not because, typically, they are admirable general-purpose means for having more freedom to lead the kind of lives we have reasons to value. The usefulness of wealth lies in the things that it allows us to do – the substantive freedom it helps us to achieve. But this relation is neither exclusive (since there

are significant influences on our lives other than wealth) nor uniform (since the impact of wealth on our lives varies with other influences). It is as important to recognize the crucial role of wealth determining living conditions and the quality of life as it is to understand the qualified and contingent nature of this relationship. (Sen 2000: 14)

Sen's thought emerges like an underground (carsic) river that has been flowing for years, carrying with it the conviction that happiness is a matter of politics. It began its course with Aristotle, re-emerged to cross the Middle Ages (Thomas Aquinas) and civic humanism (fifteenth-century Tuscany), and again to irrigate the period of Enlightenment in Scotland (Smith) and Italy. In the mid-eighteenth century in Milan and Naples, men like Muratori, Genovesi, and Verri drank from it and articulated a vision of economics into a science of 'public happiness'. We do not believe that political economists must tell people how to be happy – happiness remains a subjective matter and everyone must find his or her own way – but work only to create the objective conditions for a good living, which make a happy life possible, and maybe 'complicating economics' in order to spot non-intentional mechanisms (treadmills) or externalities. And although we recognize that psychological mechanisms are operating, which tend to subjectively neutralize improvements in material conditions, economic theory can orientate policy.

1.2   METHODS FOR THE ECONOMICS OF HAPPINESS

In the spirit of policy orientation, the last decade has seen growing literature in economics, social science and development studies on the measurement of happiness, wellbeing and quality of life. Yet, even though these concepts pursue the same objective of understanding wellbeing and human development with multidisciplinary tools, they certainly differ (Bruni et al. 2008). Indeed, if on one side, subjective wellbeing refers to the self-reported status of being well and it is methodologically grounded in the well-known happiness approach (HA), on the other side, the objective evaluation of wellbeing aims at identifying those factors and statuses objectively considered to be important for a worthwhile life and it grounds in the CA.

In the context of the CA, Amartya Sen moved not few critics to subjective wellbeing. First, individuals may be driven by adaptations, adjusting their aspirations downwards or upwards to reflect respectively hardship or new opportunities (Comim et al. 2008; Clark et al. 2008). Second, since perceptions depend on individuals' position, influencing beliefs, understanding and decisions, the concept of positional objectivism cannot be overlooked (Sen 1992). Third, subjective measures may risk providing self-regarding metrics and unreliable results for inter-individual comparison (Bruni et al. 2008). According to the CA, the capability of being happy constitutes one of the most important aspects of life and there are very good reasons for valuing it. However, happiness has to be considered as one of the capabilities in the capabilities list, whereas overall quality of life has to be assessed in terms of the capability to achieve valuable functionings (Nussbaum and Sen 1993: 27) and the set of functionings needs to be normatively defined.

On the contrary, the HA critics the paternalistic spirit embedded in the CA and it affirms that the best way to assess individual wellbeing is just asking people how well they feel. Yet, the HA covers very different aspects (Samman 2007) than pure 'people asking' or individual emotional self-reporting. Indeed, there are eudemonic measures (psychological wellbeing) and hedonic measures (subjective wellbeing). The latter distinguish between the cognitive component of life satisfaction and the positive and negative affect components of happiness. These measures come from survey questions which ask, for example, 'On the whole, are you satisfied, fairly satisfied, not very satisfied or not at all satisfied with the life you lead?' or 'Taken all together, how would you say things are these days – would you say that you are very happy, pretty happy, or not too happy?' These questions are getting common in many international surveys such as the Eurobarometer Surveys, the US General Social Surveys, the World Values Surveys and the Gallup pool Surveys, just to mention some. Yet, these capture both the emotional part and the cognitive evaluation of subjective wellbeing and the stability of such measures has been widely debated in the literature. According to Frey and Stutzer (2002), the measures of subjective wellbeing/happiness, prove to be consistent and reliable and also reported subjective wellbeing is quite stable and rather sensitive to changing life circumstances (see Diener et al. 1999).

Eudemonic measures are instead grounded in positive psychology and include other aspects of a person's psychological processes. In particular, sound literature focused on the concept of good psychological functioning refer to 'flourishing' or 'eudemonic' wellbeing (Huppert 2009; Clark and Senik 2011; Ryan and Deci 2006), which goes beyond the respondent's reflective evaluation and emotional states to focus on the functioning and the realization of the person's potential. Several psychometric scales are proposed for the measurement of psychological wellbeing or in this case of 'flourishing' (see Hone et al. 2014 for a full discussion). Among these, Diener et al. (2010) created the Flourishing Scale as a summary measure of psychological functioning in a eight-item format (Purpose/meaning, Positive relationships, Engagement, Social contribution, Competence, Self-respect, Optimism, Social relationships). Similarly, Huppert and So

(2013) tested a flourishing index on a sample of 43 000 Europeans in the European Social Survey, identifying three main factors: (1) 'positive characteristics' (comprising emotional stability, vitality, optimism, resilience and self-esteem); (2) 'positive functioning' (comprising engagement, competence, meaning, and positive relationships); and (3) 'positive appraisal' (comprising life satisfaction and positive emotion).

In this eudemonic perspective, a possible overlapping of the two approaches is understandable: on one side the CA attaches great importance to issues of autonomy and agency (Sen 1985) on the other eudemonia meant as a commitment to a set of goals provides a sense of personal agency and a sense of structure and meaning to daily life (Diener et al. 1999: 284). According to Comim et al. (2008), 'eudemonic informational spaces' can provide clear guidance in terms of what both approaches can additionally offer.

From a strictly technical and methodological viewpoint, a wide range of data collection methods and statistical techniques have been used in empirical applications to assess wellbeing in the sense of quality of life. In this context, a widely recognized practice, until now, has been to consider subjective wellbeing as a dimension of overall wellbeing. In particular, among the non-statistical methods[1] for assessing quality of life, there is the use of a dashboard of indicators and composite indicators. The Dashboard of Indicators applies a 'standard one-dimensional measure to each dimension' (Alkire et al. 2011) and because it is collected through the use of the best data source for each particular indicator it provides a rich amount of information allowing for a better impact assessment of specific policies. In this context, objective and subjective measures of wellbeing coexist and subjective wellbeing is considered as one of the aspects of overall wellbeing. This is the case for the Millennium Development Goals, the Sustainable Development Goals and the numerous national attempts to create similar informational frameworks. The use composite indicator overcomes the dashboard's heterogeneity and the weakness in communicability, converting the set of indicators into a real number. Still, the aggregation process imposes set relative weights on different indicators making this process vulnerable to the risk of arbitrariness. In both methods the procedure implies the setting of the normative framework, namely the need to define which factors (dimensions) capture a worthwhile life and which do not. Hence the risks of paternalism and arbitrariness are issues to be tackled.

On the other hand, among the statistical techniques the idea is to identify the joint distribution of achievements based on different methodologies, which statistically define the space of quality of life. To this purpose the use of micro-data is required in which information on each dimension is available for each unit of analysis. It is the case of (1) fuzzy set theory (Betti and Verma 2008; Chakravarty 2006; Martinetti 1994; 2000; 2009; Qizilbash 2006; Roche 2008); (2) multivariate data reduction techniques (Schokkaert and Van Ootegem 1990; Balestrino and Sciclone 2001; Kalsen 2000; Hirschberg et al. 2001; Lelli 2001; Neff 2007); (3) regression analysis and structural equation modeling (Kuklys 2005; Krishnakumar 2007; Krishnakumar and Ballon 2008; Di Tommaso 2007; Wagle 2009; De Rosa 2017).

1.3 EMPIRICAL APPLICATIONS AND POLICY IMPLICATIONS IN THE ECONOMICS OF HAPPINESS

Hand in hand with the setting of measurement methodologies, many scholars offered deep investigation into the dynamics which make a life worthwhile.

In particular, with respect to both subjective wellbeing and psychological wellbeing, several empirical applications analyzed the so-called determinants of happiness, life satisfaction and life sense. In this context the outcome subjective measure is considered as the individual utility function depending on many life factors, both context-related and individual-related; this is income, employment, inequality, but also marital status, fertility dynamics, social relations, relational goods and physical and mental health, just to mention the most explored relations. Similarly, with respect to quality of life many empirical applications tried to disentangle the trade-off and the interlinkages among the different dimensions of quality of life and analyzed the individual and contextual factors determining a certain level of life achievement. In this context the outcome measure is generally a composite measure or the result of some aggregation techniques, hence the empirical applications follow two levels of analysis: (1) the analysis of the relations among the different dimensions and the contribution each dimension gives to the overall composite measure, and (2) the analysis of the factors, others than those included in the composite measure, which affect quality of life.

Going deep into the debate of what makes a life worthwhile, empirical and theoretical literature showed the strong correlation between different forms of social capital and wellbeing: as a matter of fact, civil virtues and growth are positively correlated (Fukuyama 2001) and civically engaged people tend to be happier (Morrow-Howell et al. 2003), and have a greater sense of purpose in life (Greenfield and Marks 2004). Moreover, individuals located in places with higher levels of trust report higher levels of subjective wellbeing (Helliwell and Putnam 2004; Helliwell and Wang 2010; Bartolini et al. 2013) and higher levels of institutional trust determine better outcomes in subjective wellbeing (Hudson 2006). Similarly, more social interactions, relational activities and volunteering were found to significantly increase happiness and life satisfaction (Helliwell and Putnam 2004; Becchetti et al. 2008; Bartolini and Sarracino 2014; Colombo et al. 2018). In particular, a strong positive link emerges between relational goods and happiness, where relational goods, more than social capital, emphasize identity and motivation in personalized (face-to-face) interactions (Bruni and Stanca 2008). Also in the field of family studies great attention was devoted to family dynamics and wellbeing. Some scholars found that married people tend to be happier and more satisfied, with a higher level of purpose in life, optimism and energy and displaying a better wage premium and financial resources than single individuals (Cohen 1988; Gove et al. 1990; Stutzer and Frey 2006; Blanchflower and Oswald 2004; Bierman et al. 2006). Other scholars studied how children affect their parents' wellbeing. In the latter context the evidence is mixed: some found a positive relationship between parenthood and subjective wellbeing, with parents reporting higher levels of happiness, life satisfaction, self-esteem, positive emotions and meaning in life (Stutzer and Frey 2006; Haller and Hadler 2006; Hansen et al. 2009; Angeles 2010; Nelson et al. 2013; Aassve et al. 2012); while others highlighted a significant and positive effect on happiness only for the first child (Kohler et al. 2005). On the other hand, some researchers reported that having children is negatively related to subjective wellbeing and that the negative relation is mostly explained by the negative impact on financial satisfaction (Stanca 2012; Beja 2015; Bhargava et al. 2014). With respect to health and wellbeing, researchers extensively investigated such a relationship, becoming increasingly aware of the complex mutual interdependencies it encompasses (see Deaton 2008; Gwozdz and Sousa-Poza 2010). More specifically, bad mental health conditions were found to lead to much stronger decreases in life satisfaction than bad physical health conditions (Binder and Coad 2013). While physical activities, both in terms of frequency and volume, were found to be essential factors in the relationship between physical activities and happiness, numerous studies support the evidence that a small change in physical activity makes a difference to happiness (Zhang and Chen 2019). On the other hand, some applications highlighted that higher levels of happiness lead to increased physical activity (Baruth et al. 2011) and similarly that both subjective health satisfaction and eudemonic wellbeing indicators have to be considered as reliable predictors of future health outcomes (Becchetti et al. 2018; Becchetti et al. 2019).

With respect to the economic dimension of wellbeing and its relation to subjective wellbeing, Easterlin (2015) highlighted how rising unemployment is inversely related to life satisfaction. Similarly, some scholars investigated the link between income inequality and happiness, pointing out that increasing income inequality is consistently negatively related to wellbeing (Bartolini and Sarracino 2015; Bartolini et al. 2017; Mikucka et al. 2017) and that income inequality is a good explanation for the Easterlin paradox, that is to say economic growth does not always translate to an increase in happiness (Oishi and Kesebir 2015).

This is to say, in the recent past such evidence sheds light on the power the perspective of wellbeing has in informing public policy as in ensuring the effectiveness of social policies to shape individual life satisfaction.

1.4   THE CONTENT OF THE BOOK

The book is organized into three sections, each depicting a pillar of the economics of the happiness: (1) the historical and philosophical foundations of the debate; (2) the methodological and measurements issues and its political implications; and (3) the empirical applications and the debate on what determines a happy life.

Bruno S. Frey opens the discussion in Chapter 2, recalling the contribution of happiness research as part of modern economics and social psychology and designing the future of happiness research. According to the author, due to the large number of studies published, diminishing marginal insights begin to be observable, yet it is to be expected that future happiness research will pursue such well-trodden paths.

In Chapter 3 Jeffrey Sachs recollects the ancient roots of happiness, back to Aristotle, in the form of eudaimonia, and reconnects such a conception to modern psychology and neuroscience. Also Maurizio Pugno, in Chapter 4, focuses on the eudaimonic side of wellbeing, by discussing the objective/subjective dichotomy, the greater robustness of eudaimonia with respect to hedonism and the advantages of the policy implications of eudaimonia.

In Chapter 5 Luigino Bruni offers the perspective of civil economy, the southern spirit of capitalism and the account of *Felicitas Publica*, whereas Paolo Santori, in Chapter 6, completes this vision by offering the thought of Tomas Aquinas on happiness.

Chapter 7 moves on to the measurement issues and the complexity such an approach has to deal with. Filomena Maggino and Leonardo Salvatore Alaimo elaborate on complex systems and its components and report the case of wellbeing indicators as a modern example of complexity.

In Chapter 8 Easterlin, Fei Wang and Shun Wang describe the evolution of China's wellbeing in the quarter century since 1990, and suggest the likely reasons for the disparate trajectories of subjective wellbeing and GDP per capita. Chapter 9 also focuses on happiness and growth:

Francesco Sarracino and Kelsey J. O'Connor discuss the relation between economic growth and wellbeing in Luxembourg, in the presence of generous social safety nets, increasing social capital and declining income inequality. They suggest the latter condition to be a promising starting point for designing new policies to durably improve wellbeing.

In Chapter 10 the discussion encompasses the empirical evidence the literature has to offer on the determinants of subjective wellbeing. Mario Lucchini, Egidio Riva and Luca Crivelli examine the causal effect of physical activity on the three main components of subjective wellbeing in Switzerland (i.e. life satisfaction, positive affect and negative affect) while controlling for a wide set of potential socio-demographic, health, relational and environmental confounders. Dalila De Rosa and Matteo Rizzolli, in Chapter 11, explore the role of different family types on life satisfaction and satisfaction with life domains in Italy. Then Luigino Bruni, Dalila De Rosa and Giovanni Ferri, in Chapter 12, offer cross-country empirical evidence on the role of relational capital, in the form of cooperativeness, for the promotion of happiness.

In Chapter 13, Neli Esipova, Julie Ray and Anita Pugliese use Gallup data to show results coming from the Migrant Acceptance Index, created by using subjective measures from the World Gallup Poll.

NOTE

1. Non-statistical method refers to the description of wellbeing through the use of indicators appropriately identified under a normative framework.

REFERENCES

Aassve, A., A. Goisis and M. Sironi (2012), Happiness and childbearing across Europe. *Social Indicators Research*, 108(1), 65–86.
Alkire, S., J. Foster and M. E. Santos (2011), Where did identification go? OPHI Working Paper 43b. September 1. http://dx.doi.org/10.2139/ssrn.2118556.
Angeles, L. (2010), Children and life satisfaction. *Journal of Happiness Studies*, 11(4), 523–38.
Balestrino, A. and N. Sciclone (2001), Should we use functionings instead of income to measure well-being? Theory, and some evidence from Italy. *Rivista internazionale di scienze sociali*, 3(561), 3–22.
Bartolini, S., E. Bilancini and M. Pugno (2013), Did the decline in social connections depress Americans' happiness? *Social Indicators Research*, 110(3), 1033–59.
Bartolini, S. and F. Sarracino (2014), Happy for how long? How social capital and economic growth relate to happiness over time. *Ecological Economics*, 108, 242–56.

Bartolini, S. and F. Sarracino (2015), The dark side of Chinese growth: declining social capital and well-being in times of economic boom. *World Development*, 74, 333–51.

Bartolini, S., M. Mikucka and F. Sarracino (2017), Money, trust and happiness in transition countries: evidence from time series. *Social Indicators Research*, 130(1), 87–106.

Baruth, M., D. C. Lee, X. Sui, T. S. Church, B. H. Marcus, S. Wilcox and S. N. Blair (2011), Emotional outlook on life predicts increases in physical activity among initially inactive men. *Health Education & Behavior*, 38(2), 150–8.

Becchetti, L., A. Pelloni and F. Rossetti (2008), Relational goods, sociability, and happiness. *Kyklos*, 61(3), 343–63.

Becchetti, L., M. Bachelet and F. Riccardini (2018), Not feeling well . . . true or exaggerated? Self-assessed health as a leading health indicator. *Health Economics*, 27(2), e153–e170.

Becchetti, L., M. Bachelet and F. Pisani (2019), Poor eudaimonic subjective wellbeing as a mortality risk factor. *Economia Politica*, 36(1), 245–72.

Becker, G. (1996), *Accounting for Tastes*. Cambridge, MA: Harvard University Press.

Beja, E. L. (2015), Direct and indirect impacts of parenthood on happiness. *International Review of Economics*, 62(4), 307–18.

Bentham, J. (1789), *An Introduction to the Principles of Morals and Legislation*, ed. by J. H. Burns and HLA Hart, London.

Betti, G. and V. Verma (2008), Fuzzy measures of the incidence of relative poverty and deprivation: a multi-dimensional perspective. *Statistical Methods and Applications*, 17(2), 225–50.

Bhargava, S., K. S. Kassam and G. Loewenstein (2014), A reassessment of the defense of parenthood. *Psychological Science*, 25(1), 299–302.

Bierman, A., E. M. Fazio and M. A. Milkie (2006), A multifaceted approach to the mental health advantage of the married: assessing how explanations vary by outcome measure and unmarried group. *Journal of Family Issues*, 27(4), 554–82.

Binder, M. and A. Coad (2013), Life satisfaction and self-employment: a matching approach. *Small Business Economics*, 40(4), 1009–33.

Blanchflower, D. G. and A. J. Oswald (2004), Well-being over time in Britain and the USA. *Journal of Public Economics*, 88(7), 1359–86.

Bruni, L. and P. L. Porta (2003), *Œconomies in the Age of Newton. Natural Science and Political Economy in the Italian Enlightenment*. Milan: Universita di Milano-Bicocca. Mimeo.

Bruni, L., F. Comim and M. Pugno (eds) (2008), *Capabilities and Happiness*. Oxford: Oxford University Press.

Bruni, L. and L. Stanca (2008), Watching alone: relational goods, television and happiness. *Journal of Economic Behavior & Organization*, 65(3–4), 506–28.

Chakravarty, S. R. (2006), An axiomatic approach to multidimensional poverty measurement via fuzzy sets. In A. Lemmi and G. Betti (eds), *Fuzzy Set Approach to Multidimensional Poverty Measurement* (pp. 49–72). New York: Springer.

Clark, A. E., P. Frijters and M. A. Shields (2008), Relative income, happiness, and utility: an explanation for the Easterlin paradox and other puzzles. *Journal of Economic Literature*, 46(1), 95–144.

Clark, A. E. and C. Senik (2011), Will GDP growth increase happiness in developing countries? *Revue d'économie développement*, 19(2), 113–90.

Cohen, S. (1988), Psychosocial models of the role of social support in the etiology of physical disease. *Health Psychology*, 7(3), 269–97.

Colombo, E., V. Rotondi and L. Stanca (2018), Macroeconomic conditions and well-being: do social interactions matter? *Applied Economics*, 50(28), 3029–38.

Comim, F., M. Qizilbash and S. Alkire (eds) (2008), *The Capability Approach: Concepts, Measures and Applications*. Cambridge: Cambridge University Press.

De Rosa, D. (2017), Capability approach and multidimensional well-being: the Italian case of BES. *Social Indicators Research*, 140(1), 125–55.

Deaton, A. (2008), Income, health, and well-being around the world: evidence from the Gallup World Poll. *Journal of Economic Perspectives*, 22(2), 53–72.

Di Tommaso, M. L. (2007), Children capabilities: a structural equation model for India. *The Journal of Socio-Economics*, 36, 436–50.

Diener, E., E. M. Suh, R. E. Lucas and H. L. Smith (1999), Subjective well-being: three decades of progress. *Psychological Bulletin*, 125(2), 276–302.

Diener, E., D. Wirtz, W. Tov, C. Kim-Prieto, D. W. Choi, S. Oishi and R. Biswas-Diener (2010), New well-being measures: short scales to assess flourishing and positive and negative feelings. *Social Indicators Research*, 97(2), 143–56.

Easterlin, R. A. (1974), Does economic growth improve the human lot? Some empirical evidence. In *Nations and Households in Economic Growth* (pp. 89–125). London: Academic Press.

Easterlin, R. A. (2005), Feeding the illusion of growth and happiness: a reply to Hagerty and Veenhoven. *Social Indicators Research*, 74(3), 429–43.

Easterlin, R. A. (2015), Happiness and economic growth: the evidence. In *Global Handbook of Quality of Life* (pp. 283–99). Dordrecht: Springer.

Edgeworth, F. Y. (1881), *Mathematical Psychics*. London: Kegan.

Frey, B. S. and A. Stutzer (2002), What can economists learn from happiness research? *Journal of Economic Literature*, 40(2), 402–35.

Fukuyama, F. (2001), Social capital, civil society and development. *Third World Quarterly*, 22(1), 7–20.

Gove, W. R., C. B. Style and M. Hughes (1990), The effect of marriage on the well-being of adults: a theoretical analysis. *Journal of Family Issues*, 11(1), 4–35.

Greenfield, E. A. and N. F. Marks (2004), Formal volunteering as a protective factor for older adults' psychological well-being. *The Journals of Gerontology Series B: Psychological Sciences and Social Sciences*, 59(5), S258–S264.

Gwozdz, W. and A. Sousa-Poza (2010), Ageing, health and life satisfaction of the oldest old: an analysis for Germany. *Social Indicators Research*, 97(3), 397–417.

Haller, M. and M. Hadler (2006), How social relations and structures can produce happiness and unhappiness: an international comparative analysis. *Social Indicators Research*, 75(2), 169–216.

Hansen, T., B. Slagsvold and T. Moum (2009), Childlessness and psychological well-being in midlife and old age: an examination of parental status effects across a range of outcomes. *Social Indicators Research*, 94(2), 343–62.

Helliwell, J. F. and R. D. Putnam (2004), The social context of well–being. *Philosophical Transactions of the Royal Society of London. Series B: Biological Sciences*, 359(1449), 1435–46.

Helliwell, J. F. and S. Wang (2010), Trust and well-being (No. w15911). National Bureau of Economic Research.

Herbst, C. M. and J. Ifcher (2016), The increasing happiness of US parents. *Review of Economics of the Household*, 14(3), 529–51.

Hirschberg, J. G., E. Maasoumi and D. J. Slottje (2001), Clusters of attributes and well-being in the USA. *Journal of Applied Econometrics*, 16, 445–60.

Hone, L. C., A. Jarden, G. M. Schofield and S. Duncan (2014), Measuring flourishing: the impact of operational definitions on the prevalence of high levels of wellbeing. *International Journal of Wellbeing*, 4(1), 62–90.

Hudson, J. (2006). Institutional trust and subjective well-being across the EU. *Kyklos*, 59(1), 43–62.

Huppert, F. A. (2009). Psychological well-being: evidence regarding its causes and consequences. *Applied Psychology: Health and Well-Being*, 1(2), 137–64.

Huppert, F. A. and T. C. So (2013), Flourishing across Europe: application of a new conceptual framework for defining well-being. *Social Indicators Research*, 110(3), 837–61.

Jevons, W. S. (1871), *The Theory of Political Economy*. New York: Penguin Books.

Kalsen, S. (2000), Measuring poverty and deprivation in South Africa. *Review of Income and Wealth*, 46, 33–58.

Kohler, H. P., J. R. Behrman and A. Skytthe (2005), Partner + children = happiness? The effects of partnerships and fertility on well-being. *Population and Development Review*, 31(3), 407–45.

Krishnakumar, J. (2007), Going beyond functionings to capabilities: an econometric model to explain and estimate capabilities. *Journal of Human Development*, 8(1), 39–63.

Krishnakumar, J. and P. Ballon (2008), Estimating basic capabilities: a structural equation model applied to Bolivia. *World Development*, 36(6), 992–1010.

Kuklys, W. (2005), *Amartya Sen's Capability Approach: Theoretical Insights and Empirical Applications*. New York: Springer.

Lelli, S. (2001), Factor analysis vs. fuzzy sets theory: assessing the influence of different techniques on Sen's functioning approach. Kath. Univ., Department Economie, Center for Economic Studies.

Malthus, Th.R. (1798), *An Essay on the Principle of Population*. London: Macmillan.

Marshall, A. (1890), *Principles of Economics*. London: Macmillan.

Martinetti, E. C. (1994), A new approach to evaluation of well-being and poverty by fuzzy set theory. *Giornale degli economisti e annali di economia*, 7(9), 367–88.

Martinetti, E. C. (2000), A multidimensional assessment of well-being based on Sen's functioning approach. *Rivista internazionale di scienze sociali*, 2, 207–39.

Martinetti, E. C. (ed.) (2009), *Debating Global Society: Reach and Limits of the Capability Approach*. Milan: Fondazione Giangiacomo Feltrinelli.

Mikucka, M., F. Sarracino and J. K. Dubrow (2017), When does economic growth improve life satisfaction? Multilevel analysis of the roles of social trust and income inequality in 46 countries, 1981–2012. *World Development*, 93, 447–59.

Mill, J. S. (1861). (1969), Utilitarianism. In J. M. Robson (ed.), *Collected Works of John Stuart Mill* (Vol. 10, pp. 203–59). Toronto: University of Toronto Press.

Morrow-Howell, N., J. Hinterlong, P. A. Rozario and F. Tang (2003), Effects of volunteering on the well-being of older adults. *The Journals of Gerontology Series B: Psychological Sciences and Social Sciences*, 58(3), S137–S145.

Neff, D. F. (2007), Subjective well-being, poverty and ethnicity in South Africa: insights from an explanatory analysis. *Social Indicators Research*, 80, 313–41.

Nelson, S. K., K. Kushlev, T. English, E. W. Dunn and S. Lyubomirsky (2013), In defense of parenthood: children are associated with more joy than misery. *Psychological Science*, 24(1), 3–10.

Nussbaum, M. and A. Sen (eds) (1993), *The Quality of Life*. Oxford: Oxford University Press.

Oishi, S. and S. Kesebir (2015), Income inequality explains why economic growth does not always translate to an increase in happiness. *Psychological Science*, 26(10), 1630–38.

Qizilbash, M. (2006), Philosophical accounts of vagueness, fuzzy poverty measures and multidimensionality. In A. Lemmi and G. Betti (eds), *Fuzzy Set Approach to Multidimensional Poverty Measurement: Economic Studies in Inequality, Social Exclusion and Well-being*, vol. 3. Boston, MA: Springer.

Robbins, L. (1998), *A History of Economic Thought. The LSE Lectures*, ed. by S. G. Medema and W. J. Samuels. Princeton: Princeton University Press.

Roche, J. M. (2008), Monitoring inequality among social groups: a methodology combining fuzzy set theory and principal component analysis. *Journal of Human Development*, 9(3), 427–52.

Ryan, R. M. and E. L. Deci (2006), Self-regulation and the problem of human autonomy: does psychology need choice, self-determination, and will? *Journal of Personality*, 74(6), 1557–86.

Samman, E. (2007), Psychological and subjective well-being: a proposal for internationally comparable indicators. *Oxford Development Studies*, 35(4), 459–86.

Schabas, M. (1990), *A World Ruled by Numbers: William Stanley Jevons and the Rise of Mathematical Economics*. Princeton: Princeton University Press.

Schokkaert, E. and L. Van Ootegem (1990), Sen's concept of the living standard applied to the Belgian unemployed. *Louvain Economic Review*, 56(3–4), 429–50.

Sen, A. (1985), Well-being, agency and freedom: The Dewey lectures 1984. *The Journal of Philosophy*, 82(4), 169–221.

Sen, A. (1992), *Inequality Reexamined*. Oxford: Oxford University Press.

Sen, A. (2000), *Development as Freedom*. New York: A. Knopf.

Stanca, L. (2012), Suffer the little children: measuring the effects of parenthood on well-being worldwide. *Journal of Economic Behavior & Organization*, 81(3), 742–50.

Stiglitz, J. E., A. Sen and J. P. Fitoussi (2009), Report by the commission on the measurement of economic performance and social progress.

Stutzer, A. and B. S. Frey (2006), Does marriage make people happy, or do happy people get married? *The Journal of Socio-Economics*, 35(2), 326–47.

Wagle, U. (2009), *Multidimensional Poverty Measurement: Concepts and Applications*, vol. 4. New York: Springer.

Zhang, Z. and W. Chen (2019), A systematic review of the relationship between physical activity and happiness. *Journal of Happiness Studies*, 20(4), 1305–22.

2. What future happiness research?

Bruno S. Frey

2.1 THE BEQUEST OF HAPPINESS RESEARCH

At the end of the last century and the beginning of the new century economists gained great insights into the determinants of subjective well-being.[1] They were informed by social psychologists, who dealt with the issue earlier than economists did (Kahneman et al. 1999). Happiness research was taken up by the media and was recognized by the general public. It became general knowledge that national income per capita is not directly linked to people's well-being. The Kingdom of Bhutan officially proclaimed that its policy is to further happiness and not gross national product (GNP). In the social sciences, happiness research is an excellent example of an interdisciplinary approach not dictated from above but an efficient way to learn from each other. This applies in particular to economics and psychology, but beyond also to philosophy, sociology and political science. They are all engaged in finding ways and means to raise human happiness.

For economists educated in strict neoclassics it came as a surprise that human well-being can be measured, and that it can serve as a useful approximation to the theoretical concept of utility (see e.g. Weimann et al. 2015; Kahneman and Krueger 2006). Sir John Hicks and Baron Lionel Robbins, who in the 1920s and 1930s were dominant scholars, were convinced that it is impossible to measure utility. As a result, a microeconomic theory was developed which does not rely on measured utility. Above all, this approach made it possible to empirically estimate demand function. This was quite an achievement but over time it became clear that this approach cannot cope with important behavioural regularities (for an early statement see Sen 1977). These shortcomings have at least partly been overcome by happiness research which starts from the – well-founded – assumption that subjective well-being can be captured by careful representative surveys.

Happiness research has produced many novel and also surprising insights into what individuals value. It is important to emphasize and to clearly work out the differences to the views held by laypeople as well as to classical neoclassical theory as taught at universities. If there are indeed diminishing returns to research on happiness as suggested above, interest must be maintained by demonstrating that there are nevertheless new insights to be gained. If this is not done, it may well happen that economics returns to the previously orthodox position claiming that there is no need to measure and analyse happiness.

These are some examples of surprising and unexpected results of research on subjective well-being:

- One of the largest negative effects on happiness occurs when people lose their job and become unemployed. This is only partly due to the concomitant income loss (this effect is kept constant in the multiple regression approaches) but rather to the fact that people experience a strongly reduced feeling of self-worth, and that they are no longer part of society. In contrast, in neoclassical economics work is taken as a burden or cost, and receiving an income without work would be optimal. That unemployment has a strong negative effect on well-being has been found in a large number of studies. It has, for instance, been shown that the self-employed, who work harder and on average receive lower incomes than people employed in organizations, are happier (Benz and Frey 2008).
- Happiness research emphasizes the importance of social relationships to one's family and friends, an aspect disregarded as a welfare contributor in orthodox economics. This is an aspect long ago focused on by the Italian movement of civil economy (see recently Becchetti and Cermelli 2018; also Bruni 2006, 2012; Bruni and Porta 2005, 2007; Bruni and Stanca 2008; Bruni and Zamagni 2004, 2015; Bartolini et al. 2007; Gui and Sugden 2005).
- Giving and volunteering are found to raise happiness. This stands in contrast to orthodox economics where it is assumed that gaining additional income raises utility.
- Happiness theory supports the notion that procedural fairness matters for individuals. There are conditions under which a less favourable outcome is preferred if the process has been considered fair (e.g. Lind and Tyler 1988; Hollander-Blumoff and Tyler 2008).
- Adaptation, aspirations, overoptimism and mispredictions have the capacity to strongly influence human decisions, drawing them away from rational choice prediction (e.g. Stutzer 2004; Frey and Stutzer 2014; Odermatt et al. 2017; Deaton 2018). The same consequence is likely to result from social comparisons (see Bartolini et al. 2019).

Today, economic happiness research has been widely accepted in the academic profession though there are still quite a number of scholars who find that utility is not well approximated by empirical measures of happiness. Especially young researchers have become strongly engaged in the subject. Hundreds of scientific articles have appeared since the beginning of the twenty-first century. There are several extensive survey articles (e.g. Easterlin 2003; Dolan et al. 2008; Frey and Stutzer 2002a; Stutzer and Frey 2010), monographs and books (e.g. Diener et al. 2018; Sgroi et al. 2017; Clark et al. 2018; OECD 2017; Frey 2008, 2018; Layard 2005; Frey and Stutzer 2002b), and hundreds of scholarly articles.

In view of this explosion of literature it is no surprise that *marginally decreasing* insights can be observed. It is difficult for scholars to come up with really new results. Rather, most contributions are devoted to quite specific issues, and the advance in our knowledge about happiness is restricted. This is a normal process in every new field.

2.2 REACTIONS TO DECREASING MARGINAL INSIGHTS

Within economics, five different reactions to the large number of previous publications, results and insights may be distinguished.

Continuation of Existing Research Approaches

The already existing research can be, and has been, amended in various directions (see e.g. Clark 2018; Frey et al. 2014), such as:

- Use more and better statistics, in particular panel data. They could extend, for instance, to what kind of subjective well-being is captured. In addition to the normally used 'life satisfaction' data, researchers may look on the one hand at short-run happiness, or on the other hand at long-run, deeply felt happiness (eudaimonia, see e.g. Ryff 2017). An effort can be made to develop 'well-being indices' designed to substitute for national income as a welfare measure (e.g. Benjamin et al. 2014). It can also be attempted to capture subjective well-being in diverse ways. A fascinating approach is to derive it from language corpora from millions of digitized books going back at least 200 years (Hills et al. 2015). It turns out that a rise in national income indeed raises subjective well-being. However, on the basis of these data the authors cannot find a long-run positive trend in subjective well-being.
- More refined econometrics may be employed, most importantly in order to capture causal links. They are of considerable importance in

happiness research. It is, for instance, well known that higher income raises happiness, but that happier persons are better equipped to get good jobs with higher income. Similarly, healthy people are happier, but happiness to some extent contributes to health.

- Results from the natural sciences can be used to better understand the conditions of happiness. This applies most importantly to the role of genes (e.g. De Neve et al. 2012), but also to less obvious aspects such as the use of molecular fingerprints (e.g. Probst-Hensch 2017).
- The analysis may be extended to more countries above and beyond developed economies. In addition, particularly surprising developments for particular countries can be compared to other countries. Thus, for example, Americans seem to suffer greater pain than persons from other countries (Blanchflower and Oswald 2017).
- The happiness of particular groups and parts of society can be studied more deeply. For example, the subjective well-being of government compared to private employees has been identified for 21 European and 17 Latin American countries (Luechinger et al. 2008). Many groups in the United States have experienced a downward trend in happiness while the happiness of black Americans has strongly increased since the 1970s (Blanchflower and Oswald 2017). Another important area is the specific impact on happiness in groups suffering from poverty (Clark 2017). Families with children are less happy than those without children. Children are expensive and reduce the money available for other purposes. But once this finding is controlled for the financial condition of a family, it turns out that children tend to raise the well-being of parents (Blanchflower and Clark 2019).
- Both psychic and physical health affects happiness greatly. It is important to identify the many different connections more deeply (see e.g. the survey by Crivelli and Lucchini 2017).
- The state of the natural environment impacts life satisfaction in a systematic way. Over recent years many studies have been undertaken in this direction, see for example Luechinger (2009), Luechinger and Raschky (2009), or Welsch (2002, 2006).
- It is difficult to imagine people being happy in times of war or intense civil conflict but a more refined analysis suggests that even war may have some positive effects on the happiness of some persons (Welsch 2008; Frey 2012a, 2012b). It has been found that terrorist incidents strongly reduce people's well-being (Frey et al. 2007; Clark et al. 2020). More work on these issues is strongly needed; it is a rather neglected aspect in happiness research.

- An aspect of great importance in modern times is the impact of the digital world on happiness. It has, for instance, been found that Facebook usage decreases happiness because it strengthens users' engagement in upward social comparisons (Arad et al. 2017). There are, of course, many other aspects of digitization possibly impacting subjective well-being that are worth studying.
- The effect of income on life satisfaction depends on what kind of income is received. It has been shown (Lindqvist et al. 2018) that a lottery win gained without effort produces only 30 per cent of the satisfaction from the same income gained by (hard) work. This may also be relevant for rents and for programs suggesting unconditional income.
- Research has shown the general importance of happiness and income inequality, trust and social capital in society (e.g. Coleman 1990; Putnam 2000; Bennett and Nikolaev 2017). This also holds for social welfare (e.g. Musson and Rousselière 2017). There are many different aspects of trust whose effects on happiness are well worth studying (e.g. Mikucka et al. 2017).

This discussion shows that there are hundreds of worthwhile topics to be analysed. It can safely be predicted that this will be the road taken by a great many future researchers on happiness. The major reason is that young scholars today are under immense pressure to publish within a rather short time span. As a result they are induced, if not forced, to engage in a subject that is already generally accepted, and to publish by adding some small extension to already existing publications. Established scholars are increasingly subject to similar publication pressures. While this development can be criticized (e.g. Frey 2003, 2009), the reaction to pursue the trodden path is most likely to be undertaken by many future contributors to happiness research.

A Larger Picture Is Worthwhile

In the tradition of Aristotle, happiness may be taken to be the overarching goal of human beings. Alternatively, it may stand next to other goals of humans such as personal development, loyalty, solidarity, justice or religious fulfilment. Some scholars (e.g. Glaeser et al. 2016) in the context of cities identify trade-offs between individual happiness and other goals. Individuals may willingly make choices reducing happiness in order to achieve other goals.

To look at happiness in a broader way, and to compare it to other goals, has been an important and fruitful contribution of Italian economists following Genovesi (1765–87) and his insights regarding civil economy (Bruni 2006; Bruni and Porta 2005, 2007). They emphasize the importance of interpersonal concepts of public happiness (*pubblica felicità*), public trust (*fede pubblica*), reciprocity and relational goods, and that interaction may raise happiness. This direction of analysis of human well-being should be further pursued.

The Political Use of Happiness Results

There is a strong tendency to apply the results of happiness research in a direct way via happiness policies (see e.g. in the context of the United Nations, Layard and O'Donnell 2015; O'Donnell and Oswald 2015; Diener et al. 2009). However, much thought should be applied before engaging in such policy-making. According to one author, 'happiness is a poor guide for policy' because the concept is vague, multifaceted and subjective (White 2015).

In some firms there already exists a 'chief happiness officer' next to the chief executive officer, chief operating officer, chief patent officer, etc. They endeavour to create happiness by sending their employees on mindfulness courses, yoga lessons and many other things demonstrating that the top managers are interested in the 'whole person' of their employees. Such a mistaken cult of happiness constitutes an 'unacceptable invasion of individual liberty' (*The Economist* 2016: 60). To employ happiness instrumentally is moreover unlikely to work. Only 'rational fools' (Sen 1977) take such actions seriously.

The Kingdom of Bhutan measures its gross national happiness and claims to build all their policies to further happiness. A substantial number of governments (the United States, Britain, France, Germany, Australia, etc.) regularly publish reports informing their citizens on the relationship of their policies to happiness. The United Arab Emirates even has a minister of state for happiness and well-being. The United Nations General Assembly has unanimously adopted a resolution that governments should pursue the happiness of their citizens. The happiness goal is boasted irrespective of whether a country is democratic or authoritarian. It is difficult, or even impossible, to argue against the idea that governments should raise the happiness of their citizens (see Farrow et al. 2018 for the importance of words in the policy context).

To impose policies designed to raise happiness from above is mistaken. The insights of happiness research should not be used to substitute for the democratic participation of citizens but rather should serve to inform them about the determinants of happiness. What policies they favour should be left to the citizens (Odermatt ad Stutzer 2018).

There are moreover two fundamental reasons why a policy of happiness maximization by governments is mistaken (Frey and Stutzer 2000):

- Once respondents are aware that governments pay attention to the easured level of happiness they no longer answer in an unbiased way. Consider, say, a left-wing citizen. He or she will be reluctant to state they are happy when living under a strongly right-wing government. As a result the happiness surveys no longer reflect the true-life satisfaction level of the population, and therefore can no longer be used as a reasonable policy guide.
- Once governments have committed themselves to raising the happiness of their citizens they have a strong incentive to systematically manipulate the happiness statistics. This is easy to do, in particular because the data are subjective, and because it is easy to exclude answers considered being outliers, or parts of the population (for instance persons imprisoned).

In future research on happiness these considerations must be taken into account. It should be analysed in what way the population can be informed about the results of happiness research. Obviously, the classical and the new media play a large role in this context.

Another important issue is the consequences of happiness on politics, in particular on voting. This is a large area so far not widely analysed. An exception is a study suggesting that individuals satisfied with their life are 1.6 per cent more likely to support the incumbent (Liberini et al. 2017). Such results may be of great relevance in a period in which disgruntled voters tend to support extreme parties, often of the right wing.

Institutional Prerequisites of Happiness

To find out under what institutional conditions happiness flourishes, and under what conditions it is hampered, has so far been undertaken too rarely. One of the reasons for this neglect is that many economists engaged in happiness research are strongly influenced by psychology and endeavour to follow that path. The analysis of institutions is beyond the realm of psychological analyses; it is the area of political economists, political scientists, sociologists and lawyers (see e.g. Huang 2018). This is indeed an area of research in which economists could make a major contribution.

Some contributions in happiness research have isolated institutional determinants of happiness, among them democracy versus authoritarian regimes (e.g. Dorn et al. 2007), direct democracy versus more representative systems (Frey and Stutzer 2000, 2002a, 2002b), decentralization (e.g.

Diaz-Serrano and Rodríguez-Pose 2012; Rodríguez-Pose and Tselios 2019) or governance systems (Helliwell and Huang 2008; OECD 2017: 157–98). But much is still unknown, for instance the importance on happiness of the rule of law, of basic human rights, or of types of bureaucracy.

2.3   CONCLUSIONS

There are many fruitful opportunities for future happiness research. Some are rather obvious, others are too little considered despite their great importance, and others have not been exploited so far. The further pursuing of the direction indicated by the (large) literature already existing on subjective well-being is likely to happen but there are even more challenging and worthwhile opportunities.

This author does not hide his preference for more enterprising directions. In particular, happiness should be put in a larger perspective. It should be compared to other goals of human beings and it should be carefully analysed as to whether these goals are complements or rather substitutes. To prevent happiness research from becoming a handmaiden of authoritarian political tendencies it is also important to inquire carefully as to what institutional conditions favour raising the happiness of the population.

NOTE

1.   This chapter is partly based on an article by the author published in 2019 in the *International Review of Economics*. The author declares that he has no conflict of interest.

REFERENCES

Arad, A., O. Barzilay and M. Perchick (2017), The impact of Facebook on social comparison and happiness: evidence from a natural experiment. *SSRN Electronic Journal.* https://doi.org/10.2139/ssrn.2916158.

Bartolini, S., E. Bilancini and M. Pugno (2007), Did the decline in social capital decrease American happiness? A relational explanation of the happiness paradox. Working Paper 513, Department of Economics, University of Siena.

Bartolini, S., M. Piekalkiewicz and F. Sarracino (2019), A social cure for social comparisons. Working Paper 797, Department of Economics, University of Siena.

Becchetti, L. and M. Cermelli (2018), Civil economy: definition and strategies for sustainable well-living. *International Review of Economics*, 65(3), 329–57.

Benjamin, D. J., O. Heffetz, M. S. Kimball and N. Szembrot (2014), Beyond happiness and satisfaction: toward well-being indices based on stated preference. *American Economic Review*, 104(9), 2698–735.

Bennett, D. L. and B. Nikolaev (2017), Economic freedom and happiness inequality: friends or foes? *Contemporary Economic Policy*, 35(2), 373–91.

Benz, M. and B. S. Frey (2008), Being independent is a great thing: subjective evaluations of self-employment and hierarchy. *Economica*, 75(298), 362–83.

Blanchflower, D. G. and A. E. Clark (2019), Children, unhappiness and family finances: evidence from one million Europeans. Working Paper 25597, National Bureau of Economic Research Working Paper Series.

Blanchflower, D. G. and A. Oswald (2017), Unhappiness and pain in modern America: a review essay, and further evidence, on Carol Graham's happiness for all? Working Paper 24087, National Bureau of Economic Research Working Paper Series.

Bruni, L. (2006), *Civil Happiness: Economics and Human Flourishing in Historical Perspective*. London: Routledge.

Bruni, L. (ed.) (2012), Market and happiness. *International Review of Economics*, special issue, 59(4).

Bruni, L. and P. L. Porta (eds) (2005), *Economics and Happiness: Framing the Analysis*. Oxford: Oxford University Press.

Bruni, L. and P. L. Porta (eds) (2007), *Handbook on the Economics of Happiness*. Cheltenham, UK and Northampton, MA, USA: Edward Elgar Publishing.

Bruni, L. and L. Stanca (2008), Watching alone: relational goods, television and happiness. *Journal of Economic Behavior & Organization*, 65(3–4), 506–28.

Bruni, L. and S. Zamagni (2004), *Economia civile: Efficienza, equità, felicità pubblica*. Bologna: Il mulino.

Bruni, L. and S. Zamagni (2015), *L' economia civile: Un'altra idea di mercato*. Bologna: Il mulino.

Clark, A. E. (2017), Happiness, income and poverty. *International Review of Economics*, 64(2), 145–58.

Clark, A. E. (2018), Four decades of the economics of happiness: where next? *The Review of Income and Wealth*, 64(2), 245–69.

Clark, A. E., O. Doyle and E. Stancanelli (2020), The impact of terrorism on individual well-being: evidence from the Boston marathon bombing. *Economic Journal*, 130(631), 2065–2104.

Clark, A. E., S. Flèche, R. Layard, N. Powdthavee and G. Ward (2018), *The Origins of Happiness: The Science of Well-being over the Life Course*. Princeton: Princeton University Press.

Coleman, J. S. (1990), *Foundations of Social Theory*. Cambridge, MA: Belknap Press of Harvard University Press.

Crivelli, L. and M. Lucchini (2017), Health and happiness: an introduction. *International Review of Economics*, 64(2), 105–11.

De Neve, J.-E., N. A. Christakis, J. H. Fowler and B. S. Frey (2012), Genes, economics, and happiness. *Journal of Neuroscience, Psychology, and Economics*, 5(4), 193–211.

Deaton, A. (2018), What do self-reports of wellbeing say about life-cycle theory and policy? *Journal of Public Economics*, 162, 18–25.

Diaz-Serrano, L. and A. Rodríguez-Pose (2012), Decentralization, subjective well-being, and the perception of institutions. *Kyklos*, 65(2), 179–93.

Diener, E., R. Lucas, U. Schimmack and J. Helliwell (2009), *Well-being for Public Policy*. Oxford and New York: Oxford University Press.

Diener, E., S. Oishi and L. Tay (eds) (2018), *Handbook of Well-being*. Salt Lake City, UT: DEF Publishers.

Dolan, P., T. Peasgood and M. White (2008), Do we really know what makes us happy? A review of the economic literature on the factors associated with subjective well-being. *Journal of Economic Psychology*, 29(1), 94–122.

Dorn, D., J. A. V. Fischer, G. Kirchgässner and A. Sousa-Poza (2007), Is it culture or democracy? The impact of democracy and culture on happiness. *Social Indicators Research*, 82(3), 505–26.

Easterlin, R. A. (2003), Explaining happiness. *PNAS, Proceedings of the National Academy of Sciences*, 100(19), 11176–83.

Farrow, K., G. Grolleau and N. Mzoughi (2018), What in the word! The scope for the effect of word choice on economic behavior. *Kyklos*, 71(4), 557–80.

Frey, B. S. (2003), Publishing as prostitution? Choosing between one's own ideas and academic success. *Public Choice*, 116(1–2), 205–23.

Frey, B. S. (2008), *Happiness: A Revolution in Economics*. Cambridge, MA: MIT Press.

Frey, B. S. (2009), Economists in the PITS? *International Review of Economics*, 56(4), 335–46.

Frey, B. S. (2012a), Peace, war, and happiness: Bruder Klaus as wellbeing facilitator. *International Journal of Wellbeing*, 1(2), 226–34.

Frey, B. S. (2012b), Well-being and war. *International Review of Economics*, 59(4), 363–75.

Frey, B. S. (2018), *Economics of Happiness*. Cham: Springer.

Frey, B. S. (2019), What are the opportunities for future happiness research? *International Review of Economics*, https://doi.org/10.1007/s12232-019-00318-9.

Frey, B. S., J. Gallus and L. Steiner (2014), Open issues in happiness research. *International Review of Economics*, 61(2), 115–25.

Frey, B. S., S. Luechinger and A. Stutzer (2007), Calculating tragedy: assessing the costs of terrorism. *Journal of Economic Surveys*, 21(1), 1–24.

Frey, B. S. and A. Stutzer (2000), Happiness, economy and institutions. *The Economic Journal*, 110(466), 918–38.

Frey, B. S. and A. Stutzer (2002a), What can economists learn from happiness research? *Journal of Economic Literature*, 40(2), 402–35.

Frey, B. S. and A. Stutzer (2002b), *Happiness and Economics: How the Economy and Institutions Affect Well-being*. Princeton: Princeton University Press.

Frey, B. S. and A. Stutzer (2014), Economic consequences of mispredicting utility. *Journal of Happiness Studies*, 15(4), 937–56.

Glaeser, E. L., J. D. Gottlieb and O. Ziv (2016), Unhappy cities. *Journal of Labor Economics*, 34(S2), S129–S182.

Gui, B. and R. Sugden (eds) (2005), *Economics and Social Interaction: Accounting for Interpersonal Relations*. Cambridge: Cambridge University Press.

Helliwell, J. and H. Huang (2008), How's your government? International evidence linking good government and well-being. *British Journal of Political Science*, 38(04), 595–619.

Hills, T., E. Proto and D. Sgroi (2015), Historical analysis of national subjective wellbeing using millions of digitized books: introducing the HPS Index. VoxEU.org, September 18. https://voxeu.org/article/building-historical-index-happiness-using-google-books.

Hollander-Blumoff, R. and T. R. Tyler (2008), Procedural justice in negotiation: procedural fairness, outcome acceptance, and integrative potential. *Law & Social Inquiry*, 33(2), 473–500.

Huang, P. H. (2018), Subjective well-being and the law. In E. Diener, S. Oishi and L. Tay (eds), *Handbook of Well-being* (pp. 932–44). Salt Lake City, UT: DEF Publishers.

Kahneman, D., E. Diener and N. Schwarz (eds) (1999), *Well-being: The Foundations of Hedonic Psychology*. New York: Russell Sage Foundation.

Kahneman, D. and A. B. Krueger (2006), Developments in the measurement of subjective well-being. *Journal of Economic Perspectives*, 20(1), 3–24.

Layard, R. (2005), *Happiness: Lessons from a New Science*. New York: Penguin Press.

Layard, R. and G. O'Donnell (2015), How to make policy when happiness is the goal. *World Happiness Report*, 76–87. ISBN: 978-0-9968513-2-9

Liberini, F., M. Redoano and E. Proto (2017), Happy voters. *Journal of Public Economics*, 146(C), 41–57.

Lind, E. A. and T. R. Tyler (1988), *The Social Psychology of Procedural Justice*. New York: Plenum Press.

Lindqvist, E., R. Östling and D. Cesarini (2018), *Long-Run Effects of Lottery Wealth on Psychological Well-being*. Research Working Paper 24667, National Bureau of Economic Research.

Luechinger, S. (2009), Valuing air quality using the life satisfaction approach. *The Economic Journal*, 119(536), 482–515.

Luechinger, S., S. Meier and A. Stutzer (2008), Bureaucratic rents and life satisfaction. *Journal of Law, Economics, and Organization*, 24(2), 476–88.

Luechinger, S. and P. A. Raschky (2009), Valuing flood disasters using the life satisfaction approach. *Journal of Public Economics*, 93(3–4), 620–33.

Mikucka, M., F. Sarracino and J. K. Dubrow (2017), When does economic growth improve life satisfaction? Multilevel analysis of the roles of social trust and income inequality in 46 countries, 1981–2012. *World Development*, 93, 447–59.

Musson, A. and D. Rousselière (2017), Clap along if you know what happiness is to you! Wealth, trust and subjective well-being. CIRIEC Working Paper 2017/02, CIRIEC, Université de Liège.

Odermatt, R., N. Powdthavee and A. Stutzer (2017), Overoptimistic entrepreneurs: predicting wellbeing consequences of self-employment. Discussion Paper 11098, IZA.

Odermatt, R. and A. Stutzer (2018), Subjective well-being and public policy. In E. Diener, S. Oishi and L. Tay (eds), *Handbook of Well-being* (pp. 954–68). Salt Lake City, UT: DEF Publishers.

O'Donnell, G. and A. J. Oswald (2015), National well-being policy and a weighted approach to human feelings. *Ecological Economics*, 120, 59–70.

OECD (2017), *How's Life? 2017: Measuring Well-being*. Paris: OECD Publishing.

Probst-Hensch, N. (2017), Happiness and its molecular fingerprints. *International Review of Economics*, 64(2), 197–211.

Putnam, R. D. (2000), *Bowling Alone: The Collapse and Revival of American Community*. New York: Simon & Schuster.

Rodríguez-Pose, A. and V. Tselios (2019), Well-being, political decentralisation and governance quality in Europe. *Journal of Human Development and Capabilities*, 20(1), 69–93.

Ryff, C. D. (2017), Eudaimonic well-being, inequality, and health: recent findings and future directions. *International Review of Economics*, 64(2), 159–78.

Sen, A. K. (1977), Rational fools: a critique of the behavioral foundations of economic theory. *Philosophy & Public Affairs*, 6(4), 317–44.

Sgroi, D., T. Hills, G. O'Donnell and A. J. Oswald (2017), Understanding happiness: a Cage policy report. Centre for Competitive Advantage in the Global Economy, University of Warwick.

Stutzer, A. (2004), The role of income aspirations in individual happiness. *Journal of Economic Behavior & Organization*, 54(1), 89–109.

Stutzer, A. and B. S. Frey (2010), Recent advances in the economics of individual subjective well-being. *Social Research: An International Quarterly*, 77(2), 679–714.

The Economist. (2016), Schumpeter: against happiness. September 24, 60.

Weimann, J., A. Knabe and R. Schöb (2015), *Measuring Happiness: The Economics of Well-being*. Cambridge, MA: MIT Press.

Welsch, H. (2002), Preferences over prosperity and pollution: environmental valuation based on happiness surveys. *Kyklos*, 55(4), 473–94.

Welsch, H. (2006), Environment and happiness: valuation of air pollution using life satisfaction data. *Ecological Economics*, 58(4), 801–13.

Welsch, H. (2008), The social costs of civil conflict: evidence from surveys of happiness. *Kyklos*, 61(2), 320–40.

White, M. D. (2015), The problems with measuring and using happiness for policy purposes. Mercatus Research, Mercatus Center, George Mason University, Arlington, VA.

PART I

Historical and philosophical perspectives
on the Economics of Happiness

3. Aristotle, eudaimonia, neuroscience and economics

Jeffrey Sachs

3.1 ARISTOTLE AND EUDAIMONIA

Eudaimonia for Aristotle means a good life, a live well lived. The term *eudaimonia* is sometimes translated as 'thriving' and sometimes as 'happiness'. In either case, Aristotle means it to refer to life considered as a whole, rather than to a momentary experience, psychological state or emotion.

To understand Aristotle's conception of *eudaimonia*, we should start with Aristotle's theory of the *psyche* (*anima* in Latin), or soul. Aristotle believed the human soul to be divided into three capacities or faculties: the vegetative or nutritive faculty; the sensitive faculty; and the rational faculty (*nous*).[1]

In Aristotle's understanding, the first faculty is shared by all life, plants and animals. It is the ability to survive through nutrition and reproduction. The second faculty is shared only with animals, and includes the sensory capacities that guide motion towards pleasurable stimuli and away from aversive stimuli. The sensitive faculty may also be called the appetitive faculty, focusing on the appetitive desires of the senses. The third faculty is purely human, the ability to reason and deliberate. The rational faculty includes both intellectual abilities, such as logic, and moral abilities, notably the ability to pursue pleasures in moderation rather than excess.

Eudaimonia, for Aristotle, is a life lived according to *arete*, translated as virtue or excellence. Aristotle is referring to a particular kind of excellence: the excellence of the faculty of reason. Aristotle distinguishes two kinds of virtues, or excellences, of reason: intellectual virtues and moral virtues. Intellectual virtues are excellences of wisdom, both theoretical wisdom and practical wisdom. Theoretical wisdom is knowledge that can be learned through study: logic and information. Practical wisdom (*phronesis*) is knowledge gained mainly by being mentored and through experience: how to choose the right action in the right context for wellbeing.

Moral virtues are the excellences of reason guiding the sensitive faculty. The sensitive faculty moves all animals, human and others, towards pleasures and away from pain. Yet pleasures can be pursued in excess (too much of a good thing) or in deficiency (too little of a good thing). Similarly, the aversion to pain can be pursued in excess, as with cowardice, or in deficiency, as with recklessness for one's safety. Moral virtues are the excellences of using reason to steer the pursuit of pleasures and the avoidance of pain, in both cases towards moderation. Aristotle argues that wellbeing depends on moderate pursuit of pleasures and aversion to pain. Aristotle's emphasis on moderation in the pursuit of pleasures is aligned with Greek wisdom more generally, as exemplified by the inscription in the Temple of Apollo at Delphi, *Meden Agan*, Nothing in Excess.

Aristotle identifies three main moral virtues: *temperance* (*sophrosyne*), meaning the moderate pursuit of pleasures (the mean of insensibility and licentiousness); *courage* (*andreia*), meaning the moderate aversion to pain (the mean of cowardice and recklessness); and *justice* (*dikaiosyne*), meaning the proportionate treatment of other people, receiving neither too much nor too little. When *practical wisdom* is added to these three moral virtues we have the four virtues that have come down through the ages as Christianity's four cardinal virtues. Aristotle in fact discusses several other moral virtues as well, including generosity (the mean of stinginess and extravagance), gentleness (the mean of apathy and short temper), high-mindedness (the mean of pettiness and vanity) and magnanimity (the mean of meanness and vulgarity in giving by the rich).

It is worth underscoring that the excellence of justice, which is an excellence of interpersonal relations, reflects Aristotle's judgment that man is a political animal (*zoon politikon*), dependent on family, friends and fellow citizens for *eudaimonia*. The moral virtue of justice is therefore necessary for a good life. Aristotle famously writes in *The Politics*, 'Anyone who either cannot lead the common life or is so self-sufficient as not to need to, and therefore does not partake of society, is either a beast or a god'. In this context, writes Aristotle, 'justice is the bond of men in states' (*The Politics*, 1253, 35). He also underscores that 'nobody would choose to live without friends, although he were in possession of every other good' (NE, bk VIII, ch. I).

We can summarize by saying that *eudaimonia* is life lived according to the virtues, that is, according to the excellences of reason. A virtuous life does not reject the pursuit of pleasure, but calls for the pursuit of pleasure in moderation, as guided by the virtue of temperance. The crowning glory of the virtues is *phronesis*, practical wisdom, as that is nothing less than knowing how to choose the right action at the right time for the individual's highest good, *eudaimonia*. The great difficulty, notes Aristotle, is that the right choice at the right time depends on the context of each choice. The right action cannot be determined by a rigid set of rules. *Phronesis* is therefore a character trait gained by experience, the exercise of reason over time, rather than by a checklist of precepts. According to Aristotle, only older people can achieve *phronesis*, a view that seems (to me) more accurate with each passing year. In fact, each of the virtues must be cultivated throughout a lifetime, by being mentored, through formal education, and as the result of practice. Practice leads to learning, and learning leads to habits and the formation of character. In essence, *eudaimonia* is to be achieved by cultivating the excellences of character.

Aristotle recognizes that the four virtues are necessary but not sufficient for *eudaimonia*. There is also the question of material life and luck. Individuals must be able to meet their needs for food, shelter, clothing and other basic needs in order to thrive. A certain level of wealth is needed in order to be able to afford the leisure needed for contemplation and political activity, both of which are parts of a good life. We may call this condition 'material sufficiency'. Also, the individual needs good fortune for good health, adequately good looks, and the like.

Aristotle emphasizes that pleasures can easily lead to excesses unless controlled by reason. While Aristotle doesn't invoke the concept of addiction, this seems to be what Aristotle has in mind when he warns against a slavish (or animal-like) devotion to bodily pleasures. 'If then this disposition [to bodily pleasures] is not obedient and subject to authority, it will greatly develop. For the longing for pleasure which a foolish person has is insatiable and universal, and the active exercise of the desire augments its native strength, until the desires, if they are strong or vehement actually expel the reasoning power' (NE, bk II,I ch. XV). Yet Aristotle clearly rejects a life of asceticism. 'In the temperate man then the concupiscent element ought to live in harmony with reason, as nobleness is the object of them both, and the temperate man desires what is right, and desires it in the right way, and at the right time, i.e. according to the law of reason' (NE, bk III, ch. XV).

Aristotle notes that because human souls have both a sensitive faculty and a rational faculty, they have conflicting desires, or motivations, for action. (See Pearson 2012 for an excellent discussion.) Aristotle's general term for desire is *orexis*. He distinguishes three types of desires. Desire for *eudaimonia*, that is desire guided by reason, is *boulêsis*. It is linked to the term *boulesusis*, meaning deliberation. Desire for pleasure, especially through the sensation of touch, is termed *epithumia*. In accord with Aristotle's classification of the sensitive faculty as the part of the soul shared with other animals, bodily pleasures are the kind of pleasures 'the lower animals are generally capable of, and it hence that these pleasures appear slavish and brutish' (NE, bk III, ch. XIII). Desire led by anger or threat is *thumos*, another kind of irrational desire. Aristotle describes how people under the influence of *thumos* 'turn like wild beasts upon those who have wounded them' (NE, bk III, ch. X). Passion, notes Aristotle, 'is preeminently eager to encounter perils'.

The three kinds of desire give rise to internal conflicts, that is, whether to act according to reason, pleasure or passion (anger). An *akratic*, or incontinent, individual chooses pleasure over reason, acting according to *epithumia* rather than *boulêsis*. (Similarly, an *akratic* individual will pursue an action according to anger, *thumos*, rather than reason.) An *enkratic*, or continent, individual is guided by reason over pleasure, and by reason over anger, acting according to *bouleseis* rather than *epithumia* or *thumos*. The *enkratic* individual feels the tug of pleasure, but overcomes it in the pursuit of the good life. He or she craves the chocolate cake but resists the temptation to eat it. Modern psychologists use the term *inhibitory control* and *self-regulation* to describe the psychological state by which a deliberative choice based on longer-term considerations outweighs a craving.

In *De Anima* (*On the Soul*), Aristotle observes that acting according to *boulêsis* rather than *epithumia* means choosing future benefits instead of immediate but ultimately harmful pleasures. Only humans can make such a choice, because it requires the (rational) ability to see into the future. As Aristotle puts it: 'The opposition of reason and the appetites ... is confined to those creatures enjoying resistance, while the appetite supports its case with immediate facts. Inability to see into the future underwrites the appearance that what is immediately pleasant both is so absolutely and is absolutely good' (DA, bk III, ch. X). This is in line with the modern notion that addiction can be considered a kind of excessive time discounting, that is, an underweighting of adverse future consequences.

A virtuous person, a *phronimos* (an individual with *phronesis*), has a harmonized soul. Not only does reason predominate, but even the desire for pleasure is moderated. While the *enkratic* soul pushes away the chocolate cake despite the urge to eat it, the *phronimos* doesn't feel the urge to eat it. The *phronimos* is not an ascetic but rather desires pleasures in moderation, as honed by reason. The result is temperance, achieved through mentorship, education, practice and eventually habit formation.

3.2 NEUROSCIENCE AND WELLBEING

Aristotle had no knowledge of neuroscience, that is, of a scientific understanding of the brain and its interactions with the body, but he was a remarkably keen and shrewd observer of human nature. His categorization of desires into *boulêsis*, *epithumia* and *thumos*, and of the psyche into the nutritive, perceptive and rational faculties, resonates with cognitive neuroscience, which has also identified distinct circuits within the brain in ways that relate to Aristotle's concepts.

Consider the questions of desires and behavior. Aristotle argued that behavior could be guided by irrational or rational desires. In the first, some kind of appetitive pleasure (food, sex) would give rise to desire; in the latter, the individual would deliberate over the right kind of action. Cognitive neuroscientists similarly distinguish between behaviors with and without deliberation. A fascinating six-way taxonomy in this regard is proposed by LeDoux and Daw (2018).

In the LeDoux–Daw taxonomy, there are four kinds of non-deliberative behaviors. The first are *reflexes*, which are innate, species-specific stimulus–response patterns. The second are *fixed reaction patterns*, which are also innate and species-specific, but more complex than reflexes (and include freezing or defensive fighting). The third are *habits*, which are stimulus–response behaviors that are acquired through instrumental learning, but that continue to occur in response to the stimulus even when the reinforcements are no longer present. The fourth are *action–outcome behaviors* that are learned responses where the stimulus–response behavior continues to depend on the presence of the reinforcement.

LeDoux and Daw also suggest two kinds of deliberative behavior: unconscious and conscious. In *unconscious deliberative actions* the individual (or animal) considers the best actions according to cognitive calculations, but these cognitive processes are not conscious, that is, they do not involve the self-awareness of the individual. Nonetheless, they are goal-directed, and based on calculations of likely outcomes of alternative actions relative to goals. The final category is conscious deliberative actions. In this case the individual is aware of the decision making, and aims to calculate the best actions to achieve specific goals. Conscious deliberative action comes closest to Aristotle's idea of actions based on rational desire.

Loosely speaking, then, the non-deliberative actions are related to Aristotle's category of actions guided by *epithumia*, since both innate behaviors and conditioned learning generally relate to the pursuit of somatic pleasures (food, sex, comfort, addictive substances) and to the avoidance of pain or danger. Such behaviors are shared by humans and other animals. Deliberative behaviors, on the other hand, are related to Aristotle's category of actions guided by *boulêsis*. In both the Aristotelian and neuroscientific accounts, deliberative actions are goal-directed. (Note, though, that Aristotle did not distinguish between conscious and nonconscious goal-directed deliberation.)

Of course, this kind of mapping is not precise. For example, Aristotle argues that choosing actions aimed at *eudaimonia* will eventually become habitual rather than deliberative, as the result of experience. Still, the habits learned through repeated 'deliberation will be different in kind from the repertoire of habits learned through stimulus–response conditioning. Yet another key difference is that when cognitive neuroscientists discuss goal-based deliberation they are not generally specifying the *kinds of goals* being pursued, while for Aristotle rational desires aim specifically at the goal of *eudaimonia*, a thriving life. Cognitive neuroscience has not yet taken up the challenge of defining or describing the neurobiology of a thriving life.

LeDoux and Daw link their six modes of behavior to distinct neural circuitry. We can forgive Aristotle for not taking that step 2340 years ago. Most of the neural circuitry understood today has been investigated only within the past 50 years, and indeed most of the hard-won knowledge has come much more recently than that! Neuroscientific discoveries are burgeoning, so that the circuitry proposed today is still novel, somewhat speculative and contested among scholars.

Nonetheless, as a broad generalization it's fair to say that the neuroscientific findings on neural circuitry tend to support rather than refute Aristotle's claim that there is something unique about the human capacity for goal-based deliberation, while the behavioral capacities of the reflexes and conditioned learning are shared with other animals. Broadly speaking, goal-based deliberation depends on the neocortex, and especially the prefrontal cortex (PFC), parts of the human brain anatomy that grew massively in size and functionality in the course of human evolution compared with the brains of other animal species including of our closest relatives, the great apes.

Some of the circuitry recently identified by neuroscience includes:

- *Circuitry for deliberative actions*: linkages of the medial temporal lobe and other cortical areas (for episodic memory, semantic memories, cognitive maps, schema) with cortical cognitive circuitry (for conscious and nonconscious deliberation) and other systems (sensory, subcortical).
- *Circuitry for appetitive conditioning*: linkages of the basal ganglia (ventral tegmental area, ventral striatum, dorsal striatum) with cortical and other subcortical systems.
- *Circuitry for defensive action–outcome behaviors*: linkages of the sensory system with the amygdala and descending to the ventral striatum.
- *Circuitry for innate threat reactions*: linkages of the sensory system with the amygdala and descending to the periaqueductal grey (PAG).

There is no single conductor of this orchestra of brain circuitry, though the anterior cingulate cortex (ACC), which receives signals from the other brain networks, is sometimes hypothesized to play at least a limited role as an aggregator of the circuitry for deliberative, sensory, and conditioned behaviors, and to be a key part of metacognition, that is, the self-aware thinking about one's own thinking (Metcalfe and Schwartz 2016). The insula too has been identified as playing an integrative function.

What seems clear, and is the subject of considerable ongoing research, is that the various brain circuits can give rise to competing behavioral responses. A conditioned stimulus might trigger the circuitry for appetitive conditioning and cause an addict to crave the addictive substance or behavior, but simultaneously trigger the circuitry for deliberative actions to resist the craving. The individual feels like two minds, just as Aristotle described the battle between desires for the good (*eudaimonia*) and desires for the appetitive pleasures.

A great deal of addiction-related research therefore examines when behaviors are based on deliberation or conditioned learning. Both kinds of decision making are present and indeed important in a healthy individual. Deliberative decision making is appropriate for more complex and novel situations when the possible future consequences of alternative actions must be assessed. Such decision making is arduous, time-consuming and burdensome in terms of attention, working memory, energy inputs and time commitment. Conditioned responses, by contrast, are much faster, with far lighter loads on cognitive circuitry, and the outcomes can be highly desirable if circumstances are familiar, speed is of the essence and the conditioning is to appropriate stimuli, not to cues for addiction or other self-harms.

The key behavioral question is which one of the motivation systems wins out when there is a conflict between the outputs of the deliberative circuitry and the conditioning circuitry. Neuroscience is beginning to give answers, and again Aristotle had some crucial intuitions more than 2300 years ago. Certain kinds of pleasures, those that are associated with a phasic release of the neurotransmitter dopamine from the ventral tegmental area to the ventral and dorsal striatum, seem to be most addictive, and therefore most likely to elicit behaviors that are conditioned rather than deliberative.

The brain apparently produces the sensations of pleasure both in response to the *anticipation* of a reward and also to the *consummation* of the reward. The anticipation of a reward is closely linked with a phasic release of dopamine, leading to the sensation of 'craving'. The consummation of a reward is apparently linked with other non-dopamine systems, such as the release of endogenous opioids such as endorphins in response to satiety. Amazingly, addiction can persist on the basis of craving alone, even when the consummation of the reward is no longer present, and indeed when the addictive behavior leads to an aversive outcome rather than a reward outcome. This has led Berridge and Kringelbach (2013) to differentiate the brain mechanisms that cause 'wanting' (craving or anticipatory pleasure) versus 'liking' (consummatory pleasure).

It is hypothesized that both the release of dopamine (craving) and endorphins (consummation) are closely linked to *homeostasis*, the tendency of the brain and body to seek a return to normal operating parameters for physical functions (adequate water, food, salt, sexual function) and for social attachments (aversion to physical isolation). Craving is then associated with stimuli that signal the ability to restore homeostasis, and consummatory pleasure is the signal that homeostasis has been achieved (through rehydration, ingestion of food, sexual activity, etc.). For this reason, many of the most powerful addictions are related to the craving and consummation of basic bodily functions (food, sex). Aristotle intuited the same when he noted that the active exercise of appetitive pleasure 'augments its native strength, until the desires, if they are strong or vehement, actually expel the reasoning power'.

Yet the circuitry for appetitive conditioning also creates other kinds of addictions that similarly stimulate the phasic release of dopamine and thereby lead to conditioned learning that creates a craving for the behavior. Various addictive drugs, alcohol, compulsive shopping, gambling, online pornography, online gaming and other behaviors have been linked experimentally with such dopamine-mediated craving. The irony – indeed at the profound cost of suffering in our modern economy – is that businesses have widely recognized the profitability of selling addictive goods and services and marketing them through advertising stimuli that aggressively promote the addictions, a point recently emphasized by Courtwright (2019).

A key challenge, therefore, for Aristotle and for modern neuroscience, and for each of us as individuals, is to understand how the various brain networks – cognitive, conditioned, emotional, defensive – determine actual behavior. When does the *akratic* individual give in to pleasure? When does the addict succumb to craving? Or when does Aristotle's rational faculty, or neuroscience's goal-based cognition, win the battle over motivation?

Addiction researchers aim to understand why deliberative behavior sometimes dominates (the addict successfully stays away from the addictive substance or behavior) and sometimes fails (the addict relapses). By scanning the brains of addicts confronted with addictive stimuli, the evidence suggests that addictive behaviors reflect both the hyperactivation of the reward-conditioning circuitry of the basal ganglia and a weakening of the cortical deliberative circuitry, especially the ventral medial PFC. Addiction seems to be a manifestation both of heightened craving due to conditioned learning and weakened goal orientation.

This has been characterized by Bickel and colleagues (2015) as a steep rise in the addict's time discounting of future adverse consequences, recalling Aristotle's observation that appetitive pleasures tend to block out consideration of the future. In Bickel's interpretation, the current 'benefits' of anticipatory and consummatory pleasure (even when consummatory pleasure is not attained) outweigh the discounted long-term costs because of a high discount rate attached to the future costs. The addiction disorder is characterized as a disorder of time discounting, suggesting a therapeutic goal of reducing the individual's time rate of discount.

Bickel et al. (2015) report two kinds of cognitive training to reduce the discount rate: working memory training and episodic future thinking (EFT). In memory training, subjects are given various working memory tasks over a number of sessions. Alcohol-addicted subjects and obese children both showed significant therapeutic benefits of the working memory training. In EFT, subjects are asked to consider themselves in various future scenarios ('mental time travel'). This treatment too is shown to result in a significant reduction of addictive behaviors. The authors suggest that self-control, or inhibitory processes emanating from the PFC, work like a muscle, in that they need exercise and strengthening, especially when individuals are suffering from addictions.

Aside from addictions, and other behavioral disorders such as obsessive-compulsive disorders that also relate to the dysregulation of the conditioning circuitry, there are mood and anxiety disorders that deeply compromise the attainment of *eudaimonia*. Mood disorders include massive depressive disorders (MDD) and bipolar disorder, and anxiety disorders include panic disorders, post-traumatic stress disorder (PTSD), generalized anxiety and phobias. One persistent theme in all of these cases is that life experience matters enormously. One important finding is that *chronic stress*, leading to a chronically excessive load of stress-related cortisol (through the release of cortisol stimulated by the hypothalamus-pituitary-adrenal network), can damage the PFC and other brain circuitry and thereby lead to lifelong impairments of brain functioning. It is hypothesized, for example, that exposure to chronic stress in the highly vulnerable years of early childhood development (under the age of five) significantly raises the risk of adult-onset depression.

3.3   ECONOMICS AND WELLBEING

Neoclassical economics, especially before the recent advances of neuroeconomics, adopted a model of human nature that dropped the Aristotelian notions of a divided psyche and rejected any objective standards of a good life. The core notion of the virtues was replaced in nineteenth- and twentieth-century economics by a theory based on individual preferences, or utility, without reference to benchmarks of a good life or the need to cultivate virtue. The story of this shift in perspective has recently been described by Wootton (2018). The broad cultural abandonment of virtue as a shared benchmark for human wellbeing was famously and persuasively described by MacIntyre (1981).

According to the new economic viewpoint, each individual has his or her own tastes or preferences, and these preferences cannot and *should not* be judged by the standards of reason. The individual is not torn between desires of reason and pleasure, as in Aristotle (or neuroscience). Individuals have one motivation and one motivation alone: to maximize wellbeing according to their own personalized preferences, whatever those might be. Economists in this line also lost any interest in accounting for those preferences, and instead invoked the Latin saying, 'De gustibus non est disputandem' (tastes should not be disputed or debated). In other words, each to his own tastes. Neoclassical economics also assumes that preferences do not change over time, or that if they do they change in a way that is known to the individual beforehand, and therefore in a way that can be taken into account in advance. Individuals are not torn by temptation, addictions, compulsions or other internal conflicts, and are not beset by regrets. Even if addictions occur, in this view, they are rational addictions in the sense that the addict knew what was coming, and rationally balanced the short-term pleasures of the addiction with the long-term costs.

These assumptions are taught to economics students today around the world, and described by introductory economics textbooks. The six main assumptions are:

- Utility is egoistic, meaning that each individual's utility depends only on individual consumption of goods and services, not on relations with others or the wellbeing of others.
- Moment-to-moment (flow) utility is based on the consumption of goods and services.
- Lifetime utility is determined by the discounted sum of moment-to-moment utility.
- The utility function is based on a consistent set of preferences over goods and services, with minimal consistency standards such as the transitivity of preferences.
- The utility function is stable over time, not subject to experience or learning, or subject to learning in a known and predictable manner.
- The individual maximizes utility through the choice of market transactions subject to a budget constraint.

Notice that three features of utility theory are deeply contrary to Aristotle's theory of the psyche and to the findings of modern neuroscience:

- Utility (wellbeing) is defined only relative to the consumption of market goods and services, not to personal relationships (with family, friends, and fellow citizens).
- Utility is a single-value function, rather than the result of distinct valuations arising from different faculties of the psyche.
- Preferences do not change in response to experience and learning, or only in ways that the individual knows beforehand and takes into account in utility maximization.

These features of modern utility theory do not withstand empirical scrutiny, either by economists when examining economic behavior or by psychologists examining decision making and wellbeing more generally. For example, individuals clearly make choices (such as altruistic gifts, or highly cooperative actions) based on interpersonal relationships and norms of fairness and friendship. Individuals battle with conflicting desires, and sometimes succumb to addictions that cause great remorse and unhappiness. Individuals change their preferences over time as the result of experience, learning, coaching and reflection. Choices in the marketplace and laboratory settings are subject to subliminal cues, priming, framing, stress and the presence of irrelevant alternatives. Individuals have a shaky conceptualization of healthful behaviors, risks of addiction, vulnerabilities to priming and biases in reasoning. Individuals are notoriously weak at managing probabilities and uncertainties in a consistent manner. And individuals are poor forecasters of their own emotional responses to future behaviors.

Modern neuroeconomics and its close cousin, behavioral economics, aim to update the assumptions of economic decision making to take into account the anomalies and inconsistencies. There is now a widespread recognition of the importance of social norms, temptations and addictions, interpersonal relations and weak capacities to maximize utility, for example to forecast the affective states that will result from alternative future conditions. Yet these fields have not yet produced a new 'standard' model of behavior aligned with the empirical findings. Instead, the field of neuroeconomics has mainly catalogued the behavioral anomalies (measured against the standard utility theory) and proposed to address those anomalies mainly through policies that 'nudge' individuals into making better choices. Little headway has been made on more fundamental challenges, such as the pervasive addictions and consequent unhappiness that is widespread in modern societies.

3.4   TOWARDS A NEW SYNTHESIS OF ARISTOTLE, NEUROSCIENCE, POSITIVE PSYCHOLOGY AND ECONOMICS

The basic aim of economic science should be *eudaimonia*, thriving and well-lived lives, taken as a whole, for members of society. To put *eudaimonia* at the center of economics and public policy, we will need a framework to measure *eudaimonia* and relate it to life choices, and to identify the pathways to achieve *eudaimonia*. This in turn will require an accurate science of individual motivations and the ways to cultivate human actions consistent with *eudaimonia*. The way forward must be deeper and more consequent than 'nudging' individuals to counteract their *akratic* or poorly motivated behaviors.

I propose the following basic approach. First, in line with Aristotle, we should recognize that *eudaimonia* depends on the combination of two factors: life circumstances (wealth, health, friendship, family, citizenship, etc.) and personal traits (virtues, personality, brain circuitry). This proposition is illustrated in Figure 3.1.

Wellbeing cannot be achieved when life circumstances are harsh (such as ill-health or poverty), but neither can wellbeing be achieved without adequate personal traits (such as practical wisdom and temperance) and mental health (such as freedom from addiction and from mood and anxiety disorders). The two-way arrow linking circumstances and traits emphasizes that the two domains inevitably interact. Poor personal traits diminish life circumstances (e.g. by occasioning the loss of friends or business opportunities), while poor life circumstances (e.g. loneliness, absence of friends, poverty) cause stress and possibly a weakening of character traits and mental stability.

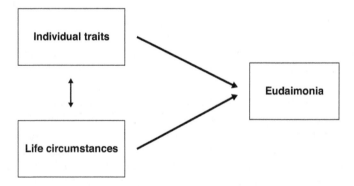

Figure 3.1   The two pillars of eudaimonia: individual and life circumstances

Second, again following Aristotle, the individual virtues include both personal virtues (such as practical wisdom and temperance) and interpersonal virtues (notably justice). Individual wellbeing depends on choices over goods and on relations with other people. In both cases, actions need to be guided by the rational pursuit of the good rather than the irrational craving for pleasure. On the personal level that means cultivating moderation in the pursuit of pleasures. On the interpersonal plane it means treating others in a manner that leads to trust, friendship, mutual support and love. In interactions that are characterized by a 'social dilemma', where an individual may gain personal wealth, fame or glory by deliberately hurting others, the interpersonal virtue of justice requires choosing sociality (trust, honesty, adherence to norms) rather than short-term personal advantage.

Third, personal character is shaped by early upbringing, education and habit formation, as depicted in Figure 3.2.

The virtues are not merely inborn personality traits, though they surely depend in part on genetics. They also depend on family and socialization, not least of which is through education and the good examples and guidance of mentors. Early socialization and a safe family environment matter enormously. Early lifetime stress, for example, predisposes the individual towards adult psychopathologies such as addictions and mood and anxiety disorders.

Aristotle's substantive recommendations regarding *eudaimonia* hold up very well in the research findings of positive psychology and cognitive neuroscience. Some of the most pertinent findings of positive psychology

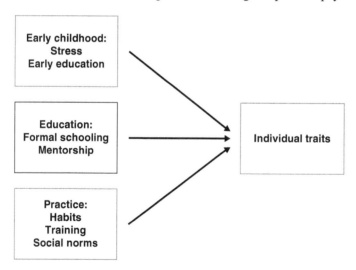

Figure 3.2   The fostering of individual traits

```
┌─────────────────────────────────────────────┐
│               Material sufficiency            │
│                                               │
│               Brain health:                   │
│          Trait emotional intelligence         │
│      Positive character, interpersonal values │
│               Mental health                   │
│                                               │
│               Physical health                 │
│                                               │
│            Strong social bonds:               │
│                  Marriage                     │
│                   Family                      │
│                 Friendship                    │
│                 Citizenship                   │
│                                               │
│               Excellences:                    │
│                   Skills                      │
│                  Purpose                      │
│              Accomplishments                  │
└─────────────────────────────────────────────┘
```

Figure 3.3   The conditions of eudaimonia: life well lived

come from studies of subjective wellbeing (SWB), meaning the subjective evaluations of the life course in survey data. One of the key measures of SWB is the Cantril ladder, which asks individuals to evaluate the quality of their life according to a ladder with rungs ranging from the bottom 0th rung (worst life imaginable) to the top 10th rung (best life imaginable). By design, the Cantril ladder requires a conscious, reflective evaluation. It is the PFC's standard of a good life.

According to the extensive range of studies of SWB using the Cantril ladder and other related measures, a good life is promoted by the following, as summarized in Figure 3.3:

- *Personality traits*, including the 'big five' (neurosis, extraversion, openness, conscientiousness and agreeableness). As expected, greater interpersonal skills (extraversion and agreeableness) and rational skills (openness to new ideas, people, and circumstances, conscientiousness) are conducive to happiness, while neuroticism results in lower happiness.
- *The ability to regulate emotions* as a key character trait. Studies demonstrate that 'trait emotional intelligence' (TEI) is conducive to happiness. TEI measures whether individuals believe that they are

'in touch' with their emotions and able to regulate them effectively to promote wellbeing.

- *Strong interpersonal relations*, measured by friendships, marriage and social support networks. The evidence suggests that interpersonal relations are key for happiness (humans are social animals after all) and that interpersonal traits including honesty, agreeableness, trust and generosity are inputs to successful interpersonal relations. Again, *eudaimonia* depends both on circumstances and character. (See Helliwell and Aknin 2018.)
- *Good mental (and brain) health*. The single most important group of factors leading to low SWB is mental illness, including mood disorders (such as massive depressive disorders), anxiety disorders (PTSD and others) and impulsive/compulsive disorders such as substance abuse and behavioral addictions.
- *Favorable life conditions*. These include adequate income, with a sharply declining marginal utility of income once basic needs have been met, good health and physical safety (e.g. absence of war and rule of law). (See Helliwell and Aknin 2018.)
- *Meaning in life*. Individuals find meaning and satisfaction in the exercise of their reason, that is, in making good life decisions. Achieving virtue is itself a source of meaning, and so too are developing satisfying relations with others. Mastery of skills and contributions to society are further sources of meaning. According to Aristotle (NE, bk X), the life of politics (of a citizen of the *polis*) can bring happiness, but the most sublime happiness comes through contemplation or 'speculative activity' according to reason.

Positive psychology (Seligman 2011) has coined the acronym PERMA to summarize: *P*ositive emotions, *E*ngagement (in activities of excellence), *R*elationships, *M*eaning and *A*chievement.

Psychological and sociological studies have also suggested several ways that the organization of high-income modern society is directly inimical to the achievement of *eudaimonia*. These include:

- *Hyper-consumerism*, overemphasizing the importance of market goods over interpersonal relations.
- *Hot-button advertising*, designed to appeal to the mesolimbic system through Pavlovian and operant conditioning (selling jeans through sexual imagery, obesogenic beverages through smiling faces of young people engaged in social activities, etc.).
- *Unregulated marketing of addictive substances*, such as synthetic opioids, online gambling, social media and processed foods

with addictive additives (salt, sugar, fats, processed grains) (Sachs 2019).

- *High inequalities of income and social status*, leading to chronic stresses and cortisol loading (Wilkinson and Pickett 2019).
- *Weakening social ties*, disrupting interpersonal relations and social support networks.
- *The political appeal to fear*, through broadcast and social media.
- *Childhood poverty and chronic stress*, leading to lifetime impairments of brain physiology.
- *Social norms of libertarianism*, which emphasize personal freedom over wellbeing. Libertarianism is based on the false proposition that humans are by nature solitary and that they come together in a political community only as contractual matter for individual benefit, with politics properly limited to the minimal functions of security and property protection under that social contract.

Achieving a new synthesis around *eudaimonia* is at once a scientific task, to identify empirically the attributes of good lives and how they can be pursued; a social task, to create a broader consensus around the ideas and goals of *eudaimonia*; an economic task, to shift society's resources (including the limited attention span of citizens and economic institutions) towards *eudaimonia*; and a political task, to mobilize politics towards the thriving lives of the citizenry. This challenge also must be carried out in the context of rapid technological change, massive economic upheavals (including mass urbanization, globalization and migration) and enormous global diversity and indeed distrust.

A starting point will be for economics and neuroscience to turn increased attention to the ancient aims of Greek philosophy and the modern aims of positive psychology: to understand the sources of human thriving and thereby to raise the happiness of individuals and societies. Adam Smith, under the influence of British empiricism, launched modern economics as the study of *The Wealth of Nations*. With the end of poverty easily within reach (if indeed the world were more just in its treatment of the poor), it is certainly overdue to relaunch economics as the study of *The Happiness of Nations*.

NOTE

1. In a general way Aristotle follows Plato, who in *The Republic* also divides the soul into three parts, though not exactly the same as Aristotle's three parts: the rational (*logistikon*), appetitive (*epithymetikon*) and spirited (*thymoeides*) faculties. Plato holds

that the three parts of the soul should function in harmony, and uses the word *dikaiosyne*, justice, for an individual with harmony of the soul. Similarly, in the dialogue *Phaedrus*, Plato imagines a human being to be a chariot with two horses. The charioteer is reason, which aims to steer the two horses, one being the appetitive faculty and the other being the willful faculty.

REFERENCES

Aristotle (1986), *De Anima* (On the Soul). Trans. Hugh Lawson-Tancred. Penguin Classics.

Aristotle., Welldon, J. E. C. (James Edward Cowell). (1912), *The Nicomachean Ethics of Aristotle*. Macmillan and Co., Limited.

Aristotle., Welldon, J. E. C. (James Edward Cowell). (1912), *The Politics of Aristotle*. Macmillan and Co., Limited.

Berridge, K. C. and M. L. Kringelbach (2013), Neuroscience of affect: brain mechanisms of pleasure and displeasure. *Current Opinion in Neurobiology*, 23, 294–303.

Bickel, W. K., A. J. Quisenberry, L. Moody and A. G. Wilson (2015), Therapeutic opportunities for self-control repair in addiction and related disorders: change and the limits of change in trans-disease processes. *Clinical Psychological Science*, 3(1), 140–53.

Courtwright, D. T. (2019), *The Age of Addiction: How Bad Habits became Big Business*. Harvard University Press.

Helliwell, J. F. and L. B. Aknin (2018), Expanding the social science of happiness. *Nature Human Behaviour*, 2(4), 248–52.

Kocher, M. G., P. Martinsson, K. O. R. Myrseth and C. E. Wollbrant (2017), Strong, bold, and kind: self-control and cooperation in social dilemmas. *Experimental Economics*, 20(1), 44–69.

LeDoux, J. E. (2015), *Anxious: Using the Brain to Understand and Treat Fear and Anxiety*. Penguin.

LeDoux, J. E. and N. D. Daw (2018), Surviving threats: neural circuit and computational implications of a new taxonomy of defensive behaviour. *Nature Reviews Neuroscience*, 19, 269–82.

MacIntyre, A. (1981), *After Virtue*. University of Notre Dame Press.

Metcalfe, J. and B. L. Schwartz (2016), The ghost in the machine: self-reflective consciousness and the neuroscience of metacognition (pp. 407–24). In J. Dunlosky and S. Tauber (eds) *Oxford Handbook of Metamemory*. Oxford University Press.

Pearson, G. (2012), *Aristotle on Desire*. Cambridge University Press.

Sachs, J. (2019), Addiction and unhappiness in America. In J. Helliwell, R. Layard and J. Sachs (eds) *World Happiness Report 2019*. Sustainable Development Solutions Network.

Seligman, M. (2011), *Flourish: A Visionary New Understanding of Happiness and Well-being*. Free Press.

Syed, S. A. and C. B. Nemeroff (2017), Early life stress, mood, and anxiety disorders. *Chronic Stress*, 1, 2470547017694461.

Wilkinson, R. and K. Pickett (2019), *The Inner Level*. Allen Lane.

Wootton, D. (2018), *Power, Pleasure, and Profit: Insatiable Appetites from Machiavelli to Madison*. Harvard University Press.

4. The economics of eudaimonia

Maurizio Pugno

4.1 INTRODUCTION

'Eudaimonia' is a difficult word, but it is increasingly mentioned by the studies in economics of happiness (e.g. Bruni 2008; Clark and Senik 2011; Benjamin et al. 2014; Graham and Nikolova 2015; Clark 2016; Pugno 2016; Sachs, Chapter 3, this volume). It has often been translated from ancient Greek as 'happiness', but recently 'flourishing' is a preferred translation. This is because – according to Aristotle's philosophy (Keyes and Annas 2009) – eudaimonia refers to living by functioning well, and by realising one's human potential, while 'happiness' rather means pleasurable feeling.

The fact that such a Greek word increasingly appears in the economics of happiness reveals that the focus of the research in this field is shifting from 'happiness' to 'eudaimonia', while frequently using 'life satisfaction' as an intermediate measure (Huta 2016). This shift may be due to the recognition that 'happiness' and 'life satisfaction' are not only correlated with economic and socio-demographic variables, but also with some subjective variables that characterise the psychology of individuals, like perceived trust in others, the confidence of being able to influence events and other variables on personality traits (e.g. Helliwell et al. 2018; Verme 2009; O'Connor 2017).[1]

Another reason for this shift may be due to the critical observation according to which the economics of happiness paves the way to the claim that people's happiness should replace gross domestic product as a policy goal to be maximised, although it is an elusive concept and easy to manipulate by policy makers (e.g. Johns and Ormerod 2007). This claim is not shared by many happiness researchers, however, who rather prefer to take happiness as a useful indicator to monitor the effectiveness of public policies (e.g. Frey and Stutzer 2011). But building a branch of economics by estimating 'happiness equations' in order to study the determinants of 'happiness' or 'life satisfaction' makes this criticism easy to raise and the reply difficult to argue convincingly. More structure in the theory and in the method to study the matter would thus be helpful, and 'eudaimonia' offers a suggestion for this purpose.

The present chapter proposes a number of contributions to the shift of the economic research towards 'eudaimonia'. Section 4.2 provides a rereading of Aristotle's conception of eudaimonia by taking a perspective typical of economists. In fact, special attention will be paid to the structure that links the variables considered by Aristotle. Section 4.3 highlights some limits to Aristotle's conception of eudaimonia, and in particular it examines how to reconcile the subjective realisation of one's potential with the objective standard that should be used to evaluate eudaimonia across people. Section 4.4 provides a reformulation of eudaimonia that adopts a dynamic approach that links stock and flow variables, so that the unique process of human development is described. The properties and advantages of this reformulation are pointed out, and empirical evidence drawn from different disciplines is addressed in support. Section 4.5 contrasts eudaimonia with hedonism as two pathways to happiness that people can choose. Section 4.6 concludes with brief remarks.

4.2 ARISTOTLE'S CONCEPTION OF EUDAIMONIA: A REREADING

Aristotle's conception of eudaimonia has long been investigated and discussed in philosophy, but it has recently also attracted interest in the economics of happiness and, some time before, in the capability approach. The conception of eudaimonia is not simple, especially if it is translated into modern words and used for modern life. Moreover, Aristotle's main work on this subject, titled *Nicomachean Ethics*, is not a complete treatise, but was written as scattered lectures notes. It is not a surprise, therefore, that only some specific issues raised by the original conception of eudaimonia are considered or stressed in the economic literature. For example, Amartya Sen finds interesting, for his capability approach, Aristotle's claim that wealth is not the final good for people (Sen 1999). John Helliwell refers to Aristotle in arguing that people's answer to the survey question about life satisfaction depends on many aspects of conceptions of a good life (Helliwell and Aknin 2018). Luigino Bruni finds interesting the role of friendship in Aristotle's conception of eudaimonia in support to his claim that relational goods should be non-instrumental in order to contribute to happiness (Bruni 2008).

In this section we reformulate Aristotle's *Nicomachean Ethics* so that it can be easily understood by economists. In particular, the structure that links the various concepts in an input–output process is emphasised, thus highlighting many issues and implications.

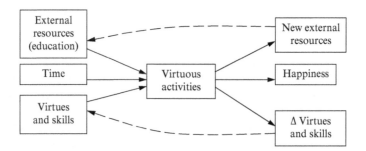

Figure 4.1   A representation of Aristotle's conception of eudaimonia

Our central argument is that Aristotle's eudaimonia is not only a dynamic process over people's life-cycle, but it is an *endogenous* process that can become a collective process. The contrast with the other well-known conception of happiness in the ancient Greek thought, namely *hedonism*, thus becomes even starker. In fact, pleasure in hedonism can be obtained in exchange for costly exogenous resources only. This implies competition for resources and vulnerability to external shocks. We further show that eudaimonia and hedonism are not simply two abstract conceptions of happiness, but – as Aristotle observed – two alternatives that people choose to practise in their daily lives.

Let us reread Aristotle's original conception of eudaimonia with the help of the chart represented in Figure 4.1. The main concepts used as building blocks of eudaimonia are indicated by boxes, which, through the links between them indicated by arrows, can describe how eudaimonia works as a process.

The only box in Figure 4.1 that receives but does not give arrows is that of 'happiness' (i.e. the English translation of eudaimonia), which is – according to Aristotle – the final good of human life. 'Final good' does not only mean that it is not intermediate or instrumental for other ends, but also that it includes all ends valued for their own sake, and that it does not need any other end, that is, it is both 'complete' and 'self-sufficient'. Eudaimonia thus includes many incommensurable dimensions of human life,[2] and it does not simply refer to momentary events but to the entire life of human beings (*NE-R*, I.1 and I.7).[3]

The box for 'happiness' in the chart receives the arrow from the box for 'virtuous activities', thus indicating that happiness materialises by realising practical projects when these are 'in accordance with the best and most complete [. . .] virtue' (*NE-R*, I.7). 'Virtue' – according to Aristotle – is a 'state of character' (*NE-R*, II.5), which should be intended as a 'disposition' (*NE-C*, introduction) that enables the person to accomplish activities in an excellent way. When virtue is 'the best and most complete' in performing activities, then the activities become pleasurable (*NE-R*, I.8). In this case, the person finds it pleasant to think about his actions, and he is thus self-confident (*NE-C*, IX.4.1166a). Indeed, 'the good person should be a self-lover' (*NE-C*, IX.8.1169a).

Since 'activity' is a flow, and virtuous activities are pleasurable intermediate ends for the final good, then eudaimonia is not a state but it takes place over time. And since only the beginning of this dynamic can be controlled, eudaimonia is difficult to predict (*NE-R*, III.5). Therefore, in economic terms, happiness is not an object that can be easily maximised, and virtuous activities are not costly means for it.

Activities need a person's 'skills' (*NE-C*, I.1) to be performed (i.e. dexterity and competence). Virtuous activities thus need both 'skills and virtues' as endowments that are distinctive for each person (see the box in Figure 4.1).[4]

In order to use these skills for virtuous activities, investigation and decisions (i.e. evaluation and choice) are necessary, and must be guided by rationality (*NE-R*, I.7 and III.2).[5] This is the distinctive property of human beings, in contrast to the other animals (*NE-R*, III.1), so that human life is a rational life (*NE-R*, I.7).

Virtuous activities need 'resources' like 'friends, wealth, and political power' besides virtues and skills (*NE-C*, I.8).[6] In fact, it is impossible to perform virtuous activities if these resources are not available. But, differently from virtuous activities, such resources are pure instruments for eudaimonia, that is, they do not bring happiness in themselves (*NE-C*, I.5.1096a). Therefore, 'it is enough to have moderate resources' (*NE-C*, X.8.1179a), that is, resources are not essential above some subsistence threshold. Aristotle goes even further: if someone pursues money making, he does it 'under compulsion' (*NE-R*, I.5), that is, he is subject to a form of addiction.

Eudaimonia is thus theoretically possible in human life, but how can it be actually pursued? Proper virtues and skills are not given by nature (*NE-C*, I.12.1103a), so that both of them must be pursued as intermediate ends. Indeed – according to Aristotle – virtues present at birth can be developed not only through education, as a particular 'external resource' that implies the activity of learning (see the chart), but also through autonomous 'personal effort' (*NE-C*, I.9.1099b) and 'experience' (*NE-R*, II.1.1103a), that is, by 'exercising' (*NE-R*, II.1103a) the virtues and skills themselves through the activities.[7] Then, over time (a further input box in Figure 4.1), practising virtues becomes a habit, and skills can be similarly developed (*NE-R*, II.1.1103a). Therefore the 'increase' of virtues and skills, indicated by the symbol 'Δ' in Figure 4.1, is both an outcome of exercising virtuous activities, and the source of the positive feedback going to the endowment of virtues and skills, which can thus be used as an increased input for the next round.

Since virtuous activities are both pleasurable and able to exert positive feedback, an *endogenous dynamics* emerges in which virtues and skills grow by themselves, if they are not constrained by inadequate external resources and education. The realisation of individual potential to perform virtuous activities is thus not simply due to the relaxation of external constraints, but also to individual rational choices and the overall pursuit of the good.

The person does not develop by living happiness in isolation, because 'a human is a social being, and his nature is to live in the company of others [. . .]. So the happy person does need friends' (*NE-C*, IX.9.1169b), or 'personal relationships' – according to an alternative translation (*NE-C*, glossary, p. 207). Aristotle's definition of 'friendship' is broad, and he distinguishes friendship for the good, for pleasure and for utility. Complete friendship is found only between virtuous people who wish goods for the sake of the other (*NE-R*, VIII.2). In this case, the 'friend is another self' (*NE-C*, IX.9.1170b), as the person was completely identified with the friend, so that having many close friends is unlikely (*NE-C*, IX.10.1171a). In the case of friendships for pleasure and for utility, Aristotle observes the presence of instrumentality (*NE-C*, IX.5.1167a), so that friendship becomes an 'external resource' (*NE-C*, IX.9.1169b) (see Figure 4.1).

Human sociality is even wider – according to Aristotle – '[f]or even if the good is the same for an individual as for a city, that of the city is obviously a greater and more complete thing to obtain and preserve' (*NE-C*, I.2.1094b). Sociality thus means pursuing the good of the community while pursuing personal good at the same time. The most evident example is political activity. According to Aristotle, 'political science is concerned most of all with producing citizens [. . .] who are both good and the sort to perform noble actions' (*NE-C*, I.9.1099b). A more subtle example is the theoretical research of knowledge, namely the 'contemplation of the truth' (*NE-C*, I.7.1098a). This is a virtuous activity that brings no other end than eudaimonia (*NE-C*, I.10.1100b). But the community can clearly benefit from this activity when new knowledge becomes common principles that govern action.

Therefore, another positive loop emerges because of human sociality. In fact, social relationships receive benefit through education and learning common principles, as well as social norms, and it gives benefit through teaching, political action and theoretical research, that is, 'new external resources' (see Figure 4.1). This is again *endogenous dynamics* but in this case *for the community as a whole*. Eudaimonia is not only a process for individuals, but also for the community, and the pursuit of virtuous activities benefits both.

Nevertheless, people can also pursue happiness through a different pathway, usually known as *hedonism*, although the term does not appear in *NE*. People, in fact, can seek pleasure for its own sake, and hence without requiring virtues (*NE-C*, VII.12.1153a).

Aristotle proposes a clarifying distinction on this point: 'By things *pleasant incidentally*, I mean those that are remedial [. . .] Things *pleasant by nature* are those that produce action in a healthy nature' (*NE-C*, VII.14.1154a–b, emphasis added). In other words, a thing is remedial when it restores the natural healthy state. Although this is an activity, it is not a virtuous activity. In fact, virtuous activities add something new on the basis of the healthy state, like individual political action. Therefore, restoring the healthy state is a self-exhausting dynamics, whereas eudaimonia can be a never-ending process.

Hedonism thus becomes attractive for people who want to escape from pains (*NE-C*, VII.14.1154a). These people, called 'self-indulgent', have such an appetite for pleasant things that they choose them 'at the cost of everything else' (*NE-R*, III.11). This is against eudaimonia (*NE-C*, I.5.1095b) because it hinders the exercise of virtuous activities. People can choose hedonism just because it is naturally attractive (*NE-C*, VI.13.1144b), but then they lose the opportunity to know eudaimonia and they cannot exercise rationality (*NE-C*, III.1.1110b). They do not develop their virtues and skills, although nature provides such potential to human beings (*NE-R*, II.1).

4.3 BEYOND ARISTOTLE'S CONCEPTION OF EUDAIMONIA

Aristotle wrote *Nicomachean Ethics* more than two millennia ago, so finding interesting suggestions for the modern life in such work is exceptional in itself. Nevertheless, *Nicomachean Ethics* exhibits limits, weaknesses and ambiguities according to a number of studies of this text, especially in philosophy. Section 4.2 focused on eudaimonia as an endogenous process, while the present section shows that some important aspects of *Nicomachean Ethics* are inconsistent with this type of dynamics. All our analysis about Aristotle, however, does not claim to establish 'what he really said', but it rather attempts to identify useful suggestions for building an 'economic approach to eudamonia'.

The point of attack may appear a minor one, and in fact it is usually overlooked. The point concerns how Aristotle considers children in relation to eudaimonia. His position is clear from the following quotation:

> children live in accordance with appetite [. . .] If, then, it is not going to be obedient and subject to its ruler, it will get out of hand. For the desire of an irrational being for what is pleasant is insatiable and indiscriminate, and the activity of desire will strengthen the tendency he is born with. And if appetites are strong and excessive, they actually expel calculation. They should therefore be moderate and few in number, and in no kind of opposition to reason – this is what we mean by 'obedient' and 'disciplined'. (*NE-C*, III.12.1119b)

Therefore, children, like animals, are not happy – according to Aristotle – because they cannot exercise virtuous activities. Nevertheless, they can be properly disciplined because they have the potential to develop their virtues (*NE-C*, I.9.1100a).

However, recent research on early human development tells us a different story. Let us report some results of this research in order to give an idea of what children are able to do. Laboratory research with one-year-old children suggests that their ability to acquire knowledge is similar to that of scientists: they formulate a hypothesis, they test it through observation and then they try to correct it in accordance with the facts. They are able to anticipate the solution of simple problems before applying the trial-and-error method, which is typical of the other animals (Gopnik 2009). Studies on the sociality of small children show that they are spontaneously cooperative and aware that human interaction is governed by social norms. For example, children before the age of two exhibit greater happiness when giving a treat to others than receiving it, even in cases of costly giving (Aknin et al. 2012). In another set of comparative experiments, one-year-old children are already able to cooperate by pointing to a desired object, thus directing the experimenter's attention, even if they could take it by themselves. By contrast, chimpanzees point to a desired object only when they cannot take it (van der Goot et al. 2014). Other studies show that three-year-old children are able to recognise property rights (Rossano et al. 2011), and to acknowledge merit when sharing resources with others, even when sharing is costly for the child (Kanngiesser and Warneken 2012).

Economists, too, have recently provided interesting evidence on the development of children. They have found that both cognitive and socio-emotional skills begin to develop early in human life and interact one with the other from then on (Heckman 2008), and that a child's emotional health (and not a child's intellectual development) is the most powerful predictor of adult life satisfaction (Layard et al. 2014). Childcare is obviously important for children's development, but markedly better results are obtained if childcare is formally structured by following the pedagogical theories where the teacher stimulates children insofar as they realise their skills (Biroli et al. 2017).

To sum up, human development is a continuous process in which children are naturally disposed to learn, to self-grow and to understand social norms. They thus reveal pleasure while learning, and rationality is not the only guide for them.

Indeed, Aristotle himself attaches two positive roles to pleasure in the pursuit of eudaimonia. First – as observed by a commentator – 'the lack of the appropriate feeling is a *sign* of the agent's not fully virtuous disposition insofar as not taking pleasure in virtuous action may reveal that the agent has not fully realized that virtues are to be sought for their own sake' (Melo 2011: 36). One can thus interpret feeling pleasure as providing some useful information that rational choice can take into account. Second, pleasure can strengthen the choices made, or, as Aristotle explains:

> the pleasure proper to an activity enhances it, because those who engage in activity with pleasure show better and more accurate judgement. It is people who enjoy geometry, for example, who become geometricians and understand each aspect of it better, and similarly lovers of music, building and so on improve in their own proper sphere by finding enjoyment in it. And the pleasures enhance the activities, and what enhances an activity is proper to it. (*NE-C*, X.5.1175a–b)

In this second role, pleasure arises from what is now called 'intrinsic motivation', which contrasts with the motivation to do something in order to receive something else in exchange.[8] Intrinsic motivation thus contrasts with the rational motivation that is typical in economics.

The case of children can help us understand another debated issue: if the eudaimonia of a person means that s/he develops the best virtues and skills according to her/his natural potential, like the 'shoemaker [who] makes the noblest shoe out of the leather [s/]he is given' (*NE-C*, I.10.1101a), and if s/he does not obviously lead a life of contemplation that would guarantee her/him the maximum eudaimonia, then what is the standard with which to evaluate *her/his* eudaimonia?

To make this issue clear let us take the paradoxical example suggested by Daniel Haybron, that is, 'Genghis Khan, who directed the slaughter of tens of millions. He appears to have done so largely with the blessing of his culture's moral code. It is not hard to imagine – thus comments the philosopher – that his relatively long life, which appeared to be rather successful on his terms, went very well for him indeed' (Haybron 2008a, ch.11). This is an example of 'self-fulfilment' – thus argues Haybron (2008b) – while Aristotle addressed 'nature-fulfilment'. But what is the standard that enables one to evaluate whether 'self-fulfilment' does fit 'nature-fulfilment' or not? Or, in Aristotle's example, whether the wise shoemaker really pursues the 'final good'?

Having discarded pleasure as the standard, since this may be hedonistic, Aristotle would argue that the standard for such an evaluation is in continuous refinement by those who live a contemplating life, and precisely by those who exercise the theoretical study of ethics. This is a discipline that is still actively studied today.[9] However, both ancient philosophy and recent studies seem to be far from achieving a definite conclusion on this matter.[10]

The case of children indicates another route: the study of ontogeny and, as suggested by the comparison of children with the other animals, the phylogeny of human beings (Tomasello 2011; Suddendorf 2013). This route may not enable us to evaluate human behaviours in detail, as Aristotle did in the discussion of the various virtues (*NE*, III-IX).[11] But going back to the early development of human beings can help to explain what their fundamental skills are, that is, those skills that generate and condition the other human skills and that can provide a resilient well-being. This route can lead research to better understand some interesting issues, such as the engine of human development, the actual choices made by people between eudaimonia and hedonism, the greater strength of eudaimonia and what the implicit suggestions are to improve people's lives.

This route promises to be far-reaching, but Section 4.4 will attempt to take just one step forward.

4.4   AN ECONOMIC APPROACH TO EUDAIMONIA

The philosophy of eudaimonia is essentially normative and theoretical, although Aristotle describes various psychological mechanisms of persons. The capability approach is, again, normative and theoretical, although the attempts to apply it to empirical cases are several. Instead, the psychology of eudaimonia, as it emerges from the bulk of recent studies on this matter, is mainly descriptive and empirical (Tiberius and Hall 2010; Melo 2011; Crespo and Mesurado 2015). The economics of happiness, which usually refers to 'life satisfaction' and 'happiness as a state of mind', provides an increasing number of studies on eudaimonia which are, again, descriptive and empirical (e.g. Clark and Senik 2011; Graham and Nikolova 2015; Clark 2016; Bachelet et al. 2016; Nikolaev 2018). Nevertheless, the psychology of eudaimonia and the economics of happiness do not abstain from normative implications; the former normally addresses advice to individual persons, as the various self-help books on happiness show, and the latter is rather addressed to the policy maker, although in different ways (Layard 2005; Frey and Stutzer 2011).

This section proposes an approach to eudaimonia which is theoretical, but easily applicable to empirical cases, and descriptive, but with straightforward normative implications that may be useful to both individual persons and the policy maker. Section 4.5 extends the approach to the contrast between eudaimonia and hedonism, which are described as two distinct pathways to happiness. The approach is economic in method because it is based on individual choice and on the individual's attempts to correct errors in choices, while taking into account resource constraints. The approach is not focused on the different feelings that characterise happiness as the outcome of the two different pathways, which is a typical psychological focus. Indeed, characterising eudaimonia and hedonism as how these are pursued makes the feeling of happiness less important. Happiness can rather be evaluated over long stretches of time, as in the case of the measure of 'life satisfaction'. As psychological studies show, life satisfaction is correlated with both eudaimonia and hedonism, both being measured in a variety of ways (e.g. Huta and Waterman 2014; Huta 2016).

Let us characterise eudaimonia as 'home production' in Becker's sense,[12] that is, as an activity performed by the individual in which they employ resources to produce what they enjoy. It thus becomes possible to identify 'the technology of eudaimonia', which employs some definite inputs and transforms them into some definite outputs, subject to definite constraints. This technology is represented in Figure 4.2, which clearly exhibits a similarity with Figure 4.1, representing Aristotle's conception of eudaimonia.

The inputs of eudaimonic home production are a person's 'human skills', time and external resources, such as market goods, skills and the time of close others.

Human skills are mental skills that possibly involve body skills, since our body skills as such are not particularly special with respect to the skills of other animals. Developmental and comparative psychologists, as well as palaeoanthropologists and economists, provide evidence from both the ontogenetic and phylogenetic perspective that there are two interconnected fundamental human skills, namely the skills that made possible the rise of other typical human skills: creativity and sociality. The most elementary 'creativity' is the skill to imagine counterfactual scenarios, which may

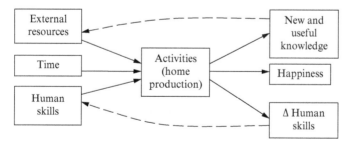

Figure 4.2   A modern representation of eudaimonia

become useful in social life, that is, it can become knowledge that is useful for actions with others and for the creation of new knowledge by others (Suddendorf 2013). This is the origin of the human skill to intentionally change humans' course of life, thus making our adaptation capacity more effective. The derived human skill that is most well known is language, which arises in babies in their first few months, that is, after exercising their elementary creativity skill (Gopnik et al. 1999; Gopnik 2009).

Evidence of the presence of a species-specific 'sociality' in small children was mentioned in Section 4.3, while its origin in our ancestors is revealed through economic studies on how early humans became cooperative (Bowles and Gintis 2013). Creativity and sociality, together with language, give rise, at the societal level, to culture, which is the typical product of the human species (Tomasello 2011).

The two skills of creativity and sociality provide a general and demanding standard to evaluate people's behaviours. They are general because many types of behaviour are both creative and social. But they are also demanding because many human behaviours imply either little creativity, like repetitive but pleasurable activities, or little sociality, like the search for personal visibility and power, or even little creativity with apparently high sociality, like conformism to others' behaviours.

Exercising creativity and sociality requires a person's time as a second essential input for the home production of eudaimonia. For example, learning, which creates a person's stock of knowledge by exploiting others' knowledge, requires time because the new information should be integrated with acquired knowledge in order to be useful. The neurobiologists confirm this by observing that effective learning entails special internal changes to the human body (Immordino-Yang 2016).

Market goods are useful but not essential inputs, after personal subsistence has been guaranteed. Skills and the time of close others are also useful inputs but they may become less important in adulthood.

There are three outputs of eudaimonia: an increase of the fundamental human skills (i.e. creativity and sociality); possible new and useful knowledge and things for the community; and 'happiness' over the long run. The increase in fundamental human skills follows from exercising a person's initial human skills in eudaimonic activities. Supporting evidence for both cognitive and socio-emotional skills is provided by Heckman (2008) when addressing the 'self-productivity' of skills.

The knowledge and things that the community regards as new and useful, or simply interesting to others, is the output of eudaimonia in adults. Social recognition does not necessarily arise only in the cases of scientific discoveries, innovations and artistic works, which remain the top outputs, but also in cases of intuitions and new solutions to old problems.

'Happiness' as an output of the eudaimonic process should be evaluated over the long run, because both the increase in fundamental human skills and the realisation of new ideas and things takes time. As some psychologists observe, living eudaimonia involves integrating past, present and future, while happiness as a state of mind is largely present-oriented (Baumeister et al. 2013).

Eudaimonia can be thus represented as the transformation of the mentioned inputs into the mentioned outputs, but with a special meaning. By 'transformation' we mean *seeking to optimise the matching of a person's human skills, as articulated in specialised skills, with the available activities to her/him.*[13] To give an idea, let us take the metaphor of a mountaineer. This person is endowed with climbing skills, which are derived from her/his early passion for mountains. By climbing, s/he expects to realise a challenging undertaking that gives her/him more self-confidence and social recognition, and hence more happiness. S/he has to decide which mountain to climb, and which way to climb it, but also which of her/his specific skills, which goods and whose help to use. The climb should be neither too easy for her/his skills, because this would miss the aims of self-confidence and social recognition, nor too difficult, because this would damage her/his happiness.

This metaphor also makes clear a structural aspect of happiness as eudaimonia: that the achievement of the peak, which is the immediate goal, is not the only source of happiness because the climbing activity itself, which deals with the challenge during the enterprise, also yields happiness for the climber. This latter source of happiness is intriguing because it is fused with effort, which is usually considered as a cost by economists. Indeed, if the climber was transported to the peak of a challenging mountain by helicopter, s/he would have achieved the immediate goal, but s/he would have missed the challenge thus damaging her/his happiness.

Therefore, optimising the matching of human skills, which are differently articulated in specific skills according to how the initial talent was initially cultivated, with the available activities, which exhibit a variety of difficulties, brings the person to happiness maximisation. However, the person cannot take happiness as an object to be directly maximised, because the matching introduces a strong form of uncertainty. In fact, the person cannot know the distribution of probability of success of their undertaking, because, in the case of challenging activities, the undertaking cannot be repeated without changing a person's skills and hence the premises for further action. Optimising the matching is thus a searching process through activities and their degrees of difficulty, while skills continuously change through experience.

As a result this dynamic becomes *endogenous*, because exercising the eudaimonic activity is both satisfying and effective in increasing human skills. If the person remained heavily dissatisfied they would choose more rewarding options. If human skills did not increase, the dynamics would require external incentives only. In both cases the activity would cease to be eudaimonic.

Learning and experience may lead the person to approach, over her/his life-cycle, a time path in which the skills/activity matching is continuously improving, that is, her/his optimum path. However, external shocks to the budget and time constraints recalibrate the necessity of seeking the best matching, so that the person's life is made up of continuous learning.

The similarities between this economic approach to eudaimonia and Aristotle's conception of eudaimonia are evident if Figures 4.1 and 4.2 are compared. Both of them display endogenous dynamics, in which performing proper activities plays a key role, and, by contrast, pleasure and material wealth are not pursued in themselves. In both of them such proper activities enable the person to lead a happy life (in which pleasure plays some role), and trigger improvements in the community's life. According to Aristotle, activities are proper if performed in accordance with virtues or excellence. In our economic approach to eudaimonia, activities are proper if human skills are 'excellently' matched with their difficulty.

The main differences between Aristotle's conception and our approach lie in the role of rationality, and in the standard to be used to evaluate the 'final good of human life'. According to Aristotle, what distinguishes human life is rationality, which both governs the choice of activities and, as 'rational reflection' or 'thoughtful consideration', investigates the 'final good', possibly in a 'contemplative life'. In our approach, what distinguishes human life is the combined skill of creativity and sociality, which affects preferences with limited voluntary decision, and *then* it affects the rational choice of activities, thus developing inner talent and aptitude from childhood to adulthood.

Such combined skill can also provide the standard to evaluate people's eudaimonia, because creativity and sociality are not only rooted in the nature of human beings, like other skills and needs (see, e.g. Doyal and Gough 1991), but are distinctive and fundamental for the healthy development of the others' skills in the human species. In this way inner individual endowment provides an objective basis for the subjective state of happiness, which thus takes specific qualities such as resilience to adverse shocks.

4.5   EUDAIMONIA AND HEDONISM AS TWO PATHWAYS TO HAPPINESS

According to Aristotle, human nature drives people from childhood towards the pursuit of pleasure, unless they are educated to use reason, which is in their natural potential. According to our approach, human nature drives people from childhood towards eudaimonia, unless they are constrained by adverse material and social conditions. Despite this difference, rational choice between pleasure and eudaimonia plays a role in both cases, so that hedonism and eudaimonia can be described as two distinct choices leading to happiness.

The two pathways, however, are not symmetric, but differ in structure. Whereas the immediate object of pursuit in hedonism is happiness, in the form of pleasure, the immediate object of pursuit in eudaimonia is the activity performed in the excellent way, so that happiness derives as a consequence that includes pleasure.

In psychology the contrast between hedonism and eudaimonia, although variously defined, has been extensively investigated and confirmed from the empirical point of view (Thorsteinsen and Vittersø 2018). Eudaimonia has often been measured by posing questions regarding 'personal growth', 'purpose in life', 'positive relationships' and 'life meaning', thus capturing aspects that are consistent with our approach. Questions that capture hedonism often include comfort as well as pleasure (Huta 2016; Huta and Ryan 2010). This is a welcome extension because the term 'comfort' in particular calls for the consumption of goods and services, and it makes it evident that certain economic conditions are essential for hedonism at every level of opulence. In this way, consumer theory as presented in economics textbooks can offer a clear interpretation of hedonism.

Differently from eudaimonia, human skills are not so important in hedonism. Mental skills are not important for enjoying pleasure, while some skills are necessary to acquire goods and services for comfort, but these are specific skills that are not specifically 'human'. In fact, typical skills of this type are skills for work, which require routine behaviours rather than creativity, and competition with other workers rather than socialisation. In order to enjoy more comfort, more specialised skills for production are required, and more formal education is usually needed. Work, and even education, may thus be more orientated towards hedonism than to eudaimonia.

Time is an essential input to 'produce' and enjoy eudaimonia, but it is important and not always essential to acquire goods and services for hedonism, in which case it is a cost rather than a benefit. Even time to enjoy consumption is irrelevant according to textbook economics.

Social relationships are also essential in eudaimonia because they are both essential means and essential ends within the process of the development of human skills, and of the enjoyment of happiness. By contrast, in hedonism social relationships are only a means to achieve pleasure, and to produce more goods and services through the division of labour.

Therefore, people have to choose between two very different options in order to achieve happiness. The social and material constraints are primarily important to condition this choice, especially in the first part of people's lives. If the material constraint is not too binding, and if early education is adequate for the development of human skills, the endogenous dynamics of eudaimonia generates new skills that reinforce the choice for the eudaimonic option. When human skills are thus strengthened people become more resilient to adverse shocks in both material and social conditions. By contrast, if the material conditions are deprived, and the social conditions are inadequate, hedonism becomes attractive because immediate pleasure appears to be a remedy. In this case the endogenous dynamics of eudaimonia may be not triggered, and human skills may languish. People remain thus vulnerable to adverse shocks.

The two pathways can be complementary, but eudaimonia strengthens by practising, and weakens by abstaining, so that the two pathways tend to become substitutable over people's life-cycle. Some forms of addiction to consumption in the pursuit of hedonism, as suggested by Aristotle himself, can reinforce this decoupling. A strong shock is thus necessary to switch from one pathway to the other.

In order to illustrate the different robustness of happiness achieved through the two pathways let us consider the link of, respectively, eudaimonia and hedonism with physical health and physiological states conducive to health. An increasing number of studies in psychology and epidemiology show that self-reported measures of eudaimonia have positive effects on physical health and on recovery from adverse states, measured with specific morbidities, biomarkers and longevity. Specific neurobiological correlates for the eudaimonic measures are also found (Ryff 2017). By contrast, hedonic measures of happiness, like positive and negative affects, exhibit a far weaker link with physical health (Ryff et al. 2004; Cross et al. 2018). Happiness measured as life satisfaction seems to lie in between, because studies on the link with physical health give mixed results (Cross et al. 2018).[14] This contrast between the two pathways seems to confirm that eudaimonia goes deeper into mental stock-and-flow dynamics, which are typically human, while hedonism is focused on body expressions, which can be common to other animals.[15]

4.6   CONCLUDING REMARKS

The economic research on people's well-being is shifting the focus from 'happiness', as a pleasant state of mind, to eudaimonia, as realising one's potential by functioning well. In other words, the shift is from studying the determinants of a goal to studying a structure that produces a dynamic. The new research is thus more ambitious, but also more rewarding, because it makes the analysis more robust and powerful, and the policy implications easier to agree.

This chapter has taken a step in this direction. It has shown how a rereading of Aristotle's work through the lens of an economist can provide the basis for building a modern economic approach to eudaimonia. Specifically, the conception that 'eudaimonia means realising one's potential by functioning well' has been spelled out in modern terms as follows. First, people's happiness is the outcome of activities both when these are underway and when the planned goals are achieved. Second, the activities are chosen rationally, that is, in the most effective way, by pursuing the matching of the skills with which people are endowed with appropriate activities, and by employing external resources. Third, performing the activities reinforces the skills, refines the ability to choose and contributes to improving resources for others, thus triggering an endogenous dynamics that sustain happiness at both the individual and societal level. Fourth, a minimum of social and material resources are necessary to perform the activities, but opulence is unnecessary.

Aristotle's conception of eudaimonia also exhibits some weaknesses. The main one is found in the unconvincing reconciliation between its objective basis in human nature and its subjective expression in individual self-realisation. Some philosophers regard this reconciliation as logically untenable, and the application of objective standards to evaluate individual self-realisation as paternalistic (Haybron 2008b). By contrast, some psychologists attempt to identify the objective standard in specific psychological constructs that are universally linked to happiness, thus making possible the evaluation of individual eudaimonia (Ryff and Singer 2008; Ryan et al. 2008).

This chapter has followed this latter line of research, enriched with further scientific studies on human development. It proposes to focus on two interconnected and fundamental skills that are specifically human because they are not detectable in other animals but are clearly present in small children, that is, when the influence of the environment is at a minimum. These skills are creativity, meaning the skill to imagine counterfactual scenarios, and sociality, meaning the skill to collaborate in intentional common goals.[16]

This suggestion has enabled us to amend Aristotle's conception of eudaimonia. First, children are no longer excluded from eudaimonia being non-rational, as Aristotle claimed, but are integrated into the human development of adults. Second, the development of creativity and sociality, which are linked to personality traits and preferences, cannot be easily predicted in direction and speed, but can heavily affect choices through changes in motivations. Therefore the role of rationality is limited because choices become sensitive to these changes in motivations, rather than only to static preferences.

The chapter concludes with the contrast between eudaimonia and hedonism. Having reformulated eudaimonia in economic terms, a clear distinction arises in the two pathways to happiness that the individual can choose. Moreover, since eudaimonia tends to self-reinforce, the two pathways tend to be substitutable. This opens up the research on the conditions that favour or hinder eudaimonia against hedonism. As Aristotle suggested, hedonism may be very appealing, and we can add that modern producers push in this direction by offering increasingly pleasurable consumption goods. Eudaimonia thus emerges as a more robust pathway to happiness because it relies on internal resources, namely individual skills, while hedonism is more vulnerable to external shocks because it only relies on external resources.

Although the policy implication appears obvious, namely encouraging eudaimonia, the advantage of this policy should be stressed. The direct goal for policy is not people's happiness, but rather people's formation of human skills. Activities, goods, material conditions, social arrangements and organisations should not be evaluated for their effects on happiness, but for their effects on people's human skills. Happiness thus becomes simply an indicator for monitoring the effectiveness of public policies over the long run. Finally, human skills can be more objectively measured than happiness, and policies for their development less paternalistic than, for example, imposing taxes on pleasurable goods.

ACKNOWLEDGEMENTS

I wish to thank, for comments on an earlier version of this chapter, the participants at my seminars at STATEC, Luxembourg, 16 May 2018, at the University of Trento, 2 February 2017, at the SIPP, University of Bergamo, 12 June 2015, and at the conferences on happiness held in Rome, 15 March 2016, and in Rotterdam, 21 March 2017. Special thanks go to Ricardo Crespo for very useful suggestions. Any remaining errors are my responsibility.

NOTES

1. These variables do not even remain fixed over time (Bartolini et al. 2013; Mikucka et al. 2017; Cobb-Clark and Schurer 2013; Boyce et al. 2013), as the frequent assumption of fixed effects in individual panel data implies.

2. This is the characteristic of eudaimonia that Helliwell and Aknin (2018) seem to refer to.

3. References to *Nicomachean Ethics* are indicated by *NE*, followed by the Roman number of the book, and then by the number/s of the chapter/s. The extension '-*R*' or '-*C*' means that the English words used are taken from the translation of, respectively, William D. Ross or Roger Crisp. In the citations, a four-digit number indicates the row of the original work.

4. According to Julia Annas, who is a scholar of Aristotle, skills and virtues are similar because both of them are characterised by the need to learn and the drive to self-improve (Annas 2011: 16), but only virtues require 'having the right feelings and attitudes' (Annas 2011: 5).

5. In Aristotle's words: 'the virtues are rational choices or at any rate involve rational choice' (*NE-R*, II.5.1106a).

6. A further external resource is 'law', which has the role of educating the masses, according to Aristotle. Indeed, 'the masses, especially the young, do not find it pleasant to live temperately and with endurance. For this reason, their upbringing and pursuits should be regulated by laws' (*NE-C*, X.9.1179b).

7. Crisp notes that 'activity' translates the Greek word *energeia*, but this can be also translated as 'actualization' (*NE-C*, glossary, p. 206).

8. For the difference between 'intrinsic' and 'extrinsic' motivations see Deci and Ryan (2000), whose conception has been formalised in Pugno (2008).

9. See Hirata (2016) for an economic discussion on ethics and eudaimonia.

10. For example, Annas (2011: 103) discards Genghis Khan as a virtuous person because he cannot be admired. On the contrary, 'honest, loyal, and generous' persons should be admired (Annas (2011: 21). However, an economist would observe that honesty, loyalty and generosity are difficult to evaluate in actual behaviours because these may hide extrinsic incentives (see, e.g. Kreps 1997).

11. In fact, we will maintain our evaluation at a higher generality, and closer to that of the capability approach. More precisely, our generality will be less than that in Sen's capability approach, which even abstains from indicating the priorities among the capabilities, but more than that in Martha Nussbaum's (1999) capability approach, which lists many central capabilities.

12. Indeed, Becker (1965) talked about 'household production', thus including the case of the 'production' of children.

13. This idea is an elaboration of Scitovsky (1976) and Csikszentmihalyi (1990), and it is developed and formalised in Pugno (2016).

14. The economists Fleurbaey and Schwandt (2016) also find that individual maximisation of subjective well-being, whether happiness or life satisfaction, turns out to be self-defeating in the long term with respect to more eudaimonic goals.

15. In fact, while creativity and sociality have been investigated by focusing on the *differences* between humans and the other animals (Suddendorf 2013; Tomasello 2011), the investigation of emotional states such as stress rather focuses on the *similarities* of humans with the other animals (Diener et al. 2017).

16. The concept of 'human development' adopted by the United Nations Development Programme, for example UNDP (1990), is different from ours, as evidenced in Pugno (2019).

REFERENCES

Aknin, L. A., J. K. Hamlin and E. W. Dunn (2012), Giving leads to happiness in young children. *PlosOne* 7: e39211.

Annas, J. (2011), *Intelligent Virtue*. Oxford: Oxford University Press.

Aristotle (2000), *Nicomachean Ethics*. Trans. R. Crisp. New York: Cambridge University Press.

Bachelet, M., L. Becchetti and F. Pisani (2016), Eudaimonic happiness as a leading health indicator. *Aiccon wp*, 150 (online).

Bartolini, S., E. Bilancini and M. Pugno (2013), Did the decline in social connections depress Americans' happiness. *Social Indicators Research* 110(3): 1033–59.

Baumeister, R. F., K. D. Vohs, J. L. Aaker and E. N. Garbinsky (2013), Some key differences between a happy life and a meaningful life. *Journal of Positive Psychology* 8(6): 505–16.

Becker, G. (1965), A theory of allocation of time. *Economic Journal* 75: 493–517.

Benjamin, D. J., O. Heffetz, M. S. Kimball and N. Szembrot (2014), Beyond happiness and satisfaction: toward well-being indices based on stated preference. *American Economic Review* 104(9): 2698–735.

Biroli, P., D. Del Boca, J. J. Heckman et al. (2017), Evaluation of the Reggio approach to early education. NBER Working Paper No. 23390, National Bureau of Economic Research, Cambridge, MA.

Bowles, S. and H. Gintis (2013), *A Cooperative Species*. Oxford: Oxford University Press.

Boyce, C. L., A. M. Wood and N. Powdthavee (2013), Is personality fixed? *Social Indicators Research* 111(1): 287–305.

Bruni, L. (2008), Back to Aristotle? Happiness, eudaimonia, and relational goods. In L. Bruni, F. Comim and M. Pugno (eds) *Capabilities and Happiness*. Oxford: Oxford University Press, pp. 114–39.

Clark, A. E. (2016), SWB as a measure of individual well-being. In M. Adler and M. Fleurbaey (eds), *Oxford Handbook of Well-being and Public Policy*. Oxford: Oxford University Press, pp. 518–52.

Clark, A. E. and C. Senik (2011), Is happiness different from flourishing? *Revue d'économie politique* 121: 17–34.

Cobb-Clark, D. A. and S. Schurer (2013), Two economists' musings on the stability of locus of control. *Economic Journal* 123: F358–F400.

Crespo, R. F. and B. Mesurado (2015), Happiness economics, eudaimonia and positive psychology: from happiness economics to flourishing. *Journal of Happiness Studies* 16: 931–46.

Cross, M. P., L. Hofschneider, M. Grimm and S. D. Pressman (2018), Subjective well-being and physical health. In E. Diener, S. Oishi and L. Tay (eds) *Handbook of Well-being*. Salt Lake City, UT: DEF Publisher.

Csikszentmihalyi, M. (1990), *Flow*. London: Rider.

Deci, E. L. and R. M. Ryan (2000), The 'what' and 'why' of goal pursuits. *Psychological Inquiry* 11: 227–68.

Diener, E., M. D. Pressman, J. Hunter and D. Delgadillo-Chase (2017), If, why, and when subjective well-being influences physical health, and future needed research. *Applied Psychology: Health and Well-being* 9: 133–67.

Doyal, L. and I. Gough (1991), *A Theory of Human Need*. Basingstoke: Macmillan Education.

Fleurbaey, M. and H. Schwandt (2016), Do people seek to maximise their subjective well-being – and fail? Available at: http://cep.lse.ac.uk/seminarpapers/WB-28–04–16-SCHpaper.pdf (accessed 15 September 2019).

Frey, B. and A. Stutzer (2011), The use of happiness research for public policy. *Social Choice and Welfare* 38(4): 659–74.

Gopnik, A. (2009), *The Philosophical Baby*. New York: Farrar, Straus, & Giroux.

Gopnik, A., A. N. Meltzoff and P. K. Kuhl (1999), *The Scientist in the Crib.* New York: William Morris and Company.

Graham, C. N. and M. Nikolova (2015), Bentham or Aristotle in the development process? An empirical investigation of capabilities and subjective well being. *World Development* 68: 163–79.

Haybron, D. M. (2008a), *The Pursuit of Unhappiness.* Oxford: Oxford University Press.

Haybron, D. M. (2008b), Happiness, the self, and human flourishing. *Utilitas* 22: 21–49.

Heckman, J. J. (2008), School, skills, and synapses. *Economic Inquiry* 46(3): 289–324.

Helliwell, J. F. and L. B. Aknin (2018), Expanding the social science of happiness. *Nature Human Behaviour* 2: 248–52.

Helliwell, J. F., M. B. Norton, H. Huang and S. Wang (2018), Happiness at different ages: the social context matters. NBER Working Paper 25121.

Hirata, J. (2016), Ethics and eudaimonic well-being. In J. Vittersø (ed.) *Handbook of Eudaimonic Well-being.* Tromsø, Norway: Springer, pp. 55–66.

Huta, V. (2016), Eudaimonic and hedonic orientations: theoretical considerations and research findings. In J. Vittersø (ed.) *Handbook of Eudaimonic Well-being.* Tromsø, Norway: Springer, pp. 215–31.

Huta, V. and R. M. Ryan (2010), Pursuing pleasure or virtue. *Journal of Happiness Studies* 11: 735–62.

Huta, V. and A. S. Waterman (2014), Eudaimonia and its distinction from hedonia. *Journal of Happiness Studies* 15: 1425–56.

Immordino-Yang, M. H. (2016), *Emotions, Learning, and the Brain: Exploring the Educational Implications of Affective Neuroscience.* New York: W. W. Norton.

Johns, H. and P. Ormerod (2007), *Happiness, Economics, and Public Policy.* London: Institute of Economic Affairs.

Kanngiesser, P. and F. Warneken (2012), Young children consider merit when sharing resources. *Plos One* 7: e43979.

Keyes, C. L. M. and J. Annas (2009), Feeling good and functioning well: distinctive concepts in ancient philosophy and contemporary science. *Journal of Positive Psychology* 4: 197–201.

Kreps, D. M. (1997), Intrinsic motivation and extrinsic incentives. *The American Economic Review* 87(2), 359–64.

Layard, R. (2005), *Happiness.* New York: Penguin.

Layard, R., A. E. Clark, F. Cornaglia, N. Powdthavee and J. Vernoit (2014), What predicts a successful life? *Economic Journal* 124: F720–38.

Melo, S. (2011), Eudaimonia and the Economics of Happiness. Documentos CEDE 008730, Universidad de los Andes – CEDE.

Mikucka, M., F. Sarracino and J. K. Dubrow (2017), When does economic growth improve life satisfaction? Multilevel analysis of the roles of social trust and income. *World Development* 93: 447–59.

Nikolaev, B. (2018), Does higher education increase hedonic and eudaimonic happiness? *Journal of Happiness Studies* 19: 483–504.

Nussbaum, M. C. (1999), *Sex and Social Justice.* Oxford: Oxford University Press.

O'Connor, K. (2017), Happier people are less likely to be unemployed: evidence longitudinal data in Germany. USCDornsife Working Paper No.17–17. Available at: https://papers.ssrn.com/sol3/papers.cfm?abstract_id=2959118 (accessed 2 September 2019).

Pugno, M. (2008), Economics and the self: a formalisation of self-determination theory. *Journal of Socio-Economics* 37: 1328–46.

Pugno, M. (2016), *On The Foundations of Happiness in Economics*. London: Routledge.

Pugno, M. (2019), Happiness, human development, and economic (de) growth. *Annali della Fondazione Luigi Einaudi* 53, 151–71.

Ross, W. D. (2014), *The Nicomachean Ethics of Aristotle*. Netlancers Inc.

Rossano, F., H. Rakoczy and M. Tomasello (2011), Young children's understanding of violations of property rights. *Cognition* 121: 219–27.

Ryan, R. R., V. Huta and L. Deci (2008), Living well: a self-determination theory perspective on eudaimonia. *Journal of Happiness Studies* 9: 139–70.

Ryff, C. D. (2017), Eudaimonic well-being, inequality, and health: recent findings and future directions. *International Review of Economics* 64: 159–78.

Ryff, C. D. and B. Singer (2008), Know thyself and become what you are: a eudaimonic approach to psychological well-being. *Journal of Happiness Studies* 9: 13–39.

Ryff, C. D., B. H. Singer and G. D. Love (2004), Positive health: connecting well-being with biology. *Philosophical Transactions of the Royal Society of London B* 359: 1383–94.

Scitovsky, T. (1976), *The Joyless Economy: An Inquiry into Human Satisfaction and Consumer Dissatisfaction*. Oxford: Oxford University Press.

Sen, A. K. (1999), *Development as Freedom*. New York: Knopf.

Suddendorf, T. (2013), *The Gap: The Science of What Separates Us from Other Animals*. New York: Basic Books.

Thorsteinsen, K. and J. Vittersø (2018), Striving for wellbeing: the different roles of hedonia and eudaimonia in goal pursuit and goal achievement. *International Journal of Wellbeing* 8(2): 89–109.

Tiberius, V. and A. Hall (2010), Normative theory and psychological research: hedonism, eudaimonism, and why it matters. *Journal of Positive Psychology* 5(3): 212–25.

Tomasello, M. (2011), Human culture in evolutionary perspective. In M. J. Gelfand, C. Chiu and Y. Hong (eds) *Advances in Culture and Psychology*, vol. 1. Oxford: Oxford University Press, pp. 5–52.

UNDP (1990), *Human Development Report 1990: Concept and Measurement of Human Development*. New York: Oxford University Press.

van der Goot, M. H., U. Liszkowsyi and M. Tomasello (2014), Differences in the non verbal requests of great apes and human infants. *Child Development* 85: 444–55.

Verme, P. (2009), Happiness, freedom and control. *Journal of Economic Behavior & Organization* 71(2): 146–61.

5. *Felicitas publica*: the southern spirit of capitalism

Luigino Bruni

> Merchant spirit and greed for large gains have brought so much ineptitude in all human things that it's truly pitiful. (Antonio Genovesi, extract from private correspondence, December 1757)

5.1 INTRODUCTION: THE MANY SPIRITS OF THE MARKET

Theology has been for centuries at the centre of the work of economic and social thinkers. From the very beginning of Christianity up to modern political economy, a cross-fertilization between theology and *oikonomia* has occurred. Smith, Marx, Vico and Genovesi used theological languages and their theoretical systems were influenced by theological debates.

According to Benjamin ([1921] 1985), capitalism is a new form of religion that calls for an exclusive form of worship and aims at replacing Christianity (not any religion), because it spawned from Jewish-Christian humanism. According to this view (which is consistent with Marx's vision of capitalism, less with Weber's), modernity is not characterized by a *disenchantment* of the world, but instead by the affirmation of a new religion, that is, by the transformation of the Christian spirit into the 'spirit' of capitalism (Bruni and Milbank 2018).

A key passage in the interconnections between theology and economy is the Protestant Reformation and the Catholic Counter-Reformation (*Controriforma*) in the sixteenth to seventeenth centuries. Before this crucial crossroads of Western civilization the market economy had grown as a unique European movement, from Sicily to London, from Lisbon to Prague. Christian faith had represented the new *philia* (*fides*) that, as in the *polis* of Aristotle and Pericles, made possible trust and trading among different people belonging to different clans and villages. The scholastic philosophers and theologians – Aquinas above all – built up a first ethics of the proto-market economy based on the pivotal idea of the common good, namely the thesis according to which the good of the individual has to be seen in deep and necessary connection with the good of the community. This view gave rise to a conception of the economy – money, usury, just price, etc. – that was ontologically communitarian and hierarchical, because the mediators (priest, king, father, etc.) were the basic mechanism to implement the harmonization of public and private goods. Furthermore, in the late Middle Ages the cross-contamination between market and religion reached a huge dimension: the granting of indulgences, poor people paid by rich ones for making prayers and penitence in their place, donations from bankers for buying a reduction in years of purgatory, etc.

Martin Luther reacted strongly against at least two elements of southern Christianity: (1) the excessive and often insane mixture of money–grace, (2) the magnificence of Rome and Italy, which was also the fruit of the wealth created by a new and positive attitude towards luxury and money during the fourteenth and fifteenth centuries. Luther was deeply shocked and appalled by the worldly and market-based society he saw in Italy, which he considered far from the original message of austerity and poverty of the Gospel. The strong reaction of the Lutheran and later Calvinist Reformation was not only against the theology of the Roman Church but also against the lifestyle in the Italian Renaissance, its palaces, masterpieces of art, Michelangelo, Leonardo. Therefore the Protestant cultural program was also the re-establishment of a more authentic and less money-oriented society. Nevertheless, paradoxically, due to the elimination of the hierarchical mediation of the Church, the Protestant culture created an environment far more favourable to the development of the capitalist economy (Barbieri [1940] 2013). As a matter of fact, while in southern Europe the Counter-Reformation stopped the process of freedom in commerce and politics started with civic humanism, in the northern Protestant countries individual freedom (produced by the elimination of hierarchy of the Church) was the engine of capitalistic revolution. Then there was northern Protestant Europe where civic humanism and renaissance continued, although in Catholic countries, such as Italy or Spain, there was a refeudalization of society that brought those countries back to a situation close to the Middle Ages, before civic humanism.

The mediation of the Catholic Church is a key point here. Unlike the Protestant world, in the Roman context the Church and its institutions played a central role in the legislation of commerce and money, using a theological view – that of the Scholastics, of Aquinas in a special way – written in a different historical period (thirteenth to early fourteenth centuries) that was more static and based upon Aristotelian categories (the sterility of money) that in the *Rinascimento* were no longer able to encompass the new economic reality after the commercial revolution in Italian and European cities. The mediation and control of the institutions of the Catholic Church upon individual economic activity, and the strong tools of implementation of this control (i.e. *Inquisitione*), put the countries of southern Europe (Italy, Spain, Portugal, part of France) in a condition of economic and financial disadvantage with respect to northern Europe. Hence, due also to a lack of religious hierarchy, in Holland and in other Protestant countries finance and money lending were allowed, and so commerce and wealth grew (Barbieri [1940] 2013).

Parallel to this, whereas in northern Europe and later in the US, thanks to Calvinist ethics, labour and business were considered to be morally acceptable ways of engaging in ordinary life, in Italy, after the *Controriforma*, there was a refeudalization of culture, with a new praise for rural life and diffidence towards urban life (and its commerce). Also the condemnation of money lending and usury flourished once again in Italy in the *Seicento*, which clashed with what was going on in the northern part of Europe – Bentham's 'defence of usury' is a radicalization of a widely shared idea in this context. It is true that most ecclesiastic, political thinkers – theologians of the post-*Controriforma* era – were *laudatores* of labour, but the praised labour was agricultural and intellectual work, whereas the manual or artisan's activity in the cities (smiths, carpenters, shoemakers, etc.) were considered to be servile and not noble. Most of the present-day differences in labour culture, public debt, private and public ethics, welfare states, individual rights and the idea of the market lay in the two different routes that Europe took after the Protestant Reformation and *Controriforma* era.

The *Cinquecento* and *Seicento* were therefore a return to the Middle Ages (Aquinas) as far as economic ethics is concerned. The modernization and openness to the market of the *Quattrocento*, with the key role of figures such as Bernardino da Siena or Leon Battista Alberti, were not able to fully flourish in Italy and southern Europe. Furthermore, the age of *Controriforma* embraced – with few exceptions – praise for agriculture and rural life and criticism of urban and civic activities (i.e. commerce). As a consequence, starting with the second half of the sixteenth century, southern Europe witnessed a refeudalization of society and the centrality of rent over the profits of merchants and salaries of workers. After the Reformation neo-Platonic thought replaced the Aristotelian one of the *Quattrocento*; then solitude and esoteric and magic practices took the place of social and political activities pertaining to the Aristotelian view of Leonardo Bruni and other civic humanists from the previous century.

Finally, in this chapter I claim that theology is relevant for understanding the still significant differences between Anglo-Saxon (Protestant) capitalism and Latin European capitalism – the differences between the economic spirit of the north and the spirit of the south of Europe – by discussing the ideas of the economic historian Amintore Fanfani and his school at the Catholic University in Milan, whose golden era was from the 1930s to the 1960s. The Reformation and the *Controriforma* was a turning point in modern Europe, and the contemporary gaps, in economic and social terms, between northern and southern Europe are the results of an interrupted path. Social pathologies, 'amoral familism' and the corruption of 'mediated society' pertaining to Italian and Mediterranean societies are well known and serious. At the same time Protestant humanism, its individualism, is facing a different but not less relevant crisis that equally calls for something new.

5.2   WEALTH OR HAPPINESS?

Modern political economy was meant to be a by-product of the modern need to make the search for wealth and individual self-interest socially and morally legitimate. However, before Adam Smith published his *Wealth of Nations* in 1776, where he defined 'wealth' as the subject of the newborn discipline, a different approach had gained ground. In the mid-eighteenth century, in French and Italian traditions, the issue placed at the core of modern economic reflection was 'public happiness'. The first author who used the expression '*pubblica felicità*' as the title of one of his books was the Italian philosopher Ludovico Antonio Muratori (*On Public Happiness*) in 1749, and after him the term 'happiness' appeared in the title of many books and pamphlets by Italian economists of that time: examples include Giuseppe Palmieri (1788: *Reflections on the Public Happiness*) and Pietro Verri (1781: *Discourse on Happiness*). Happiness became a landmark of the Italian classical political (civil) economy: 'All our [Italian] economists, from whatever regional background, are dealing not so much, like Adam Smith, with the wealth of nations, but with public happiness' (Loria 1893: 85).

   The eighteenth-century Italian tradition was in continuity with civic humanism, and with the idea in particular that comes from the Aristotelian–Tomistic tradition that happiness is 'social' by nature – man is a social animal, and therefore the happy man needs friends.

   It should also be noted that in Italy the theme of public happiness was coupled with the idea of *ben-vivere sociale* (social well-being), an association that had been characteristic of the Italian civic humanist tradition, from Francesco Petrarca to Leon Battista Alberti and Ludovico Antonio Muratori. A special Neapolitan echo of that tradition stayed alive in Naples thanks to Giambattista Vico, Pietro Giannone and Paolo Mattia Doria. Some years later, in France, philosopher-economists such as Rousseau, Linguet, Maupertuis, Necker, Turgot, Condorcet and Sismondi all gave a place to happiness in their analyses, and the '*félicité publique*' was one of the key ideas of the French Enlightenment movement: 'The mass of the [English] nation seems to forget, as do philosophers, that the increase in riches is not the end of political economy, but the means by which to provide the happiness for all' (Simonde de Sismondi 1819: 52).

Loria's and Sismondi's thesis has to be circumstantiated. As a matter of fact, if it is true that Smith or Ricardo did not give happiness a central role in their economic theories, nonetheless the issue of happiness was far from being absent in the British debate of their time – it suffices to remember that classical utilitarianism was an offspring of that intellectual climate. At the same time, we must however recognize that English classical political economy did not choose public happiness as a direct object of its enquiries, focusing instead on the wealth of nations and its distribution, creation and growth.

Smith's position is well known. In the *Theory of Moral Sentiments* (*TMS*) one can find the classical (Aristotelian) idea of happiness as the final goal of human life (Smith [1759] 1976: 166). Human happiness does not present a peculiar characteristic for human beings compared to other creatures, and under the Stoic influence happiness is defined as 'tranquillity and enjoyment' (Smith [1759] 1976: 149). The idea that happiness is related to interpersonal relationships is not emphasized, although Smith's moral system is built on relational categories such as 'fellow-feeling' – categories, however, that are absent in his economic theory of the *Wealth of Nations*.

The key idea in the relationship between wealth and happiness is that the former is instrumental for the latter; wealth is just a means for being happy (Smith [1759] 1976: 166), a thesis not far away from the classical one. However, Smith's vision of happiness in relation to the economic field is more complex than the simple equivalence 'more wealth for more happiness'. The argument runs as follows. The emulation of the wealth and greatness of the rich is the engine of both social mobility and economic development. So the 'poor man's son' submits 'to more fatigue of body and more uneasiness of mind [. . .] he labours night and day to acquire talents superior to all his competitors' (Smith [1759] 1976: 181).

This dynamic, however, is based upon a *deception*, namely the idea that the rich man is happier than the poor, or that he possesses 'more means for happiness' (Smith [1759] 1976: 182). In reality this is not true, but it is the engine for social and economic development (by means of the 'invisible hand' argument). This 'good deception' (for the common good) is at the core of Smith's theory of the 'invisible hand'.

Smith's illustration of how deceived human imagination works is a piece of psychological analysis which achieves its completion in the description of the *real* and actual condition of the rich, as people paradoxically sharing the same lot as the poor:

> It is to no purpose, that the proud and unfeeling landlord views his extensive fields, and without a thought for the wants of his brethren, in imagination consumes himself the whole harvest that grows upon them. The homely and vulgar proverb, that the eye is larger than the belly, never was more fully verified than with regard to him. The capacity of his stomach bears no proportion to the immensity of his desire, and will receive no more than that of the meanest peasant. (*TMS*, IV, 1, 10)

The fate of the rich, in fact, is *merely* that:

> they only select from the heap what is most precious and agreeable. They consume little more than the poor, and in spite of their natural selfishness and rapacity, though they mean only their own conveniency, though the sole end which they propose from the labours of all the thousands whom they employ, be the gratification of their own vain and insatiable desires, they divide with the poor the produce of all their improvements. They are led by an invisible hand to make nearly the same distribution of the necessaries of life, which would have been made, had the earth been divided into equal portions among all its inhabitants, and thus without intending it, without knowing it, advance the interest of the society, and afford means to the multiplication of the species. When Providence divided the earth among a few lordly masters, it neither forgot nor abandoned those who seemed to have been left out in the partition. These last too enjoy their share of all that it produces. In what constitutes the real happiness of human life, they are in no respect inferior to those who would seem so much above them. In ease of body and peace of mind, all the different ranks of life are nearly upon a level, and the beggar, who suns himself by the side of the highway, possesses that security which kings are fighting for. (*TMS*, IV, 1, 10)

Smith's use of the *invisible hand* metaphor in *The Theory of Moral Sentiments* parallels the logic of the *happiness paradox* in the current literature. In Smith's moral theory the rich and the ambitious are moved by frivolous and temporary illusions. 'Power and riches (IV, 1, 8) appear then to be, *what they are*, enormous and operose machines contrived to produce a few trifling conveniences to the body ... which in spite of all our care are ready every moment to burst into pieces, and crush in their ruins their unfortunate possessor' (*TMS*, VI, 1, 9, italics added).

In the *Wealth of Nations* the issue of happiness is almost totally absent. The title of the book itself defines the object of the newborn political economy: it deals with wealth not with happiness, even if in Smith's choice of the word 'wealth' instead of 'riches' one can rightly see the idea that wealth (weal or well-being) is more and something different from simply possessing riches.

Malthus, 'the first of the Cambridge economists', as J. M. Keynes (1933: 95) defined him, followed a different path. His *Essay on the Principle of Population* (Malthus [1798] 1966) plays an important role for the issue of happiness, a word that appears even in the title of the second edition (1803) of the book. In a very central passage, he writes:

> The professed object of Dr Adam Smith's inquiry is the nature and causes of the wealth of nations. There is another inquiry however perhaps even more interesting, which he occasionally includes in his studies and that is the inquiry into the causes which affect the happiness of nations [. . .] I am sufficiently aware of the near connection of these two subjects and that the causes which tend to increase the wealth of a state tend also, generally speaking, to increase happiness [. . .] But perhaps Dr Adam Smith has considered these two inquiries as still more nearly connected than they really are. (Malthus [1798] 1966: 303–4)

From this sentence we have the main elements for us to be able to understand the key points of Malthus's idea of happiness and his evaluation of Smith's position. Malthus claims that happiness is not wealth, but in general he agrees with Smith that more wealth leads to more happiness. According to Malthus, however, Smith was not sufficiently aware that the relation between these two concepts is complex and worth investigating on its own: he was aware, then, of the 'happiness transformation problem'. In particular, Malthus belongs to those economists (Sismondi, Genovesi and many Italians) who thought that the 'happiness of the nations' is 'another inquiry, however, perhaps still more interesting' (Malthus [1798] 1966: 304) than that of wealth, as the modern theorists of happiness also believe.

Nevertheless, it is important to notice that Malthus's wish to directly study happiness as the object of political economy did not last long. In his *Principles of Political Economy* (Malthus [1820] 1986) there are no references to happiness, and the object of his enquiries becomes wealth, as in Smith and the classical mainstream tradition of economics (something similar would also occur with Marshall, as we will see later). In particular, although he was fully aware that political economy, in focusing on material and quantitative aspects of human interactions, was losing important elements of well-being, he left out all interpersonal dimensions of wealth:

> A man of fortune has the means of [. . .] collecting at his table persons from whom he is likely to hear the most agreeable and instructive conversation [. . .] It would not be denied, that these are some of the modes of employing wealth, which are always, and most justly, considered as much superior in respectability, to the purchase of fine clothes, spending on furniture, or costly jewels [. . .] But it is a wide step in advance of these concessions, at once to place in the category

of wealth, leisure, agreeable conversation [. . .] The fact really is, that if we once desert matter in definition of wealth, there is no subsequent line of demarcation which has any tolerable degree of distinctness, or can be maintained with any tolerable consistency, till we have included such a mass of immaterial objects as utterly to confuse the meaning of the term, and render it impossible to speak with any approach towards precision, either of the wealth of different individuals, or different nations. (Malthus [1820] 1986: 31–2)

Here the main reason that led political economy to avoid dealing with interpersonal qualitative aspects of economic transactions is clearly stated. Malthus was convinced not only that 'enjoying conversations' with friends is an important and 'superior' form of using wealth, but even that 'leisure and agreeable conversations' can rightly be considered as components of the wealth and welfare of a person. These components, however, he considered to be too ill-defined to be included within the economic domain that instead needs data and objective measurement, namely, it needs 'matter' – a methodological position very close to the Austrian school of Menger, at the end of the nineteenth century. Something had to be sacrificed on the altar of the new science of objective and scientific measurements, and one victim was the social and immaterial components of wealth. A science seeking to encompass the first 'scientific' reflections on economic relations chose to focus its analyses upon objective elements, such as labour value or redistribution of income. However, such a science does not have the tools to study the 'happiness of nations', as the young Malthus claimed.

5.3   CAPITALISM AND CATHOLICISM

Just as Hobbes was developing his theory in England, the Protestant Reformation was spreading across Europe, the ideas and doctrines of Jansenism were growing in the Netherlands and in France and the Protestant pilgrims were occupying the new 'promised land' in North America. At the very same time the Counter-Reformation, the doctrine and practice of the Jesuits and the action of the Holy Office were gathering momentum across Italy, Spain and Portugal. It is from the evolution of these early signs that civil economy would arise in the eighteenth century.

Even before Martin Luther a remarkable difference existed between Latin Catholic humanism, that is, the spirit of the south, and the spirit of the north. Prior to the Christian saints the Italians worshipped the Penates and other Roman deities and held processions in their temples. Roman Christianity influenced the social culture they had created, but it found space in it to grow. Below the Alps the market already existed before the diffusion of the Calvinist spirit and, to this day, it continues to exist with its own distinctive character.

Early in his appointment as historian at the newly established Catholic University of the Sacred Heart, Amintore Fanfani focused his efforts on the study of the Catholic spirit of capitalism. His analysis hinges upon the comparison between the Middle Ages and Renaissance humanism. Fanfani's writings remind us that in medieval times the accumulation of wealth drew such strong opposition that greed was labelled as a capital vice; people were taught to cultivate an ethics of self-contentment and not to envy those above them. The Gospels and the message of Christ were unambiguous about money and wealth, and the economic ethics of the first millennium AD, as shaped first and foremost by the Early Church Fathers, contained a strong critique of money and of the pursuit of wealth in which the attainment of true wealth was deferred to the heavens. Even the notion of private property, while sanctioned as a legitimate individual right, was 'much tempered and closely bound up with the rules as to the social use of property' (Fanfani [1934] 1935: 126).

The development of early trade practices and the foundation of the Franciscan and Dominican orders favoured the shift to a more open view of money lending and economic activity (for instance, think of Peter John Olivi and the Franciscan economists). Nonetheless, Christian ethics did not evolve into a capitalist ethics; nor did it encourage the accumulation of wealth in the 'valley of tears': 'Wealth is thus a gift of God, and therefore not to be condemned. But men must not seek it so eagerly as to forget to lay up treasure in heaven, and they must walk carefully' (Fanfani [1934] 1935: 127). From the first centuries of the Christian era wealth was sublimated into a means and a sign: 'The most striking aspect for someone trying to comprehend the social views inherent in early Christianity is the radical transformation and broadening of the idea of wealth from a means to satisfy earthly needs and pleasures into a nobler path to the heavens' (Barbieri 1960: 116). The framework established by the Church Fathers, which went on to be a major influence in medieval culture, and was itself informed by the Greeks, and by Seneca, Cicero and the Romans, hinges on the notion of need: wealth that is not meant for, or exceeds, the satisfaction of needs is illicit, 'His [of the miser] horse, his land, his servant, his gold is worth 15 talents; he is worth 3 soldi' (quoted in Barbieri 1960: 118).

From the Book of Proverbs to Aquinas, the figure of the ant is famously praised for working hard and gathering resources instead of spending them. In addition, the general mistrust of the market and commerce was fuelled by antipathy towards merchants, who were seen in Christianity as parasites creating no value and earning their living from speculation. It is not incorrect to say that:

Christian and capitalistic virtues correspond in name but not in signification [. . .] Certainly no-one can deny that such men as the Bardi, Pitti, Datini, acted in a capitalistic manner, and, though baptized Christians, introduced a capitalistic mode of life among their Catholic contemporaries. But we deny that in so doing they were acting in conformity with Catholic social ethics [. . .] Only unawares can Catholics truly conforming to their faith have favoured the development of capitalism – as understood in the sense we have already many times defined. Or else, only by consequences that humanly and practically could not be foreseen, could certain actions on the part of real and true Catholics have favoured capitalism. (Fanfani [1934] 1935: 151–4)

Yet it was exactly this brand of anti-wealth and anti-capitalist Christian spirit during the second millennium that allowed Florence, Venice, Paris, Lisbon and London to thrive with wealth and usurers, as well as Rome with its boundless luxury. Fanfani then raises another interesting point: 'This fact makes us ask ourselves if it be indeed true that Catholicism always opposed the capitalistic spirit as it revealed itself in a Catholic age' (Fanfani [1934] 1935: 170). And: 'If Catholicism and Catholics did not pave the way for the advent of capitalism, when and where did this come about? In Protestant countries after Luther's revolt? Many declare that it flourished in such countries, but as for its birth, no one now denies that it took place before the Reformation, and hence in Catholic countries, among Catholics' (Fanfani [1934] 1935: 160).

His answer is that the capitalist spirit emerged prior to the Reformation out of certain 'deviations' from Catholic ethics, as a reaction to a new set of circumstances affecting Europe between the fifteenth and sixteenth centuries. The merchant began to benefit from a set of exemptions unavailable to other social actors: 'In medieval economic society the only individual who could easily and often find himself in a position to act otherwise than in conformity with pre-capitalist economic ideals was the merchant' (Fanfani [1934] 1935: 177). Among such 'deviations' or 'transgressions' the most striking occurred in the sphere of long-distance international commerce and in response to a substantial increase in the risks (which legitimated otherwise inadmissible profits). In those situations, merchants were able to act outside the moral control of their cities. Aquinas made the same argument, moving beyond the case of international trade:

If the citizens themselves engage in commerce, they open the way to many vices. For since the aim of merchants is wholly one of gain, greed takes root in the heart of the citizens, by which everything, in the city, becomes venal, and, with the disappearance of good faith, the way is open to fraud; the general good is despised, and each man will seek his own particular advantage; the taste for virtue will be lost when the honour which is normally the reward of virtue is accorded to all. Hence, in such a city civil life cannot fail to grow corrupt. (*De Regimine principum*, Book II, chap.3, quoted in Fanfani [1934] 1935: 176)[1]

This extensive quotation provides a clear insight into the prevailing opinion of the morality of commerce and of the markets in the Middle Ages. Suspicion and caution towards merchants and their activity remained ingrained within southern European humanism, whereas after the Reformation and through the Calvinist equivalence of wealth as blessing the pursuit of profit turned from vice into the highest virtue of capitalist ethics – a transformation that has come to affect all forms of life on our planet.

Another important role in this process was played by the displacement of the Jews in the sixteenth century from the south to the north of Europe, as well as the reconfiguration of trade routes from the Mediterranean to the Atlantic and the effect of the Protestant spirit, which Fanfani (unlike Weber) considers to be only one in a wider set of elements that led to the rise of capitalism in modern Europe.

However, the main point in Fanfani's argument is that the real conflict behind the Reformation was not theological but civil: a clash between the Germanic world, organized around an archaic and feudal order, and the Italian and Latin humanism: 'As it came into contact with the Latin world imbued with a new humanistic vocation and exhibiting the soft traits of the Renaissance, the Germanic world retreated in horror. Luther thought ill of the nature of this renewed spirit and responded' (Fanfani 1968: 508). Hence: 'The Reformation, which in him found its beginning and its energy, was first and foremost a protest, and only afterward a restoration [. . .] That world that revolved around man, in which others – objects, time, mind, pray – were aimed at enhancing the individual enjoyment of life was seen as heresy in the eyes of his/its first followers' (Fanfani 1968: 508). This argument is not dissimilar from Max Weber's: 'And what the reformers complained of in those areas of high economic development was not too much supervision of life on the part of the Church, but too little' (Weber [1905] 2005: 5).

Even though this statement might sound odd today, it has the potential to enhance our understanding of the historical origin of capitalism, if we can set aside its apology of Catholicism, its relatively unconcealed anti-Protestant stance (a common attitude at that time), its disguised antisemitism and its professed corporatism – quite an undertaking!

Luther's protest, even more than Calvin's, mostly targeted the Roman and Italian humanism and Renaissance and not exclusively their theological deviations (like the indulgences) or the corruption of the clergy. It was, all in all, an anti-humanistic and anti-Renaissance critique that extended to the Counter-Reformation:

> The Latin world reacted to the Protestant critique, but its reaction was primarily ecclesiastical. Thus came the Counter-Reformation that, sharing into the

original criticism of Protestantism to the ideals of Humanism and of the Renaissance, detached the latter from its own and made it so that men, without forgetting the arts, the letters, and the discoveries that had been perfected with Humanism and the Renaissance, could use them to live a life lightened by Christian values. (Fanfani 1968: 509)

Therefore, according to Fanfani: 'Humanism-Renaissance and Protestantism walked the same path, they were two moments of a single revelation that man gave to himself: the "naturalistic" revelation' (Fanfani 1968: 509). We shall take a closer look at this point.

5.4 THE ECONOMICS OF THE COUNTER-REFORMATION

When the Counter-Reformation set out to restore the Middle Ages, the Protestant Reformation took on an attitude of increasing amenability to commerce and to modern attitudes that had originated in humanism and the Renaissance. In the northern countries the view of individualism endorsed by the Reformation laid the groundwork for the production and creation of wealth. In Catholic countries, still permeated by the decadent culture of the late Roman Empire, the Counter-Reformation abruptly halted that revolution of the subject and brought back the ethical values of the Middle Ages: in doing so it encouraged an ostentatious type of consumption based on positional goods, as well as the pursuit of revenues, land ownership, and property holdings; at the same time it discouraged economic activity, crafts, commerce and private initiative (see Fanfani 1968: 512ff.).

The reaction of the Catholic Church against the values of the Reformation thus also led to a re-evaluation of the values of humanism and the Renaissance and, ultimately, to the end of the fledgling market economy that European humanism had been building upon the notion of liberty. Then, the northern cities gave rise to a capitalism of their own, just as the southern cities witnessed the reinstatement of an earlier set of values that were static, conservative and anti-modern, enforced by newly established institutions like the High Office and the Inquisition. The same amount of effort poured by these institutions into the fight against heresy was devoted in the north to the creation of companies and banks. In other words, the Counter-Reformation brought to a halt the proto-capitalism that emerged in the Middle Ages and evolved into civic humanism, which was both personalistic and communal, capable of reconciling individual freedom and the common good with the fundamental role of the great charismata and medieval theology, and of civic institutions free within the walls. Protestantism criticized the customs of the Renaissance and humanism displaying a view of luxury and wealth that was even more conservative than the Catholic Church of the time. However, by eliminating Church mediation and control from the citizens' daily lives Protestantism established a climate of personal freedom, which paved the way for the development of modern capitalism as a continuation – and this is the main hermeneutical point – of the European market economy of the thirteenth and fourteenth centuries: a continuation predicated on new terms and stripped of its original social dimension (with the exception of philanthropy and of the ethical principle of restitution).

We cannot try to understand the eighteenth century and the major antifeudal shift that took place in southern Europe, where providence became central to the view of the market and commerce, without considering the special context of Catholic Europe. After the sixteenth century and for the following two or three hundred years the path to the 'civil' market seemed lost. The civil and commercial virtues of Siena, Florence, Venice, Barcelona and Lisbon were replaced by the desire for land and revenues. Civil economy is what was needed. However, let us take a closer look at the economic underpinnings of the Counter-Reformation.

The capitalism stemming from Catholic Europe was predicated upon a view of the economy and society that lay at the heart of the monastic movements, primarily the Franciscans and the Dominicans, and Dominican Thomas Aquinas in particular. Only a short time after Luther's and Calvin's revolution, the Counter-Reformation presented a new breaking point in the economic and civil process, which had begun in the Middle Ages. If this did not happen right away it is because the economic impact of the Counter-Reformation was not immediately perceived. It was not until the second half of the sixteenth, and into the seventeenth, century that its characteristic traits became manifest, like the 're-feudalization' of southern Europe and the return to the land. Therefore, in the very same years that Luther was carrying out his Reformation, Cardinal Cajetano in his commentary of Aquinas' *Summa* affirmed the ethical legitimacy of seeking wealth beyond the conservation of the individual social and economic status within the hierarchy (Barbieri [1940] 2013). This attitude was actually a rupture with Aquinas' scholasticism, which advocated the conservation of one's social status. It came closer, instead, to the positions of Franciscan Bernardino of Siena (first half of the fifteenth century), Dominican Bishop Antoninus of Florence (latter part of the century) or lay humanists Leon Battista Alberti, Coluccio Salutati and Poggio Bracciolini, who were among the main interpreters of civic humanism. During the Reformation moral philosophers like Cajetan and Garimberto concentrated their hermeneutical efforts on finding arguments to legitimate interest-bearing loans (the ban of usury was still the prevailing view within the Church given its derivation from the Bible). Among such arguments fell the distinctions between *lucrum cessans* (ceasing profit) and *damnum emergens* (loss suffered), and between *usura* (excessive interest rate resulting from monetary speculation) and fair interest (*equo*) on loans towards complex and risky trade ventures. In civic humanism and during the Renaissance such analytic distinctions had made it easier for trade and economic activity to gain acceptance by the Church compared to earlier (and later) centuries. The real shift, however, came a few decades after the beginning of the Counter-Reformation with its actual implementation in civil and economic life.

The writings of the Jesuit preachers (*inter alia*), which appeared between the sixteenth and seventeenth centuries, show that the Counter-Reformation effectively set the moral evaluation of economic activities back by a few centuries to scholasticism and to Aquinas. The leaders of the Counter-Reformation – Castiglione, Bartolomeo of Salutio, Gattioli, Segneri, etc. – deemed guilty of a 'mortal sin' (*peccatum mortale*) those 'not content with their condition and status' (Castiglione, quoted in Barbieri [1940] 2013: 12).

5.5   VOLUNTARISM AND NATURALISM: ONE MORE DIFFERENCE BETWEEN NORTH AND SOUTH

Fanfani's writings help to cast light on another meaningful difference in the socio-economic perspectives of north and south. According to him, humanism-Renaissance and the Protestant Reformation constituted *two reforms* of the medieval spirit, two different transitions from 'voluntarism' (i.e. human beings are ill and *it falls on the institutions, and hence on the hierarchy*, to steer them towards good) to 'naturalism' (i.e. natural interests and passions are good).

In turn, the distinction between voluntarism and naturalism provides relevant insights into Fanfani's work. The medieval (and Greek-Roman) world was based on voluntarism, which gave primacy to politics. In the modern world, on the contrary, naturalism prevailed and primacy has shifted to economics, thereby eliminating the need for mediation:

> Finally, the politician has been deposed. He is no longer the regulator of human existence [. . .] Having discovered the immanence of the rational order, his exertion became superfluous and even harmful. His mission is to live at the

margins of the economy and of the 'crumbs' the latter reluctantly accords him. The relationships established by modern voluntarists between economics and politics have been turned upside-down. Even politics has been exempted from the task of maintaining economics on the plane of morality. Freely competing egoisms deliver this prodigious result, too, of giving rise to an order that not only fares better economically, but is even more just and better. (Fanfani 1942: 1, 176)

Classic voluntarism, especially in its medieval and proto-modern articulations, begins with the idea that the human being is ill with selfishness, but *remains a social animal capable of relationality*. This notion was rooted in the Bible and was later grafted on to the Greek world (where it can be found in Aristotle and, differently stated, in Plato and in Stoicism). In the remarkable synthesis, represented by (St Thomas') scholasticism, we find an acknowledgement, and reassertion, of this biblical root as well as of the need for institutions and social rules to prevent such fragile nature to fall 'ill' (on this point, see Aristotle's view of chrematistics, which remained virtually unchanged in St Thomas and throughout the Middle Ages).

In this anthropological perspective (particularly in Christian anthropology), man is seen as ambivalent and being capable of virtue and vice together: 'A positive and optimistic view of human nature became prevalent after Thomas Aquinas: in spite of the original sin, humankind has preserved the ability to discern good from evil and the impulse to choose good and regret evil' (Prosperi 2017: 74). Erasmus of Rotterdam, one of modern Europe's most fundamental figures (whom Luther thus accused of neo-Pelagianism in his private letters), held the same positive view.

Moreover, institutions had the crucial and twofold task of enabling man's virtuous social soul to find expression, while restraining his 'vicious' side. In human beings virtue is a natural and co-essential trait. The main message of virtue ethics, as we will see shortly, is imbued with anthropological realism: man is at the same time virtue and vice, *agape* and egoism. In order to strengthen virtue we need to foster education, schooling, rewards and institutions. It is at this point that voluntarism comes in: the common good must be institutionally constructed, not just accepted as the product of vices. A critical element in such humanism is the mediating role of the institutions, which are here 'communal' and relational (rather than automatic and anonymous).[2]

Also in this respect, the Reformation was an epoch-making shift. The anthropological approach at work in Protestantism, steeped as it was in Augustinian pessimism (and even overemphasized by Luther), no longer depicts human beings as truly capable of positive reciprocity (at least outside of the public or economic sphere). In this perspective the direct cooperation of men and women ought to be discouraged and the common good (a major theme) ought to be understood as a game of interests, for the *incivil animal* is incapable of nothing beyond this.

In the voluntaristic view widely held within Catholic humanism the economic order is not a *spontaneous order*. Therefore, Fanfani claims:

> As to whether or not the economic order may arise spontaneously, three are the possible conceptions: either one considers the rational and most beneficial economic order to be immanent; or one might believe that, since it cannot come about spontaneously, man may actually be capable of realizing the beneficial and rational economic order, obsequiously abiding by human reason and not giving himself up to invincible resistances; or finally one might believe that such order, which cannot arise spontaneously, may be realized by man, abiding by human reason, but giving himself up to a rotten resistance, at times vincible, at times invincible. (Fanfani 1942)

Then he adds:

> The economic doctrines based on the second conception of the economic order, which postulate the nonexistence of an immanent order that may be rational and beneficial . . . [and] assuming, instead, the need to rationalize economic life in accordance to the principles of righteous reason and to the ideals the latter ingenerates, will enumerate numerous *norms*, capable of guiding man towards the realization of the rational economic order that will be the reflection and the fruit of will guided by reason. In consideration of the confidence that these doctrines ascribe to human will as the force capable of realizing the ideals suggested by said reason, it is hereby proposed that they be called *voluntaristic* and *economic voluntarism*. (Fanfani 1942)

In line with its Catholic cultural origin, civil economy – and generally the Latin and Italian economic and political tradition – has maintained its voluntaristic approach, which ascribes a fundamental role to the mediation of institutions and of the state (consider the example of mixed economy and the weight of the state within the economy). As a matter of fact, this was the case up until recently, when a naturalist-based *pensée unique* has become prevalent across the world.

On the topic of medieval economics, Fanfani argues: 'Economic instincts and economic forces left to act freely generate an order that, insofar as it is natural, being the result of physical forces and human instincts, is not the ideal rational order, the reflection of reason, the order outside of which every human creature cannot maintain the position she deserves in the nature of things and according to the supernatural order' (Fanfani 1942: 89–90).

Medieval 'voluntaristic' theories then should not be seen as overlooking the 'true' nature of the market, understood as the intertwining of mutually advantageous relationships or as a 'positive-sum' game (an insight held by several of these authors); nor do these theories fail to acknowledge the incentivizing nature of interests and profits. Rather, voluntarism is the expression of a view of man and society in which the good of all and of each does not arise from the sum of interests, but from the encounter of virtues: 'They remark [quoting Montcrétien and Botero] ... that man operates in view of utility [. . .] They value the importance of such a force in that it animates economic life [. . .] Notwithstanding, they refuse to believe that the free action of individuals moved by this very instinct may actually lead to social well-being' (Fanfani 1942: 167).

It is no surprise, then, that Fanfani should quote Antonio Genovesi and acknowledge the importance of his *Lessons in Civil Economy*. After mentioning the Neapolitan abbot's book, he remarks:

> Liberty without rules always has pernicious effects on people and on civil societies. On people because it ushers them to the excesses of passions; and on societies because, by leading men solely to their personal or domestic interest, it corrupts the public good in countless ways ... because the profit of the merchant should not be confused with the profit of the State. It may well leave the merchant rich and the State ruined. (Fanfani 1942: 167)

At the height of the Middle Ages, southern Europe with its long history and broad biodiversity gave rise to a market economy informed by the Catholic paradigm and which was, therefore, the expression of a community-based and institutionally 'mediated' idea of society. In the north, Protestantism produced the idea of a society of individuals rid of the intermediate institutions, as visible in the humanism of the 'invisible hand' and in the Leviathan. In the space of freedom of the state-Leviathan established by the social contract, the common good is not left to the mediation of institutions; it is the unintentional outcome of the action of separate and independent individuals. The Reformation and the Counter-Reformation were major turning points in the development of modern Europe and the current socio-economic gaps between the north and south of Italy may be seen as the end of an interrupted journey. Social pathologies, 'amoral familism' and the corruption of the 'mediated society' created by Italian and Mediterranean societies are serious and widely known matters. At the same time Protestant humanism, with its loneliness and unhappy individualism, has undergone a crisis of its own, which is different, albeit no less significant, and which invites us to search further in hopes of finding something new.

The work of Antonio Genovesi has to be placed within this context.

5.6　THE TRADITION OF COMMON GOOD ENTERS ECONOMICS: CIVIL ECONOMY

In the latter half of the eighteenth century, civil economy was thriving in Naples and spreading to the rest of Italy. Its most prominent figure was Antonio Genovesi (Naples, 1713–69).

Genovesi (or Genovese) was born on 1 November 1713 in Castiglione (today Castiglione del Genovesi), a small town eight miles from Salerno. He was the second youngest son of Salvatore, a craftsman and shoe trader, and Adriana Alfinito of San Mango, who passed away at the age of twenty-four after giving birth to four children. Antonio pursued his earliest studies in Castiglione (back then a lively commercial centre inhabited by over 10000 people, founded in the pre-Roman era by the Piceni) and in Salerno, where he entered ecclesiastical life. In 1736 he was ordained a priest and the following year he moved to Naples.

On his father's advice he initially:

> Considered becoming a Lawyer of the Forum: but, fortunately for science and for his native land, due to utter indisposition he elected to pursue philosophy and set to reform his studies. Here more than anywhere else he had the ease and great opportunity to study at pleasure, thanks to the freedom he enjoyed and to the aid of the libraries he required. He first attended public University listening to the most renowned Professors. (Galanti 1774: 11)[3]

For a few years he offered private lessons in philosophy and ethics, while he attended the lessons of philosopher Giambattista Vico.[4] In the same years he met and befriended Celestino Galliani (uncle of the famous economist Ferdinando), an important figure in the ecclesiastical world and prefect of education in Naples. Thanks to him, in November 1741 he obtained the first professorship in metaphysics: 'Abbot Genovesi began lecturing on metaphysical matters at the University as extraordinary Professor' (Galanti 1774: 21). In 1743 he published his first philosophical work, the first part of the *Elementa Metaphysicae Mathematicum in Morem Adornata* (the fourth and final part would appear in 1752).

Young Genovesi talked about pantheism, cosmography, reason and faith with such latitude that he came off as exceedingly innovative in his time. In particular, his interest in Locke and his theory of the origin of ideas, as well as his empirical approach, were too distant from neo-scholasticism.[5] In 1744, on Galliani's advice, and in order to avert excommunication, he wrote an appendix to his oeuvre that reads as a declaration of Catholic faith: 'It was agreed therefore that Abbot Genovesi should elucidate some aspects of his Metaphysics [. . .] He proceeded to do so by means of an Appendix addressed to the Cardinal himself' (Galanti 1774: 31).

Nevertheless, his theological and philosophical oeuvre drew such severe criticism from the clergy that the work had to be published without the ecclesiastical stamp of approval (*imprimatur*) of the archbishop of Naples, Cardinal Spinelli, following Genovesi's refusal to eliminate some passages from the text.[6] Having lost the teaching post in metaphysics, in 1745, thanks once again to the mediation of Celestino Galliani, he obtained the recently re-established post of professor of ethics. In the same year he published a new book of logic (*Elementorum Artis Logico-Criticae*).

Throughout Genovesi's career his relationship with the religious authorities remained problematic; so much so that in 1817 his *Lezioni di Economia Civile* appeared on the Index of Forbidden Books. Notwithstanding the disagreement with the Church's temporal and political choices, Genovesi always maintained an authentic Christian spirit and genuine Catholic faith. Critics scorned his *Metaphysics*: 'As soon as the first part came out, calumnies and detractions ensued [. . .] Theologians on another side, used to dismiss as atheist anyone who failed to share their views, already regarded Abbot Genovesi as a man without religion' (Galanti 1774: 29, 48). In 1748 a rival of Genovesi (Abbot Molinari) competing for a professorship in theology 'presented the Pope with a list of 14 heretical propositions . . . that he claimed had been extracted from the theological manuscripts of Abbot Genovesi' (Galanti 1774: 49). Additional attacks and accusations came from Father Maria T. Mamachi, a friar from Puglia whose book *On the Free Right of the Church to Acquire and Possess Temporal Goods, Both Moveable and Immoveable* was published in the year of Genovesi's death (1769). The main points of Mamachi's allegations are contained in an appendix to Galanti's *Historical Eulogy* (1774, first edition 1772), which shows the student firmly and decidedly defending his master against the charges of heresy (see also Tisi 1937).

Genovesi ultimately obtained an appointment in economics, commerce and mechanics. Among the first ever recorded in Europe,[7] this position had been conceived and endowed by Bartolomeo Intieri (administrator in Campania for the properties of the Medici family) upon condition that it be assigned to Genovesi and that the lectures be held in Italian rather than Latin – a choice informed by a specific educational and reformatory intention.[8] The challenges faced by Genovesi in his pursuit of theology had hindered the free flow of his ideas, which thus deviated towards a less controversial sphere of theology, namely economics; here references to Locke and Hume drew less suspicion and posed less of a threat to the salvation of the soul. In the last 15 years of his life Genovesi applied himself almost exclusively to economic subjects, a field in which he excelled and attained universal recognition.[9]

Like the first civil humanists, Genovesi saw civil life as the place where 'civil happiness' (an expression used by Vico) can be achieved in full, thanks to good and just laws, to institutions, to commerce and to civil bodies in which men may express their sociability: 'While companionship entails some evils, it is nonetheless the assurance of life and of good; from it come the greatest pleasures, unknown to men of nature' ([1766] 1973: 37). And in *Lezioni*: 'Man is a naturally social animal, this is a common dictum. But not every man will believe that no animal exists on earth that is not sociable[10] [. . .] In what regard may we then say man to be more sociable than others? [It is] the reciprocal right to be helped and, as a consequence, a reciprocal obligation to help each other in our times of need' ([1765–76] 1824: ch. 1, §XVII, 283).

Reciprocity, or mutual aid, is for Genovesi the primary law of both civil society and economics. Unlike Adam Smith he does not believe the 'propensity in human nature . . . to truck, barter, and Exchange one thing for another' (1776: 25) to be the defining trait of human relationality.[11] If, on one side, he criticizes the Hobbesian–Augustinian view that sees man as interest driven, Genovesi is nonetheless unwilling to embrace the opposite anthropological view that regards man's virtue as merely natural – this idea was then popular among the philosophers of *moral sense* associated with a certain romantic literature of his generation (see Shaftesbury). His anthropological framework is quite complex in that it emphasizes reciprocity over altruism. Human beings are moved by a plurality of forces, by interests and love simultaneously – and this applies to all spheres of life, including economics. We shall examine this point shortly.

Genovesi wrote his *Trattato di Economia* while in Naples, at the time of Enlightenment and of the city's highest cultural splendour; for his work he chose the title *Lezioni di commercio o sia di economia civile* (1765–76). This title is a synthesis of his thought: commerce, that is to say, civil economy. Commercial activities *are* civil, the market *is* civility. On this topic Leopardi wrote in *Zibaldone*: 'What if Genovesi had given his *Lessons in Commerce* the title of *Lessons in Merchant Practice*?' (1898–1900: n.1423).

However, his appointment had a different title: 'commerce and mechanics'. This is significant because it alerts us to a key link between economic (and generally academic) culture and the techniques and applications essential to civilization and to the material improvement of people's conditions. Genovesi was a staunch reformer; he was personally committed to the dissemination of technical skills in rural areas and was a champion of school education for youth and for all people. Europe's ability to foster economic and civil development has been (and is) greatest when it manages to combine practical and intellectual knowledge, the intelligence of the mind and the intelligence of the hands.

Lezioni was written throughout the years of his teaching appointment in economics (1754–69), building upon the previous *Elementi di Commercio*, written for his students in 1758. Published by M. L. Perna as part of a critical edition of the *Lezioni*, its manuscript is held at the National Library in Naples.[12]

In *Lezioni*, economic matters are treated unsystematically, even though the structure of the work is more linear than generally acknowledged. The most beautiful and innovative pages and ideas are the ones about trust, reciprocity and happiness; less so are the pages about price or gold (even though many surprises are scattered here and there).[13] Genovesi's oeuvre, despite its absolute modernity (which unsettled the ecclesiastical authorities of his time), belongs to the classical tradition and to virtue ethics: 'In nature the words just, honest, virtue, useful, interest cannot be disjoined, if not foolishly' ([1766] 1973: 49).

The keywords of Genovesi's civil economy are trust, reciprocity and happiness. Nowadays these words have regained the centre of the economic debate; they differ from the words of Smith and of the founders of political economy. *Lezioni di economia civile* deals almost with the same themes found in the books of the European economists of Genovesi's generation (themes like money, internal and external trade, public debt, taxation, the role of the government, the price system, gold), but the ethical premises and the socio-anthropological perspective are different, as we have had the chance to observe.

Consider trust. Like the Franciscans and Aquinas, as well as fifteenth-century humanists, Genovesi sees the market as a matter of *fides* and, in particular, of 'public faith', which he considers the real precondition for economic and civil development. A few years later another important exponent of the Neapolitan school, Gaetano Filangieri, wrote: 'Confidence is the soul of commerce, [. . .] without it the parts that compose its edifice fall in on themselves' (Filangieri [1780] 2003: 93). *Private* trust (similar to today's notion of reputation) is different from public faith, because the latter is not a simple sum of private trusts. It is similar to what modern social theorists call *social capital*, which is the very fabric of trust and civil virtues that enables human and economic development to be set in motion and continue over time. Public faith is born out of 'private faiths', but it also requires the role of the government, of religion, of education, of law, etc. Also for this reason, not only is public faith a means, but it is equally *part of the wealth* of a nation (Bianchini 1845: 21). According to Genovesi, the absence of 'public faith' accounted for the low civil and economic development in the Kingdom of Naples – an analysis that has lost none of its currency two and a half centuries later.

In that kingdom – wrote a concerned Genovesi at the beginning of his career – there was much 'private faith' (particularistic and tied to clans, bound by blood or feudal pacts of vassalage), but too little 'public faith'. And while it is true that the development of the markets brings along civil and economic development, according to the Neapolitan school it is even more urgent to emphasize that the *cultivation* of public faith is the precondition for any discourse on economic and civil development: 'Nothing is more necessary for a great and prompt circulation than public faith' (Genovesi [1765–76] 1824: 751). Additionally, Genovesi makes this important remark in one of the notes: 'The word *fides* means rope, which ties and unites. Public faith is then the bond of families united in a life of companionship' (Genovesi [1765–76] 1824: 751). Those who study the role of social capital today will no doubt appreciate the prophetic value of this argument made both by Genovesi and by civil economy.

5.7   VIRTUE ETHICS

Another important distinction between *civil economy* and *political economy* lies in their ethical underpinnings: while civil economy is founded on virtue ethics, political economy adopted Bentham's principles of utilitarianism. Virtue is related to the ethics of common good, to Aristotle and Aquinas, and less to Augustine, whose ideas had a major influence on the Reformation and informed the economic doctrine of Protestantism. Every ethical approach modelled on the notion of virtue (like Aristotle's, Aquinas' or today MacIntyre's) hinges on the assumption that human beings are capable of genuine sociality; or, in other terms, that self-interest does not prevent them from cultivating *philia*, or even *agape*, in public, civil and economic life. The anthropological pessimism embedded in the Protestant Reformation effectively chased away virtue ethics from the northern spirit, whereas it lived on in the works of Catholic authors like Genovesi and other prominent theorists of civil economy.

As a matter of fact, Genovesi was not the only one among such authors to be living in Naples in the years of the Enlightenment: among his students we remember Giacinto Dragonetti from L'Aquila, whose pamphlet *Delle Virtù e Dei Premi* (*Of Virtues and Rewards*) had wide international circulation – for instance it was cited by Thomas Paine, one of the fathers of the American Revolution, in his *Common Sense* (1776).

But what is *virtue*? And what does *virtue ethics* actually mean? The concept of virtue does not fit neatly into any of the categories formulated in modern and contemporary economics to capture human choices. The anthropological and methodological framework established by economic theory, mostly in the last century (the so-called 'neoclassical paradigm'), was not designed to accommodate the idea of virtue, which grew out of the philosophical context 'of the Mediterranean' at far distance from the birthplace of contemporary economic science.[14] Virtue is neither a matter of preferences, nor of expectations; it is, rather, *a trait in one's character*, a long-term disposition, a behaviour that society recognizes as upstanding and commendable, which leads to excellence in those who practise it (and which should therefore be upheld).[15] We can draw the logical conclusion that economic behaviour might also possess some virtues of its own, some upstanding and commendable dispositions to exercise in doing business, exchanging and trading in pursuit of excellence. And, as a matter of fact, virtue (*areté* in Greek) has to do with excellence.[16]

According to the Greek view of virtue, it is not the excellence of scientists' discoveries that make them virtuous, but the quest for truth regardless of the results: what is essential is the ongoing search; its aim is excellence itself and not primarily the fruits that excellence delivers.[17] Similarly, happiness (the Aristotelian *eudaimonia*) is attained by those who, while they may not be pursuing it directly, lead a virtuous life. A very close relationship, therefore, exists between virtue and non-instrumental behaviour or, as we might call it today, a behaviour arising from intrinsic motivations: we would not regard as virtuous an artist who painted for the sake of fame rather than beauty; nor an athlete only seeking excellence in view of its gains; nor a scientist or a university professor who engaged in research as a means to further their career. The following corollary thus applies: in the perspective of virtue ethics, those who engage in an activity or practice solely motivated by its extrinsic benefits (fame, money, career, etc.) will never achieve excellence therein.

Contemporary virtue philosophers have introduced the concept of *practice*[18] (which effectively replaces the Aristotelian *telos*) in light of the fact that the criteria for excellence in any given activity are ultimately defined by a specific *community* (whether of artists, of athletes, of entrepreneurs, etc.).[19] In the game of chess excellence is defined by a set of *goods* that are *internal*, or intrinsic, to the game, just as art's internal goods are defined by the nature of each artistic discipline. We can therefore conclude that virtue is scarce and that it is unlikely to be achieved every day by everyone and in every field of activity, given that excellence, to which one may aspire, is hard to achieve within the wider perspective of dynamic historical processes.[20]

In conclusion, we can argue that virtue ethics is predicated upon the prevalence of virtue over vice, which warrants resort to rewards at least as much as punishments. Yet, this project of modernity was completely disavowed, partly because of Napoleon (whose penal codes did not envision rewards) and because of the European Restoration. Together these elements led to the interruption of this Enlightenment program that had been championed first and foremost by the civil economy tradition.

NOTES

1. Fanfani does not mention (and perhaps ignored) that book III of *De Regimine princi-pum*, from which this citation has been taken, was actually written by Bartholomew of Lucca, a student of Aquinas.

2. The Catholic wariness of contractualist theories is partially the result of the assumption (central to Thomism and *mainstream* Catholic thought) that human beings are sociable by nature: we do not *become* sociable through the social contract, we already were – the social contract famously embodies a pessimistic anthropology (apparent in Hobbes as well as in Rousseau, even though the latter believed humankind was once sociable and later spoiled by civilization). On the other hand, according to the Thomistic view: *homo homini naturaliter amicus*.

3. Galanti writes of Genovesi: 'Nature, that in its provisions had him destined for great things, in addition to granting greatness to his person and beauty to his body, as well as anything anyone could ever wish for, making him of endearing and attractive figure, also gave him sound health, proper and elegant manners, and the talent, as precious as it is singular, to communicate his mind with clarity and grace. It coupled such fortunate dispositions with vast memory, straight thinking, great spirit; and, even more rare, with a superior genius unlike those of ordinary saviours who neither think nor reason, except on the ideas of others' (1774: 20).

4. The subject of Vico's influence on Genovesi has always been controversial. According to Galanti, who was a student of Genovesi and his first biographer, such influence hardly existed: 'Giambattista Vico left us with the suspicion that he might have been a man of genius by means of a body of work that is obscure and enigmatic, which is to say, useless' (1774: 17).

5. Giovanni Gentile wrote: 'Genovesi is in fact the initiator of the entire philosophical movement of Empiricism emerged in Naples toward the end of the eighteenth century and the beginning of the following century' (1930: 2).

6. As Galanti explains: 'The revision had been commissioned by him [the Archbishop] to a priest who was ignorant and yet presumptuous and who believed, in reason of his degree in Theology, to have a universal understanding as well as the right to judge everything. But being hardly capable of discerning science from folly, the new truths he encountered in the work of Mister Genovesi seemed to him suspicious and he therefore wanted to fill it with the most appalling corrections' (1774: 29). Thus: 'eagerly misguided theologians rose against the author with their ordinary absurdity ... Mister Genovesi was then regarded as a monster, because he had introduced in Italy the freedom to think; and because he quoted the works of Galilei, Newton, and Grotius. This is how the good and the true are invariably saluted by the apostles of error' (Galanti 1774: 30).

7. A teaching post specifically dedicated to civil economy was established in Modena in 1772 and offered to Francesco III Agostino Paradisi, an eclectic personality whose expertise stretched well beyond economics. The manuscript of his *Lezioni di Economia Civile* (undoubtedly inspired by Genovesi) is held at the Library of Modena and Reggio Emilia, where it awaits to be discovered and its value acknowledged. Genovesi, partly through his friendship with Muratori, was very well connected with Modena's cultural milieu (as is apparent in his correspondence, which has been successfully preserved).

8. Cesare Beccaria made the same choice in Milan. In the outline for the post in public economics he wrote: 'And it is redundant to suggest that to treat this science in Italian is to render its insights more common and familiar to any class of people, in order to timely train the young to speak the language of business, given the sterility of the Latin language in these matters' (Beccaria 2014: 57). And in his *Prolusion* to the post we read: 'it is hereby prescribed with eager predilection that the teaching of the science previously subtracted from the eyes of public examination by reason of useless, and even harmful, prudence, be taught in vernacular language' (Beccaria 2014: 82). The choice of Italian was therefore a civil choice, motivated by the demands of democratic participation

in knowledge and power. Genovesi similarly remarked in his *Lezioni*: 'What I wish to establish as an absolutely certain political axiom is that a nation will never be perfectly versed in the sciences, the arts, and the manners, unless it has laws, sciences, schools, and books of arts in its own language, for otherwise it will have to rely on a foreign language; and since the latter won't be understood, except by the smallest part of the population, everything else will remain outside of the luminous sphere of the letters' ([1765–76] 1824: ch. 24, 90, Bk VIII).

9. Between 1765 and 1769 Genovesi published his most important writings: *Lezioni di economia civile*, immediately translated into German and Spanish (and partially in French); *Logica Italiana* (1766), *Diceosina o sia della Filosofia del Giusto e dell'Onesto* (1766). He also produced a commentary (appeared posthumously and incomplete in 1777; De Mas 1971) of Montesquieu's *De l'Esprit des Lois*. Posthumous was also the publication in 1779 of a volume about Newtonian mechanics, where Genovesi reprised and further developed an earlier academic theme – in 1745, with his friend P. Orlandi, professor of experimental physics at the University of Naples, he curated the Neapolitan edition of Pieter van Musschembroek's *Elementa Physicae* (*Elements of Natural Philosophy*). Abbot Genovesi died prematurely in Naples in September 1769. Due to his troubled relationship with the ecclesiastical authorities, his funeral was held privately and he was buried in Naples in the crypt of a church (Sant'Eramo Nuovo), without public honours or recognition.

10. The Italian economist Vilfredo Pareto wrote to his friend and colleague Maffeo Pantaleoni that cats are an exception to the universal rule of sociability (something he knew well being himself a notorious cat lover, who even named his villa in Céligny near Lausanne after the breed living around him: Villa Angora).

11. Owing partly to the Christian roots of his philosophical framework, we find hints in Genovesi's work of an idea of reciprocity that goes beyond mutual advantage and is amenable to gratuitousness. In several passages (chiefly in *Diceosina*) the gain of another is not a precondition for one's own behaviour: at the same time, however, reciprocity is necessary for another's gain.

12. A comparative reading of *Elements* and *Lezioni* shows a growing critical attitude towards commerce. In one of Genovesi's last works on economics – the commentary to Montesquieu's *L'Esprit des Lois* – in discussing the famous passages about the 'spirit of commerce' ('the natural effect of commerce is to bring peace') Genovesi makes a claim that seems to contradict all his other works. We read in one of the notes: 'Commerce is the main source of wars. He is jealous, and jealousy harms Men. The wars of the Carthaginians and of the Romans, the Venetians, the Genoese, the Pisans, the Portuguese, and the Dutch, the French, and the English bear witness to this fact. If two nations trade with each other for reciprocal needs, it is these needs that prevent war, not the spirit of commerce' (Genovesi 1777: II, 195). Here too, however, in order to understand the meaning of this sentence we must dig beneath the surface and read this claim in light of the ideas we have been unpacking on the topic of mutual advantage and mutual assistance. The Salerno-born economist criticizes the mercantilist view of the *spirit* of commerce (still dominant until the Enlightenment), whereby commerce is profoundly related to the spirit of conquest and predation of the states; commerce is thus conceived and experienced not as mutual assistance, but as a 'zero-sum game'. On the contrary, Genovesi and civil economy praise trade among individuals and people when it stems from their respective needs and from mutual assistance: 'They trade with each other for mutual needs'. And in the last Neapolitan edition of his *Lezioni* (1769) he adds this very significant remark: 'Many have thought it utterly strange that I shall describe the spirit of commerce as spirit of conquest. But so it is: many read to avoid thinking. Let them say, then: why trade, if not to seize?' ([1765–76] 1824: 523, note a).

13. For instance: 'In every country, more in some places and less in others, there is a certain number of poor and beggars. Were it possible to incorporate them into the mass of workers and repaying borrowers, two good deeds would be accomplished. Firstly, this

would increase the general revenue of the nation. Secondly, It would be of service to public morals' (Genovesi 2013: ch. 1, I, bk I). Or: 'Price is the child of need: who could ever know my need better than myself? The needs of an entire family are suffered by the family, and those of a nation by the entire nation [. . .] Man's needs are the primary source of the price of every thing and every exertion' (Genovesi 2013: ch. 1, 17, bk II).

14. Nevertheless, neoclassical theory could, in principle, accommodate a soft concept of virtue. On this point, see Bruni and Sugden (2013).

15. Some authors (e.g. McCloskey 2008) detect in instrumental rationality (this being the kind known to economic science) traces of the virtue of prudence. However, this reading does not seem entirely convincing.

16. In the Aristotelian view, which relies on virtue ethics, *areté* relates to nature and is closely associated with the idea of *telos* (end/purpose): virtue consists in acting according to nature, namely the authentic reality of things, because things carry within themselves their end, namely their *telos*. Similarly, happiness comes from acting in accordance with virtue and therefore with the *telos* of a specific area of life. For instance, Aristotle argues that victory is the *telos* of war and in order to achieve this *telos* the warrior must cultivate, among others, the virtue of courage (2009: 7). As MacIntyre (2013) points out, however, unlike the mythical and Homeric conception, in Aristotle (as in the later Aristotelian–Thomistic and Christian tradition) the good life must be connected to *all* virtues, stressing that virtue requires the person's overall orientation to Good.

17. When scientists or artists operate in their respective fields in accordance with their *telos*, be it truth (science) or beauty (art), they attain excellence, but its mark is not merely, nor primarily, the quality of its fruits: rather, it is reflected in the person acting in accordance with the nature or intrinsic scope of her activity, thereby revealing her own virtue-excellence. Walzer (2008), as well as Sandel (2013), uses the word 'sphere' to denote a certain area of activity; however, 'sphere' does not fully convey the classic concept of *telos*, or of practice-field).

18. The concept of practice has been formulated to make sense of virtue ethics in today's world, where the notions of nature and *telos* have fallen out of the current sensitivity and lost part of their effectiveness in communicating the purport of being virtuous or excellent. For instance, what would be the *telos* or the authentic nature of the game of golf (upon which the international golf federation ought to base the rules of the game in order to reward excellence-*areté*)?

19. Practice, however, is always defined in relation to a specific field. Therefore, virtue in a given practice depends on the achievement of certain goods inherent to the practice, which are non-instrumental (insofar as they relate to the intrinsic aim of that practice in that field). It is also worth noticing that such intrinsic goods aren't established by a single individual, but by a community: unlike Hume's or Smith's rather pragmatic and conventional views, the idea here is that a community does not define the virtuosity of a behaviour simply by means of consent, but through the unfolding of history and tradition, which exceed the consent given by a single community member in a specific moment in history, and are hence changeless. We should also point out that for MacIntyre excelling in a certain practice is not enough to be called virtuous. Virtue also requires excellence in character. For instance, a soccer player who excelled in the practice of soccer, but not in other aspects of his or her existence, may not be called virtuous. The same is true of artists, scientists, etc. For a critical analysis of these observations see Bruni and Sugden (2013).

20. In Italy at the beginning of the twentieth century Mario Calderoni and Giovanni Vailati came up with an 'economic' approach to virtue which falls within the same philosophical tradition: altruism is considered virtuous because it is scarce, but in a society of altruistic individuals it's self-interested actions that should be called virtuous and hence encouraged.

REFERENCES

Aristotle (2009), *The Nicomachean Ethics.* Translated by David Ross and edited by Lesley Brown. Oxford: Oxford University Press.

Barbieri, G. [1940] (2013), *Decline and Economic Ideals in Italy in the Early Modern Age.* Florence: Leo S. Olschki.

Barbieri, G. (1960), *Il pensiero economico dall'antichità alla scolastica.* Bari: Istituto di Storia Economica dell'Università di Bari.

Beccaria, C. (2014), *Edizione Nazionale delle Opere di Cesare Beccaria.* Under the general editorship of L. Firpo and G. Francioni, vol. 3, *Scritti economici,* edited by G. Gaspari. Milano: Mediobanca.

Benjamin, W. [1921] (1985), Capitalism as religion, in *GesammelteSchriften,* vol. 6, ed. Ralph Liedemann and Hermann. Schweppenhäuser, Frankfurt: Suhrkamp Verlag.

Bianchini, L. (1845), *Della Scienza del ben Vivere Sociale e della Economia Degli Stati.* Palermo: Stamperia di Francesco Lao.

Bruni, L. and J. Milbank (eds) (2018), Martin Luther's heritage in modern economic and social sciences. Special issue of the *International Review of Economics.*

Bruni, L. and R. Sugden (2013), Reclaiming virtue ethics for economics. *The Journal of Economic Perspectives,* 27(4): 141–64.

De Mas, E. (1971), *Montesquieu, Genovesi e le edizioni italiane dello «Spirito delle leggi».* Milano: Mondadori.

Fanfani, A. (1934), *Cattolicesimo e protestantesimo nella formazione storica del capitalismo.* Milan: Vita e Pensiero.

Fanfani, A. [1934] (1935), *Catholicism, Protestantism and Capitalism.* London: Sheed and Ward.

Fanfani, A. (1942), *Il volontarismo* (Voluntarism). Como: Cavalleri.

Fanfani, A. (1968), *Storia economica, I: Antichità, Medioevo, età moderna* (Economic History, I: Antiquity, the Middle Ages, and the Modern Age). Torino: Utet.

Filangieri, G. [1780] (2003), *La scienza della legislazione.* Napoli: Grimaldi & C. Editori.

Galanti, G. M. (1774), *Elogio storico del signor abate Antonio Genovesi.* Napoli.

Genovesi, A. [1765–76] (1824), *Lezioni di commercio o sia di economia civile.* Milan: Società Tipografica dei Classici Italiani.

Genovesi, A. [1766] (1973), *Della diceosina o sia della filosofia del giusto e dell'onesto.* Milan: Marzorati.

Genovesi, A. (1777), *Spirito delle leggi del Signore di Montesquieu, con le note dell'Abbate Antonio Genovesi.* 2nd edition. Napoli: Domenico Terres Libraio.

Genovesi, A. (2013), *Lezioni di economia civile.* Edited by F. Dal Degan. Milano: Vita e Pensiero.

Gentile, G. (1930), *Storia della filosofia italiana dal Genovesi al Galluppi, seconda edizione con correzioni ed aggiunte.* Firenze: Sansoni.

Keynes, J. M. (1933), *Essays in Biography.* London: Macmillan.

Leopardi, G. (1898–1900), *Zibaldone,* in *Pensieri di varia filosofia e di bella letteratura.* Firenze: Le Monnier.

Loria, A. (1893) [1904]), *Verso la Giustizia Sociale.* Milan: Società Editrice Libraria.

MacIntyre, A. (2013), *After Virtue.* London and New York: Bloomsbury.

Malthus, T. R. [1798] (1966), *An Essay on the Principle of Population*. London: Macmillan.

Malthus, T. R. [1820] (1986), *Principles of Political Economy*. Edited by E. A. Wrigley and D. Souden. London: Pickering.

McCloskey, D. (2008), Adam Smith, the last of the former virtue ethicists. *History of Political Economy*, 40(1): 43–71.

Muratori, L. A. (1749), *Della Pubblica Felicità*. LOESCHER Edition. Lucca.

Palmieri, G. (1788), *Riflessioni sulla Pubblica Felicità Relativamente al Regno di Napoli*. Milan: Pirotta e Maspero.

Prosperi, A. (2017), *Lutero: Gli anni della fede e della libertà*. Milan: Mondadori.

Sandel, M. J. (2013), Justice beyond fairness. In *Reading Walzer* (pp. 185–192). London: Routledge.

Simonde de Sismondi, J. C. L. [1819] (1971), *Nouveaux Principes d'Economie Politique*. Paris: Calmann-Lévy.

Smith, A. [1759] (1976), *The Theory of Moral Sentiments*. Edited by A. L. Macfie and D. D. Raphael. Oxford: Oxford University Press.

Smith, A. (1776). *An inquiry into the nature and causes of the wealth of nations: Volume One*. London: printed for W. Strahan and T. Cadell, 1776.

Tisi, A. (1937), *Il pensiero religioso di Antonio Genovesi*. Amalfi: De Luca.

Verri, P. (1781), *Sull'indole del Piacere e del Dolore*. Milan: Giuseppe Marelli.

Walzer, M. (2008), *Spheres of Justice: A Defense of Pluralism and Equality*. New York: Basic Books.

Weber, M. [1905] (2005), *The Protestant Ethic and the Spirit of Capitalism*. New York and London: Routledge.

6. 'Naturaliter homo homini amicus est': economy, happiness and relationships in Aquinas' thought[1]

Paolo Santori

6.1 INTRODUCTION

The happiness paradox raised by Easterlin's (1974) empirical investigation advanced an unsettling thesis for economics: self-reported happiness decreases (or remains steady) after a rise in income. This is valid *over time* at an aggregate level for a single country (Layard, 2005), even if the correlation between the rise in income and happiness *in a given moment of time* is robust (Frey and Stutzer, 2002), and *cross-country analyses* have produced controversial results (Frey and Stutzer, 2002; Hagerty and Veenhoven, 2003; Easterlin, 2005). Several explanations have been advanced. The positionality theory, grounded on the relation between absolute and relative income, appeared to be a clear explanation for the lack of growth in the level of happiness (Clark and Oswald, 1996; Frank, 1997, 1999; Holländer, 2001; Layard, 2005; Clark, 2017; Grasseni and Origo, 2018). Interdisciplinary scholars (those studying economics and psychology) merged two psychological (treadmill and set-point) theories into a single account: there are two treadmills bringing people back to their inner-decided level of happiness after an increase in income, one treadmill working on pleasure and the other on aspirations (Kahneman et al., 1999; Frey and Stutzer, 2005; Kahneman, 2011; Frey, 2018). Eventually some academics suggested considering the missing ingredient of the happiness paradox – the role of non-intrinsically motivated sociality (Bruni, 2010), that is, relational goods (Pugno, 2007; Becchetti et al., 2008; Bruni and Stanca, 2008; Gui and Stanca, 2010; Bartolini, 2014).

This last stream of research is small but growing. Some Italian economists[2] are trying to recover insights from modern economic traditions, specifically from the Neapolitan school of civil economy of the eighteenth century (Bruni and Porta, 2003; Bruni and Zamagni, 2016), to enrich the debate on economics and happiness through empirical analyses. Among them, Bruni (2006, 2007, 2010) combines an historical approach with a theoretical claim to 'bring back' the discourse of genuine relationality in economics. He establishes that the modern discourse on happiness (Frey and Stutzer, 2002; Easterlin, 2005) rejects the rational choice theory as developed after Pareto's turn, but in doing so it turns back to the utilitarian-hedonistic view of happiness: 'The Three Main lines are the classical (from Aristotle to Genovesi), the classical English and the hedonist-utilitarian. The first two traditions are closer to each other and both are far removed from the third' (Bruni, 2007, p. 44).[3]

This chapter aims at continuing Bruni's work while adopting the same methodology. Bruni (2006, 2007, 2010) not only clarified the features of Aristotle's and Genovesi's views on happiness, economy and interpersonal relations but also the theoretical messages for contemporary debate. The present work aims to add a missing, yet fundamental, protagonist to this story: Thomas Aquinas (1225–74). The central role that the Aristotelian categories play in Aquinas' philosophy is undisputable (MacIntyre, 1988; Gilson, 2002; Franks, 2015; Hirschfeld, 2018). Less evident is the importance of Aquinas' thought in Genovesi and in the civil economy tradition, even though some scholars attempt to make the case for this new notion (Bruni and Santori, 2018; Santori, 2019, 2020). The analysis on Aquinas' view on happiness and wealth will show the similarities and differences between his perspective and Aristotle's, as well as the influence that Aquinas had on Genovesi's theory.

Hence, this chapter will show that Aquinas' notion of happiness is closer to Aristotle's *eudaimonia* than to Bentham's happiness, but at the same time Aquinas' anthropological view, very different from Aristotle's, provides a unique account of happiness and relationality, which has become the foundation for civil economists' views on public happiness (*pubblica felicità*). The dimensions of gratuitousness and mutual assistance will appear as the core elements of *beatitudo* – happiness in Aquinas' lexicon – but also as elements characterising man's attitude towards the economic sphere and wealth.

The renewed interest on Aquinas' interpretation on human beings and economy (Hirschfeld, 2018; Melé and Pastor, 2018; Sison, 2018) supports this line of inquiry. However, the scope of this chapter is not merely historical. Attention must also be directed towards demonstrating the novelty of the topics analysed. All historical research is research on contemporary history, as it becomes a tool to ask the right questions in the present. Hence, we should ask how Aquinas' views on happiness, economy and interpersonal relations add value to the debate. This will be part of the final remarks, following the discussion of Aquinas' theory.

6.2 DISCUSSION

In the eighteenth century, Genovesi defined economy as the science of public happiness (Bruni and Zamagni, 2016). The roots of this tradition have been debated (D'Onofrio, 2015; Bruni, 2017), resulting in the establishment of its proximity to the Aristotelian and Thomistic tradition, but what does it mean to state that Genovesi's view on public happiness is connected to Aquinas' philosophy? The answer is given directly by Genovesi in a postscript to his own letter (Santori, 2020): 'This is because he – Genovesi is talking about himself – considers natural and civil happiness which [. . .] not differently from philosophical virtue is natural, and *acquiritur per naturalia*, as stated by St. Thomas' (Genovesi, [1764] 1791, p. 260). Some elements emerge from this passage: (1) natural and civil happiness are connected, quasi-identified with one another; (2) happiness and virtue 'naturally acquired' are strictly intertwined. Another fundamental element arises if we frame this passage within the broader scope of Genovesi's corpus: 'The end of civil economy – stated Genovesi – is [. . .] the natural and civil happiness' (Genovesi, [1765–7] 2013, p. 170). Therefore, (3) happiness, virtue and relationality are all constitutive parts of the science of civil economy. Since Aquinas is Genovesi's source, we consider Aquinas' stance on the three points and, consequently, the main features of his ideas of happiness, relationality and the economic domain.

6.3 AQUINAS ON HAPPINESS

Aquinas deemed man as a free and rational agent who, in seeking the utmost good (*summum bonum*), naturally pursues specific goals or goods. Happiness (*beatitudo*) is defined both as the operation (*operatio*) in the achievement and enjoyment of the good and as the good itself. The attainment of a good is an end consistent with the fundamental inclinations of a human being, and this consistency (*similitudo*) can be both potential, since the good is present in the subject as one of his or her possible perfections, and actual, since the good is attained in operation. In this respect, Hirschfeld rightly argued: 'So the principle we use to order our own goods in this life is to do so toward our own perfection, which is to say to our becoming excellent versions of ourselves' (2014, p. 181). The reason why happiness is defined as an operation becomes immediately intelligible: 'human beings . . . act through the intellect, which characteristically and manifestly works toward an end' (*agens per intellectum, cuius est manifeste propter finem operari*) (Aquinas, 1997, p. 61).

By regarding the intellect as the highest expression of human nature (*optima potentia*), and God as its object (*optimum obiectum*), Aquinas defines perfect beatitude (*beatitudo perfecta*) as the solitary contemplation of God, that is, participation in His own beatitude. However, one can experience perfect beatitude only in eternal life. During his permanence on Earth man can reach imperfect happiness (*beatitudo imperfecta*) in contemplative and active life. This imperfection seems also to be determined by two characteristics of happiness inherited from Aristotle – completeness and self-sufficiency – which Aquinas believed could not characterise happiness obtained in this life due to the mutability of conditions and circumstances (Adams, 1991).

So far Aquinas seems distant from an account of happiness strongly related to relationality. He seemed to attribute happiness to the solitary activity of the intellect and to relegate the active life, the one typical of the *civitas* and its numerous relationships to an imperfect form. Hirschfeld (2018) demonstrated the extent to which this account of happiness can be used to better understand our relationships with instrumental goods (necessary goods, wealth), an issue discussed below. But one problem persists: what is the space for relationships in Aquinas' view of happiness?

We discover that Aquinas' view is relational in all aspects, including the contemplative one. An acute commentator of Aquinas, Jean Pierre Torrell, advised readers to identify perfect happiness as just a matter of the intellect. Beatitude, for Aquinas, is God's gift, and therefore it is experienced within a relation: 'Given that there is a certain communication of man with God since he communicates his beatitude to us, a certain friendship must be based on this communication' (Aquinas in Torrell, 2003, p. 339). Torrell also commented: 'Differently stated, God not only wants us to be happy, he wants us to be happy with the happiness with which he himself is happy, his beatitude' (Torrell, 2003, p. 339).

This reference to friendship implies that for Aquinas, *relationality is a constitutive part of perfect happiness* (Torrell, 2003; Kimbriel, 2014). This is not only related to the theological sphere, perfect happiness and the man–God relation, but also analogically connected to the natural sphere, imperfect happiness and the relation between human beings.

According to Aquinas, happiness concerns goods and operations. The passion of love (*amor*) has a central role in both. Aquinas describes love as the principle of movement towards the goods. All human acts derive from love: 'It is evident that every agent, whatever it be, does every action from love of some kind' (*S. Th.*, I-II, q. 28, a. 6, corp). In this process, love plays both a passive and an active role, depending on whether it is intended as a passion (*passio*) or as an act of the will (*actus voluntatis*). In regard to the former meaning, somehow the good, perceived by the intellect, shapes our appetite (*immutatio appetitus*) by preparing it for the motion towards itself. Love consists in a moment of pure appreciation of the value of the good (*amor complacentiae*), which corresponds to moving from indifference to interest in this value.[4] The highest form in which love expresses itself is the love of friendship (*amor amicitiae*), whereas the subject of love is appreciated for its own value.[5] As the Latin term discloses, Aquinas envisioned the love directed to another person as the paradigm of *amor amicitiae*. Hence, we can rightly place Aquinas in the tradition that Bruni retraced, going back from Aristotle to Genovesi, which put an emphasis on the intrinsic value of relationality:

> For Aristotle, and in the whole Western civil tradition, there is an *intrinsic* value in relational and civil life, without which human life does not fully flourish. Though human life, as seen, must be able to flourish autonomously, in the sense that it cannot be totally jeopardized by bad fortune, it is also true that in the Aristotelian line of thought some of the essential components of the good life are tied to interpersonal relationships. (Bruni, 2010, p. 394)

Aquinas, in fact, borrowed and further elaborated on Aristotle's idea: 'First of all, among all *worldly* things there is nothing which seems worthy to be preferred to friendship' (*De Reg.*, I, 11). According to Aquinas, friendship is profoundly associated with human happiness (*beatitudo imperfecta*), since a shared life leads two people to experience a higher degree of happiness than they could in a solitary life. Significantly, Aquinas defined friendship as the common good of society. The individual and social aspects of friendship are strictly intertwined. In Aquinas' words, '*naturaliter homo homini amicus*' (*ScG*, IV, chap. 54, a. 6), where *naturaliter* acquires teleological nuances: it is not only a human predisposition to friendliness towards other people, it is also the deliberate openness to creating genuine relationships with other people.

Within this broader framework, Aquinas directly asked if the fellowship of friends is necessary for happiness:

> If we speak of the happiness of this life, the happy man needs friends, as the Philosopher says (Ethic. ix, 9), not, indeed, to make use of them, since he suffices himself; nor to delight in them, since he possesses perfect delight in the operation of virtue; but for the purpose of a good operation, viz. that he may do good to them; that he may delight in seeing them do good; and again that he may be helped by them in his good work. For in order that man may do well, whether in the works of the active life, or in those of the contemplative life, he needs the fellowship of friends. (*S. Th.*, I-II, q. 4, a. 8, corp)

To further understand why a happy human being 'needs' friends, we should move to Aquinas' account of virtue.

6.4 VIRTUES, MUTUAL ASSISTANCE AND HAPPINESS

In the *Summa Theologiae* Aquinas characterises virtue as the 'good quality of the mind, by which we live righteously, of which no one can make bad use, which God works in us, without us' (*S. Th.*, I–II, q. 55, a. 4). Then, he states that the word 'habit' (*habitus*) should be adopted in place of 'quality' and that if we omit the reference to God, the definition could be applied to all virtues. The acceptance of 'habit' is Aristotelian: a quality of character which can be developed through intentional, constant exercise until it becomes second nature. The Latin *habitus*, in fact, retrieves the Greek *hexis* employed by Aristotle (Pinckaers, 1962), meaning a repeated, intentional action.

Aquinas explicitly recognised his debt to 'the Philosopher' and, to leave little room for doubt, he devoted an article inquiring 'Whether any virtue is caused in us by habituation?' (*S. Th.*, I–II, q. 63, a. 2). The answer is affirmative: intellectual and moral virtues are caused in us by habituation. Moreover, 'certain seeds or principles of acquired virtue pre-exist in us by nature' (*S. Th.*, I–II, q. 63, a. 2, ad. 3). This is a typical Aristotelian ontological category, the dual potentiality/actuality, applied by Aquinas to the view of human beings. For both philosophers, human nature is imbued with fundamental potentialities. Happiness is nothing but the actualisation of these potentialities, and virtues are qualities acquired which express the end of this process.

Like Aristotle, Aquinas employed the language of prize to talk about the relation between virtue and happiness: happiness is the 'reward (*praemium*) to virtue'. Is that a means–end relationship? The answer is both affirmative and negative. Reading Aristotle, in fact, some perplexities can be raised, as the following passage from MacIntyre's *After Virtue* demonstrates:

> The virtues are precisely those qualities the possession of which will enable an individual to achieve *eudaimonia* and the lack of which will frustrate his movement toward that *telos*. But although it would be incorrect to describe the exercise of virtues as a mere means to the end of achieving the good for man, that description is ambiguous. [. . .] [T]he exercise of virtues is not in this sense *a* means to the end of the good for man. For what constitutes the good for man is a complete human life lived at its best, and the exercise of virtues is a necessary and central part of such a life, not a mere preparatory exercise to secure such a life. (MacIntyre, 1984, pp. 148–9)

In other words, virtues are composed of an intrinsic value, their own reward, and a way to something else of more value. Given this fact, human beings are able to achieve happiness if, and only if, they consider virtue not as a means to that end but the end itself. In Aristotle this problematic issue, named significantly the 'happiness paradox' (Brennan and Pettit, 2004; Bruni, 2010), remains open and probably unsolvable.

Conversely, in Aquinas' account we discern new elements, allowing readers to grasp a comprehensive understanding of this paradox. First, Aquinas does recognise the double role of virtues in Aristotle without noticing its ambiguity:

> According to the Philosopher (Ethic. i, 7), of those things that are desired for their own sake, some are desired for their own sake alone, and never for the sake of something else, such as happiness which is the last end; while some are desired, not only for their own sake, inasmuch as they have an aspect of goodness in themselves, even if no further good accrued to us through them, but also for the sake of something else, inasmuch as they are conducive to some more perfect good. (*S. Th.*, I–II, q. 145, a. 1, ad. 1)

The lack of concern for an apparent paradox is easily explainable since, as mentioned earlier, Aquinas considers two different kinds of happiness. In his work, the theme of 'reward of virtue' is often explicitly related to perfect happiness (*beatitudo perfecta*) and rarely to imperfect happiness (*beatitudo imperfecta*).

However, there is something more profound in Aquinas' view. The message behind his acceptance of the paradox is that human beings are simultaneously focused on their own good and capable of authentic relationships. Both are fundamental for their happiness or, in other (better) words, flourishing. To better understand this key passage, let us return to Aquinas' view on virtue.

The essence of virtue is inextricably tied to the way in which virtue is acquired. Ethics means ethical life (*bios etikos*), that is, virtue is learned in the social and political spheres. In Aristotle's world virtue is first learned in the master–disciple relationship and then progressively tested and developed in political life; few can go even further by practising theoretical life (*bios theoretikos*). The Greek man walks down the long path of virtue throughout his life, but the most important step in this pursuit is being capable of ethical reasoning (practical wisdom) without needing others (master or friends).

Aquinas emphasised the need of others in developing virtues far more than Aristotle did: 'Moreover, there should be mutual friendship among man, in accord with which they assist each other in spiritual or in earthly functions' (*ScG*, IV, chap. 133, par. 4). In the passage abovementioned, Aquinas specified, 'for in order that man may do well, whether in the works of the active life, or in those of the contemplative life, he *needs* the fellowship of friends' (*S. Th.*, I–II, q. 8, a. 4, corp, my emphasis). The

Latin text discloses more subtleties than the English one. Aquinas said '*Indiget enim homo ad bene operandum auxilio amicorum*'. The Latin term *Indiget* can be rendered as 'needs', but the semantic space rather refers to 'something lacking' or 'something missing'. What does man miss, which is preventing his happiness?

These questions may be less cogent in Aristotle's philosophy, but they are perfectly contextualised in Aquinas'. The argument in this chapter is focused on the existence of a thread between Aristotle and Aquinas, namely Augustine of Hippo, that is, Christianity and its doctrine of 'Original Sin'. MacIntyre summarised this point well:

> Nonetheless Aquinas' work, especially in the *Somma Theologiae*, is informed by an overriding unity of purpose, expressed both in his conception of the ultimate unity of good and in the way he writes about it, which notably exceeds even that of Aristotle. And perhaps nothing less would have enabled him to confront the apparently incompatible and conflicting demands of two distinct and rival traditions, the Aristotelian and the Augustinian, both in their thirteenth-century versions deemed irremediably opposed to one another by many of his contemporaries, but both of which he gave allegiance. (1988, p. 166)

In other words, when Aquinas dealt with Aristotelian virtue ethics he applied it to the Christian anthropological view informed by the consequences of Original Sin. The effects of the corrupt nature of human beings, in fact, regards man's attitude towards virtue:

> the good of nature, that is diminished by sin, is the natural inclination to virtue [. . .] the aforesaid inclination is to be considered as a middle term between two others: for it is based on the rational nature as on its root, and tends to the good of virtue, as to its term and end [. . .] it is diminished on the part of the obstacle which is placed against its attaining its term, it is evident that it can be diminished indefinitely, because obstacles can be placed indefinitely, inasmuch as man can go on indefinitely adding sin to sin: and yet it cannot be destroyed entirely, because the root of this inclination always remains. (*S. Th.*, I–II, q. 85, a. 2, corp.)

To be virtuous is more difficult in Aquinas' philosophy. Hence, he emphasised a need (*indigentia*) of friends. The reasons are twofold. On the one hand, every human being needs friends to benefit from them in the spirit of the love of friendship. On the other hand, everyone needs help or assistance from other people because of the natural deficiency which is inevitable in every action performed. These are the features of the authentic/genuine (Bruni and Sugden, 2008) relationality that Aquinas saw as connected to happiness.

Given these premises, I suggest that one key category of Aquinas' account of virtue and happiness, one which is distant from Aristotle's framework but closer to Genovesi's, is mutual assistance. Aquinas compares human inclinations, especially those aimed at virtue, to city or state (*civitas*; see Finnis, 1998), as they are both related to friendship:

> there is in all men a certain natural impulse toward the city, as also toward the virtues. But nevertheless, just as the virtues are acquired through human exercise, as is stated in Book II of the Ethics, in the same way cities are founded by human industry. Now the man who first founded a city was the cause of the greatest goods for men. (*Pol.*, book 1, 40)

Civil life has to be understood as a net of relationships of mutual assistance between citizens, and the economic life, despite the limited impact during Aquinas' times, is included in it.

6.5   HAPPINESS, WEALTH AND RELATIONSHIPS

When Aquinas considered friendship, he was pursuing something very different from friendship as it is understood today. His notion of friendship involved many kinds of relationships: human being–God, father–mother, parents–children, friend–friend, citizen–citizen and so on. Regarding relationships within the city (*civitas*), Aquinas clarified, commenting on Aristotle, that they are based on mutual assistance:

> This can be shown by the fact that the citizens live together amicably because they have proportionate kindliness towards one another. Accordingly, if one does something for another, the other is anxious to do something in proportion in return [. . .] men live together because one makes a return to another for the favors he has received. (*Eth.*, V, 8)

As argued extensively elsewhere, commercial exchanges are also included within the relationship of the city (Santori, 2019, 2020). Thus, we can rightly ask: what is the relation between happiness, virtues, mutual assistance and wealth in Aquinas' thought?

The topic is widely discussed in recent literature. According to Baritz (2013), Aquinas distinguished three categories of goods – useful, pleasant and moral goods – with preference for moral goods. Baritz states:

> useful goods, referring to the material and material like goods, are tools, having no intrinsic value; they are there to further the realization of the moral and pleasant 'goods' (like bitter medicine, which does not have a value in itself but which just promotes the higher values of health and life, *S.Th.* I. q.5. a.6.). (2013, p.47)

Das Neves (2000) suggests that Aquinas may have adopted Aristotle's distinction between natural wealth (material goods) and artificial wealth (money) while rejecting it in the *Summa Theologiae*. Conversely, Hirschfeld drew on this distinction and its connection with happiness:

> After rejecting natural wealth as a possible end, Aquinas goes on to argue that artificial wealth is an even less likely candidate for final end than is natural wealth since it is (properly) sought for the sake of natural wealth [. . .] it is an instrumental good in service of an instrumental good. (2018, p. 148)

Hirschfeld goes on to criticise the rational choice model of economics because it encapsulates a problem already envisaged by Aquinas' theory:

> As Aquinas argues, happiness is the most desirable end, which has the property of being self-sufficing, that is, of setting our appetites at rest. Money gives the promise of self-sufficiency, because all things seem to obey money. That general command means that money can seem to contain all possible goods, which furthers its likeness to true happiness. (2018, p. 158)

These analyses of Aquinas' thought have many merits, but this chapter argues that they overlooked the key element of mutual assistance. In other words, for Aquinas the relationship between human beings and objects, a typical product of modernity (Dumont, 1992), is far less relevant than the relationship between people, in which the object is included. This is valid especially as far as the nexus of wealth–virtue–happiness is concerned. That wealth is connected to virtue and happiness *via* mutual assistance is explicitly recognised by Aquinas:

> As a matter of fact, external riches are necessary for the good of virtue; since by them we support our body and give assistance to other people. Now, things that are means to an end must derive their goodness from the end. So, external riches must be a good for man; not, of course, the principal one, but as a secondary good. (*ScG*, III, chap. 133, par. 1)

The term *subvenio* employed by Aquinas is often confined to the realm of gift and beneficence, what is today called charity. Reading Aquinas' thought as a whole, it is evident that assistance means much more: it is an anthropological mode which is at the basis of every human relationship, including the economic and political one.[6]

This is the paradigm found in *Summa Theologiae*, when Aquinas elucidated that 'the purpose of the Law was to accustom men to its precepts, so as to be ready to come to one another's assistance: because this is a very great incentive to friendship' (*S. Th.*, I–II, q. 105, a. 2, ad. 4). The word utilised by Aquinas in this passage is *fomentum*, which in ancient Latin signified 'to provoke', 'the log to light the fire' (Santori, 2019, p. 86). Thus, the condition of being in need, and the mutual help and utility which arises from association, is what primarily grounds civil society. Not only is political friendship, commerce and foreign trade included (Santori, 2019), an element capable of holding together the different parts of the country, but it is also intrinsically related to the practice of virtues and to human flourishing. This is a strong link and what Genovesi calls the 'right of mutual assistance': 'How is man more sociable than other animals? . . . [It is] in his reciprocal right to be assisted and consequently in his reciprocal obligation to help us in our needs' (Genovesi in Bruni, 2006, p. 89).

For Aquinas even in the relationship between seller and buyer there is space for mutual assistance, since both are concerned with one another's well-being along with their own utility (Todeschini, 2000; Koehn and Wilbratte, 2012; Santori, 2020). Aquinas conceived the commercial transaction as deeply connected to the spread of friendly relations between citizens. However, as Hirschfeld rightly indicated (2018, chap. 5), sin and bad use of money are always behind the door. Due to the disharmony between passion and reason, that is, the anthropological equivalent of Original Sin, human beings are not always willing to enter a business transaction with the perspective of mutual assistance, and often their judgement is overshadowed by the need for immoderate gain (*turpe lucrum*). Therefore, Aquinas stressed the role of the virtue of justice and the institution of a contract between two individuals, which guarantees equality in the exchange by the force of law.

In Aquinas' philosophy, contributing to the common good means not only increasing the material wealth of society but also (or almost) fostering relations of friendship (concord) among citizens. As far as market exchanges are concerned, this means encouraging buyers and sellers to adopt the logic of mutual assistance whereby a fair price – guaranteed by the institution of contract and the virtue of justice – is determined and the transaction is concluded.

Aquinas applied this logic to the wage market with an example of a fair wage (*recompensationem*):

> The same applies to the physician who attends on a sick person to heal him, and to all like persons; provided, however, they take a moderate fee, with due consideration for persons (*conditione personarum*), for the matter in hand, for the labor entailed, and for the custom of the country. If, however, they wickedly extort an immoderate fee, they sin against justice. (*S. Th.*, IIª–IIᵃᵉ, q. 71, a. 4, corp.)

> The same is valid in any market transaction, where man may intend the moderate gain which he seeks to acquire by trading for the upkeep of his household, or for the assistance of the needy: or again, a man may take to trade for some

public advantage, for instance, lest his country lack the necessaries of life, and seek gain, not as an end, but as payment for his labor. (*S. Th.*, II-II, q. 77, a. 4, corp.)

To sum up, the nexus between wealth (natural and artificial), virtue and happiness is always mediated by the nature of human relationships within which these elements are considered. In Aquinas' thought, happiness is inexorably connected to authentic relationality, and the economic domain is not excluded from this discourse.

6.6   FINAL REMARKS

Aquinas' philosophy proved to be open to analyses of authentic relationality within the economic domain. The happiness depicted by Aquinas, both in its perfect and imperfect forms, is intrinsically connected to the spread of authentic and genuine relationships. This work suggested that Aquinas was not only chronologically but also conceptually at the midpoint of Aristotle and Genovesi, at least as far as the nexus between happiness, virtue and wealth is concerned. Hence, the researches on relational goods can list another important author. As Aquinas' thought is demonstrably connected to the Aristotelian and civil economy perspectives, but irreducible to both, one wonders what elements can Aquinas' view add to the contemporary debate.

This chapter suggests two directions based on the arguments provided herein. First, there is more space for inquiry in the historical analysis on happiness and economics. If there exists a continuum from Aristotle to Aquinas to Genovesi, then nothing precludes the search for a rival tradition that arrives at Bentham, and perhaps further. In this sense, John Duns Scotus' intellectual rivalry with Aquinas seems a fruitful source. Scotus emphasised the priority of the accidental happiness over the essential one (i.e. the need to look at individuals and circumstances instead of objective dimensions and definitions). How much of Scotus is present in the Benthamite account of happiness? More intriguingly, how much of Scotus is there in the Paretian turn (Bruni, 2007) and the advent of rational choice model? These are unanswered questions and addressing them may bring new elements and insights from the past.

Second, the perspective of mutual assistance reveals new information about the research on relational goods. According to Aquinas, these goods can emerge as a result of people's reciprocity and their actions aiming at the good of others. In turn, mutual help implies the mutual recognition of being in need, what MacIntyre (1999), after his Thomistic turn, named 'acknowledged dependence'. There may have been many reasons why the dimension of mutual assistance was removed from economic science. As Smith explained, 'nobody but a beggar chooses to depend chiefly upon the benevolence of his fellow-citizens' (Smith, [1776] 1977, p. 31). This was the expression of the Illuminist concern for a transition from a hierarchical society, where 'assistance' came from a feudal landlord, to a commercial society between free and equal people. But this removal meant to throw the baby in the dirty water. As Aquinas, and then Genovesi, proved, freedom and dignity can coexist with mutual assistance. Market and civil society are based on this kind of relationship. A similar notion was envisaged when 'fraternity' accompanied freedom and equality in the famous French motto (Bruni and Sugden, 2008).

Today, relational goods bring back the dimension of mutual assistance within the realm of economics, but following Aquinas this chapter argues that relational goods seem to emerge more easily within certain institutions. Hence, this chapter proposes further research on the kinds of institutions that favour relational goods, as it would open up debate on economics and happiness. Therefore, this chapter concludes with an example of a contemporary institution which does not encourage genuine relationality in economics. The cultural dominance of the discourse on meritocracy (Frank, 2016; Young, [1958] 2017), in fact, inexorably tends to undermine the perception of acknowledged dependence. This is because meritocracy encourages individuals to overemphasise the importance of their efforts in the achievements reached and hide the role of others (and the role of luck). Market transactions are inexorably affected by this misperception. In turn, the emergence of relational goods suffers from the individualistic meritocratic discourse since people are discouraged in recognising the cooperation for mutual advantage (Sugden, 2018) which lies behind the reaching of an economic result. If we agree on the nexus between happiness and relational goods, and if we agree that the economic domain is where genuine relations could be cultivated, then the next step is to understand the context in which these elements emerge. Hence, it is necessary to revisit authors such as Aquinas, who bring forgotten yet fundamental questions to contemporary debates.

NOTES

1. This manuscript is dedicated to the memory of Luis Miguel Neto (1958–2020), who studied, loved, and lived happiness in his life.
2. The etiquette used in the text has been created for the sake of the argument. Non-Italian economists, too, are working on relational goods and happiness (Bünger, 2010; Marujo and Neto, 2014; Velásquez, 2016).

3. Bruni rightly refuses to identify the long tradition tying authors from Aristotle to Genovesi with the civil economy tradition, employing the more cautious term 'classical'. In what follows I will use the expression 'civil economy tradition' to consider the Neapolitan school of the eighteenth century (Genovesi, Filangieri), whose forerunners may be identified as Aristotle and Aquinas.
4. To explain this capability of gratuitousness, the concept of good (*bonum*) can be related to the aesthetic concept of beauty (*pulchrum*). The following extract from the fundamental manual of Wladyslaw Tatarkiewicz on the history of aesthetic will help clarify this connection: 'Moreover, Thomas affirms, it is privilege of man to be the only creature capable of loving the beauty and to enjoy it for itself. Thomas proves the difference between these two kinds of pleasures, following Aristotle, using the example of the voice of deer. The voice of deer – he says – is relished both by the lion and the man, but for different reasons: it is liked by lion because it represents a promise of nourishment, but it is liked by men for its harmony ('*propter convenientiam sensibilium*'). The lion enjoys auditive sensations because he links them to other sensations, biologically important for him, but man enjoys them for their autonomous value; the pleasure that man benefits from harmonious sounds has no connection with the preservation of life; even if it has its source in sensible perception, in color or sound, it not coming from the relation between them and the biological activity, but only from their harmony. The aesthetic sensibilities are not purely sensible, as some sensibilities that are important from a biological point of view, but they are neither purely intelligible as the morals: they are situated halfway between the two' (Tatarkiewicz, [1970] 1979, p. 284).
5. Aquinas classifies love into love of concupiscence (*amor concupiscentiae*) and love of friendship (*amor amicitiae*). The former is always directed towards a further aim, whereas the object of love in the latter is pursued for its own value. However, the conquest of the beloved describing love of friendship is not to be thought of as a stagnant achievement, since the lover tries to achieve a deep knowledge of the other to attain their goals, to support them in bad times and to share their happiness. Aquinas shows that between the two individuals involved, it emerges not only a real union (*unio realis*) but also an emotional one (*unio affectuum*).
6. Gilson rightly noted that mutual assistance is connected to Aquinas' account of natural law, as developed in the I–II of *Quaestio* 94: 'The third devolves upon us as rational beings and enjoins upon us the task of seeking whatever is good according to the order of reason. To live in society in order to unite the efforts of all and to help one another; to seek truth in the realm of the natural sciences or, what is better, in what concerns the highest intelligible being, namely, God; correlatively, not to injure those with whom we are called to live; to avoid ignorance and to do what we can to dispel it. All these are the binding prescriptions of the natural law, which is but one aspect of the eternal law willed by God' (Gilson, 2002, p. 304).

REFERENCES

Adams, D. (1991), Aquinas on Aristotle on happiness. *Medieval Philosophy & Theology*, 1, 98–118.

Aquinas, St [1256–9] (1956), *Summa contra gentiles*. New York: Doubleday & Company. (*ScG.*)

Aquinas, St [1270] (1947), *Summa theologiae*. New York: Benzinger Brothers. (*S. Th.*)

Aquinas, St [1271–2] (1964), *In decem libros ethicorum Aristotelis ad nicomachum exposition*. Chicago: Henry Regnery. (*Eth.*)

Aquinas, St (1951), *Sententia libri Politicorum*. Bologna: Marietti. (*Pol.*)

Aquinas, St (1997), *On the Government of Rulers: De Regimine Principum*.

Translated by J. M. Blythe. Philadelphia: University of Pennsylvania Press. (*De Reg.*)

Baritz, L. S. (2013), The three dimensional economy and the common good model: an alternative approach to mainstream economic theory. *Journal of Ethics & Social Sciences*, 1, 43–57.

Bartolini, S. (2014), Relational goods. In *Encyclopedia of Quality of Life and Well-Being Research*, ed. by A. C. Michalos (pp. 5428–9). Verlag GmbH: Springer Netherlands.

Becchetti, L., A. Pelloni and F. Rossetti (2008), Relational goods, sociability, and happiness. *Kyklos*, 61(3), 343–63.

Brennan, G. and P. Pettit (2004), *The Economy of Esteem: An Essay on Civil and Political Society*. New York: Oxford University Press.

Bruni, L. (2006), *Civil Happiness: Economics and Human Flourishing in Historical Perspective*. London and New York: Routledge.

Bruni, L. (2007), The 'technology of happiness' and the tradition of economic science. *Handbook on the Economics of Happiness*, 24, 19–44.

Bruni, L. (2010), The happiness of sociality. Economics and eudaimonia: a necessary encounter. *Rationality and Society*, 22(4), 383–406.

Bruni, L. (2017), On the concept of economia civile and 'felicitas publica': a comment on Federico D'Onofrio. *Journal of the History of Economic Thought*, 39(2), 273–9.

Bruni, L. and P. L. Porta (2003), Economia civile e pubblica felicità in the Italian Enlightenment. *History of Political Economy*, 35(5), 361–85.

Bruni, L. and L. Stanca (2008), Watching alone: relational goods, television and happiness. *Journal of Economic Behavior & Organization*, 65(3–4), 506–28.

Bruni, L. and R. Sugden (2008), Fraternity: why the market need not be a morally free zone. *Economics & Philosophy*, 24(1), 35–64.

Bruni, L. and S. Zamagni (2016), *Civil Economy: Another Idea of the Market*. Newcastle upon Tyne: Agenda Publishing Limited.

Bruni, L. and P. Santori (2018), The plural roots of rewards: awards and incentives in Aquinas and Genovesi. *The European Journal of the History of Economic Thought*, 25(4), 637–57.

Bünger, B. (2010), The demand for relational goods: empirical evidence from the European Social Survey. *International Review of Economics*, 57(2), 177–98.

Clark, A. E. (2017), Happiness, income and poverty. *International Review of Economics*, 64(2), 145–58.

Clark, A. E. and A. J. Oswald (1996), Satisfaction and comparison income. *Journal of Public Economics*, 61(3), 359–81.

Das Neves, J. L. C. (2000), Aquinas and Aristotle's distinction on wealth. *History of Political Economy*, 32(3), 649–57.

Dumont, L. (1992), *Essays on Individualism: Modern Ideology in Anthropological Perspective*. Chicago: University of Chicago Press.

D'Onofrio, F. (2015), On the concept of 'felicitas publica' in eighteenth-century political economy. *Journal of the History of Economic Thought*, 37(3), 449–71.

Easterlin, R. A. (1974), Does economic growth improve the human lot? Some empirical evidence. In *Nations and Households in Economic Growth*, ed. by P. A. David and M. W. Reder (pp. 89–125). New York: Academic Press.

Easterlin, R. A. (2005), Feeding the illusion of growth and happiness: a reply to Hagerty and Veenhoven. *Social Indicators Research*, 74(3), 429–43.

Finnis, J. (1998), *Aquinas: Moral, Political, and Legal Theory*. Oxford: Oxford University Press.

Frank, R. H. (1997), The frame of reference as a public good. *Economic Journal*, 107, 1832–47.

Frank, R. H. (1999), *Luxury Fever*. New York: Free Press.

Frank, R. H. (2016), *Success and Luck: Good Fortune and the Myth of Meritocracy*. Princeton: Princeton University Press.

Franks, C. A. (2015), Aristotelian doctrines in Aquinas's treatment of justice. In *Aristotle in Aquinas's Theology*, ed. by G. Emery and M. Levering (pp. 139–66). Oxford: Oxford University Press.

Frey, B. S. (2018), *Economics of Happiness*. Cham: Springer International Publishing.

Frey, B. S. and A. Stutzer (2002), What can economists learn from happiness research? *Journal of Economic Literature*, 40(2), 402–35.

Frey, B. S. and A. Stutzer (2005), Happiness research: state and prospects. *Review of Social Economy*, 63(2), 207–28.

Genovesi, A. [1764] (1791), *Lettere accademiche sulla questione se sieno più felici gli scienziati o gl'ignoranti*. Venezia: Pietro Savoni.

Genovesi, A. [1765–7] (2013), *Lezioni di economia civile*. Milano: Vita e Pensiero.

Gilson, E. (2002), *Thomism: The Philosophy of Thomas Aquinas*. Toronto: Pontifical Institute of Medieval Studies.

Grasseni, M. and F. Origo (2018), Competing for happiness: attitudes to competition, positional concerns and wellbeing. *Journal of Happiness Studies*, 19(7), 1981–2008.

Gui, B. and L. Stanca (2010), Happiness and relational goods: well-being and interpersonal relations in the economic sphere. *International Review of Economics*, 57(2), 105–18.

Hagerty, M. R. and R. Veenhoven (2003), Wealth and happiness revisited: growing national income does go with greater happiness. *Social Indicators Research*, 64(1), 1–27.

Hirschfeld, M. L. (2014), On the relationship between finite and infinite goods, or: how to avoid flattening. *Econ Journal Watch*, 11(2), 179–85.

Hirschfeld, M. L. (2018), *Aquinas and the Market: Toward a Humane Economy*. Cambridge, MA: Harvard University Press.

Holländer, H. (2001), On the validity of utility statements: standard theory versus Duesenberry's. *Journal of Economic Behavior & Organization*, 45(3), 227–49.

Kahneman, D. (2011). *Thinking, Fast and Slow*. London: Macmillan.

Kahneman, D., E. Diener and N. Schwarz (Eds.). (1999), *Well-being: Foundations of Hedonic Psychology*. New York: Russell Sage Foundation.

Kimbriel, S. (2014), *Friendship as Sacred Knowing: Overcoming Isolation*. Oxford: Oxford University Press.

Koehn, D. and B. Wilbratte (2012), A defense of a Thomistic concept of the just price. *Business Ethics Quarterly*, 22(3), 501–26.

Layard, R. (2005), Rethinking public economics: the implications of rivalry and habit. *Economics and Happiness*, 1(1), 147–70.

MacIntyre, A. (1984), *After Virtue*. Notre Dame: University of Notre Dame Press.

MacIntyre, A. C. (1988), *Whose Justice? Which Rationality?* Notre Dame: University of Notre Dame Press.

MacIntyre, A. C. (1999), *Dependent Rational Animals: Why Human Beings Need the Virtues*, vol. 20. Chicago: Open Court Publishing.

Marujo, H. Á. and L. M. Neto (2014), Felicitas publica and community well-being: nourishing relational goods through dialogic conversations between deprived and privileged populations. *Journal of Psychology in Africa*, 24(1), 102–14.

Melé, D. and A. Pastor (2019), *Aquinas and the Market: Toward a Humane Economy*, by Mary L. Hirschfeld. Cambridge: Harvard University Press, 2018. *Business Ethics Quarterly*, 29(3), 425–8.

Pinckaers, S. (1962), Virtue is not a habit. *CrossCurrents*, 12(1), 65–81.

Pugno, M. (2007), The subjective well-being paradox: a suggested solution based on relational goods. In *Handbook on the Economics of Happiness*, ed. by L. Bruni and P. L. Porta (pp. 263–89). Cheltenham, UK and Northampton, MA, USA: Edward Elgar Publishing.

Santori, P. (2019), Was Aquinas a 'universal economist?' *History of Economics Review*, 72(1), 79–91.

Santori, P. (2020), *Donum*, exchange and common good in Aquinas: the dawn of civil economy, *The European Journal of the History of Economic Thought*, 27(2), 276–97, DOI: 10.1080/09672567.2020.1720764.

Sison, A. J. G. (2018), Virtue ethics and natural law responses to human rights quandaries in business. *Business and Human Rights Journal*, 3(2), 211–232.

Smith, A. [1776] (1977), *An Inquiry into the Nature and Causes of the Wealth of Nations*. Chicago: Chicago University Press.

Sugden, R. (2018), *The Community of Advantage: A Behavioural Economist's Defence of the Market*. Oxford: Oxford University Press.

Tatarkiewicz, W. [1970] (1979), *Storia dell'estetica. Volume secondo. L'estetica medievale*. Turin: Einaudi.

Todeschini, G. (2000), Ecclesia and market in the doctrinal lexicon of Thomas Aquinas. *Quaderni Storici*, 35(3), 585–621.

Torrell, J. P. (2003), *Saint Thomas Aquinas, Volume 2: Spiritual Master*. Washington: The Catholic University of America Press.

Velásquez, L. (2016), The importance of relational goods for happiness: evidence from Manizales, Colombia. In *Handbook of Happiness Research in Latin America*, ed. by R. Montero and T. Rau (pp. 91–112). Dordrecht: Springer.

Young, M. [1958)] (2017), *The Rise of the Meritocracy*. London: Routledge.

PART II

Methods and policy implications for the
Economics of Happiness

7. Complexity and wellbeing: measurement and analysis

**Filomena Maggino and
Leonardo Salvatore Alaimo**

7.1 COMPLEXITY: DEFINITIONS AND CONCEPTUAL APPROACHES

In his 'millennium' interview on 23 January 2000 (*San Jose Mercury News*), Stephen Hawking said: 'I think this century will be the century of complexity' (Gorban and Yablonsky 2013). We can encounter this concept in different fields (e.g. physics, chemistry, biology, engineering, software, social sciences). It has no precise meaning and no unique definition (Erdi 2008). This notion does not belong to a particular theory or discipline, but rather to a 'discourse about science'. According to Morin (1984), we cannot approach the study of complexity through a preliminary definition: there is no such thing as *one* complexity, but *different* complexities. Therefore, it seems more appropriate to talk about *definitions* of complexity. This term can assume profoundly different meanings and has been influenced by the contribution of many disciplines.

7.1.1 Complexity and Knowledge

The concept of complexity is closely linked to that of knowledge. Humanity has always had the aim of reflecting on its existence and investigating the possibilities and limits of knowledge (Alaimo 2020). The study of complexity begins when we realize the lack of knowledge of phenomena: each increase in knowledge corresponds to an increase in ignorance and inability to know. In this sense, we can affirm that complexity is *subjective*: the observer, on the basis of his knowledge or non-knowledge of phenomena, establishes whether reality is more or less complex.

The 'classical' approach to knowledge tries to reduce complex concepts to their simple elements, convinced that this research is able to reach an *objective knowledge*. The true and correct knowledge of phenomena should seek their stability and unchangeability, considered essential characteristics of their objective nature. Classical science is based on a separation between subject and object, between beings and Nature, considered the only possible way to an objective knowledge. The aim is to search for a 'model', an ideal representation of the phenomena that encloses all their characteristics; to reach the *Platonic Hyperuranium*, in search of a perfection understood in terms of generalization and immutability. According to Morin (2007), in classical science the expression 'it is complex' indicates the difficulty of giving a definition or an explanation. The rejection of the concept of complexity by classical science is due to three of its fundamental principles:

- The principle of *universal determinism*, according to which it is possible to not only know all past events, but also predict all events in the future.
- The principle of *reduction*, according to which we can understand any phenomenon simply from the knowledge of its elements.
- The principle of *disjunction*, which consists in separating cognitive difficulties from one another, leading to the separation between disciplines.

Based on these assumptions the notion of 'complexity' is absolutely rejected. Conceived as a synonym for uncertainty and confusion, complexity concerns only superficial or illusory appearances, since the criterion of truth of classical science is expressed by simple laws and concepts.

The concept of complexity – initially affirmed in the physical and then in the social sciences – emerges when one realizes the impossibility of fully knowing the phenomena around us. As a result, the static and immutable image of Nature, unjustified and wrong, is lost: it becomes clear that it is dynamic, temporal, in perpetual becoming. An example of this new way is the analysis of the concept of Nature proposed by Prigogine and Stengers (1993). The authors reject the classical idea, stating that the presumed dialogue *detached* with Nature has no theoretical consistency, but only operational. 'Experimental dialogue with Nature does not imply passive observation but rather practice' (Prigogine and Stengers 1993, 41). It is not possible to study phenomena by isolating them from their context, conceptualizing them as ideal entities that are impossible in reality. Modern science is characterized, on the contrary, by the encounter of theory and practice: 'the only possible way to knowledge is the systematic alliance between the ambition to model the world and that of understanding it' (Prigogine and Stengers 1993, 40). This new conception emerges when time and dynamism break into classical physics, upsetting it. Time enters into areas from which it was traditionally excluded, where it was believed that there were 'eternal laws' (at the microscopic and cosmic level). It can be seen that the phenomena, physical or social, are all characterized by an intersection of times and different speeds that make simplification absolutely ineffective. All phenomena are complex and characterized by a plurality of times that give rise to articulated results.

It should be pointed out immediately that the multiplicity of time and its relevance in understanding phenomena have always been known, but were practically ignored and denied. It is not possible to conceive of any form of knowledge that is not oriented in time, that does not have a *before* and an *after*.

Nature is, therefore, an entity that grows and develops over time, not a static object regulated by immutable laws. Each phenomenon manifests itself in an articulated way and presents the fundamental characteristic identified by Aristotle: from the interaction of the parts emerge new properties not present in the individual parts. Morin (1977) defines them as 'emergencies', quality and properties of a system that present a character of novelty with respect to the properties and quality of the individual parts taken alone or linked by different interactions in another system. 'Emergency is a product of the organization that, although inseparable from the system as a whole, not only appears on a global level, but can appear at the level of the components' (Contini 2013, 208). According to Morin, a system is both more and less than the sum of its individual components, since it binds the parts themselves, making them different from what they were originally or could have become in a different system.

We cannot photograph reality as it is: the researcher builds a series of levels of reality, the result of his cultural preferences and cognitive abilities (Maturana and Varela 1980). The idea of an objective and immutable knowledge and of the researcher distinct from the object of his investigation collapses. The only way to know reality is a dialogue between the researcher and Nature, a dialogue that necessarily presupposes the subjective component. Knowledge is, therefore, a dialectical path between beings and reality. The myth of isolating phenomena to understand them falls. Each of us is an integral part of reality and moves in an environment in which it is conditioned and which inevitably conditions.

7.1.2 Does a Paradigm of Complexity Exist?

The issue of complexity cannot be approached by means of a preliminary definition. There is no such thing as *one* complexity, but *different* complexities. There is no one single way to complexity, but multiple ways to complexity. In this sense, Stengers (1984) states that there cannot be a *paradigm of complexity*, since it does not have an epistemological status comparable to that of other scientific notions. Complexity does not belong to a particular theory or discipline, but rather to a discourse 'about science'. 'Paradigm' is a concept of multiple meanings that has an ancient origin. Plato used it as a synonym for model; for Aristotle, however, a paradigm is an example. Masterman (1970) identifies 21 different meanings associated with this term, often in contradiction with each other. Therefore, we have to clarify what Stengers means by paradigm. It is the author herself who defines the concept, referring to the work of Thomas Kuhn: 'a systematic articulation between a set of practical and conceptual tools and an a priori definition of the object and its rules of experimental manipulation' (Stengers 1984, 62).

In *The Structure of Scientific Revolutions*, Kuhn (1962) brings back to the top of the scientific debate the concept of the paradigm. Starting with the question about how sciences develop, he states that, in the traditional conception, scientific progress is considered as a linear and progressive accumulation of new knowledge in addition to that already acquired. However, this process is sometimes interrupted by revolutionary moments, which mark a break with the past and the beginning of the construction of a new knowledge. After these scientific revolutions, the problems that are the object of scientific investigation and the criteria for assessing these problems and proposing potential solutions change. There is a *reorientation* of the discipline that consists in the transformation of its conceptual structure. Thus, a new paradigm consists in the passage from an old cognitive structure to a new one. It is a *guide* that defines an orientation and the criteria of a discipline.

As Stengers states, complexity is not affirmed in the context scientific revolution leading to profound changes in its conceptual structure. It is not a new concept. It is not a revolution. On the contrary, complexity is affirmed in the context of a science that precisely questions a pair of concepts that guides the evaluation of reality: the *simple/complicated* pair. This pair is linked to the concept of paradigm as a model that represents the relationship between concepts and the possibility of experimenting with them. Complicated often has a negative meaning: it identifies the limits of the human capacity to know, the impossibility of using tools that allow the perfect understanding of simple systems. If we cannot understand a phenomenon through these tools, we define it as *complicated* and implicitly give it a negative meaning. Closely linked to this idea is the rejection of everything that we cannot understand, according to the canon of simplicity, and its labelling to 'non-scientific' and 'only subjective'. Some phenomena seem complicated because we observe them from our exclusive point of view, which is stable whereas reality is a perpetual becoming. As already mentioned, complexity removes the idea of a *simple* Nature, regulated by immutable rules.

At this point we have to clarify the difference between complicated and complex, often used as synonyms. Complicated derives from the Latin *cum plicum* where *plicum* indicates the fold of a sheet; complex comes from the Latin *cum plexum* where *plexum* indicates the weave, the node (De Toni and Comello 2009). These are different concepts and, therefore, require different approaches and analysis tools. Dealing with a complicated problem needs an *analytical* approach: we arrive at the solution by explaining the individual aspects of the problem. However difficult it may be, a solution can always be found. Faced with a complex problem, it is necessary to adopt a *synthetic* approach. It is impossible to understand the weave in its individual parts; it is necessary to renounce attempts to explain the problem analytically and try to understand the whole system as an indivisible entity. We can understand the structure and functioning of a complicated system and, over time, it is possible to reach an integral knowledge of it. On the other hand, we can have a global perception of a complex system without understanding it in its details. As Capra (1996) points out, the transition to systemic thinking coincides with the awareness of understanding systems by means of analysis:

> The relationship between the parts and the whole has been reversed. Cartesian science believed that in any complex system the behaviour of the whole could be analyzed in terms of the properties of its parts. Systems science shows that living systems cannot be understood by analysis. The properties of the parts are not intrinsic properties but can be understood only within the context of the larger whole. (Capra 1996, 37)

According to Stengers, the notion of complexity overturns the perspective between objective and subjective, questioning the objective categories derived from the simple model. Classical science favours the simplification of systems and, consequently, develops tools suitable, or rather adaptable, to these systems. In this sense a 'paradigm of complexity' does not exist. The discovery of complexity does not correspond to the answer to a problem, but rather to the 'awakening of a problem'. Complexity is a change of point of view. The description of systems based on simplification is poor, suitable for borderline cases. Systems must be analysed from multiple points of view. We can consider complexity as a new lens to observe reality in order to grasp its multiplicity and dynamism.

7.1.3 The Concept of the Complex System

Complexity is often associated with the term *system*. Before analysing the complexity of a system, we must define what a system is. This term is used both in common language and in that of many scientific disciplines.

We could trace the 'official' birth of system theory back to the foundation of the Society for General System Research in 1954 at Palo Alto. It was a group of researchers of different disciplinary fields, led by the father of systemic theory, biologist Ludwig von Bertalanffy. This group wanted to develop a theory that could relate traditionally separate fields of knowledge. The concept of the system seemed perfectly suited to this purpose. According to Bertalanffy (1968), deterministic explanations are insufficient in the analysis of complex phenomena. It is not the individual causalities, independent from one another, that determine the evolution of the systems, but entire interrelated causal complexes. A system is able to reach the same final state of dynamic equilibrium regardless of the intervention of individual causal factors (the so-called principle of *equifinality*).

The term system has many meanings. Bertalanffy (1968) defines it as a set of elements standing in interaction. This definition does not formally clarify which are the elements themselves. Furthermore, there is no reference to the criterion for choosing either objects or relations that are given a systemic character, that is, there is no observer of the system. The criterion of choice, specific to the observer, appears in the definition of Miller (1995): a system is 'a region delimited in space-time', where the term 'delimited' evidently refers to an observer who delimits and then chooses. In contemporary systemic theory, no one refuses to introduce the observer and this *observer dependence* is considered not so much a defect (as in classical science), but a fundamental quality. A more precise definition is given by Morin (1977): an organized global unit of interrelationships between elements, actions or individuals. A set of elements, to be defined as a system, must be governed by an organizational principle that establishes the rules of interaction between the elements.

What characteristics allow a system to be defined as complex? Figure 7.1 presents the main elements of complex systems. They are made up of a great variety of elements which have specialized functions. Therefore, elements are different from one another and it is precisely this diversity that makes it difficult to study complex systems.

The high density of interconnections is typical: the various elements are connected by a great variety of links. The interactions between the elements are non-linear. This is a fundamental characteristic. In linear systems the whole is strictly equal to the sum of its parts; the connections do not bring any added value. Non-linear connections are important in the definition of the structure and organization of the system: the whole is greater than the sum of its parts (the so-called *system holistic principle*). Simple systems are characterized by few elements and few linear relationships between them; they can be analysed analytically. Complex systems, on the contrary, are made up of many elements and many relations, linear and non-linear; they

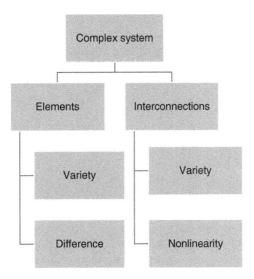

Figure 7.1   Components of complex systems

can be analysed only in a synthetic way. In a complex system, elements and connections, besides being numerous, are various and different.

A particular type of complex system is the *complex adaptive system*[1] (CAS), which adds to the other characteristics typical of complex systems the ability to adapt and 'learn'. CASs are able to adapt to the world around them by processing information and building models capable of assessing whether or not adaptation is useful. The elements of the system have the main purpose of adapting and in order to achieve it they constantly look for new ways of doing things and learning, thus giving rise to real dynamic systems. These systems challenge our ability to understand and predict. As stated by Battram (1999), they are perfectly placed in the middle of 'simple' systems, in which the connections between the elements are fixed and the behaviour is easily predictable, and 'chaotic' systems, whose components are dispersed and free to interact, generating absolutely unpredictable behaviour. Compared to the latter, the CASs have a hierarchical structure that maintains a certain control. The behaviour is emerging from the interactions between the elements and oscillating between predictability and unpredictability.

It is evident that these characteristics are typical of social phenomena, such as wellbeing. They are *multidimensional*, that is, made up of different dimensions (elements) of different types, which are linked together in a non-linear way. Social phenomena evolve over time, modifying both their dimensions and the links between them. The measurement and analysis of social phenomena requires the definition of systems of indicators capable of capturing their different aspects. As can be easily understood, these systems are dynamic, since they have to adapt to changes in the measured phenomena. In simple terms, the social phenomena are CASs and can be monitored and measured through systems of indicators that are CASs.

7.2   MEASURING AND ANALYSIS IN THE CONTEXT OF COMPLEXITY: THE CASE OF WELLBEING INDICATORS

Dealing with the study of wellbeing means dealing with the analysis of a complex adaptive system. The elements that define the concept of wellbeing are different and of various nature, as are the interconnections that bind them to each other. Elements and bonds change over time, making it necessary both to continuously update them and to measure and monitor them. The definition of indicators aimed at monitoring wellbeing at national level requires the involvement of different players (statisticians, researchers, analysts, policy makers and so on) who are capable of considering complexity by avoiding over-reductionism, oversimplification and over-redundancy, and investigating how to make observations relative.

7.2.1   Factors Defining the Complexity of Social Phenomena

Measuring and analysis of a complex social phenomenon, such as wellbeing, through indicators imply several methodological issues, in order to manage the complexity referring to several aspects. Here we present the main factors that define the complexity of a social phenomenon and with which we need to deal in order to analyse them.

The starting point in analysing social phenomena is the *definition* of what should be observed. Defining a concept is a process of abstraction, a complex stage that requires the identification and definition of theoretical constructs that involve the researcher's point of view, the applicability of the concepts and the socio-cultural, geographical and historical context. It is a demanding exercise, especially when the concept refers to a complex state, such as wellbeing. A correct conceptualization allows the identification of the model aimed at data construction, the spatial and temporal ambit of observation, the aggregation levels and the models allowing interpretation and evaluation. How can we define wellbeing? What is wellbeing? Answering these questions is a very difficult task. Along with concepts such as equity and sustainability, wellbeing is something that defines the level of progress of a country. This notion can be developed at the individual or societal level. From a general point of view, wellbeing involves dimensions such as economic and social cohesion, integration of individuals and groups, social connections and social ties (social capital), observed at both the micro level and macro level (Brulé and Maggino 2017). Thus, the main complexity in developing indicators of wellbeing concerns its definition and is due to the multidimensionality of this concept. In fact, the wellbeing of a nation involves several concepts, which can be defined by different dimensions and subdimensions. The conceptual approaches trying to define the idea of wellbeing are many and can be classified according to different criteria.[2] As shown by Maggino (2016), no approach is able to fully describe wellbeing. Different perspectives only focus on certain aspects and do not consider the complexity of the phenomenon. Identifying a comprehensive definition of wellbeing is difficult. We have to consider the individual and societal level, both defined by objective and subjective aspects and measured through objective and subjective indicators. The following can be considered a possible multidimensional definition of wellbeing: 'A good and healthy society is that in which each individual has the possibility to participate in the community life, develop skills, abilities, capabilities and independency, adequately choose and control his/her own life, be treated with respect in a healthy and safe environment and by respecting the opportunities of future generations' (Maggino 2016, 214).

Latent variables are another factor of complexity. Each of them represents an aspect to be observed. Their identification is founded on empirical statements (each variable reflects an aspect of the considered phenomenon consistently with the conceptual model) and theoretical assumptions (requiring also an analysis of the literacy review). According to its level of complexity, the variable can be described by one or more factors. The different factors of each variable are referred to as dimensions. The concept of 'dimensionality' is quite complex, because its meaning is mainly and essentially theoretical. In this perspective, two different situations can be observed:

- *Unidimensional*, when the definition of the considered variable assumes a unique, fundamental underlying dimension.
- *Multidimensional*, when the definition of the considered variable assumes two or more underlying factors.

This identification will guide the selection of the indicators. The correspondence between the defined dimensionality and the selected indicators has to be demonstrated empirically by testing the selected model of measurement.

In dealing with concepts like wellbeing or quality of life, the consensus on what variables should be selected and on their interpretation is lower. What should be clarified is that comparing different realities (represented by countries or by areas inside a country) does not necessarily imply using the same variables but could require differentiated choices (Stiglitz et al. 2009; Sharpe and Salzman 2004). In fact, the choice of variables depends on shared societal values, which are functions of time and place. Consequently, transferring a wellbeing concept developed in a certain context could be misleading. A good example of this is the variable 'leisure time', whose definition can differ from one individual to another.

In almost all cases the defined variable can be measured only indirectly through observable elements called *indicators* of the reference variable. Each basic indicator (item, in subjective measurement) represents what can be actually measured in order to investigate the corresponding variable. In other words, *the indicator is what relates concepts to reality*. According to Land (1971, 1975), an indicator is something different from a statistical index because it presents some specific characteristics. It is a component in a model concerning a social system; it can be measured and analysed in order to compare the situations of different groups and to observe the direction (positive or negative) of its evolution over time; it can be aggregated with other indicators or disaggregated in order to specify the model. Indicators can be considered as *purposeful statistics* (Horn 1993, 7).

With reference to a latent variable, a variety of different indicators can be identified; no set of indicators exists that is able to perfectly capture a conceptual variable. Moreover, the same defined variable can find different indicators according to different (social, physical, etc.) contexts. For example, different countries could agree on the same definition of wellbeing but could then select different indicators from each other.

From the conceptual point of view, indicators can describe a phenomenon through different levels of observation:

- Indicators are said to be *micro* when the values refer to individuals or groups, while they are said to be *macro* when the values refer to communities, regions, countries, etc.
- Indicators are defined as *internal* or *external*, a duality sensitive to individual observation; in fact, the concepts defined at individual level can be observed at both 'external' (e.g. objective living conditions) and 'internal' (e.g. subjective evaluations or perceptions) levels.

How many basic indicators are there? There is no single answer to this question. This is another factor characterizing the complexity of measuring social phenomena. According to the simplest strategy, each latent variable is defined by a single element (*single indicator approach*). While undoubtedly thrifty and functioning, the single indicator approach requires the adoption of robust assumptions concerning the possibility of measuring one dimension (with reference to one domain) with just one indicator (i.e. direct correspondence between one latent variable and one indicator). Such an assumption shows some risk since each single indicator can produce a wide and considerable amount of error related to:

- *Precision* (*reliability*), since the measurement through one single indicator is strongly affected by random errors.
- *Accuracy* (*validity*), since the chance that one single indicator can describe one latent complex variable is highly dubious and questionable.
- *Relationship* with the other variables and dimensions.
- *Capacity of discriminating* and *differentiating* among observed cases.

Consequently, the adoption of the *multi-indicator approach* (i.e. several indicators for each conceptual variable) is desirable. It allows the problems produced by the single indicator approach to be overcome, or at least reduced. In fact, multiple measures allow the conceptual dimensions to be measured with more precision (multiple measures allow random errors to be compensated), accuracy and discriminant capacity.

Domains are another factor influencing the complexity of social phenomena. They can be defined as the contexts/areas within which concepts, their variables and dimensions have to be assessed and observed. Each domain represents a specific segment of reality and refers to individuals, families and territorial/social areas. Typically they are housing, health, transport, environment, leisure and culture, social security, crime and safety, education, the labour market, working conditions and so on. A shared list of domains showing explicit priority does not exist because the list depends on value judgements that are only valid and acceptable in a certain place or time (Noll 2004). However, scholars have noticed that many domains recur in empirical studies (Felce and Perry 1995; Nuvolati 1997; Johansson 2002; Stiglitz et al. 2009), highlighting how human conditions lead individuals to face challenges that are common all over the world and that require collective solutions. Generally the differences concern the importance assigned to each domain.

Dealing with complexity implies other issues to be considered in order to define indicators:

- *Multidimensionality*, which requires different aspects to be defined that are not necessarily consistent to each other.

- *Nature*, which can be:
  - *Objective and subjective*, refering to two aspects of the reality integrating each other.
  - *Quantitative and qualitative*, which implies a consistent choice of measures (e.g. 'life expectancy' represents a quantitative aspect, while 'healthy life expectancy' represents a more qualitative aspect).
- *Levels of observation*, which can be:
  - *Micro* (individuals, groups).
  - *Macro* (communities, regions, countries, etc.). Macro does not necessarily correspond to the sum of micros and micro does not necessarily reflect what emerges at the macro level. *Quality of life* is typically observed at the individual level, while other concepts like *economic and social cohesion* are observed at community level. Some concepts require both levels of observation, like *sustainability*.
- *Dynamics*, referring to:
  - *Internal levels and external conditions*. At the individual level the defined concepts can be observed at both 'external' (e.g. objective living conditions, equity and sustainability of conditions) and 'internal' (e.g. subjective evaluations about living conditions, subjective perceptions about equity and sustainability of living conditions) level.
  - *Trends*, which can be different from one dimension to another (linear, non-linear, chaotic and so on).
  - *Relationships between phenomena*.

7.2.2   Making Relative

Making relative represents a crucial need in dealing with indicators in social complex systems and concerns issues which are at the same time conceptual and technical. From the conceptual point of view, making indicators relative is related to their *consistency* with the defined concept and their *adequacy* with reference to involved territories/groups.

Let us consider the construction of wellbeing indicators. As previously described, we start with the definition of wellbeing. The second step is its *operationalization* (in terms of indicators) which aims at adapting such definition to the territorial domain in which the observation is made. Consequently, different areas could identify different domains and adopt different indicators in order to measure wellbeing. For this reason, indicators should be compared with reference to the conceptual synthesis and not with reference to single indicators (comparing synthetic indicators).

Making relative is directly related to the interpretation of the results described by the indicators and also calls for better policies. Let us consider an example. For a particular region, a high value is produced by the ratio: *number of hospital beds/dimension of population*. How should we interpret this? A flat interpretation could be that a high number of beds could reveal a region paying attention to the population's health. However, a question could be raised: does the high number of available beds in hospital fit a real need for that population in that territory?

Making relative has strong implications with reference to the *comparability* of indicators. In fact, making relative and making comparable involve the general need for harmonizing different concepts, data sources and analyses with reference to different levels of observation. Comparing concepts, data and analyses over time, across territories and between groups means considering differences in geographical, linguistic, social, cultural, political, environmental and administrative conditions as well as methodological conditions for data production (sampling design, questionnaire design, data collection methods and so on).

All these issues have direct and strong implications in the statistical treatment of indicators. From the technical point of view data comparability is, more or less, solved in the ambit of *data normalization* which aims at giving a correct and comparable meaning to each indicator in view of the creation of synthetic indicators. There are many approaches to standardization. Each of them has its strengths and weaknesses; there is no such thing as the best normalization. In selecting the more appropriate approach we have to consider the data properties; the original meaning of the indicators; values to be emphasized or penalized; whether or not absolute values are used; whether or not cases are compared to each other or to a reference unit; and whether or not units are evaluated across time.

7.2.3 Reductionism and Its Risks

The systematic identification of elementary indicators, in terms of concepts and domains, allows a *system of indicators* to be constructed. A system of indicators is more complex than a simple set of indicators; in a system, indicators are always related to a conceptual framework. In other words, the consistent application of the hierarchical design (Maggino 2017) produces a complex structure. Integrity is one of the main characteristics of a system. It may exhibit adaptive, dynamic, goal-seeking, self-preserving and sometimes evolutionary behaviour (Meadows 2008).

In order to obtain a meaningful and interpretable picture of reality, the indicators within the system must be reduced in order to allow more comprehensive measures. This issue is referred as reductionism. Reductionism cannot be avoided since it is impossible to pull an image from the pure observation of reality. On the other hand, it is dangerous to concentrate on just a few elements and statistically infer the sufficiency of the reduced observation from them.

Reductionism applied to indicators can find two solutions: reducing the number of indicators or synthesizing indicators. The former approach needs solid conceptual support. From the statistical point of view the only evidence supporting the exclusion of one of two indicators is interrelation. A high level of relation between two indicators allows us to consider just one of them, assuming that indicators showing a strong relationship are actually measuring the same concept or component. However, this assumption is not always true. The degree of freedom for such decisions is defined by reality: the relationship between two indicators (e.g. number of firemen and amount of damage in a fire) can be high but mediated by a third one (e.g. dimension of the fire). If the nature of the third indicator changes, the relationship between the other two indicators changes or disappears, even though they will continue to describe the reality autonomously. If, by observing the previous high correlation, we excluded one of the two indicators, doing without one of them could deny ourselves precious pieces of the whole picture (as represented by the indicators). This means that having a solid conceptual model allows the relationships between indicators' concepts to be identified and interpreted. This approach consists in combining the indicators in a meaningful way.

7.3   CONCLUDING CONSIDERATIONS

In this chapter we have analysed in detail the concept of wellbeing, framing it within the complexity concept. It is undoubtedly a complex system, which to be fully understood must be analysed by taking into account some guidelines. Its multidimensionality must be taken into account: wellbeing consists of several aspects that must be considered in their mutual relations for its effective understanding.

Beyond the different positions on the issue there is no doubt that the concept of complexity has led to a number of important innovations in the relationship with knowledge. In particular, the need for a new way of looking at reality emerges; the importance of going beyond empirical evidence, trying to grasp at the same time the whole and the individual components that make it up.

We can discuss whether these transformations coincide with an actual paradigm shift or not; however, their importance is not in question at all. The complex nature of social phenomena is beyond question, as is the need to analyse their temporal evolution, if we want to grasp their real meaning. In particular, we have seen how dealing with social phenomena means dealing with CASs. Social phenomena not only adapt to change, but learn from it as they evolve.

We have proposed an approach to the measurement of complex phenomena that takes into account their specificities. The measurement of social phenomena starts from their conceptual definition and unfolds through a series of phases that define the so-called hierarchical design. Following the latter, we arrive at the definition of a system of indicators, a tool that allows us to measure, and consequently understand, a specific aspect of reality. Indicators are the tools to understand complexity. They play a key role in describing, understanding and controlling complex systems. Managing indicators simultaneously introduces: a challenge, represented by the need of dealing with complexity; a need, given by the need of making indicators relative; and a risk, given by reductionism.

NOTES

1. For a review of different definitions of CASs and their main characteristics, see Turner and Baker (2019).
2. For an analysis of different conceptual approaches, see Maggino (2016).

REFERENCES

Alaimo, L. S. (2020), Complexity of Social Phenomena: Measurements, Analysis, Representations and Synthesis. Unpublished doctoral dissertation, University of Rome 'La Sapienza', Rome, Italy.

Battram, A. (1999), *Navigating Complexity: The Essential Guide to Complexity Theory in Business and Management*. London: Industrial Society.

Bertalanffy, L. von. (1968), *General System Theory*. New York: Braziller.

Brulé, G. and F. Maggino (2017), Towards more complexity in subjective well-being studies. In G. Brulé and F. Maggino (eds) *Metrics of Subjective Well-being: Limits and Improvements* (pp. 1–17). Cham: Springer.

Capra, F. (1996), *The Web of Life: A New Synthesis of Mind and Matter*. New York: Anchor Books.

Contini, R. M. (2013), The paradigm of the complex dynamic systems and sociological analysis. *Procedia-Social and Behavioral Sciences*, 92, 207–14.

De Toni, A. F. and L. Comello (2009), *Prede o ragni: uomini e organizzazioni nella ragnatela della complessità*. Torino: UTET Università.

Erdi, P. (2008), *Complexity Explained*. Berlin and Heidelberg: Springer-Verlag.

Felce, D. and J. Perry (1995), Quality of life: its definition and measurement. *Research in Developmental Disabilities*, 16(1), 51–74.

Gorban, A. N. and G. S. Yablonsky (2013), Grasping complexity. *Computers & Mathematics with Applications*, 65(10), 1421–6.

Horn, R. V. (1993), *Statistical Indicators for the Economic and Social Sciences*. Cambridge: Cambridge University Press.

Johansson, S. (2002), Conceptualizing and measuring quality of life for national policy. *Social Indicators Research*, 58, 13–32.

Kuhn, T. (1962), *The Structure of Scientific Revolutions*. Chicago: University of Chicago Press.

Land, K. C. (1971), On the definition of social indicators. *American Sociologist*, 6, 322–5.

Land, K. C. (1975), Social indicator models: an overview. In K. C. Land and S. Spilerman (eds) *Social Indicator Models* (pp. 5–36). New York: Russell Sage Foundation.

Maggino, F. (2016), Challenges, needs and risks in defining wellbeing indicators. In F. Maggino (ed.) *A Life Devoted to Quality of Life* (pp. 209–33). Cham: Springer.

Maggino, F. (2017), Developing indicators and managing the complexity. In F. Maggino (ed.) *Complexity in Society: From Indicators Construction to their Synthesis* (pp. 87–114). Cham: Springer.

Masterman, M. (1970), The nature of a paradigm. In I. Lakatos and A. Musgrave (eds) *Criticism and the Growth of Knowledge* (pp. 59–90). Cambridge: University Press.

Maturana, H. R. and F. J. Varela (1980), *Autopoiesis and Cognition: The Realization of Living*. Dordrecht: D. Reidel Pub. Co.

Meadows, D. (2008), *Thinking in Systems: A Primer*. White River Junction: Chelsea Green Publishing.

Miller, J. G. (1995), *Living Systems*. Niwot: University Press of Colorado.

Morin, E. (1977), *La méthode. I. La nature de la nature*. Paris: Le Seuil.

Morin, E. (1984), Le vie della complessità. In G. Bocchi and M. Cerruti (eds) *La sfida della complessità* (pp. 49–60). Milan: Feltrinelli.

Morin, E. (2007), *Restricted Complexity, General Complexity. Science and Us: Philosophy and Complexity*. Singapore: World Scientific.

Noll, H. H. (2004), Social indicators and indicators systems: tools for social monitoring and reporting. Paper presented at OECD, World Forum 'Statistics, Knowledge and Policy', Palermo, 10–13 November 2004.

Nuvolati, G. (1997), Uno specifico settore di applicazione degli indicatori sociali: La qualità della vita. In F. Zajczyk (ed.) *Il mondo degli indicatori sociali, una guida alla ricerca sulla qualità della vita* (pp. 69–94). Rome: La Nuova Italia Scientifica.

Prigogine, I. and I. Stengers (1993), *La nuova alleanza*. Torino: Einaudi.

Sharpe, A. and J. Salzman (2004), Methodological choices encountered in the construction of composite indices of economic and social well-being. Center for the Study of Living Standards, Ottawa.

Stengers, I. (1984), Perché non può esserci un paradigma della complessità. In G. Bocchi and M. Cerruti (eds) *La sfida della complessità* (pp. 61–83). Milan: Feltrinelli.

Stiglitz, J. E., A. Sen and J.-P. Fitoussi (2009), Report by the Commission on the Measurement of Economic Performance and Social Progress, Paris. http://www.stiglitz-sen-fitoussi.fr/en/index.htm.

Turner, J. R. and R. M. Baker (2019), Complexity theory: an overview with potential applications for the social sciences. *Systems*, 7(1), 4.

8. Growth and happiness in China, 1990–2015[1]

Richard A. Easterlin, Fei Wang and Shun Wang

As in any historical study of a developing country, quantitative data are in short supply – though typically expanding and improving with time. The task of empirical study is to assemble and evaluate the quantitative evidence available and assess its fit with the broader historical context, as is attempted here. Although the available measures of China's Subjective Wellbeing (SWB) in the period under study tend to be biased toward the urban sector, the same is true of economic growth.[2] Hence the present data should provide a reasonable perspective on the course of well-being in an area experiencing an unparalleled increase in per capita output and the consumption of goods and services.

8.1 LONG-TERM MOVEMENT

Since 1990 China's SWB has been U-shaped over time, falling to a 2000–5 trough and subsequently recovering (Figure 8.1).[3] This pattern is found in four different series that reach back into the 1990s – World Value Survey (WVS), Gallup1 and 2, and Horizon. The fifth series in Figure 8.1, based on the Chinese General Social Survey (CGSS), only starts in the 2000s, and trends upward like the other series in the same time span. The series that include 1990s data come from three different survey organizations, two American and one Chinese. In every series both pre- and post-trough values are higher than those in 2000–5, even though the series differ in their origin, measure of SWB, and sample size (see Technical Box 8.1). The consistency of the results from these different series strengthens the finding on the overall movement. Lack of annual data prevents more precise dating of the trough in SWB. Additional support for the U-shape is provided by the 95 percent confidence interval bars presented for the WVS data. There is no overlap between the confidence interval at the 2000–5 trough and the corresponding intervals for the initial value of the series in 1990 and the terminal value in 2012.

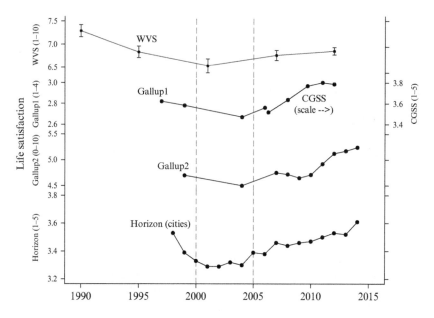

Notes: Horizon series is a three-year moving average, centered, of annual data for 1997–2015; Gallup 2, after 2004, is a three-year moving average, centered, of annual data for 2006–15; CGSS is a three-item moving average for dates given in Technical Box 8.1. Series with response options of 1–4 or 1–5 are plotted to twice the scale of series with response options of 1–10 and 0–10. For survey questions and response options, see Technical Box 8.1.

Source: Online Appendix, Table A1 (see: https://www.e-elgar.com/textbooks/bruni).

Figure 8.1   Mean subjective well-being, five series, 1990–2015

The 1990 WVS value of 7.29 for SWB seems high for what was then a poor country, but several considerations point to its plausibility.[4] China's urban labor market at that time has been described as a 'mini-welfare state', its workers as having an 'iron rice bowl'.[5] Concerns about one's current and future job and family security were virtually non-existent. Those employed by public enterprises (which accounted for the bulk of urban employment) were essentially guaranteed lifetime jobs and had benefits that included subsidized food, housing, healthcare, childcare, and pensions, as well as assurance of jobs for their grown children. Russia's labor and wage policies served as the model for communist China, and China's value of 7.29 is almost identical to the 7.26 found in the available data for pre-transition Russia.[6] In 1990 life satisfaction differences by socio-economic status in China were very small, as was true also of former Soviet Union countries prior to transition.[7] In the 1990 survey data for China, mean values exceeding 7.0 are found across the distributions by education, occupation, and

TECHNICAL BOX 8.1   SURVEYS AND MEASURES OF
SUBJECTIVE WELL-BEING

World Values Survey (sample size: *c*.1000–*c*.2000). Life satisfaction: all things considered, how satisfied are you with your life as a whole these days? Please use this card to help with your answer.
  1 (dissatisfied) 2 3 4 5 6 7 8 9 10 (satisfied).
Gallup1 (sample size: *c*.3500). Life satisfaction: overall, how satisfied or dissatisfied are you with the way things are going in your life today? Would you say you are 4, very satisfied; 3, somewhat satisfied; 2, somewhat dissatisfied; or 1, very dissatisfied?
Gallup2 1999, 2004 (sample size: *c*.4000). Ladder of life: please imagine a ladder with steps numbered from 0 at the bottom to 10 at the top. Suppose we say that the top of the ladder represents the best possible life for you, and the bottom of the ladder represents the worst possible life for you. On which step of the ladder would you say you personally stand at this time?
Gallup2: Gallup World Poll 2006–2015 (sample size: *c*.4000, except 2012 *c*.9000). Ladder of life: please imagine a ladder with steps numbered from zero at the bottom to ten at the top. Suppose we say that the top of the ladder represents the best possible life for you, and the bottom of the ladder represents the worst possible life for you. On which step of the ladder would you say you personally stand at this time, assuming that the higher the step the better you feel about your life, and the lower the step the worse you feel about it? Which step comes closest to the way you feel?
Horizon 1997–1999, 2001 (sample size: *c*.5000). [In Chinese] In general, are you satisfied with your current life: very satisfied, fairly satisfied, fairly dissatisfied, or very dissatisfied? (single answer). Coded 5, 4, 2, or 1.
Horizon 2000, 2002–2010 (sample size: *c*.2500–*c*.5500). [In Chinese] In general, are you satisfied with your current life: very satisfied, fairly satisfied, average, fairly dissatisfied, or very dissatisfied? (single answer). Coded 5, 4, 3, 2, or 1.
Chinese General Social Survey (CGSS) 2003, 2005, 2006, 2008, 2010–13 (sample size: *c*.5500–*c*.12000). [In Chinese] On the whole, do you feel happy with your life: very unhappy, unhappy, so-so, happy, or very happy? (single answer). Coded 1, 2, 3, 4, or 5.

income; hence the high overall average cannot be attributed to a disproportionate representation in the 1990 survey of those with high life satisfaction.

It is doubtful that the recovery in SWB by the end of the period reaches a value equal to that in 1990. In the WVS series, the one covering the longest time span, the terminal value of 6.85 in 2012 is significantly less than the 1990 value of 7.29. The upper bound of the 95 percent confidence interval in 2012 is 6.93, well below the lower bound of 7.16 in 1990. Another indication that China has not recovered to its 1990 value is the slippage in its worldwide ranking by SWB. If the 2012 high-to-low array of 100 countries with recent WVS data is taken as a reference,[8] China falls from 28th to

50th between 1990 and 2012. The middling position of China in the 2012 WVS ranking is fairly consistent with that in the current Gallup World Poll ladder-of-life array for 157 countries – in 2013–15 China was 83rd.[9]

In the research literature on SWB, cross-section studies typically find that happiness varies positively with gross domestic product (GDP), and this finding is frequently cited as evidence that economic growth increases subjective well-being.[10] The SWB data for China call into question the validity of this assertion. Based on the regression results of such cross-section studies, China's striking fivefold multiplication of GDP since 1990 would be expected to increase SWB by upwards of a full point or more on a 1–10 life satisfaction scale. It is noteworthy that four different surveys reaching back to the 1990s fail to give evidence of an overall increase approaching this magnitude (Figure 8.1).

The positive cross-section relation of SWB to GDP reported in prior happiness research implies that the growth rates of GDP and SWB are positively related. Yet China's GDP growth rate goes through three cycles between 1990 and 2012 while SWB goes through only one (compare Figure 8.2, left panel, with Figure 8.1). Moreover, the growth rate of GDP is highest in 2000–5 when SWB is bottoming out with a growth rate close to zero. Also noteworthy is the disparate course of the rate of inflation, which has typically been found to have an inverse relation to SWB.[11] In China in 2000–5, when SWB was at its lowest, the rate of inflation was also low – lower than in any other years between 1994 and 2015 (Figure 8.2, right panel and Table A2). Neither GDP nor inflation has a time series pattern that might by itself explain the course of SWB. As will be seen below the explanation of China's SWB rests on different factors.

A number of Eastern European countries have been transitioning from a socialist to free market economy at the same time as China, and it is of interest to ask how China's transition pattern of life satisfaction compares with that of these other countries. Indeed, China's overall trajectory of SWB is quite similar. For those European countries whose SWB data extend back into the socialist period, SWB invariably follows a U- or V-shaped pattern in the transition.[12] Unlike China, however, where GDP grows at an unprecedented rate, in the European countries GDP collapses and recovers in a pattern much like that of SWB, a difference between China and Europe to be discussed subsequently.

8.2   DETERMINANTS OF THE SWB TRAJECTORY

Two factors appear to have been of critical importance in forming the U-shaped course of subjective well-being in China – unemployment and

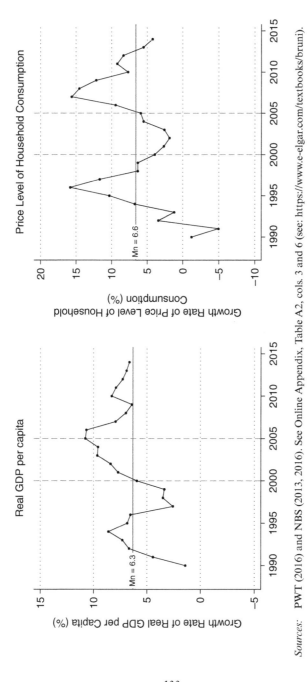

Sources: PWT (2016) and NBS (2013, 2016). See Online Appendix, Table A2, cols. 3 and 6 (see: https://www.e-elgar.com/textbooks/bruni).

Figure 8.2   Growth rate of real GDP per capita and price level, 1988–2015 (three-year moving average, centered)

the social safety net. In the 1990s severe unemployment emerged and the social safety net broke down. The 'iron rice bowl' was smashed, giving rise to urgent new concerns about jobs, income security, family, and health. Although incomes rose foremost for those who had jobs, the positive effect on well-being of income growth was offset by a concurrent rise in material aspirations. The counteracting effect to income growth of increasing aspirations has been pointed out by a number of China specialists. Shenggen Fan et al. observe: 'Happiness draws from relative comparisons. As income increases, people's aspirations aim for a new target'.[13] Research by John Knight and his collaborators provides further valuable insights into the effect of reference groups on happiness in China.[14]

In its survey of findings on subjective well-being, the high-profile Stiglitz–Sen–Fitoussi Commission states: 'One aspect where all research on subjective well-being does agree concerns the high human costs associated with unemployment'.[15] The reason why unemployment has a major adverse effect on well-being is straightforward – jobs are of critical importance for sustaining people's livelihood, family, and health, and it is concerns with these personal circumstances that are foremost in shaping people's happiness.[16]

The quantitative evidence on unemployment is consistent with the view that unemployment has been an important determinant of China's SWB trajectory. The unemployment rate rose sharply from near-zero shortly before 1990 to double-digit levels in 2000–5, and then declined moderately. Although the unemployment estimates are somewhat rudimentary,[17] this pattern appears consistently in unemployment data from several different sources (Figure 8.3). Subjective well-being largely inversely mirrors the path of the unemployment rate. As the unemployment rate rises, SWB declines; as the rate falls, SWB increases. The 2000–5 trough in SWB occurs when the unemployment rate reaches its peak.

The term 'massive' is used repeatedly by China specialists in describing the precipitous upsurge in unemployment that began in the 1990s.[18] In little more than a decade (1992–3 to 2004) 50 out of 78 million lost their jobs in state-owned enterprises (SOEs), and another 20 million were laid off in urban collectives.[19] Knight and Song aptly describe this period as one of 'draconian . . . labor shedding'.[20]

The impact of unemployment on SWB was not confined to those who lost their jobs. As has been demonstrated in the SWB literature,[21] increased unemployment also reduces the well-being of those who remain employed as they fear for their own jobs as layoffs increase. An indication of the widespread anxiety associated with a high level of unemployment in China is the answer to a nationally representative survey question that asked, 'Now thinking about our economic situation, how would

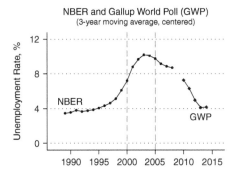

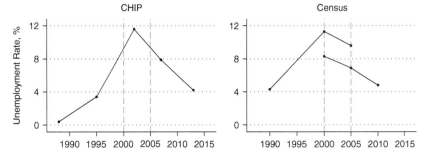

Source: Online Appendix, Table A3 (see: https://www.e-elgar.com/textbooks/bruni).

Figure 8.3　*Urban unemployment rate, four series, 1988–2015 (% of labor force)*

you describe the current economic situation in China: is it very good, somewhat good, somewhat bad or very bad?' In 2002, when unemployment was at two-digit levels, almost half of respondents (48 percent) answered somewhat or very bad; by 2014, when the unemployment rate had markedly improved, only 6 percent fell in these two categories.[22] The survey responses demonstrate that employment is what matters for SWB, not growth of GDP. The growth rate of GDP was considerably higher in 2002 than in 2014 (Table A2), but respondents assessed the state of the economy as much worse in 2002.

Along with the upsurge in unemployment, the social safety net broke down, aggravating the decline in SWB. As workers lost jobs, their benefits disappeared, though for a modest fraction temporary support was provided through an urban layoff program. Those who found jobs in private firms no longer enjoyed the benefits that they previously had in the public sector. Even for those who retained public jobs, new government policies abolished guaranteed employment and lifetime benefits. This positive

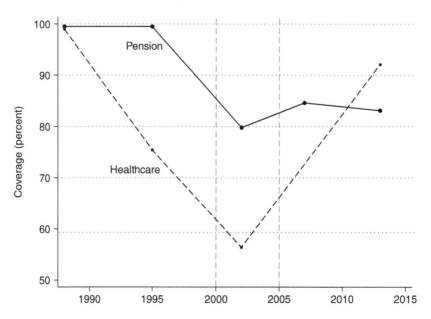

Source: CHIP. See Online Appendix, Table A4 (see: https://www.e-elgar.com/textbooks/bruni).

Figure 8.4   *Safety net indicators: pension and healthcare coverage,*
              1988–2013 (urban households)

relationship between the social safety net and SWB has been demonstrated by both economists and political scientists.[23]

The unemployment rate is itself an indicator of safety net coverage because benefits were employment-dependent. Survey data on pension and healthcare coverage provide additional quantitative evidence of the course of safety net benefits (Figure 8.4). Note that the pattern in these safety net indicators tends to be U-shaped, and the trough in coverage occurs in 2000–5 when unemployment peaks and SWB reaches its lowest point.

The emergence of extensive unemployment and dissolution of the social safety net were due to the government-initiated comprehensive policy of restructuring SOEs, many of which were inefficient and unprofitable. Although the new policy was successful in stimulating economic growth, it marked an abrupt end to the era of 'reform without losers'. As Naughton points out, urban SOE workers 'bore the brunt of reform-related costs'.[24] According to a World Bank report, 'by all measures, SOE restructuring had a profound effect on . . . the welfare of millions of urban workers'.[25] The quantitative unemployment, safety net, and SWB patterns here are consistent with these statements.

Faced with massive and rising urban unemployment, government policy shifted gears. Beginning in 2004 the rate at which SOEs were downsized diminished sharply. Between 1995 and 2003, reduced employment in SOEs far exceeded increased employment elsewhere in the urban sector; thereafter, the situation was reversed, and the unemployment rate improved (Figure 8.3).[26] The safety net, as indexed by healthcare and pension coverage, also started to improve (Figure 8.4). The result was a turnaround and gradual recovery of SWB.

In 2000–5 the growth rate of GDP was approaching its highest level at the same time that unemployment was peaking. How could output be growing, and so rapidly, when employment was falling? China's restructuring policy involved greatly expanded support for a relatively small proportion of large, capital-intensive, and high-productivity SOEs at the expense of numerous small, labor-intensive, and low-productivity SOEs, a policy officially labeled 'Grasping the big and letting go of the small'. As described by Huang:

> 'Grasping the big' meant restructuring, consolidating, and strengthening China's largest SOEs . . . 'Letting go of the small' meant that the government supported privatization of individually small but numerically numerous SOEs. These are labor-intensive firms and singling them out for privatization, with no established social protection in place, led to massive unemployment, social instability, and wrenching human costs . . . Instead of managing tens of thousands of small firms scattered around the country, the Chinese state could now focus on only a few thousand firms [which benefitted from] a massive reallocation of financial, human, and managerial resources away from the small SOEs to a handful of the largest SOEs.[27]

This redistribution of resources from low-productivity small SOEs to high-productivity large SOEs resulted in a strong upsurge in output at the same time that small SOEs shed labor, creating a large pool of unemployed. As Huang points out, 'GDP growth in the 1990s increasingly was disconnected from the welfare of Chinese citizens'.[28] The survey responses reported above on the state of the economy in 2002 and 2014 provide concrete evidence of the continuation of this disconnect. The economy was viewed by the public as much worse in 2002, even though the GDP growth rate was considerably higher than in 2014.

As previously noted, China's GDP in transition has grown at an unprecedented rate while that of European transition countries collapsed and recovered in a pattern similar to SWB. The difference between China's GDP trajectory and that of the European countries appears to be due to the difference in restructuring policies. In both cases restructuring led to massive unemployment. While the European transition countries abandoned the entire public sector to privatization and experienced a major

GDP collapse, China invested heavily in the most productive SOEs and was rewarded with significant output growth.

8.3   OTHER SOCIAL AND ECONOMIC FACTORS

Is China's SWB trajectory also a reflection of societal conditions such as social capital, income inequality, or environmental pollution? What about the 'predictors' of SWB differences among countries identified in previous *World Happiness Reports* – material, social, and institutional supports for a good life – do they explain the time series course of SWB in China?[29] To answer these questions this section examines whether changes over time in these variables conform as expected to the movement in SWB since 1990. This is the same procedure as that followed in Section 8.2 on unemployment and the social safety net.

The measures of social capital examined here – trust in others and civic cooperation – are those used in a recent article by Bartolini and Sarracino that seeks to explain the change in China's life satisfaction from 1990 to 2007, one of the rare articles addressing change over time.[30] The specific questions and responses are given in Technical Box 8.2. The two indicators of social capital are treated separately in what follows.

Trust has an overall trajectory fairly similar to SWB, falling at the beginning of the period and rising at the end (Figure 8.5). It is plausible that in the 1990s, as restructuring led to the emergence and growth of unemployment and job competition, a decline in interpersonal trust occurred. Correspondingly, the upswing in employment during the 2000s recovery may have helped restore trust. The decline and recovery of interpersonal trust may, in turn, have reinforced the U-shaped trajectory of SWB. The biggest difference between trust and SWB centers on the value in the 2000–5 period. Trust is slightly higher, but not much different from that in adjacent years, while SWB is lower. As noted previously, the lower value of SWB in the 2000–5 period is credible because it is found in four different surveys conducted independently of each other.

Another measure of social capital is civic cooperation, a term reflecting disapproval of cheating or bribery in circumstances such as paying taxes or claiming government benefits (see Technical Box 8.2). The composite measure presented here is the average of four components, each of which has a pattern fairly similar to that in the summary measure (Technical Box 8.2 and Table A5). In each interval from 1990 to 2007 the summary measure of civic cooperation moves in the same direction as trust, though the movements in civic cooperation through 2001 are slight. After 2001, however, trust and civic cooperation begin to diverge

---

**TECHNICAL BOX 8.2 MEASURES OF SOCIAL CAPITAL AND
FREEDOM OF CHOICE**

World Values Survey 1990, 1995, 2001 (sample size: *c*.1000–*c*.1500). Trust: generally speaking, would you say that most people can be trusted or that you can't be too careful in dealing with people? 1, most people can be trusted; 2, can't be too careful. Recoded 1 or 0.

World Values Survey 2007, 2012 (sample size: *c*.2000). Trust: generally speaking, would you say that most people can be trusted or that you can't be too careful in dealing with people? 1, most people can be trusted; 2, need to be very careful. Recoded 1 or 0.

World Values Survey (sample size: *c*.1000–*c*.2000). Civic cooperation: please tell me for each of the following statements whether you think it can always be justified, never be justified, or something in between, using this card.

Claiming government benefits which you are not entitled to

Never 1 / 2 / 3 / 4 / 5 / 6 / 7 / 8 / 9 / 10 Always

Avoiding a fare on public transport

Never 1 / 2 / 3 / 4 / 5 / 6 / 7 / 8 / 9 / 10 Always

Cheating on tax if you have the chance

Never 1 / 2 / 3 / 4 / 5 / 6 / 7 / 8 / 9 / 10 Always

Someone accepting a bribe in the course of their duties

Never 1 / 2 / 3 / 4 / 5 / 6 / 7 / 8 / 9 / 10 Always

Recoded 10, 9, 8, 7, 6, 5, 4, 3, 2, or 1 for each item.

World Values Survey (sample size: *c*.1000–*c*.2000). Freedom of choice: some people feel they have completely free choice and control over their lives, and other people feel that what they do has no real effect on what happens to them. Please use the scale to indicate how much freedom of choice and control you feel you have over the way your life turns out:

None at all 1 2 3 4 5 6 7 8 9 10 A great deal.

---

noticeably and, from 2007 on, in seemingly contradictory directions – a rise in trust being accompanied by a decline in civic cooperation, that is, increased acceptance of cheating and bribery. Unlike trust, the overall pattern of change in civic cooperation consequently differs considerably from that in SWB, and casts doubt on any causal connection between the two.

The results in the general literature on the relation between income inequality and happiness are mixed – some studies report no relationship, while others find that an increase in inequality reduces happiness.[31] In China income inequality as measured by the Gini coefficient has trended upward since the early 1980s, increasing when SWB is both falling and rising (Figure 8.6, panel A).[32] It is hard to see how the course of income inequality could solely explain the U-shaped movement of SWB. Indeed, as will be seen subsequently, since the beginning of the millennium the life

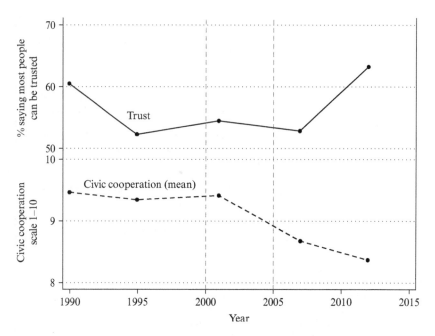

Source: Inglehart et al. (2014). See Online Appendix, Table A5 (see: https://www.e-elgar.com/textbooks/bruni).

Figure 8.5   Measures of social capital, 1990–2012

satisfaction difference between the lowest and highest income groups has diminished despite an increase in income inequality.

One might expect that the widely publicized environmental pollution problem in China would have had an adverse impact on happiness. A recent study based on cross sectional data, however, finds no relation between pollution and overall life satisfaction, although there is a shorter-term effect on day-to-day moods.[33] The time series finding in the present analysis turns out to be much like the nil cross-section finding. If the trend in coal consumption is taken as a measure of the course of environmental pollution, one finds that coal consumption trends upward throughout most of the period, rising after 2005 at close to its highest rate, while life satisfaction also rises, rather than falls (Figure 8.6, panel B).

Housing prices are also sometimes mentioned as a determinant of life satisfaction. The housing price data only start in 2000, not long after a housing market becomes widely established in China.[34] Housing prices trend steadily upward from 2000 on (Figure 8.6, panel C), a development that might be expected to reduce life satisfaction; in fact, life satisfaction rises, not falls.

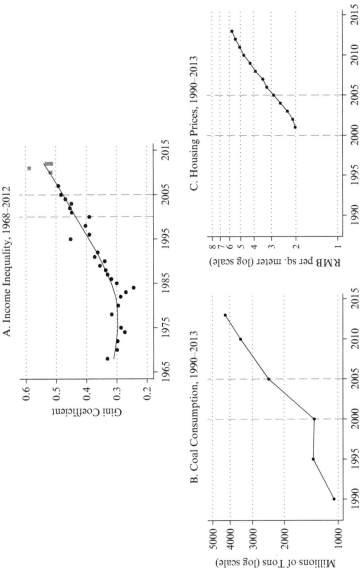

Sources: Panel A reproduced from Xie and Zhou (2014); panels B and C, NBS (2013, 2016). See Online Appendix, Table A6 (see: https://www.e-elgar.com/textbooks/bruni).

Figure 8.6   Indicators of trends in income inequality, environmental pollution, and housing prices

There are six 'predictors' of the annual national evaluations of SWB presented in the *World Happiness Reports* – GDP per capita (in log form), healthy life expectancy, freedom to control one's life, corruption, social support, and giving to charity. Of these it is possible to obtain time series measures for China that span the period covered here for the first four. (In the 2016 *World Happiness Report* the time series course of healthy life expectancy is based on that in life expectancy at birth, and the latter is consequently used in the present analysis.)[35] None of these 'predictors' has a time series pattern suggestive of a causal relation to SWB. GDP and life expectancy, which are themselves highly correlated, both trend upward throughout the period (Figure 8.7). Freedom to choose the course of one's life changes very little over time, and its movements do not conform to those in SWB. Corruption, approximated here by the acceptability of bribery, increases somewhat after 2001, but remains at a very low level. The two measures with the greatest changes – GDP and life expectancy – reach their highest values at the end of the period, but SWB does not.

The 2016 *World Happiness Report* presents a pooled time series and cross-section regression equation based on data for 156 countries in the period 2006–15, in which the six predictors are found to fit national ladder-of-life evaluations with an R-squared of 0.74.[36] Another way of examining the predictors here is to ask how accurately this equation predicts China's actual ladder-of-life values from 2006 to 2015. The answer is, not very well. If China's values for the independent variables are entered into the equation, the predicted values are uniformly higher, often by a substantial amount (Figure 8.8). Moreover, if one leaves aside the year 2006 (for which values for China are available for only three of the six independent variables) the predicted values in SWB exhibit a nil trend, while the actual trend is upward.

As pointed out in the 2016 *World Happiness Report*, the choice of 'predictors' is constrained by the limited availability of comparable data for a large number of countries worldwide, and the variables that are in fact chosen 'may be taking credit properly due to other better variables'.[37] The advantage of a country study, like the present one, is that it is not inhibited by the requirement of comparable international data. This makes it possible to explore the possible role in determining the SWB of a wider range of variables, and consequently developing a deeper understanding of the mechanisms at work. Indeed, an analysis of selected countries in the 2016 report moves in the direction of the present study. In evaluating the reasons for a decline in life satisfaction in four Eurozone countries hard hit by the Great Recession, the unemployment rate is added to the analysis and found to have an explanatory effect equal to that of all six of the present 'predictors' combined,[38] a result similar to the present findings.

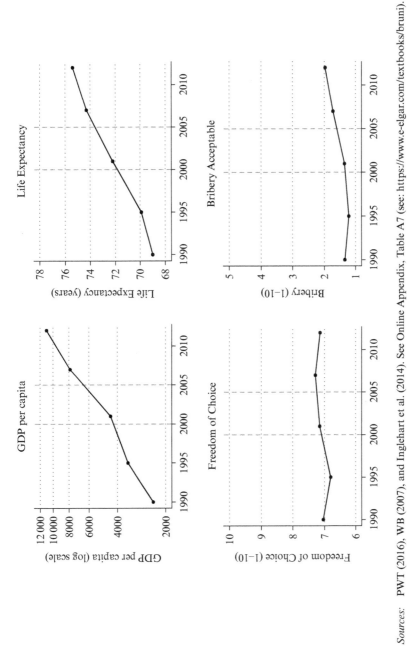

Sources: PWT (2016), WB (2007), and Inglehart et al. (2014). See Online Appendix, Table A7 (see: https://www.e-elgar.com/textbooks/bruni).

Figure 8.7 Predictors of SWB in World Happiness Reports, 1990–2012

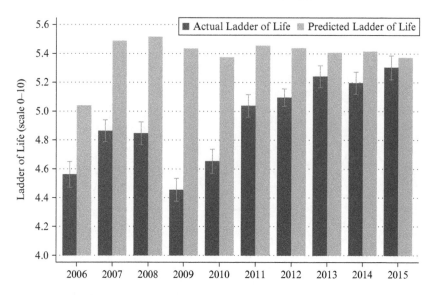

Source: Gallup World Poll micro-data 2006–2015. See Online Appendix, Table A8 (see: https://www.e-elgar.com/textbooks/bruni).

Figure 8.8   Actual and predicted mean ladder of life, 2006–15

Unfortunately, it is not possible to include unemployment as a predictor in the pooled regression equation for all countries due to lack of comparable international data.

As a brief summary of the results to this point, Table 8.1 presents the bivariate correlation and corresponding p-value between life satisfaction and each of the variables discussed in this and Section 8.2. (The housing price variable is not included because the series spans only half the period.) There are, at best, only five observations available for computing each correlation, which means each variable is evaluated singly in a bivariate analysis. Subject to the qualification that a multivariate analysis might give a fuller picture, the pattern of results is generally consistent with the observations based on the graphs. The unemployment rate and safety net indicators come quite close to the 0.10 level of significance. Trust and income inequality have the next highest correlation coefficients, but the p-values are above 0.30. The remaining variables have even worse p-values, and in some cases the sign of the correlation coefficient is contrary to what might be expected. As a whole the correlations uphold the conclusion that unemployment and the safety net have been the important forces shaping the course of China's life satisfaction.

Why are unemployment and the social safety net so important? These two factors bear most directly on the concerns foremost in shaping

Table 8.1   Time series correlation with WVS life satisfaction of indicated variable, 1990–2012

	Correlation coefficient	P-value
Unemployment rate	−0.76	0.13
Pension coverage	0.74	0.15
Healthcare coverage	0.89	0.11
Trust	0.52	0.37
Civic cooperation	0.17	0.79
Gini coefficient	−0.57	0.31
Coal consumption	−0.21	0.73
Log GDP per capita	−0.46	0.44
Life expectancy at birth	−0.50	0.40
Freedom of choice	−0.27	0.67
Bribery acceptable	−0.10	0.87

Notes: n = 5, except healthcare coverage, n = 4. The basic data are given in the Online Appendix Table A1, col.1; Table A3, col. 3; Table A4, rows 1, 6; Table A5, rows 1, 2; and Table A6a, cols. 1–4 (see: https://www.e-elgar.com/textbooks/bruni).

personal happiness – income security, family life, and the health of oneself and one's family. It is these concerns that are typically cited by people worldwide when asked an open-ended question as to what is important for their happiness.[39] In contrast, broad societal matters such as inequality, pollution, political and civil liberties, international relations, and the like, which most individuals have little ability to influence, are rarely mentioned. Abrupt changes in these conditions may affect happiness, but for the most part such circumstances are taken as given. The things that matter most are those that take up most people's time day after day, and which they think they have, or should have, some ability to control.

8.4   DIFFERENCES BY SOCIO-ECONOMIC STATUS

Although China's well-being declined, on average, and then somewhat recovered, there were significant differences among various groups in the population. Perhaps most striking was the severe impact of restructuring on those of lower socio-economic status (SES). In 1990 the difference in life satisfaction between the third of the population with the lowest incomes and that with the highest was quite small (Figure 8.9). Subsequently life satisfaction of the lowest third plunged markedly, while that of the highest actually improved slightly. The result was the emergence of a marked disparity in

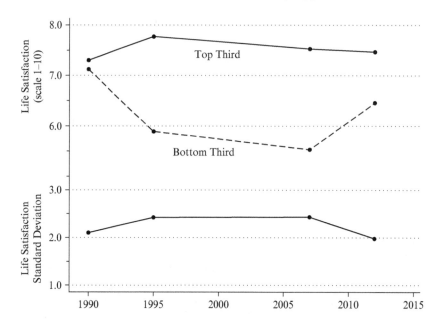

Source: Inglehart et al. (2014). See Online Appendix, Table A9 (see: https://www.e-elgar.com/textbooks/bruni).

Figure 8.9   Mean life satisfaction, top and bottom income terciles, and standard deviation of life satisfaction, 1990–2012

life satisfaction by socio-economic status. Toward the end of the period, life satisfaction of the lowest stratum somewhat recovered, and by 2012 the disparity in life satisfaction, though still sizeable, had shrunk considerably.[40] The standard deviation of life satisfaction, a measure reflecting all sources of life satisfaction differences, not just SES, follows the SES pattern of rising and decreasing inequality in life satisfaction (Figure 8.9, bottom).

The course of the life satisfaction difference by socio-economic status demonstrates the critical importance of full employment and safety net policies for the well-being of the most disadvantaged segment of the population. As these policies were abandoned in the 1990s, the lowest socio-economic group was the one that suffered severely. Data by level of education are indicative of the differential employment and safety net effects. The unemployment rate of those with a primary education or less soared to almost 20 percent in 2000–5, while that of the college-educated group remained at less than 5 percent (Figure 8.10). Similarly, pension and healthcare coverage of the less educated declined much more than that of the more educated (Figure 8.11). Consistent with these differences,

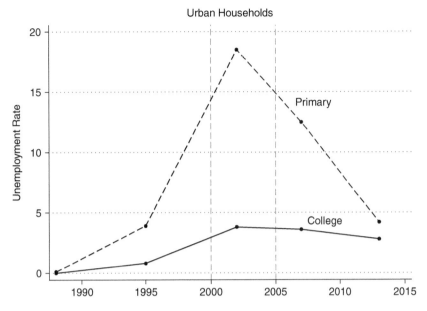

Note: 'Level of education' refers to persons with college education or more and primary school education or less.

Source: CHIP. See Online Appendix, Table A10 (see: https://www.e-elgar.com/textbooks/bruni).

Figure 8.10   Unemployment rate by level of education, 1988–2013 (% of labor force)

satisfaction with finances and self-rated health increased for the highest income stratum and decreased for the lowest (Figure 8.12).[41]

Eventually, as economic policy reversed and brought unemployment down, and substantial efforts were initiated to repair the social safety net,[42] these disparities diminished. Life satisfaction of the lowest third of the population recovered as employment and the safety net improved, though in 2012 it was still less than in 1990 (Figure 8.9).

8.5   DIFFERENCES BY AGE AND COHORT

Those aged 30 and over experienced large declines in life satisfaction over the quarter century studied here; men and women were about equally affected. In 1990 those aged 30 and over were already on a life course set under 'iron rice bowl' conditions. The collapse of the traditional environment severely

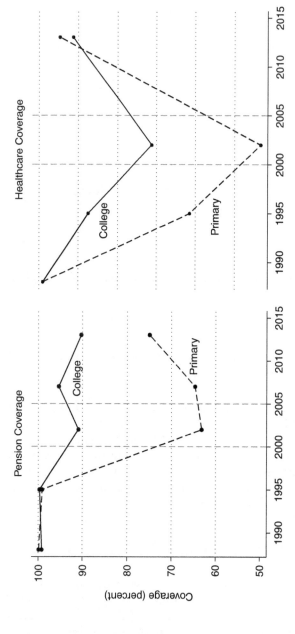

Note: 'Level of education' refers to persons with college education or more and primary school education or less.

Source: CHIP. See Online Appendix, Table A4 (see: https://www.e-elgar.com/textbooks/bruni).

Figure 8.11 Safety net indicators by level of education, 1988–2013 (urban households)

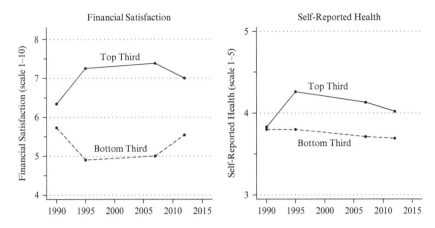

Source: Inglehart et al. (2014). See Online Appendix, Tables A11 and A12 (see: https://www.e-elgar.com/textbooks/bruni).

Figure 8.12   *Mean financial satisfaction and mean self-reported health, top and bottom income terciles, 1990–2012*

disrupted their lives and substantially reduced their well-being. As economic restructuring took hold the cohort of 1946–60, which spanned ages 30–44 in 1990, suffered the biggest decline in life satisfaction (Figure 8.13).

From an initial situation in which virtually everyone had jobs, men and women alike, in 2002 fewer than 70 percent were employed. Most of the remainder of the cohort, 21 percent, had been forced into early retirement, and 6 percent were unemployed.[43]

The next oldest cohort, that of 1936–45, also had a considerable initial drop in life satisfaction. The overall decline was somewhat cushioned, however, as by 2012 most of this cohort had reached retirement age (55 for women, 60 for men) and qualified for pensions, though these were sometimes reduced or in arrears.[44]

In contrast, the cohort of 1961–70, which in 1990 was merely in its twenties, experienced only a mild decline in life satisfaction between 1990 and 2002 and ended up with life satisfaction about the same as initially. The members of this and the successor cohorts were less wedded to traditional ways and better able to adapt to the new 'free market' conditions, most notably by acquiring a college education. Thirty-five percent of the cohort of 1961–70 had completed a college education by the time they were in their thirties; for the successor cohort, that of 1971–80, the corresponding figure was 40 percent. Among the cohorts born before the 1960s, however, the percentage with a college education was only 11 to 15 percent.[45] As seen above, those belonging to the higher SES group – which includes those with a

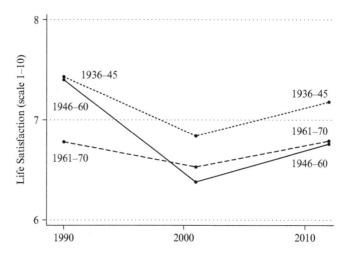

Note: In 1990 the birth cohort of 1961–70 was 20 to 29 years old; the birth cohort of 1946–60, 30 to 44; and the birth cohort of 1936–45, 45 to 54.

Source: Inglehart et al. (2014). See Online Appendix, Table A13 (see: https://www.e-elgar. com/textbooks/bruni).

Figure 8.13   Mean life satisfaction by birth cohort, 1990–2012

college education – largely escaped the adverse impact on life satisfaction of economic restructuring; clearly young adults were among the beneficiaries.

A comparison with the European transition countries is once again of interest. As has been seen, the trajectory of life satisfaction for the population as a whole is quite similar in China and the European countries. This similarity is also true of the differentials in life satisfaction that emerged in both areas. For both China and the European countries, small SES differences at the start of the transition were replaced by large disparities. [46] The lowest SES group experienced a severe decline in life satisfaction, while the upper tier typically enjoyed a mild improvement. Those under age 30 fared better than their older counterparts.[47] In both China and Europe adaptation to the new environment was greatly facilitated by a college education.[48]

8.6   DIFFERENCES BY RESIDENCE AND MIGRATION STATUS

Subjective well-being in China's urban areas has typically been greater than in rural areas, a pattern typical of developing countries.[49] The principal evidence for China is from three sources – the 1995 World Values Survey, CGSS surveys done almost annually since 2005, and surveys conducted annually since 2006 by the Gallup World Poll (Table A14).[50] The urban–rural life satisfaction differential in the 1995 WVS – about half a point (1–10 scale) – is just about the same as the average differential in the Gallup World Poll over the period 2006–15 (0–10 scale). Starting in 2010, a wider range of surveys is available – some continue to show the usual excess of urban over rural SWB, but in a few the urban and rural areas are about equal.[51]

Since 2005, when fairly continuous data become available, the trend in rural life satisfaction appears to have largely paralleled urban. Two different surveys give a highly consistent picture (Figure 8.14).

The improvement in rural life satisfaction may have been partly due to new policies strengthening the social safety net in rural areas. Also, there was a change in government policies that significantly lessened the burden placed on agriculture to support industrialization.[52] Lack of comparable data prevents generalization about the trend prior to 2005.

The 1990s saw the onset of a substantial population movement from rural to urban areas, as government restrictions on migration were increasingly relaxed. According to census data, between 1990 and 2010 the proportion of people in cities that had a rural *hukou* (identifying the holder as a resident of a rural place) rose from 17 to 36 percent.

Rural *hukou* holders in urban areas were initially treated as second-class citizens, but are gradually being assimilated.[53] The few life satisfaction surveys in the early 2000s that classified the urban population by *hukou* status uniformly found urban *hukou* holders with higher SWB than rural migrants.[54] The upward trend in life satisfaction since then has been fairly similar for the two groups (Figure 8.15).

The evidence is mixed on whether or not the gap in urban areas between urban and rural *hukou* holders has closed. In several surveys the gap persists, but in others it has disappeared.[55] A comparison between rural migrants and those remaining in rural areas is less ambiguous – initially the migrant group was higher, but in recent years there has been no difference.[56]

8.7 SUMMARY AND IMPLICATIONS

China's soaring GDP growth over the past quarter century is viewed by many analysts as the hallmark of a successful transition from socialism to capitalism. But if the welfare of the 'common man' is taken as a criterion of success, then the picture is much less favorable and more like that of European transition countries. From 1990 to 2000–5 life satisfaction in

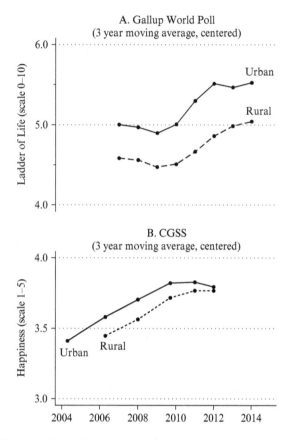

Source: Online Appendix, Table A14 (see: https://www.e-elgar.com/textbooks/bruni).

Figure 8.14   Mean life satisfaction by urban–rural residence, 2003–15

China, on average, declined. Since then it has turned upward, but at present it is probably less than a quarter century ago. China's ranking in the international array of countries by SWB appears to have declined considerably since 1990, although it has improved as of late. There is no evidence of an increase in China's life satisfaction of the sizeable magnitude that would be expected based on the international point-of-time bivariate relationship of happiness to GDP.

The lower-income and older segments of the population have suffered most, and their life satisfaction remains below that in 1990. The upper income and youngest population groups have, in contrast, enjoyed a fairly constant or a modest improvement in life satisfaction. The rather small life

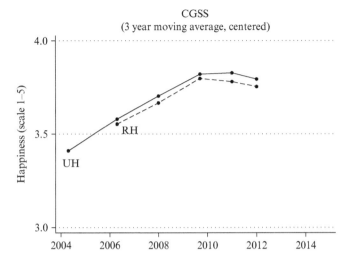

Notes: UH = Urban *hukou* holders in urban areas; RH = Rural *hukou* holders in urban areas.

Source: Online Appendix, Table A15 (see: https://www.e-elgar.com/textbooks/bruni).

Figure 8.15   Mean life satisfaction, urban and rural hukou *holders in urban areas, 2003–13*

satisfaction differential by socio-economic-status that prevailed in 1990 has been replaced by a considerably larger one, though there has been some lessening since the SWB trough of 2000–5.

The evidence on subjective well-being comes from four surveys conducted independently by three different survey organizations, and shows quite consistent results. Further support derives from the similarity between the course of SWB during China's transition and that in the European transition countries. The U-shaped pattern of SWB is a transition phenomenon common to both Europe and China.

To understand the course of well-being in China, one must recognize that few societies have undergone such wrenching change in such a short period of time. Isabelle Attané and Baochang Gu succinctly convey the essence of this transformation:

[T]he dismantling of collective structures under the reform and opening-up policy ... overturned the social organization that had prevailed in previous decades, producing an impact that extended far beyond the economy alone. Previously, each individual had depended on the state, through his or her work unit, for all aspects of daily life. Everyone enjoyed guaranteed access to employment, housing, health, education of children, and for urban dwellers, retirement and social insurance. Gradually transferred to the private sector, these areas are now governed by the market, which makes access to them less systematic, and therefore increasingly unequal.[57]

The data on life satisfaction herein provide a summary indication of the overall impact of this social transformation on people's lives. The circumstances through which SWB was most directly affected were labor market conditions and the social safety net. Briefly put, the dynamics of change are as follows. In the first part of the transition, as economic restructuring is undertaken, jobs and safety net benefits shrink markedly for the disadvantaged members of the population, and their well-being suffers severely, especially for those who are older or in the lowest economic stratum. In contrast, the life satisfaction of those who are in the highest economic stratum tends to improve slightly, while that of young adults, who are typically more educated and better able to cope with the new economic environment, remains fairly constant. The difference in life satisfaction by socio-economic status, which initially was quite small, widens substantially. Eventually, as economic recovery takes hold, the job market improves. In addition, the government, in response to symptoms of economic distress, starts to mend the social safety net. The result is that life satisfaction, on average, turns upward, and the disparity in life satisfaction between the more and less affluent shrinks somewhat. Life satisfaction of the disadvantaged, however, remains below its 1990 level.

The evidence supporting this interpretation is threefold. The first is quantitative time series on unemployment and the social safety net. These series move as one might expect in relation to SWB, in terms of both average levels and differences by SES. The second type of evidence is qualitative – descriptions by China specialists of the state of the economy and society, especially the job market and social protection. These qualitative accounts are consistent with the time series pattern in the quantitative data and contribute to its understanding. The third is the fact that the same factors explain the U-shaped trajectory of life satisfaction in the European transition countries.

Plausible causal variables other than GDP that fail the time series test of conformity to the SWB pattern are civic cooperation (one of the proxies for social capital), income inequality, environmental pollution, housing prices, life expectancy, freedom to control one's life, and corruption (as indexed by acceptance of bribery). Trust in others, another social capital proxy, is a borderline case, moving somewhat similarly to SWB, but less so than unemployment and the social safety net. The six predictors of differences in SWB in the *World Happiness Reports* do not explain the time series change in China's SWB.

The preeminence of employment and the safety net in explaining SWB lies in the evidence that it is these circumstances that bear most immediately on the personal concerns that are at the heart of people's personal happiness – jobs and income security, family life, and health. In the 1990s the emergence of massive unemployment and dissolution of the social safety net led to growing anxiety regarding these concerns, and a marked decline in overall life satisfaction. Since the 2000–5 trough, employment conditions and the social safety net have improved, and life satisfaction has returned to near its 1990 level. There remains, however, considerable opportunity for further progress. Of particular importance is attention to increasing the well-being of the disadvantaged segment of the population through improved employment opportunities and safety net policies.

Within policy circles, subjective well-being is receiving increasing attention as an alternative or complement to GDP as a measure of well-being.[58] There could hardly be a better test case than China for comparing the two measures. As indexed by GDP, well-being in China has multiplied over fivefold; based on SWB well-being is, on average, less than a quarter of a century ago. These disparate results reflect the different scope of the two measures. GDP relates to the economic aspect of life, and to just one dimension – the output of goods and services. SWB, in contrast, is a comprehensive measure of individual well-being, taking into account the variety of economic and noneconomic concerns and aspirations that principally determine people's well-being. There is no hint in GDP of the enormous structural changes that impacted people's lives in China. In contrast, SWB captures the increased anxiety and new concerns that emerged as a result of growing dependence on the labor market. If the objective of policy is to improve people's well-being, then SWB is a more meaningful measure than GDP, as China's experience attests.[59]

NOTES

1. This chapter is derived in part from an article published in Helliwell, J., R. Layard and J. Sachs (eds), (2017), *World Happiness Report 2017*, New York: Sustainable Development Solutions Network. The authors are grateful for the assistance of Kelsey J. O'Connor, and for the helpful comments of Jan-Emmanuel DeNeve, John Helliwell, John Knight, Matthew Kahn, and Kelsey J. O'Connor. Financial assistance was provided by the University of Southern California.
2. Knight and Song (2005), Xu (2011). Speaking of the period of policy reforms initiated in 1993, Cai et al. (2008, p.181) observe that 'a large amount of resources have been extracted from the agricultural and rural sector to support urban industrialization'.
3. Here and in subsequent figures vertical broken lines delimit the period when SWB

troughs. Also, in order to highlight the longer-term movement, a three-year moving average is plotted for series with annual data.

4. Data and sources for the graphs and numbers cited in the text are presented in the Online Appendix (see: https://www.e-elgar.com/textbooks/bruni).
5. Knight and Song (2005, p. 19).
6. Easterlin (2014).
7. Easterlin (2012).
8. Helliwell et al. (2012, p. 39).
9. Helliwell et al. (2016, p. 21).
10. Arrow and Dasgupta (2009), Deaton (2008), Diener et al. (2010), Frey and Stutzer (2002), Guriev and Zhuravskaya (2009), Inglehart (2002), Stevenson and Wolfers (2008), Veenhoven (1991).
11. Di Tella et al. (2001).
12. Easterlin (2009).
13. Fan et al. (2014, p. 10). See also Akay et al. (2012), Carlsson and Qin (2010), and Chen (2014).
14. For a good summary, see Knight and Gunatilaka (2011).
15. Stiglitz et al. (2008, p. 149). See also Helliwell and Huang (2014), Layard et al. (2012), and Sachs (2017).
16. See Cantril (1965), Easterlin (2013), and Radcliff (2013).
17. Feng et al. (2015), Gustafsson and Ding (2011), Knight and Xue (2006).
18. See Cai et al. (2008, p. 182), Naughton (2008, pp. 121–2), Huang (2014, p. 294).
19. Naughton (2008, p. 121).
20. Knight and Song (2005, p. 22).
21. Di Tella et al. (2001), Helliwell and Huang (2014).
22. Pew Research Center (2014).
23. Di Tella et al. (2003), O'Connor (2016), Pacek and Radcliff (2008), Radcliff (2013).
24. Naughton (2008, p. 121).
25. World Bank (2007). See Giles et al. (2006) for a comprehensive study of the impact of economic restructuring on urban workers.
26. OECD (2010), Gustafsson and Ding (2011).
27. Huang (2014, p. 294). Cf. also Huang (2008, pp. 169ff.).
28. Huang (2008, p. 273).
29. Helliwell et al. (2012, pp. 13ff., 2013, pp. 11ff., 2016, p. 17).
30. See Bartolini and Sarracino (2015). The authors include a third measure of social capital, social participation, which is measured as the percentage of the population reporting (1) membership in or (2) unpaid voluntary work for various associations. Unfortunately this measure is not comparable over time. The number of associations named in the WVS surveys varies between eight and 15, and the question on voluntary work is asked in only two surveys. As a result the total number of options presented to a respondent varies from lows of eight to 15 (in 1995, 2007, and 2012) to highs of 29 and 30 in 1990 and 2001. Not surprisingly the highest values for participation occur in the last two years, those with the largest number of respondent options.
31. Layard et al. (2012).
32. Xie and Zhou (2014); we are grateful to Professors Xie and Zhou for providing the data needed to reproduce the China series in Figure 1 of their paper. See also Cai et al. (2010), Gustafsson et al. (2008), Knight and Song (2000).
33. Zhang et al. (2015).
34. Wang and Zhou (2016).
35. Helliwell et al. (2016, p. 17).
36. Ibid., p. 16.
37. Ibid., p. 19.
38. Helliwell et al. (2013, pp. 15ff., table 2.2).
39. Cantril (1965, p. 162, table VIII: 6).
40. In this and subsequent figures depicting differences by SES based on WVS data, the

2001 WVS observations are omitted because the highest and lowest education groups were not covered in the 2001 survey. Due to this omission, SES differences in 2001 are much smaller than in the two adjacent surveys, 1995 and 2007. The mean value of SWB in 2001, however, does not seem to be affected by the omission of the highest and lowest education groups. If the highest and lowest education groups are dropped from the 1995 and 2007 surveys, one finds that the overall means in both surveys are virtually identical to those when the two education groups are included.

41. Graham et al. (2015) report an increase in mental illness from 2002 to 2012.
42. For a comprehensive overview of China's new social protection system see Cai and Du (2015); see also Fang (2014), Frazier (2014), and Ravallion (2014).
43. See CHIP surveys of 1988 and 2002.
44. Giles et al. (2006).
45. Cohort data on percentage completing college education are from CHIP surveys 1988, 2002, and 2013.
46. Easterlin (2012).
47. Easterlin (2009).
48. Demographic changes in China differed somewhat from Europe, primarily because China's 1990 situation was governed by public policies and traditional strictures regarding marriage, divorce, and childbearing. See Davis (2015) and Attané and Gu (2014).
49. Easterlin et al. (2011).
50. The 1995 WVS figures for mean life satisfaction are: places <5000 population, 6.52; places 5000+, 7.00. Unfortunately 1995 is the only WVS survey in which comprehensive size-of-place data are available.
51. The 2002 CHIP survey is noticeably different from all other surveys in that rural happiness (3.68 on a 1–5 scale) considerably exceeds urban (3.47). Unlike the 2013 CHIP survey, the 2002 survey contained a special rural module on SWB in which the question preceding that on happiness asked respondents with whom they compared themselves, offering eight options (Knight and Gunatilaka 2017, p. 20). This question elicited valuable information on reference groups, but probably tended to channel responses to the subsequent happiness question toward social comparison, precluding comparison with one's past experience. Neither the 2002 CHIP urban module nor the 2013 CHIP urban and rural modules had this reference group question before the question on happiness. In the 2013 CHIP survey, urban happiness exceeds rural by 0.14 points, a more typical result.
52. Anderson (2014, pp. 152–3). See also Cai et al. (2008, p. 181).
53. Henderson (2014).
54. See CGSS (2003), CHIP (2002), and Horizon (2003).
55. Surveys showing the persistence of the gap are the CGSS (2010–13), CFPS (2012), and CHIP (2013); those showing no gap are CFPS (2010) and (2014), and CHFS (2011).
56. See CGSS (2005–2013) and CFPS (2010–14).
57. Attané and Gu (2014, p. 3).
58. See OECD (2013) and Layard and O'Donnell (2015).
59. An objection to SWB sometimes voiced is that the SWB scale is bounded while GDP is not. In response one might note, first, that there is substantial agreement that international differences in self-reported SWB, such as those reported in the series of *World Happiness Reports*, are meaningful. The Nordic countries are invariably leaders in SWB with values in the neighborhood of 8 on scales with an upper limit of 10, while the lowest values are down around 3. This suggests that there is plenty of opportunity to improve the happiness of people worldwide even in the Nordic countries. Moreover, if well-being is the goal of public policy, then reaching a value of 10 with everyone 'completely satisfied' would seem to be a sign of remarkable policy success. By contrast, if GDP is the measure of well-being there is no clear mark of achievement other than an ever higher growth rate, which, as evidenced by China's experience, says little about what is really happening to people's lives.

REFERENCES

Akay, A., O. Bargain and K. Zimmermann (2012), Relative concerns of rural-to-urban migrants in China. *Journal of Economic Behavior & Organization*, 81, 421–41.

Anderson, K. (2014), China's evolving trade composition. In S. Fan, R. Kanbur, S-J. Wei and X. Zhang (eds) *The Oxford Companion to the Economics of China* (pp. 150–55). Oxford: Oxford University Press.

Arrow, K. J. and P. S. Dasgupta (2009), Conspicuous consumption, inconspicuous leisure. *The Economic Journal*, 119(541), F500–F513.

Attané, I. and B. Gu (eds) (2014), *Analysing China's Population: Social Change in a New Demographic Era*. New York: Springer.

Bartolini, S. and F. Sarracino (2015), The dark side of Chinese growth: declining social capital and well-being in times of economic boom. *World Development*, 74, 333–51.

Cai, F. and Y. Du (2015), The social protection system in ageing China. *Asian Economic Policy Review*, 10(2), 250–70.

Cai, F., A. Park and Y. H. Zhao (2008), The Chinese labor market in the reform era. In L. Brandt and T. G. Rawki (eds) *China's Great Economic Transition* (pp. 167–214). New York: Cambridge University Press.

Cai, H. B., Y. Y. Chen and L. A. Zhou (2010), Income and consumption inequality in urban China: 1992–2003. *Economic Development and Cultural Change*, 58(3), 385–413.

Cantril, H. (1965), *The Pattern of Human Concerns*. New Brunswick, NJ: Rutgers University Press.

Carlsson, F. and P. Qin (2010), It is better to be the head of a chicken than the tail of a phoenix: concerns for the relative standing in rural China. *Journal of Socio-Economics*, 39(2), 180–86.

Census of China (1990), 1% random sample. National Bureau of Statistics of China.

Census of China (2000), 0.1% random sample. National Bureau of Statistics of China.

Census of China (2000), Tabulation of the 2000 Population Census of the People's Republic of China. National Bureau of Statistics of China (2002), http://www.stats.gov.cn/tjsj/pcsj/rkpc/5rp/index.htm.

Census of China (2005), 20% random sample of the 1% National Population Sample Survey. National Bureau of Statistics of China.

Census of China (2010), Tabulation of the 2010 Population Census of the People's Republic of China. National Bureau of Statistics of China (2012), http://www.stats.gov.cn/tjsj/pcsj/rkpc/6rp/indexch.htm.

CFPS (2010–), Institute of Social Science Survey at Peking University, China Family Panel Studies, http://www.isss.edu.cn/cfps.

CGSS (2003–), National Survey Research Center at Renmin University of China, Chinese General Social Survey, http://www.chinagss.org/index.php?r=index/index&hl=en.

Chen, X. (2014), Relative deprivation in China. In S. Fan, R. Kanbur, S. J. Wei and X. Zhang (eds) *The Oxford Companion to the Economics of China* (pp. 406–10). Oxford and New York: Oxford University Press.

CHFS (2011–), Survey and Research Center for China Household Finance at

Southwestern University of Finance and Economics, China Household Finance Survey, http://www.chfsdata.org/chfs.html.

CHIP (1988–), China Institute for Income Distribution, China Household Income Project, http://www.ciidbnu.org/chip/index.asp.

Davis, D. R. (2015), *Continuity and Change in Mainland China's Recent Marital History*. PhD dissertation, University of California, Los Angeles.

Deaton, A. (2008), Income, health, and well-being around the world: evidence from the Gallup World Poll. *Journal of Economic Perspectives*, 22(2), 53–72.

Di Tella, R., R. J. MacCulloch and A. J. Oswald (2001), Preferences over inflation and unemployment: evidence from surveys of happiness. *American Economic Review*, 91(1), 335–41.

Di Tella, R., R. J. MacCulloch and A. J. Oswald (2003), The macro-economics of happiness. *Review of Economics and Statistics*, 85(4), 809–27.

Diener, E., W. Ng, J. Harter and R. Arora (2010), Wealth and happiness across the world: material prosperity predicts life evaluation, whereas psychosocial prosperity predicts positive feeling. *Journal of Personality and Social Psychology*, 99(1), 52–61.

Easterlin, R. A. (2009), Lost in transition: life satisfaction on the road to capitalism. *Journal of Economic Behavior and Organization*, 71(2), 130–45.

Easterlin, R. A. (2012), Life satisfaction of rich and poor under socialism and capitalism. *International Journal of Happiness and Development*, 1(1), 112–26.

Easterlin, R. A. (2013), Happiness, growth, and public policy. *Economic Inquiry*, 51(1), 1–15.

Easterlin, R. A. (2014), Life satisfaction in the transition from socialism to capitalism: Europe and China. In A. Clark and C. Senik (eds) *Happiness and Economic Growth: Lessons from Developing Countries* (pp. 6–31). Oxford: Oxford University Press.

Easterlin, R. A., L. Angelescu-McVey and J. S. Zweig (2011), The impact of modern economic growth on urban–rural differences in subjective well-being. *World Development*, 39(12), 2187–98.

Easterlin, R. A., R. Morgan, M. Switek and F. Wang (2012), China's life satisfaction, 1990–2010. *Proceedings of the National Academy of Sciences*, 109(25), 9775–80.

Fan, S., R. Kanbur, S.-J. Wei and X. Zhang (2014), Overview. The economics of China: success and challenges. In S. Fan, R. Kanbur, S.-J. Wei and X. Zhang (eds) *The Oxford Companion to the Economics of China* (pp. 1–27). Oxford and New York: Oxford University Press.

Fang, H. (2014), Insurance markets in China. In S. Fan, R. Kanbur, S.-J. Wei and X. Zhang (eds) *The Oxford Companion to the Economics of China* (pp. 279–84). Oxford and New York: Oxford University Press.

Feng, S., Y. Hu and R. Moffitt (2015), Long run trends in unemployment and labor force participation in China. Working Paper no. 21460, National Bureau of Economic Research.

Frazier, M. W. (2014), State schemes or safety nets? China's push for universal coverage. *Daedalus*, 143(2), 69–80.

Frey, B. S. and A. Stutzer (2002), *Happiness and Economics: How the Economy and Institutions Affect Well-being.* Princeton: Princeton University Press.

Giles, J., A. Park and F. Cai (2006), How has economic restructuring affected China's urban workers? *The China Quarterly*, 185, 61–95.

Graham, C., S. Zhou and J. Zhang (2015), Happiness and health in China: the paradox of progress. Global Economy & Development Working Paper 89.

Guriev, S. and E. Zhuravskaya (2009), (Un)happiness in transition. *Journal of Economic Perspectives*, 22(2), 143–68.

Gustafsson, B. and S. Ding (2011), Unemployment and the rising number of non-workers in urban China: causes and distributional consequences. In S. Li, H. Sato and T. Sicular (eds) *Rising Inequality in China: Challenge to a Harmonious Society* (pp. 289–331). New York: Cambridge University Press.

Gustafsson, B. A., S. Li and T. Sicular (2008), *Inequality and Public Policy in China*. New York: Cambridge University Press.

Helliwell, J. F. and H. Huang (2014), New measures on the costs of unemployment: evidence from the subjective well-being of 3.3 million Americans. *Economic Inquiry*, 52(4), 1485–1502.

Helliwell, J. F., R. Layard and J. Sachs (eds) (2012), *World Happiness Report 2012*. New York: Sustainable Development Solutions Network.

Helliwell, J. F., R. Layard and J. Sachs (eds) (2013), *World Happiness Report 2013*. New York: Sustainable Development Solutions Network.

Helliwell, J. F., R. Layard and J. Sachs (eds) (2016), *World Happiness Report 2016, Update*, vol. 1. New York: Sustainable Solutions Network.

Helliwell, J. F., R. Layard and J. Sachs (eds) (2017), *World Happiness Report 2017*. New York: Sustainable Development Solutions Network.

Henderson, J. V. (2014), Urbanization in China. In S. Fan, R. Kanbur, S.-J. Wei and X. Zhang (eds) *The Oxford Companion to the Economics of China* (pp. 225–9). Oxford and New York: Oxford University Press.

Horizon Research Consultancy Group (1997–2015), www.agmr.com/members/horizon.html.

Huang, Y. (2008), *Capitalism with Chinese Characteristics: Entrepreneurship and the State*. New York: Cambridge University Press.

Huang, Y. (2014), Political economy of privatization in China. In S. Fan, R. Kanbur, S.-J. Wei and X. Zhang (eds) *The Oxford Companion to the Economics of China* (pp. 291–5). Oxford and New York: Oxford University Press.

Inglehart, R. F. (2002), Globalization and postmodern values. *The Washington Quarterly*, 23(1), 215–28.

Inglehart, R., C. Haerpfer, A. Moreno, C. Welzel, K. Kizilova, J. Diez-Medrano, M. Lagos, P. Norris, E. Ponarin and B. Puranen et al. (eds.) (2014), *World Values Survey: All Rounds – Country-Pooled Datafile 1981–2014*. Madrid: JD Systems Institute.

Knight, J. and R. Gunatilaka (2011), Does economic growth raise happiness in China? *Oxford Development Studies*, 39(1), 1–24.

Knight, J. and R. Gunatilaka (2017), Is happiness infectious? *Scottish Journal of Political Economy*, 64(1), 1–24.

Knight, J. and L. Song (2000), *The Rural–Urban Divide: Economic Disparities and Interactions in China*. New York: Oxford University Press.

Knight, J. and L. Song (2005), *Towards a Labour Market in China*. New York: Oxford University Press.

Knight, J. and J. J. Xue (2006), How high is urban unemployment in China? *Journal of Chinese Economic and Business Studies*, 4, 91–107.

Layard, R., A. Clark and C. Senik (2012), The causes of happiness and misery. In J. Helliwell, R. Layard and J. Sachs (eds) *World Happiness Report 2012* (pp. 58–9). New York: The Earth Institute, Columbia University.

Layard, R. and G. O'Donnell (2015), How to make policy when happiness is the goal. In J. F. Helliwell, R. Layard and J. Sachs (eds) *World Happiness Report 2015* (pp. 76–87). New York: UN Sustainable Development Solutions Network.

National Bureau of Statistics of China (2013), *China Statistical Yearbook 2013*. Beijing: China Statistics Press.

National Bureau of Statistics of China (2016), Statistical communiqué of the People's Republic of China on the 2015 national economic and social development. Released on February 29, 2016. http://www.stats.gov.cn/english/PressRelea se/201602/t20160229_1324019.html.

Naughton, B. (2008), The demographic factor in China's transition. In L. Brandt and T. G. Rawki (eds) *China's Great Economic Transformation* (pp. 91–135). New York: Cambridge University Press.

O'Connor, K. J. (2016), Happiness and welfare state policy around the world. Working Paper, University of Southern California Department of Economics.

OECD (2010), *Economic Surveys: China*, vol. 2010/6. Paris: OECD Publishing.

OECD (2013), *OECD Guidelines for Measuring Subjective Well-being*. Paris: OECD Publishing.

Pacek, A. and B. Radcliff (2008), Assessing the welfare state. *Perspectives on Politics*, 6(2), 267–77.

Penn World Table (PWT) 9.0 (2016), Released on June 9, 2016. http://www.rug.nl/ research/ggdc/data/pwt/pwt-9.0.

Pew Research Center (2014), Spring 2014 Global Attitudes Survey. http://www. pewglobal.org/2014/06/05/spring-2014-survey-data/. Accessed July 2016.

Radcliff, B. (2013), *The Political Economy of Human Happiness: How Voters' Choices Determine the Quality of Life*. Cambridge: Cambridge University Press.

Ravallion, M. (2014), An emerging new form of social protection in 21st-century China. In S. Fan, R. Kanbur, S.-J. Wei and X. Zhang (eds) *The Oxford Companion to the Economics of China* (pp. 441–5). Oxford and New York: Oxford University Press.

Sachs, J. D. (2017), Restoring American happiness. World Happiness Report 2017, 178.

Stevenson, B. and J. Wolfers (2008), Economic growth and subjective well-being: reassessing the Easterlin paradox. *Brookings Papers on Economic Activity*, 39(1), 1–87.

Stiglitz, J. E., A. Sen and J. P. Fitoussi (2008), Report of the Commission on the Measurement of Economic Performance and Social Progress. www.stiglitz-sen-fitoussi.fr.

Veenhoven, R. (1991), Is happiness relative? *Social Indicators Research*, 24(1), 1–34.

Wang, S. and W. Zhou (2016), Family structure and home ownership: evidence from China. Working Paper, Korean Development Institute.

World Bank (2007), *China's Modernizing Labor Market: Trends and Emerging Challenges*. Washington, DC: World Bank.

Xie, Y. and X. Zhou (2014), Income inequality in today's China. *Proceedings of the National Academy of Sciences*, 111(19), 6928–33.

Xu, C. G. (2011), The fundamental institutions of China's reforms and development. *Journal of Economic Literature*, 49(4), 1076–151.

Zhang, X., X. Zhang and X. Chen (2015), Happiness in the air: how does dirty sky affect subjective well-being? IZA Discussion Papers 9312.

9. Economic growth and well-being beyond the Easterlin paradox

Francesco Sarracino and Kelsey J. O'Connor

9.1 INTRODUCTION

The finding of no long-run relationship between economic growth and subjective well-being is controversial. This result, contrasting a positive cross-sectional relation, came to be known as the Easterlin paradox (Easterlin, 1974). Since then, many scholars have contributed with diverging views. There are those who oppose (see e.g. Easterlin et al., 2010; Bruni and Stanca, 2008; Easterlin and Angelescu, 2009; Becchetti et al., 2011; Clark et al., 2014; Easterlin, 2017) and those who support (see e.g. Stevenson and Wolfers, 2008; Deaton, 2008; Sacks et al., 2012; Veenhoven and Vergunst, 2013) economic growth as a way to improve well-being. Beyond whether or not growth accompanies increasing well-being, some recent evidence suggests that the relation depends on social, political, economic, cultural and institutional conditions: if economic growth is compatible with a cohesive and inclusive society, it is reasonable to expect that well-being will improve (Oishi and Kesebir, 2015; Mikucka et al., 2017; Easterlin, 2013; Ono and Lee, 2013). In contrast, if economic growth leads to loneliness and inequality, well-being may arguably decline.

Although the quest for conditions of 'inclusive growth' – growth that benefits all the members of a society – is still in its infancy, past evidence provides a preliminary explanation of how and when a positive correlation between economic growth and well-being can exist over time. This is important because it suggests ways to promote well-being. Our aim is to distil the evidence on the conditions affecting the economic growth–well-being gradient to explain the flat trend of life satisfaction in Luxembourg.

We focus on Luxembourg as an example of the lack of correlation between economic growth and well-being in the long run. Panel a in Figure 9.1 shows that since the early 1980s Luxembourg experienced substantial economic growth, at least until the economic crisis of 2008. Yet the share of very satisfied people did not change substantially over time.[1] The economic crisis may explain what happened after 2008, but prior to 2008 it is

(a) Life satisfaction (EB data) and real GNI per capita (World Development Indicators).

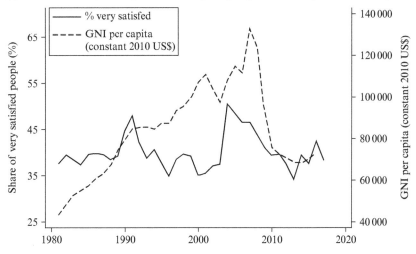

(b) Life satisfaction in Luxembourg. For the years when three different datasets are jointly available, they provide comparable information.

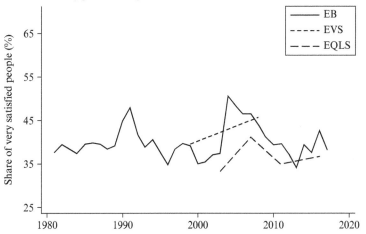

Note: The samples consist only of native-born individuals. We restrict our analysis on natives only to ensure the comparability of data on life satisfaction over time. EB data collected before 1994 provided data on nationals only, and after 1994 they included information on immigrants from other European countries. We discuss this issue in more detail in Section 9.4.

Source: EB, EVS, EQLS, and World Development Indicators, own elaboration.

Figure 9.1   Share of very satisfied people (panel A) and real GNI per capita (panel B) in Luxembourg in the period 1981–2015

not clear why economic growth did not improve people's well-being (from a traditional economics perspective).

A possible explanation is that life satisfaction is an unreliable measure. Yet we have reasons to believe that life satisfaction is reliable based on the available data and previous literature. Panel b reports the share of very satisfied people according to Eurobarometer (EB), the European Values Study (EVS) and the European Quality of Life Survey (EQLS). For the years when the data are jointly available the three surveys provide a remarkably similar picture. Moreover, a well-established literature provides evidence supporting the reliability and validity of life satisfaction as a measure of both subjective and objective well-being (Blanchflower and Oswald, 2004; Van Reekum et al., 2007; Schimmack et al., 2010; Kahneman and Krueger, 2006; Layard, 2005).

Another possible explanation is that the trends of life satisfaction are always flat – at least among the richest and most developed countries in the world. However, the evidence does not support this view. Figure 9.2 shows the trends of the share of very satisfied people in Belgium, France, Germany and the Netherlands (i.e. a set of Western European countries which are close to Luxembourg). The picture shows that the trends of

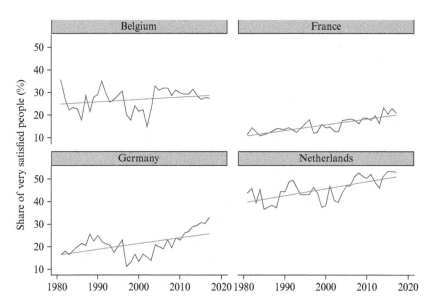

Source: EB, own elaboration.

Figure 9.2   Trends of the share of very satisfied people in a sample of Western European countries

life satisfaction are not always flat: although average levels may differ, the trends in France and the Netherlands are monotonically positive, whereas the trend is rather flat in Belgium and follows a 'J' curve in Germany. This is consistent with previous studies (Sarracino, 2012).

In sum, the flat trend of life satisfaction in Luxembourg does not have a simple explanation. We posit that economic growth and life satisfaction did not go together because four factors acted in opposite directions for well-being, namely increasing social capital and social expenditures (which are expected to have a positive impact on well-being) and increasing income inequality and unemployment (which, on the other hand, could have a negative impact).

Unfortunately we do not have micro data providing long time series for Luxembourg: the EVS includes individual data collected in 1999 and 2008, the European Social Survey was administered in 2002 and 2004, and the EQLS has provided data every four years since 2003. Thus, we adopt a macroeconomic perspective. Specifically, we apply an error correction model (ECM) to a panel of 15 Western European countries to explain country-year levels of life satisfaction using the set of potential explanatory factors identified in previous literature. The results are then used to predict life satisfaction and to assess whether and to what extent the explanatory factors explain the trend of life satisfaction in Luxembourg.

We build our argument in two steps: in Section 9.2 we review the literature on the Easterlin paradox and on the factors moderating the relationship between economic growth and well-being. Subsequently, we detail our econometric approach (Section 9.3) and the dataset used for the analysis (Section 9.4). Section 9.5 illustrates the results of the model, which we use to predict and explain the trend of life satisfaction in Luxembourg. Section 9.6 concludes.

9.2   THE EASTERLIN PARADOX AND MODERATING FACTORS

The debate on subjective well-being gained special attention in part because it concerns an important question: to what extent do modern societies benefit from economic growth? For years this question has divided social scientists among: those who claim that contemporary societies should not expect significant improvements in subjective well-being from economic growth (Easterlin, 1974); those who argue that economic growth and increasing subjective well-being are associated over time (see e.g. Stevenson and Wolfers, 2008; Deaton, 2008; Sacks et al., 2012; Veenhoven and Vergunst, 2013); those who point out that whether a relationship exists depends on the set of countries considered (developed and developing countries vs transition countries) or the period of time, that is, economic growth and the trends of well-being correlate in the short run but such correlation disappears in the long run (Easterlin and Angelescu, 2009; Becchetti et al., 2011; Easterlin et al., 2010; Clark et al., 2014; De Neve et al., 2018; Bartolini and Sarracino, 2014); and those who claim that even if the trends of subjective well-being and economic growth are statistically related, the magnitude is too small for growth to have a meaningful impact (Beja, 2014). Recently some scholars have argued that the question is not *whether* but *when* – under what conditions – economic growth correlates with increasing subjective well-being (Oishi and Kesebir, 2015; Mikucka et al., 2017). The literature identified three factors which plausibly affect the relation between economic growth and well-being over time: income inequality (Oishi and Kesebir, 2015; Mikucka et al., 2017), social capital (Uhlaner, 1989; Helliwell, 2003, 2008; Bartolini et al., 2013; Clark et al., 2014), and social policy (Easterlin, 2013; Ono and Lee, 2016).

Concerning income inequality, the evidence about the cross-sectional relationship with well-being is mixed (e.g. Alesina et al., 2004; Clark and D'Ambrosio, 2015). These contradictions may arise because the relationship between inequality and well-being depends on a country's level of development (Jiang et al., 2012; Iniguez-Montiel, 2014). However, previous studies found that *increasing* income inequality is consistently negatively related to well-being (Bartolini and Sarracino, 2015; Oishi and Kesebir, 2015; Mikucka et al., 2017). By widening the possibilities to establish social comparisons, growing income inequality undermines the positive effect of income growth for well-being. Raising income inequality can also undermine well-being by reducing feelings of fairness and trust in others (Oishi et al., 2011) or by weakening social linkages and feelings of cooperation (Graham and Felton, 2006; Oishi et al., 2011).

Social capital is defined by the Organisation for Economic Co-operation and Development (OECD, 2001, p. 41) as 'networks together with shared norms, values and understandings that facilitate co-operation within or among groups'. A well-established literature shows that social capital correlates positively with subjective well-being at both the individual (Helliwell et al., 2017; Clark et al., 2014; Becchetti et al., 2009) and aggregate level, over time within countries (Bartolini et al., 2013; Bartolini and Sarracino, 2015; Brockmann et al., 2009; Easterlin et al., 2012) and in country panels (Bartolini and Sarracino, 2014). Helliwell and Aknin (2018) discuss in detail the relationship between social capital and subjective well-being.

The experience of countries that transitioned from communist economic systems illustrates the importance of social safety nets for well-being (Ono and Lee, 2013). Survey data consistently indicate that people in European post-communist countries are among the least satisfied people in Europe. Moreover, after the transition average life satisfaction declined. The loss of jobs and the deterioration of safety nets are among the causes that explain this decline. The communist regime provided people with jobs, basic income, health insurance, education and other benefits. The transition to market capitalism was accompanied by widespread corruption and the collapse of the social insurance system, which invariably led to greater inequality and lower well-being. In recent years life satisfaction has recovered, but it took more than ten years and required an increase in gross domestic product (GDP) per capita averaging about 25 per cent above the 1990s value (Easterlin, 2009, p. 142).[2]

In China life satisfaction exhibited a similar pattern of collapse and recovery following the transition, all the while growing at an average annual rate of more than 9 per cent. Brockmann et al. (2009), Easterlin et al. (2012), Easterlin et al. (2017) and Bartolini and Sarracino (2015) discuss possible explanations for these startling facts. Each work partially attributes the decline in life satisfaction to increased social comparisons, especially facilitated by rising income inequality. Bartolini and Sarracino (2015) document the importance of social capital, estimating that nearly 19.0 per cent of the well-being loss in China is related to a decrease in social capital. Easterlin et al. (2012) and Easterlin et al. (2017) instead emphasize the role of rising unemployment,[3] which was inversely related to life satisfaction over the full cycle from 1990 to 2010 (while inequality, in contrast, rose throughout the period). And, like in the European transition countries, with unemployment came not only income losses but the elimination of social benefits. The loss of these benefits arguably significantly exacerbated the effects of unemployment. Social safety nets are positively related to life satisfaction in general (Di Tella et al., 2003; Rothstein, 2010; Pacek and Radcliff, 2008; Boarini et al., 2013; Easterlin, 2013; Ono and Lee, 2016; O'Connor, 2017), not just in transition economies, and the association is not limited to those directly affected (e.g. the unemployed) (Carr and Chung, 2014). In sum, the decline in Chinese well-being can be explained by (1) increasing income inequality which facilitated increasing social comparisons, (2) declining social capital and (3) increasing unemployment accompanied by a severely reduced social safety net. The recent recovery appears to be driven by improvements in trust, employment and the social safety net (Easterlin et al., 2017).

Previous studies investigating the Easterlin paradox and its moderating factors focused mainly on cross-country studies or on countries providing 'negative' examples, that is, countries in which economic growth and

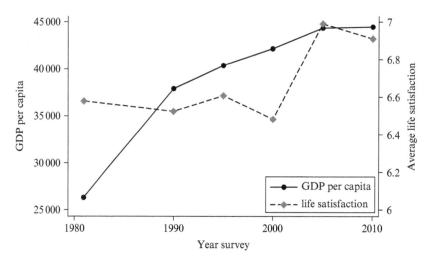

Note: Life satisfaction data are from the WVS, whereas GDP figures, presented in real dollars with base year set to 2010, are issued from the World Development Indicators of the World Bank. The trends in life satisfaction from WVS are roughly consistent with those issued from other sources.

Source: Sarracino et al. (2019).

Figure 9.3   *Trends of life satisfaction and GDP per capita (constant 2010 US$) in Japan between 1981 and 2010*

increasing well-being do not go together. The case of Japan stands out as a 'positive' example: a country where economic reforms in the early 1990s shifted the country from a pattern of rampant economic growth and stagnant well-being to one of moderate growth and increasing well-being (see Figure 9.3). The question then becomes: what made this change possible?

By the end of the 1980s Japan was in the middle of two crises: on one side, the demographic crisis; on the other, the decline in the viability of the traditional and corporate social safety net. Greater urbanization and industrialization, along with economic stagnation and international competition, put pressure on the scheme of social safety nets which traditionally relied on intergenerational support and on generous benefits for the employees of large corporations. For instance, the share of three-generation households went from 54 per cent in 1975 to 13 per cent in 2013 (Ministry of Health, Labour and Welfare, 2014), whereas the share of elderly people living alone nearly doubled. At the same time economic conditions forced companies to limit the benefits granted to their employees, and in particular to newly hired personnel. Moreover,

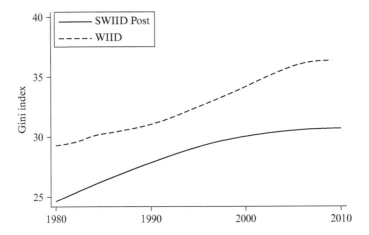

Note: Lowess smoothed curves. The two lines in the chart refer to measures of Gini issued from two different sources of data: the SWIID and the WIID. Together the two series of data provide consistent evidence that income inequality in Japan increased since 1980.

Source: Solt (2016) and UNU-WIDER (2018).

Figure 9.4   Evolution of the Gini index of income in Japan

the likelihood of lifetime employment declined (Ono, 2010). The share of workers in nonstandard employment more than doubled from 15 to 38 per cent between 1984 and 2016 (Ministry of Health, Labour and Welfare, 2014). Consequently, the population in need of social protection greatly expanded during the 1990s, as did income inequality (see Figure 9.4).

To face these challenges the government introduced a state-sponsored social support system to share social risk equitably across society (Horioka and Kanda, 2010). A number of policies targeting elderly people, as well as work–family policies were introduced in the mid-1990s with the aim of improving the living and health conditions of elderly people, alleviating the costs of having children and facilitating women's access to the job market. Figure 9.5 shows the trend of welfare state generosity in Japan (Scruggs et al., 2017).

In the years following the policy reforms that introduced a state-sponsored social safety net in Japan, people's satisfaction with life increased, and in particular the satisfaction of people in the targeted groups. By 2010 aging was associated less negatively to life satisfaction than in 1990, that is, before the introduction of the reforms; average health improved; trust in others and social participation of elderly people nearly doubled; single people reported higher life satisfaction than previously. All this happened

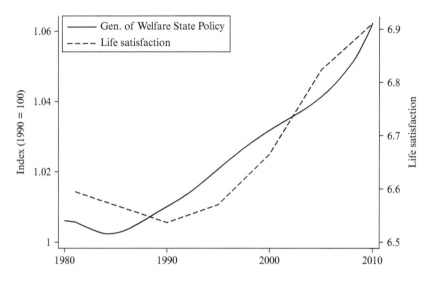

Note: Lowess smoothed curves.

Source: Sarracino et al. (2019).

Figure 9.5　Average life satisfaction and generosity of welfare state in Japan, 1981–2010

while the economy grew, although at a lower pace compared to the previous period.

9.2.1　Our Contribution

Available studies indicate that: (1) social capital, social safety nets and income inequality affect the relationship between economic growth and well-being over time; (2) policy-makers can adopt policies to promote well-being in the long run. Our aim is to assess whether the factors discussed above can help explain the flat trend of life satisfaction in Luxembourg. This test is important to evaluate the reliability of available knowledge about the conditions to promote well-being in the long run, and to identify possible areas of intervention for policy-makers. Additionally, in this chapter we extend the list of moderating conditions to include unemployment. It is well established that unemployment is one of the major causes of ill-being. Thus, it is possible that the changes in unemployment contribute to explaining the trend of life satisfaction.

9.3 METHOD

We use an ECM to analyse the factors that contribute to life satisfaction in the long run. The main reason is that ECMs allows us to estimate consistent long-run relations between the explanatory variables and dependent variable. Additional reasons are more technical. First, explanatory variables in levels (e.g. GDP per capita) often exhibit unit root properties, which could lead to the estimation of spurious relations (Engle and Granger, 1987). First-differencing the variables can be used to address such spurious relations, but first-differencing limits the interpretation of the results to short-run changes. ECMs separately estimate the short- and long-run relations to avoid spurious relations (under certain conditions discussed below). Also, the estimated long-run relations, referred to as long-run effects in the time series literature, are consistent in the presence of short-run reverse causality (Chudik and Pesaran, 2015; Pesaran, 2015).

Before presenting the ECM we begin with our assumed data-generating process, represented by Equation 9.1. LS_{it} represents life satisfaction for country i at time t, the vector $X_{i,t}$ includes the explanatory variables, and fixed country characteristics are represented by μ_i.

$$LS_{it} = \rho_i \cdot LS_{i,t-1} + \beta'_{i0} \cdot X_{i,t} + \beta'_{i1} \cdot X_{i,t-1} + \mu_i + \varepsilon_{it} \qquad (9.1)$$

The error correction form is the reparameterization of Equation 9.1 given by Equation 9.2.

$$\Delta LS_{it} = \Phi_i \cdot (LS_{i,t-1} - \theta'_i \cdot X_{i,t}) + \gamma'_i \cdot \Delta X_{i,t-1} + \mu_i + \varepsilon_{it} \qquad (9.2)$$

where $\Phi_i = (\rho_i - 1)$; $\theta'_i = (\beta'_{i0} + \beta'_{i1}) / (1 - \rho_i)$ and $\gamma' = -\beta'_{i1}$

The short-run relations are captured by γ and the long-run effects by θ. With a large change in $X_{i,t}$, the response in the $LS_{i,t}$ might overshoot the long-run equilibrium relationship. When this happens, the error correction term, Φ, serves to bring the relationship back to the long-run one.

For an error correction parameterization to be appropriate, (1) the error correction term should be statistically significant, negative, but greater than negative two, and (2) there must be a long-run cointegrating relationship between the level variables. Condition 2 is necessary for the term $(LS_{i,t-1} - \theta'_i \cdot X_{i,t})$ to be stationary, which is necessary for the error term to be stationary when Φ is statistically significant. Condition 1 is tested directly in the regression analysis. To check condition 2 we test the regression residuals for stationarity using panel unit root tests (Fisher-type augmented Dickey Fuller tests). The results indicate that the residuals are indeed stationary and condition 2 is met.

We adjust Equation 9.2 to develop our final specification (presented below). Notice the coefficients are indexed by i in Equation 9.2, indicating that they are allowed to vary across countries. We allow the short-run relations to be heterogeneous in order to capture flexibly any reverse causality. However, in our final specification we assume the long-run effects (θ) are common across countries. Without this assumption we could not simultaneously assess each of the factors discussed in Section 9.2 that may explain the trend of life satisfaction in Luxembourg. This specification is referred to as a pooled mean group model (PMG).

In our final specification we address two further issues: cross-sectional dependence and lag order for serial correlation. Cross-sectional dependence occurs when there is omitted correlation across countries. A commonly correlated effect, such as the impact of European Union policies, can be a source of cross-sectional dependence. To address cross-sectional dependence we add to Equation 9.2 cross-sectional means of both the dependent and independent variables (as suggested by Chudik and Pesaran, 2015). This approach is similar to adding year dummies, but has some advantages: adding year dummies greatly increases the number of controls, and cross-sectional means allow the commonly correlated effect to affect each country through multiple channels and to different degrees according to their different variable values. Cross-sectional means are also included among short-run variables in the PMG model, meaning their coefficients vary across countries. Concerning lags, we chose one lag in levels (as specified in Equation 9.1) because the full model did not converge when using additional lags. However, we ran regressions using one explanatory variable at a time including up to six lags (in levels). Generally the long-run effects maintain significance and direction and the magnitudes are larger when including additional lags, suggesting our estimates represent lower bounds. The exception is for social expenditures, which is insignificant (presented with the results).

Our final specification is presented as Equation 9.3.

$$\Delta LS_{it} = \Phi_i \cdot (LS_{i,t-1} - \theta' \cdot X_{i,t}) + \gamma'_i \cdot \Delta X_{i,t-1} + \varphi_i \overline{LS}_t + \delta_i \overline{X}_t + \mu_i + \varepsilon_{it}$$

(9.3)

9.4   DATA

Individual life satisfaction data are from repeated cross-sectional EB surveys (European Commission, 2018). Life satisfaction is measured on a scale from 1 to 4 using the responses to the question: 'On the whole, are you very satisfied, fairly satisfied, not very satisfied or not at all satisfied with the life you lead?' This question was first asked in 1973 in seven countries and continues today for more than the present 28 EU countries. In each year multiple surveys are conducted that ask about life satisfaction. Annual observations of life satisfaction were constructed in each country as the weighted proportion of native-born individuals reporting the top response category, 'very satisfied'. Foreign-born individuals were necessarily excluded, because prior to 1994, the EB target population only included native-born individuals, and in 1994 the target population expanded but still excluded individuals born in non-EU countries (Schmitt et al., 2009, p. 56).

The explanatory variables include the natural log of real gross national income (GNI) per capita, unemployment rate, the Gini coefficient of income, social expenditures and trust in others. GNI and unemployment data (national estimate) are from the World Development Indicators (WDI) (World Bank, 2018). We use the Gini coefficient of inequality in equivalent household disposable (post-tax, post-transfer) income from the Standardized World Income Inequality Database (SWIID) (Solt, 2016).[4]

Data for social expenditures per capita are available every five years from 1980–2015 and 2016 from the OECD Social Expenditures Database (OECD, 2019). The variable includes all public social expenditures on active labour market programmes, family, health, housing, incapacity, old age, other social policy areas, survivors and unemployment. We adjusted the variable to more closely represent the generosity of the welfare state policy. Conceptually subjective well-being relates to the generosity of policies not to expenditures; that is because social expenditures increase mechanically when people retire or when unemployment increases. Indeed O'Connor (2017) finds that social expenditures relate to subjective well-being, but the relation becomes statistically insignificant when excluding a control for the old age dependency ratio. In the present analysis we could also include the old age dependency ratio, but given the small number of degrees of freedom we chose instead to separate out the effects of the old age dependency ratio and unemployment rate on social expenditures. Specifically, we used the residuals from a regression of social expenditures on the old age dependency ratio and unemployment rate. We then linearly interpolate the residuals to facilitate annual analysis.

Trust in others is based on responses to the question: 'Generally speaking, would you say that most people can be trusted, or that you could not be too careful in dealing with people?' Individual responses are obtained from EB surveys in the years 1986, 2004, 2009, 2010 and 2014. These responses are then aggregated at the country level for each year as the portion of people feeling most people can be trusted. However, comparison over time is limited by differences in the response scales. The largest change occurred beginning in 2009, when the scale went from two discrete choices to a scale ranging from 1 to 10. In order to produce annual estimates and account for the change in scale, we impute trust through the following steps:

1. The weighted percentage of people stating most people can be trusted is calculated by country year. For the years 2009, 2010 and 2014 responses 7–10 are recorded as most people can be trusted.
2. These scores are de-meaned by subtracting the average level of trust within a country over the years 1986 and 2004 (the years based on the previous response scale).
3. The de-meaned trust values are then linearly interpolated and extrapolated over the sample period with an exception – trust is not extrapolated to the years before 2004 if it is unobserved in 1986.
4. Additional data from the World Values Survey (WVS, 2014) and EVS (EVS, 2011) is used to provide additional information on trust. The two surveys provide dichotomous answers to a question asking respondents whether people can be trusted. As in step 1, the answers are de-meaned (within country) and extrapolated.
5. To remove the effect of the change in scale that occurred from 2004 to 2009, EB trust from step 3 is regressed on EVS/WVS trust from step 4, a dummy variable demarking the period post-2004, a quadratic trend and interactions between EVS/WVS trust and both the dummy and trend. Trust is predicted after excluding the impact from the interaction between post-2004 and EVS/WVS trust.
6. The country means from step 2 were added back to obtain our final prediction of trust.

Our sample of countries includes the first 15 European Union member states (EU15) because only these countries have suitably long enough series to be included. The period of analysis includes the years 1991–2016. Our sample for regression analysis begins in 1991 to ensure there were at least ten countries observed in each year. Prior to 1991 data for fewer countries were available when including lags. It is important to use as many countries as possible because the analysis includes cross-sectional means in each period. We would prefer to begin the sample with more than ten countries, but data for all 15 countries are not available until 1995, and with lags that would significantly reduce the time dimension. Table 9.1 presents the sample characteristics and average variable values for each country.

Table 9.1 Descriptive statistics

Country	First year	Last year	Life satisfaction (% very happy)	GNI ln(US$ per capita)	Gini index (0–100)	Unemployment rate (%)	Trust (% can be trusted)	Adj. social expenditures ln(US$ per capita)
Austria	2001	2016	23.95	10.74	27.58	5.10	47.78	0.42
Belgium	1991	2016	27.35	10.62	25.75	7.99	35.10	0.16
Denmark	1991	2016	65.82	10.92	23.85	6.16	78.45	0.51
Finland	2001	2016	33.11	10.73	25.37	8.63	70.02	0.27
France	1991	2015	15.90	10.57	28.69	9.83	29.14	0.15
Germany	1991	2015	17.85	10.57	27.38	7.86	45.06	0.13
Greece	1991	2016	8.29	10.07	33.58	12.98	37.04	−0.67
Ireland	1991	2016	36.02	10.51	31.13	9.48	37.67	−0.22
Italy	1991	2015	11.41	10.45	32.99	9.83	30.93	−0.07
Luxembourg	1991	2015	43.39	11.25	26.67	3.80	35.68	0.89
Netherlands	1991	2016	47.47	10.73	26.14	4.96	64.32	0.17
Portugal	1992	2015	4.01	9.93	34.03	8.03	31.60	−0.73
Spain	1992	2016	18.17	10.24	32.93	17.38	35.53	−0.44
Sweden	2001	2016	46.83	10.86	25.20	6.77	71.07	0.40
United Kingdom	1991	2016	35.30	10.49	33.83	6.74	44.17	−0.24
Sample average			28.76	10.57	29.22	8.48	45.06	0.02

9.5   RESULTS

Simple descriptive statistics suggest that income inequality, unemployment, social trust and social expenditures increased in Luxembourg from the early 1980s. Panel a in Figure 9.6 shows that income inequality increased by about 5 points, from 23.9 to 28.7, between 1985 and 2015. Similarly, Panel b indicates that unemployment as a percentage of the total labour force was 0.7 per cent in 1980 and 6.7 per cent in 2015, a nearly ninefold increase in 35 years. According to the previous literature we should expect that such increases hindered life satisfaction, probably overcoming the positive contribution of economic growth expected from traditional economic theory.

The increases in social trust and social expenditures, on the other hand, are expected to have positively contributed to life satisfaction. Since 1980 the share of people who feel that others can be trusted nearly doubled (see panel a in Figure 9.7), whereas social expenditures rose from US$8190 per capita (base year 2013) in 1980 to US$23 880 in 2015, that is, a nearly threefold increase (panel b). It is possible that the effects on life satisfaction of increasing income inequality and unemployment, on one side, and increasing social trust and expenditures, on the other, offset each other. To test this hypothesis formally we turn to the results of the ECM.

Table 9.2 presents the results of the ECM. The first five rows present the long-run relations corresponding to the θ in Equation 9.3; ECT corresponds to the error correction term Φ; the middle rows present the short-run-change relations corresponding to the γs, and the final rows the cross-sectional means of life satisfaction and the independent variables in levels. The first five columns use one explanatory variable at a time, column 6 reports the results from the model including each explanatory variable, and column 7 lists the standardized coefficients of the long-run effects from the full model.

The long-run effects generally correspond with our expectations, with the exception of the Gini coefficient, which is statistically significant and positive. Permanent increases in GNI per capita, income inequality, social trust and adjusted social expenditures are positively related to life satisfaction in the long run, and unemployment negatively.[5] The long-run effects are generally consistent between the reduced models (columns 1–5) and the full model (column 6). The magnitudes and significance of GNI per capita and social expenditures are reduced. Indeed, social expenditures are no longer statistically significant. This finding is surprising in light of the positive relations found in cross-sectional evidence; however, insignificance could be due to multicollinearity and low statistical power (recall adjusted social expenditures are positive and significant in column 5). The

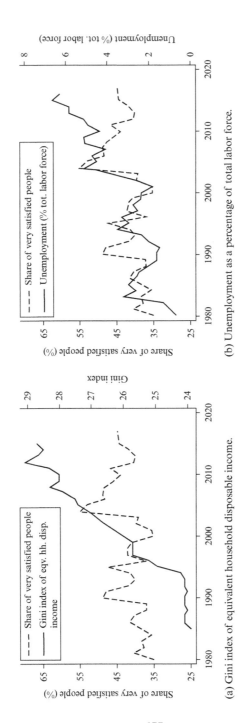

(a) Gini index of equivalent household disposable income.

(b) Unemployment as a percentage of total labor force.

Source: Authors' own elaboration.

Figure 9.6   Increasing income inequality (panel a) and unemployment (panel b) in Luxembourg

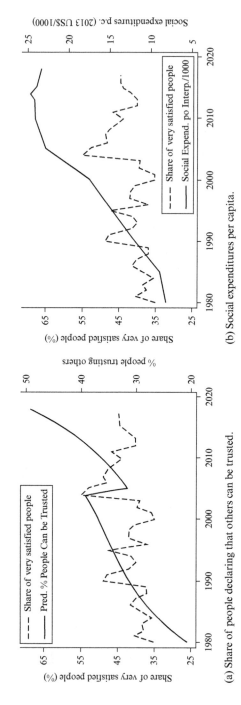

(a) Share of people declaring that others can be trusted.

(b) Social expenditures per capita.

Source: Authors' own elaboration.

Figure 9.7 Increasing social trust (panel a) and social expenditures (panel b) in Luxembourg

178

Table 9.2   Results from the ECM applied to the panel of 15 Western European countries, 1991–2016

| | | | Δ Life satisfaction | | | | |
	(1)	(2)	(3)	(4)	(5)	(6)	(7)
							Standardized
Long-run effects							
GNI	38.274***					10.648*	0.259*
	(3.990)					(6.004)	(6.004)
Gini		0.526**				0.734***	0.190***
		(0.249)				(0.231)	(0.231)
Unemployment rate			−0.437***			−0.572***	−0.181***
			(0.058)			(0.134)	(0.134)
Trust in others				0.175**		0.494***	0.570***
				(0.082)		(0.046)	(0.046)
Social expenditures					19.689***	0.695	0.023
					(3.449)	(3.101)	(3.101)
Coefficients							
ECT	−0.745***	−0.741***	−0.693***	−0.610***	−0.770***	−1.036***	
	(0.049)	(0.062)	(0.061)	(0.075)	(0.043)	(0.090)	
Δ GNI	−6.238					8.324	
	(9.132)					(12.123)	
Δ Gini		−0.424				0.441	
		(0.538)				(1.183)	
Δ Unemployment rate			0.085			0.202	
			(0.212)			(0.309)	
Δ Trust in others				0.162***		−0.170	
				(0.060)		(0.171)	
Δ Social expenditures					5.943	−15.673	
					(16.668)	(28.448)	

Table 9.2 (continued)

	Δ Life satisfaction						
	(1)	(2)	(3)	(4)	(5)	(6)	(7)
Mean life satisfaction	0.955***	0.869***	0.860***	0.868***	0.926***	0.984***	
	(0.139)	(0.140)	(0.137)	(0.149)	(0.123)	(0.169)	
Mean GNI	−30.443***					−27.442*	
	(5.410)					(16.434)	
Mean Gini		−0.475				−2.541***	
		(0.923)				(0.877)	
Mean unemployment rate			0.352***			0.319	
			(0.131)			(0.291)	
Mean trust in others				−0.118		−0.399*	
				(0.124)		(0.232)	
Mean social expenditures					−15.231***	15.418	
					(4.621)	(11.047)	
Constant	14.287	−2.074	−5.714**	−5.191	−5.112	222.303	
	(63.727)	(25.398)	(2.846)	(6.063)	(3.342)	(173.954)	
N	353	353	353	353	353	353	

Notes: Long-run effects correspond to θ in Equation 9.3 and ECT corresponds with the mean of estimated Φ_i (over all sample countries). Other coefficients represent the means of estimated of γ_s, φ_s, and δ_s in Equation 9.3. GNI is per capita and transformed in natural logarithms. Social expenditures are per capita, adjusted and transformed in natural logarithms. Trust is partially imputed. For more details, please refer to Section 9.4. Standard errors in parentheses. * p < 0.10, ** p < 0.05, *** p < 0.01

magnitudes of the other variables (Gini, unemployment rate and trust) increase in size. Across variables trust has the largest standardized coefficient. The coefficient of trust in others is more than twice as large as the one for GNI and nearly three times larger than the one for inequality or unemployment (in absolute terms). This indicates that trust in others is the strongest correlate of the changes of life satisfaction in the long run among the considered variables. The magnitude, however, is small: a one standard deviation difference in trust is related to 0.6 percentage point greater life satisfaction. The standard deviation of life satisfaction over the full sample is 17.5 percentage points.

It is surprising that the Gini coefficient is positively related to life satisfaction; however, as mentioned in the literature section, positive relations have been obtained in cross-sectional studies. The Hirschman tunnel effect could explain the relation – increasing the income of a few, leading to greater inequality – may signal that the incomes of everyone are increasing, thereby raising subjective well-being. Future research should focus further on inequality and revaluate it in a time series context.

Part of the overall trend in life satisfaction is captured by the cross-sectional means. As controls their coefficients should not be interpreted as if they provide economic meaning, especially because the means are calculated on a small number of countries. Additionally, the coefficients on means do not apply in a *ceteris paribus* manner. For clarity, we provide an example calculation using GNI. To calculate the relation of long-run GNI growth in all countries, the long-run effect of GNI should be added to the long-run relation for mean GNI. The latter needs to be calculated because although the table displays the long-run effects of GNI (in an individual country), the raw coefficients are displayed for the cross-sectional means. The long-run relation for mean GNI is calculated as the negative of the coefficient divided by the ECT, that is, for column 6: $-\delta/\Phi = -1 * -27.44/(-1.04) = -26.49$. Thus, based on the estimates in column 6, GNI growth in all countries is associated with a decrease in life satisfaction, that is, $10.65 - 26.49 = -15.84$. As an example, 3 per cent growth is associated with a decrease in life satisfaction of 0.48 percentage points per year ($-0.48 = 0.03 * -15.84$). This suggests that GNI positively affects life satisfaction in a particular country only if it grows at a greater rate than in the other countries: to break even, the GNI change in a country needs to be $26.49/10.65 = 2.49$ times the average change across countries. For mean life satisfaction, the long-run relation is $-1 * 0.98/-1.04 = 0.95$, but like the other cross-sectional means, economic meaning should not be applied to the coefficient. If life satisfaction increases in one country, then life satisfaction will increase in the other countries by nearly one-fifteenth of that increase (from column 6, $1/15 * 0.95$).

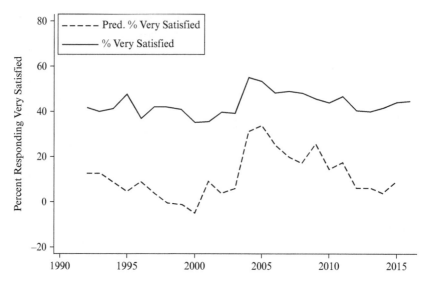

Figure 9.8   Predicted life satisfaction vs observed data

Short-run variation in various factors has theoretically distinct impacts on life satisfaction compared to permanent increases, especially for income as illustrated in Bartolini and Sarracino (2014). For instance, we would expect short-run changes in unemployment to be significantly (and negatively) correlated to the changes of life satisfaction. However, the present study cannot comment on the short-run relations. The short-run variation is not independent and the relations are generally statistically insignificant.

Perhaps the most intuitive way to illustrate our results is to use the model's prediction of life satisfaction, which includes the impacts of each variable and their interdependencies. Figure 9.8 presents the prediction and observed share of very satisfied people in Luxembourg, based on the estimates presented in Table 9.1, column 6. From this figure it is clear the model has high predictive power. Indeed, predicted and observed life satisfaction are strongly correlated at 84 per cent (significant at 1 per cent). The model does not get the level of life satisfaction right, but the short-run changes and long-run trend match well. The difference in level is due to a strong error correction term being applied to a relatively high level of life satisfaction (Luxembourg averages 43.4 compared to 28.8 in all countries), which brings the predicted level of life satisfaction in Luxembourg towards the average. Although we included country fixed effects in the model, they are treated as short-run deviations that are counterbalanced by the error correction term. The results indicate that the flat trend of life satisfaction in Luxembourg is due, at least in part, to offsetting influences of increases in: GNI per capita, income inequality, unemployment, social trust and social expenditures.

9.6   CONCLUSIONS

The previous literature suggests that the relationship between well-being and economic growth depends on a set of conditions: if economic growth is accompanied by extensive social safety nets, high social capital and low income inequality then it is likely to be associated with increasing well-being. In this chapter we test this view. In particular, we check whether the flat trend of life satisfaction in Luxembourg, despite a growing economy, can be explained by the conditions identified in the previous literature.

Between 1980 and 2008 – the year of the economic crisis – the GNI per capita in Luxembourg grew by 6.35 per cent yearly, while the share of very satisfied people remained constant at about 35 per cent. If the evidence from previous studies is correct, we should expect that the conditions mentioned above have a zero net effect on life satisfaction. Unfortunately the lack of long time series of micro data prevents a microeconomic analysis in Luxembourg. We thus adopt a macroeconomic perspective and apply an ECM to a panel of 15 Western European countries to predict life satisfaction in Luxembourg on the basis of a known set of explanatory factors. These are: income inequality, unemployment, social expenditures and trust in others – a commonly used proxy of social capital.

We find that the factors explain the flat trend of life satisfaction in Luxembourg reasonably well and broadly consistently with expectations. Increases in unemployment partially offset the positive influences of increasing social trust and economic growth. On the other hand, increases in income inequality apparently positively affected life satisfaction, and social expenditures did not have the statistically robust impact on well-being that we expected. Across factors, the single most impactful is trust in others. Standardized coefficients indicate that the long-run effect of trust is nearly twice the effect of economic growth. We also found that the cross-sectional mean of GNI per capita attracts a significant and negative coefficient. However, this relation should not be interpreted as having much economic meaning. Cross-sectional means are included in the regressions solely to control bias due to cross-country correlations, such as from the impact of European Union policies. If one were to interpret the relationship for the cross-sectional mean of GNI, it would imply that mean GNI offsets the positive effects of idiosyncratic GNI – indeed, when each country grows at a similar pace the total effect on well-being would be negative. This finding is reminiscent of a 'social comparisons' effect, but this time across countries. As far as we know this is the first time that such evidence has been documented in a panel of countries. As more data become available, this relationship should be assessed further.

Our findings should be viewed with caution. They are based on the best available data, but several assumptions were necessary to develop the long time series. In particular, social trust is adjusted to improve comparability over time and social expenditures is adjusted to obtain a better proxy for social safety nets. Moreover, the sample size limits the degrees of freedom and our ability to include additional control variables and time lags. Our results reflect a preliminary assessment that could change with new data or methods.

Nonetheless, we believe our results are encouraging. They support the view that the quality of growth matters for well-being. The quest to determine the conditions that characterize this 'quality' is still in its infancy, but we have a promising starting point. Further assessment is necessary, but it is plausible that jointly considering economic growth, social safety nets, social capital, unemployment and income inequality is the best route to promote lasting well-being.

NOTES

1. EB is the only dataset that provides long time series about life satisfaction in Luxembourg. The answers to the question are organized on a four-point scale. The distribution of this variable over time is remarkably stable with a consistently fat right tail. Hence, our measure of life satisfaction, the share of very satisfied people, is conservative because the trend would be even flatter than observed if we focused on the share of satisfied people.
2. It is possible that asymmetric responses to economic collapse and positive income growth could explain why life satisfaction did not fully recover at the same time as GDP (e.g. from loss aversion, De Neve et al., 2018), but that is insufficient to explain the pattern in China as discussed in the next paragraph.
3. Due to government restructuring of state-owned enterprises and large rural to urban migration associated with relaxed internal migration laws.
4. The SWIID provides the longest, most complete, and comparable set of data on income inequality. It is based on data from the World Income Inequality Database (WIID), but it hinges on additional assumptions to ease cross-sectional comparability and to impute missing data. For these reasons some scholars have expressed criticism towards the SWIID (Jenkins, 2015). However, we find that in our case, figures from the SWIID positively and significantly correlate with data from WIID and the World Inequality Database in the years and countries when the three data sources are jointly available.
5. We use the word permanent to distinguish the changes in levels that trigger the long-run effects from annual deviations associated with short-run differences in life satisfaction.

REFERENCES

Alesina, A., R. Di Tella and R. MacCulloch (2004), Inequality and happiness: are Europeans and Americans different? *Journal of Public Economics*, 88(9): 2009–42.

Bartolini, S., E. Bilancini and M. Pugno (2013), Did the decline in social connections depress Americans' happiness? *Social Indicators Research*, 110(3): 1033–59.

Bartolini, S. and F. Sarracino (2014), Happy for how long? How social capital and economic growth relate to happiness over time. *Ecological Economics*, 108: 242–56.

Bartolini, S. and F. Sarracino (2015), The dark side of Chinese growth: declining social capital and well-being in times of economic boom. *World Development*, 74: 333–51.

Becchetti, L., E. Giachin Ricca and A. Pelloni (2009), The 60es turnaround as a test on the causal relationship between sociability and happiness. *Working Paper wp07, Econometica.*

Becchetti, L., G. Trovato and D. Bedoya (2011), Income, relational goods and happiness. *Applied Economics*, 43(3): 273–90.

Beja, E. L. (2014), Income growth and happiness: reassessment of the Easterlin paradox. *International Review of Economics*, 61(4): 329–46.

Blanchflower, D. and A. Oswald (2004), Money, sex and happiness: an empirical study. *The Scandinavian Journal of Economics*, 106(3): 393–415.

Boarini, R., M. Comola, F. de Keulenaer, R. Manchin and C. Smith (2013), Can governments boost people's sense of well-being? The impact of selected labour market and health policies on life satisfaction. *Social Indicators Research*, 114(1): 105–20.

Brockmann, H., J. Delhey, C. Welzel and H. Yuan (2009), The China puzzle: falling happiness in a rising economy. *Journal of Happiness Studies*, 10: 387–405.

Bruni, L. and L. Stanca (2008), Watching alone: relational goods, television and happiness. *Journal of Economic Behavior and Organization*, 65(3–4): 506–28.

Carr, E. and H. Chung (2014), Employment insecurity and life satisfaction: the moderating influence of labour market policies across Europe. *Journal of European Social Policy*, 24(4): 383–99.

Chudik, A. and M. H. Pesaran (2015), Common correlated effects estimation of heterogeneous dynamic panel data models with weakly exogenous regressors. *Journal of Econometrics*, 188(2): 393–420.

Clark, A. E. and C. D'Ambrosio (2015), Attitudes to income inequality: experimental and survey evidence. In A. B. Atkinson and F. Bourguignon (eds) *Handbook of Income Distribution*, vol. 2A (pp. 1147–208). Amsterdam: Elsevier.

Clark, A. E., S. Flèche, C. Senik, et al. (2014), The great happiness moderation: well-being inequality during episodes of income growth. In A. Clark and C. Senik (eds) *Happiness and Economic Growth: Lessons from Developing Countries* (pp. 32–139). Oxford: Oxford University Press.

De Neve, J.-E., G. Ward, F. De Keulenaer, B. Van Landeghem, G. Kavetsos and M. I. Norton (2018), The asymmetric experience of positive and negative economic growth: global evidence using subjective well-being data. *Review of Economics and Statistics*, 100(2): 362–75.

Deaton, A. (2008), Income, health, and well-being around the world: evidence from the Gallup World Poll. *The Journal of Economic Perspectives*, 22(2): 53–72.

Di Tella, R., R. MacCulloch and A. Oswald (2003), The macroeconomics of happiness. *The Review of Economics and Statistics*, 85(4): 809–27.

Easterlin, R. A. (1974), Does economic growth improve the human lot? Some empirical evidence. In P. David and W. Melvin (eds) *Nations and Households in Economic Growth* (pp. 98–125). Palo Alto, CA: Stanford University Press.

Easterlin, R. A. (2009), Lost in transition: life satisfaction on the road to capitalism. *Journal of Economic Behavior & Organization*, 71(2): 130–45.

Easterlin, R. A. (2013), Happiness, growth, and public policy. *Economic Inquiry*, 51(1): 1–15.

Easterlin, R. A. (2017), Paradox lost? *Review of Behavioral Economics*, 4(4): 311–39.

Easterlin, R. A. and L. Angelescu (2009), Happiness and growth the world over: time series evidence on the happiness–income paradox. *IZA Discussion Paper*, 4060.

Easterlin, R. A., L. Angelescu, M. Switek, O. Sawangfa and J. S. Zweig (2010), The happiness–income paradox revisited. *Proceedings of the National Academy of Sciences*, 107(52): 1–6.

Easterlin, R. A., R. Morgan, M. Switek and F. Wang (2012), China's life satisfaction, 1990–2010. *Proceedings of the National Academy of Sciences*, 109(25): 9775–80.

Easterlin, R. A., F. Wang and S. Wang (2017), Growth and happiness in China, 1990–2015. In J. F. Helliwell, R. Layard and J. D. Sachs (eds) *World Happiness Report 2017* (pp. 48–83). New York: The Sustainable Development Solutions Network.

Engle, R. F. and C. W. Granger (1987), Co-integration and error correction: representation, estimation, and testing. *Econometrica: Journal of the Econometric Society*, 55: 251–76.

European Commission (2018), Eurobarometer. Technical report, GESIS Data Archive for the Social Sciences.

EVS (2011), European values study 1981–2008, longitudinal data file. Technical report, GESIS Data Archive, Cologne. ZA4804 Data File Version 2.0.0.

Graham, C. and A. Felton (2006), Inequality and happiness: insights from Latin America. *Journal of Economic Inequality*, 4(1): 107–22.

Helliwell, J. F. (2003), How's life? Combining individual and national variables to explain subjective well-being. *Economic Modelling*, 20(2): 331–60.

Helliwell, J. (2008), Life satisfaction and quality of development. Working Paper 14507, National Bureau of Economic Research.

Helliwell, J. F. and L. B. Aknin (2018), Expanding the social science of happiness. *Nature Human Behaviour*, (2): 248–52.

Helliwell, J. F., L. B. Aknin, H. Shiplett, H. Huang and S. Wang (2017), Social capital and prosocial behaviour as sources of well-being. Working Paper 23761, National Bureau of Economic Research.

Horioka, C. Y. and R. Kanda (2010), Revitalizing the Japanese economy by socializing risk. *Japanese Economy*, 37(3): 3–36.

Iniguez-Montiel, A. J. (2014), Growth with equity for the development of Mexico: poverty, inequality, and economic growth (1992–2008). *World Development*, 59: 313–26.

Jenkins, S. P. (2015), World income inequality databases: an assessment of WIID and SWIID. *The Journal of Economic Inequality*, 13(4): 629–71.

Jiang, S., M. Lu and H. Sato (2012), Identity, inequality, and happiness: evidence from urban China. *World Development*, 40(6): 1190–200.

Kahneman, D. and A. Krueger (2006), Developments in the measurement of subjective well-being. *Journal of Economic Perspectives*, 20: 3–24.

Layard, R. (2005), *Happiness: Lessons from a New Science*. New York: Penguin.

Mikucka, M., F. Sarracino and J. K. Dubrow (2017), When does economic growth improve life satisfaction? Multilevel analysis of the roles of social trust and income inequality in 46 countries, 1981–2012. *World Development*, 93: 447–59.

Ministry of Health, Labour and Welfare (2014), *Graphical Review of Japanese Household*. Tokyo: Ministry of Health, Labour and Welfare.

O'Connor, K. J. (2017), Happiness and welfare state policy around the world. *Review of Behavioral Economics*, 4(4): 397–420.

OECD (2001), The evidence on social capital. In *The Well-being of Nations: The Role of Human and Social Capital* (pp. 39–63). Paris: OECD.

OECD (2019), *The OECD SOCX Manual: 2019 Edition. A Guide to the OECD Social Expenditure Database*. Paris: OECD.

Oishi, S. and S. Kesebir (2015), Income inequality explains why economic growth does not always translate to an increase in happiness. *Psychological Science*, 26(10): 1630–38.

Oishi, S., S. Kesebir and E. Diener (2011), Income inequality and happiness. *Psychological Science*, 22(9): 1095–100.

Ono, H. (2010), Lifetime employment in Japan: concepts and measurements. *Journal of the Japanese and International Economies*, 24(1): 1–27.

Ono, H. and K. S. Lee (2013), Welfare states and the redistribution of happiness. *Social Forces*, 92(2): 789–814.

Ono, H. and K. S. Lee (2016), *Redistributing Happiness: How Social Policies Shape Life Satisfaction*. Santa Barbara: Praeger.

Pacek, A. C. and B. Radcliff (2008), Welfare policy and subjective well-being across nations: an individual-level assessment. *Social Indicators Research*, 89(1): 179–91.

Pesaran, M. H. (2015), *Time Series and Panel Data Econometrics*. Oxford: Oxford University Press.

Rothstein, B. (2010), Happiness and the welfare state. *Social Research: An International Quarterly*, 77(2): 441–68.

Sacks, D. W., B. Stevenson and J. Wolfers (2012), Subjective well-being, income, economic development and growth. In P. Booth (ed.) *The Pursuit of Happiness* (pp. 59–98). London: The Institute of Economic Affairs.

Sarracino, F. (2012), Money, sociability and happiness: are developed countries doomed to social erosion and unhappiness? *Social Indicators Research*, 109(2): 135–88.

Sarracino, F., K. J. O' Connor and H. Ono (2019), Making economic growth and well-being compatible: evidence from Japan. Working Paper, MPRA paper n. 93010.

Schimmack, U., P. Krause, G. Wagner and J. Schupp (2010), Stability and change of well-being: an experimentally enhanced latent state-trait-error analysis. *Social Indicators Research*, 95(1): 19–31.

Schmitt, H., E. Scholz, I. Leim and M. Moschner (2009), *The Mannheim Eurobarometer Trend File Codebook and Unweighted Frequency Distributions*.

Scruggs, L., J. Detlef and K. Kati (2017), Comparative welfare entitlements dataset 2. Technical report, University of Connecticut and University of Greifswald. Version 2017-09.

Solt, F. (2016), The Standardized World Income Inequality Database. *Social Science Quarterly*, 97(5): 1267–81. SWIID Version 7.0, July 2018.

Stevenson, B. and J. Wolfers (2008), Economic growth and subjective well-being: reassessing the Easterlin paradox. *Brookings Papers on Economic Activity*, 1: 1–87.

Uhlaner, C. (1989), Relational goods and participation: incorporating sociability into a theory of rational action. *Public Choice*, 62: 253–85.

UNU-WIDER (2018), World income inequality database.

Van Reekum, C., H. Urry, T. Johnstone, M. Thurow, C. Frye, C. Jackson, H. Schaefer, A. Alexander and R. Davidson (2007), Individual differences in amygdala and ventromedial prefrontal cortex activity are associated with evaluation speed and psychological well-being. *Journal of Cognitive Neuroscience*, 19(2): 237–48.

Veenhoven, R. and F. Vergunst (2013), The Easterlin illusion: economic growth does go with greater happiness. *EHERO Working Paper 2013/1*.

World Bank (2018), World Development Indicators. Technical report, World Bank. Accessed May 2018.

WVS (2014), World values survey 1981–2014 longitudinal aggregate v.20150418. Technical report, World Values Survey Association. Aggregate File Producer: JDSystems, Madrid.

PART III

Empirical applications in the Economics
of Happiness

10. The effect of physical activity on subjective well-being: the case for exercise

Mario Lucchini, Egidio Riva and Luca Crivelli

10.1 INTRODUCTION

Sedentary behaviours, which are the consequence of numerous and intertwined social, economic and technological factors, are among the main 'silent' killers worldwide. Indeed, they are a relevant risk factor for a wide set of non-communicable diseases and chronic conditions (e.g. coronary heart or cardiovascular disease, diabetes, obesity and being overweight, and some types of cancer) and significantly raise the chances of premature mortality (for a review, see, e.g. Blair et al., 2004; Samitz et al., 2011). In contrast, being physically active has a preventive and curative effect on physical health. It also has a positive effect on different components of mental health. In particular, exercise (a term that is used interchangeably with physical activity in this study) reduces negative emotions, such as stress, blues and depression, and anxiety, and stimulates positive feelings, such as happiness, joy, energy, optimism, life satisfaction, self-confidence and self-esteem (for a review, see, e.g. Biddle et al., 2000; Mammen and Faulkner, 2013; Wang et al., 2012). In sum, evidence suggests that increased physical activity and a reduced sedentary lifestyle are major elements of healthy and happy living.

Physical activity is generally defined as any form of bodily movement produced by the contraction of skeletal muscle that results in substantial energy expenditure (World Health Organization, 2018). Accordingly, in addition to participation in competitive sports, games and other active forms of recreation, exercise can be carried out in several ways in daily living: working, doing housework and domestic chores, caring for others, walking or cycling to commute and engaging in hobbies. However, the multiple benefits that the different forms of physical activity can engender depend on the frequency, duration and intensity of exercise, in addition to the type or domain of activity performed (e.g. recreational or utilitarian/

occupational) (for a review, see, e.g. Downward and Rasciute, 2011; Huang and Humphreys, 2012; Warburton et al., 2006). In this regard, regular exercise sessions of at least moderate-intensity activity, based on an individual's capacity, that cause increased heart rate, breathing rate, sweating and muscle fatigue are currently recommended to maintain physical and mental health (World Health Organization, 2018).

Although a growing body of literature has examined, from different standpoints, the positive linkage between physical activity and health and well-being outcomes, there are still a few gaps to fill. Meta-analytic and narrative review papers suggest, first, that many earlier studies have suffered from methodological shortcomings. Much of the research that has been conducted so far draws on cross-sectional data that may not adequately assess the direction and strength of causal effects and rarely utilized randomized controlled trial design (some notable exceptions are: Mack et al., 2000; Yook et al., 2017) or similarly strong research designs. Another issue requiring more attention is exercise dose–response. The physical and mental benefits of exercise seem to be well documented. Nonetheless, most studies have not considered the linkage between the dose or volume of exercise, which equals the energy expended and impacts on several health outcomes (Kesaniemi et al., 2001). In addition, systematic reviews indicate that the findings on the dose–response relationship between physical activity and health and well-being benefits are mixed (Bernard et al., 2018; Samitz et al., 2011). Finally, an overview of the evidence reveals that positive components of mental health have been underinvestigated. When considering the role of physical activity in psychological well-being, evidence of positive mental health outcomes, such as happiness, is comparatively lower. In contrast, much more research has been conducted on the protective or restorative effect of exercise on mental disorders and illnesses (for a review, see, e.g. Richards et al., 2015; Zhang and Chen, 2019).

Against this background, this chapter has a twofold aim. First, it intends to prove the beneficial effect of physical activity on subjective well-being. In an attempt to produce sound empirical evidence, it draws on a longitudinal dataset from the Swiss population, the Swiss Household Panel, and employs specific panel data models (i.e. random and fixed effects estimators) to control for unobserved time-invariant individual heterogeneity. Subsequently it quantifies causal relationships between physical activity and the three fundamental components of subjective well-being, namely: life satisfaction, frequent pleasant affect and infrequent unpleasant affect. Indeed, based on the most authoritative literature these components should be measured and studied separately (Diener et al., 1985, 1999). Doing so extends the literature in the field by shedding more light on positive psychology-related concepts. Second, this study aims at assessing the causal effect of greater weekly participation in exercise on subjective well-being. Hence it contributes to the ongoing debate on the dose–response effect of exercise; namely, it addresses the call for further research that could ascertain whether there is an optimal dose of physical activity for the promotion of health and well-being (Zhang and Chen, 2019).

The remaining part of the study has been organized in the following way. Section 10.2 provides a critical summary of published research literature on the relationship between physical activity and health and well-being outcomes. Section 10.3 discusses the data and the methodology used for this study. Section 10.4 presents the main findings of the research, focusing on the effects of both physical activity and its increments on the three main components of subjective well-being separately. Section 10.5 concludes the chapter and comments on the importance of this study for future research.

10.2   LITERATURE REVIEW AND RESEARCH PROPOSITIONS

10.2.1   Physical Activity and Subjective Well-being

The investigation of subjective well-being and its correlates, which has a longstanding tradition in psychology and in the economic literature, is still a promising area of interdisciplinary research. It may also inform policymakers, as long as much empirical evidence suggests that there is only a partial overlap between wealth and subjective well-being (Diener and Seligman, 2004; McDaid and Cooper, 2014). The concept of subjective well-being refers to people's overall evaluation of their lives and reflects the influence of different factors and circumstances on good mental functioning. It is not just a measure of happiness; rather, it covers several aspects of people's subjective state, such as satisfaction, affective states and psychological flourishing (Diener, 2006). The conceptual and operational framework used in this chapter comprises the main components of subjective well-being, which are people's cognitive evaluation of their lives, measures of affect and sense of purpose and engagement.

Over the past few decades interest in the positive effects of physical activity on subjective well-being has grown, but the influence of exercise on different aspects of people's subjective experience has been overlooked. Literature examining the link between physical activity and health-related outcomes is comparatively much more developed (Rasciute and Downward, 2010). Moreover, other material correlates of subjective well-being, such as income or work and employment conditions, have attracted more attention

(Dolan et al., 2008). Accordingly, literature reviews indicate that prior studies have relied on several subjective well-being measures that are somewhat biased towards the negative components of mental functioning as well as on the assessment of the preventive and restorative effect of physical activity. Hence, some calls have been issued to extend the literature to components of well-being such as life satisfaction, and feelings or emotional states such as optimism and hope (e.g. Zhang and Chen, 2019).

Physical activity may boost joy and happiness, life satisfaction and quality of life and reduce depression and anxiety symptoms (Brown et al., 2004; Fox, 1999; Maher et al., 2015; Richards et al., 2015). Certain physiological mechanisms can explain these relationships. At the molecular level, physical activity promotes hippocampal neurogenesis, triggers dendritic remodelling, stimulates serotonin and endorphin release, and reduces the levels of cortisol in the brain (Huang and Humphreys, 2012). All these biochemical modifications contribute to increased well-being. Furthermore, indirect associations of physical activity with health and well-being outcomes have also been found. In this regard, current literature has hypothesized several physiological, psychological and environmental mediators of the relationship between physical activity and subjective well-being. Namely, physical activity promotes health, which is probably the most important determinant of subjective well-being (De Mello and Tiongson, 2009), as it provides opportunities for socialization, improves self-esteem and environmental mastery, strengthens resilience to stress and mitigates the effects of anxiety (Biddle et al., 2000; Dolan et al., 2008; Lathia et al., 2017). Accordingly, we may anticipate that physical activity has a positive effect on the main components of subjective well-being.

10.2.2 The Dose–Response Mechanism

While abundant empirical evidence supports the positive effects of regular physical activity on health-related outcomes, a search of the literature revealed few studies addressing the dose–response mechanism, that is, the relationship between duration (time), frequency (sessions per time period) and intensity (absolute or relative) of physical activity on the one hand, and health and well-being benefits on the other hand (Brown et al., 2004; Samitz et al., 2011). Hence the results concerning the dose–response pattern are inconsistent (Kesaniemi et al., 2001). Different levels of physical activity do not necessarily produce the same health outcomes (Lee, 2007; Rodriguez et al., 2011). Specific health benefits may result from increasing amounts and intensities of physical activity (e.g. Kohl, 2001); however, beyond a certain threshold any increment in exercise may not bring about any further health benefit or it may be even associated with higher relative risk of negative events (e.g. injuries) or adverse effects (Bouchard and Rankinen, 2001; Brown et al., 2004; Hootman et al., 2002). Numerous studies have found an inverse relationship between an increased level of physical activity and good health or that low levels (e.g. a non-vigorous dose) of physical activity provide enough health benefits for most people (e.g. Rodriguez et al., 2011; Samitz et al., 2011; Woodcock et al., 2011). Following these controversial findings, the appropriate dose or volume of exercise necessary to improve health has been debated, and indeed divergent recommendations for physical activity have been promulgated over time by public health agencies (Blair et al., 2004). In this regard, the most recent guidelines created by public health authorities, such as the National Health Service or World Health Organization, suggest that adults should get at least moderate-intensity physical activity for a minimum of 30 minutes a day at least five days a week. These are usually considered as health-enhancing physical activity levels. Coherently, we may postulate that increments in physical activity in terms of frequency will positively affect subjective well-being.

10.3   DATA AND METHODS

10.3.1   Sample

This chapter investigates the relationship between physical activity and subjective well-being using data coming from waves 2004–16 of the Swiss Household Panel. The sample for this study consists of respondents for whom complete data for all variables included in the models were available across the 13 waves. More specifically, we selected 95 858 person-year observations nested within 18 396 subjects (8633 men and 9763 women) aged at least 14; 1875 individuals have been followed for 13 waves and the average number of observations per subject is 5.2.

10.3.2   Variables

Subjective well-being. Following the definition of Diener and colleagues (1999), subjective well-being was operationalized as an umbrella construct that accounted for the presence of positive affect, the absence of negative affect and the cognitive evaluation of one's life. In particular, subjective well-being was measured using three different indicators: (1) satisfaction with life in general (i.e. the cognitive component, hereafter life satisfaction), (2) energy and optimism (i.e. the positive component), and (3) depression, blues and anxiety (i.e. the negative component, hereafter depression). All these indicators were measured on an 11-point rating scale (0 'never' to 10 'always').

Physical activity. The outcome variable was measured with one item that encompassed the recommendations on the optimal amount of at least moderate-intensity physical activity throughout the week to stay healthy: 'At present, how many days a week do you practice for half an hour minimum a physical activity which makes you slightly breathless?' Examples of physical activity included walking quickly, dancing, gardening or other types of sporting activities. Frequency of physical activity was coded as follows: 'None'; '1–2'; '3 or more' days per week. This choice was justified by the fact that people practicing physical activity for more than three days a week were relatively scarce in the sample.

Covariates. We first included in the models, as control variables, some of the most important correlates of subjective well-being and physical activity. These were: age; age squared; family status [single/never married (ref. category), married, separated or divorced, widowed]; household size; number of children in the household; education [compulsory education (ref. category), apprenticeship, university entrance diploma, post-apprenticeship diploma, university degree]; employment status [employed (ref. category), unemployed, not in the labour force]; Swiss nationality [dummy recoded]; quartiles of net total annual household income [ref. category (1st quartile)]; the death of a closely related person [dummy recoded]; end of a close relationship [dummy recoded]; conflict with or among related persons [dummy recoded]; region of residence [Lake Geneva (ref. category), Middleland, North-West Switzerland, Zurich, East Switzerland, Central Switzerland, Ticino]; wave of the survey [2004 (ref. category) to 2016, dummy recoded]. In a second step we included in the model the following health status variables as additional covariates: health-related factors, such as back pain [not at all (ref. category), somewhat, very much]; headaches [not at all (ref. category), somewhat, very much]; chronic illness or long-term health problem [10-point scale ranging from 0 'not at all' to 10 'a great deal']; health impediment in everyday activities [10-point scale ranging from 0 'not at all' to 10 'a great deal']; body mass index. Some scholars consider these health status variables as potential mediators of the causal pathway from physical activity to subjective well-being. If this assumption is correct they should not be considered as confounders, otherwise their presence would lead to the underestimation of the strength of the causal effect (Rothon et al., 2010).

10.3.3 Analytic Strategy

This study aims at estimating the effect of physical activity on subjective well-being using analytic strategies that are appropriate for panel data.

More specifically, we developed two types of models in which subjective well-being was regressed on physical activity, controlling for observed and unobserved individual heterogeneity factors. We used the following equation:

$$\text{SWB}_{it} = \sum_{k=1}^{K} \beta_k X_{it} + \sum_{q=1}^{Q} \gamma_q Z_{it} + \sum_{r=1}^{R} \delta_r W_i + \alpha_i + \psi_t + \varepsilon_{it} \quad (10.1)$$

where SWB_{it} is a specific indicator of subjective well-being of individual i at occasion t; X_{it} is a vector of K time-varying physical activity dummies weighted for their respective coefficients β_k; Z_{it} and W_i represent, respectively, a vector of Q time-varying and R time-constant characteristics weighted for their respective coefficients γ_q and δ_r treated as control variables; α_i is a time-invariant individual-specific effect removed in the fixed effect models by applying the within-demeaning transformation; finally, ψ_t corresponds to wave effects and ε_{it} is the idiosyncratic error term.

We estimated this equation with different estimators, namely random effects (RE) and fixed effects (FE). An RE model assumes the covariates to be uncorrelated with the individual specific error term. If the individual effects correlate with covariates, RE provide biased estimates. If this assumption cannot be met, an FE estimator is a better choice because it yields unbiased parameter estimates by erasing time-constant unobserved heterogeneity due to personality or genetic traits, if there is enough intra-individual variation in the covariates of interest. In addition to RE and FE models, we implemented pooled ordinary least squared (OLS) regressions to get an idea of the upward bias in the parameter estimates due to unobserved heterogeneity. Analyses were stratified by gender. Indeed, previous empirical studies or systematic reviews (e.g. Huang and Humphreys, 2012; Morgan and Bath, 1998; Richards et al., 2015; Samitz et al., 2011) have suggested that men and women differ substantially in the occurrence of mental diseases, the prevalence of moderate physical activity and the effect of physical activity on health and well-being outcomes.

10.4   FINDINGS

10.4.1   Descriptive Statistics

Table 10.1 reports unconditional summary statistics by gender, which were obtained by pooling data over the 2004–16 waves, and displays the total

Table 10.1   Summary statistics by gender

	Males	Mean	SD	Females	Mean	SD
Life satisfaction	overall	8.059	1.359	overall	8.046	1.427
	between		1.216	between		1.258
	within		0.835	within		0.901
Energy and optimism	overall	7.283	1.782	overall	7.128	1.765
	between		1.483	between		1.481
	within		1.229	within		1.217
Depression	overall	1.727	1.913	overall	2.381	2.147
	between		1.691	between		1.879
	within		1.139	within		1.305
Physical activity (frequency)						
none	overall	0.240	0.427	overall	0.272	0.445
	between		0.348	between		0.363
	within		0.303	within		0.313
1–2 days per week	overall	0.329	0.470	overall	0.320	0.466
	between		0.355	between		0.343
	within		0.354	within		0.361
3 or more days per week	overall	0.431	0.495	overall	0.408	0.492
	between		0.397	between		0.385
	within		0.347	within		0.352
Person-period observations (N)	43 700			52 128		
Number of respondents (n)	8633			9763		

variation of the key variables as decomposed into: (1) within variation over time for each individual; (2) between variation across individuals. In the three indicators of subjective well-being and in the physical activity covariate, the between variation is higher compared to the within variation. Nevertheless, there is enough within variation to justify the application of FE models.

The distributions of life satisfaction and energy and optimism indicators were negatively skewed, as commonly found in research in this field, indicating that most respondents were satisfied rather than dissatisfied with their lives or were rather optimistic than pessimistic. On the other hand, the item measuring depression showed a positively skewed distribution. Moreover, the average scores of life satisfaction and optimism displayed little variation between the male and female samples (Figures 10.1 and 10.2). However, in line with several studies carried out in European countries (e.g. Kessler et al., 1993; Van de Velde et al., 2010), depression scores were higher for women (2.38) than for men (1.73) (Figure 10.3).

Turning to physical activity (Figure 10.4), women were more likely to report sedentary lifestyle compared to their male counterparts (27 per cent

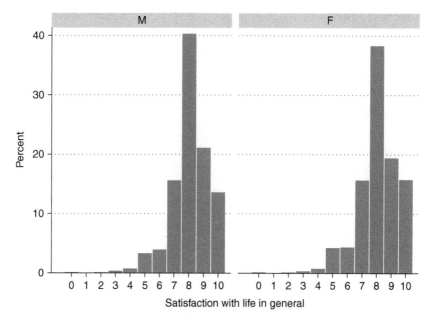

Figure 10.1 Life satisfaction scores, by gender (pooled data)

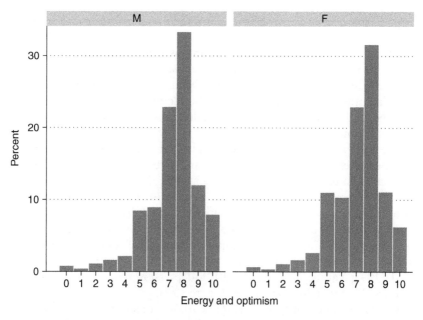

Figure 10.2 Energy and optimism scores, by gender (pooled data)

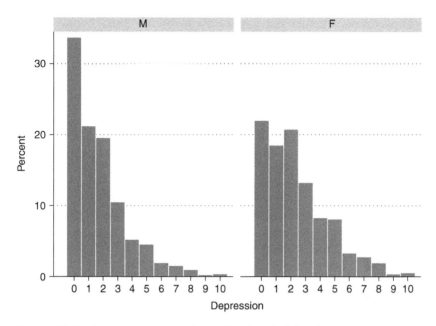

Figure 10.3   Depression scores, by gender (pooled data)

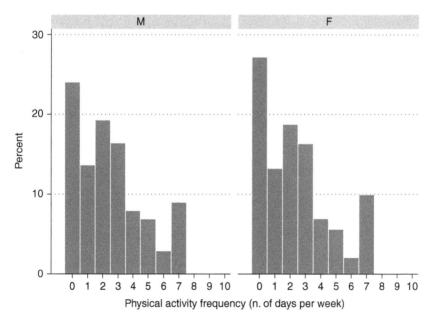

Figure 10.4   Physical activity, by gender (pooled data)

vs 24 per cent), although the shape of the probability distribution was very similar for both genders.

10.4.2   Bivariate Analysis

Bivariate analysis carried out on a subsample that accounted for only the first person-year observation (Table 10.1A in the Appendix) indicated that, in the Swiss sample, life satisfaction followed a U-shaped curve by age, while the other two indicators of subjective well-being did not have the same shape. Turning to family and household-related variables, married people reported a higher level of subjective well-being *while* one-person household and the absence of children were negatively associated with subjective well-being. Concerning socio-economic characteristics, respondents who were unemployed and belonged to the bottom income quartile showed the lowest levels of life satisfaction and optimism and the highest levels of depression. Education did not reveal a clear gradient. As expected, stressful life events, such as the death of a closely related person, the end of a close relationship and the conflicts with or among related persons were more likely to be associated with a lower level of subjective well-being. Health problems (such as back pain, headaches, long-term illness, chronic illness or long-term health problems, health impediment in daily activities, obesity and being overweight) were negatively associated with life satisfaction and optimism and positively associated with depression. Turning to contextual variables, individuals living in the Lake Geneva and Ticino regions reported lower life satisfaction and a higher risk of depression. Finally, Swiss citizens seemed to be happier and less depressed compared to their foreign counterparts.

10.4.3   Regression Analysis

Table 10.2 displays the results of the regression analyses conducted separately for men and women and adjusted for demographics and socio-economics confounders. As mentioned previously, in the first step health problems indicators and body mass index were not included in the equation. As expected, parameter estimates indicate that physically active individuals reported higher levels of life satisfaction and energy and optimism, and a lower level of depression compared to inactive people. However, moving from an OLS pooled estimator to more appropriate specifications, the magnitude of the effect of physical activity on the different components of subjective well-being decreased, although the coefficient estimates remained statistically significant. Roughly speaking, the strength of parameter estimates halved when using RE as opposed to

Table 10.2 Parameter estimates of physical activity on subjective well-being indicators, by gender: OLS, RE and FE specifications

	OLS		RE		FE	
	M	F	M	F	M	F
	b/se	b/se	b/se	b/se	b/se	b/se
Life satisfaction						
0 days per week (ref. cat.)						
1–2 days per week	0.219***	0.228***	0.101***	0.114***	0.051**	0.069***
	(0.02)	(0.02)	(0.02)	(0.02)	(0.02)	(0.02)
3 or more days per week	0.317***	0.298***	0.163***	0.136***	0.097***	0.075***
	(0.03)	(0.02)	(0.02)	(0.02)	(0.02)	(0.02)
Unemployed					−0.521***	−0.411***
					(0.09)	(0.08)
Termination of a close relationship					−0.213***	−0.174***
					(0.03)	(0.02)
Conflicts with persons closely related					−0.220***	−0.231***
					(0.03)	(0.02)
Energy and optimism						
0 days per week (ref. cat.)						
1–2 days per week	0.230***	0.191***	0.134***	0.132***	0.078**	0.101***
	(0.03)	(0.03)	(0.02)	(0.02)	(0.03)	(0.02)
3 or more days per week	0.479***	0.446***	0.266***	0.262***	0.156***	0.183***
	(0.03)	(0.03)	(0.02)	(0.02)	(0.03)	(0.02)

Table 10.2 (continued)

	OLS		RE		FE	
	M b/se	F b/se	M b/se	F b/se	M b/se	F b/se
Unemployed					-0.228* (0.10)	-0.143 (0.09)
Termination of a close relationship					-0.105** (0.03)	-0.103*** (0.03)
Conflicts with persons closely related					-0.142*** (0.03)	-0.184*** (0.02)
Depression 0 days per week (ref. cat.)						
1–2 days per week	-0.215*** (0.04)	-0.225*** (0.04)	-0.086*** (0.02)	-0.129*** (0.02)	-0.034 (0.02)	-0.096*** (0.02)
3 or more days per week	-0.318*** (0.04)	-0.378*** (0.04)	-0.135*** (0.02)	-0.161*** (0.02)	-0.064* (0.03)	-0.103*** (0.03)
Unemployed					-0.162** (0.05)	0.074 (0.04)
Termination of a close relationship					0.316*** (0.04)	0.280*** (0.03)
Conflicts with persons closely related					0.281*** (0.03)	0.340*** (0.03)

Notes: * p<.05 ** p<.01 *** p<.001. Adjusted for: age, age^2, household size, number of children, marital status, education, employment status, household equivalent income (quartiles), death of closely related person, nationality, region of residence, wave.

202

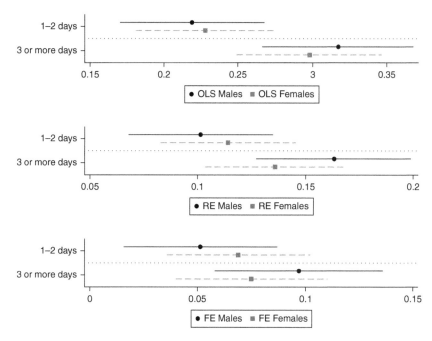

*Figure 10.5   Life satisfaction: parameter estimates and 95% confidence
intervals*

OLS, and it halved further when using FE models rather than RE. In more
detail, in the FE specification, as physical activity frequency increased
from none to 1–2 days and 3 or more days per week, life satisfaction scores
increased in the male (by 0.051 and 0.097 point respectively) and female
(by 0.069 and 0.075 point respectively) samples (see also Figure 10.5).
Comparisons of parameter estimates across physical activity levels indicated that the dose–response mechanism was statistically significant only
in the male sample (Table 10.3). Turning to depression scores (see also
Figure 10.6), while in the female sample as physical activity increased,
depression scores slightly decreased (by 0.096 point for 1–2 days per week
and by 0.103 point for 3 or more days per week), in the male sample only
high levels of physical activity were impactful. Nonetheless, the difference
of estimated parameters across physical activity frequency levels was not
statistically significant in either sample. Lastly, physical activity had the
strongest effects on energy and optimism (see also Figure 10.7). Exercise
conducted on 1 or 2 days per week raised the average value on the energy
and optimism scale by 0.078 in the male sample and 0.101 in the female
one. A further increase in physical activity frequency was associated with

Table 10.3 *Test of the difference of estimated parameters across physical activity frequency levels (1–2 days per week vs 3 or more days per week)*

	Life satisfaction		Energy and optimism		Depression	
	F	Prob. > F	F	Prob. > F	F	Prob. > F
OLS Males	26.71	0.0000	99.30	0.0000	12.82	0.0003
OLS Females	15.43	0.0001	125.58	0.0000	27.96	0.0000
RE Males	21.64	0.0000	51.03	0.0000	7.14	0.0075
RE Females	3.05	0.0808	61.85	0.0000	2.95	0.0861
FE Males	10.07	0.0015	61.85	0.0000	2.43	0.1187
FE Females	0.20	0.6533	21.31	0.0000	0.14	0.7083

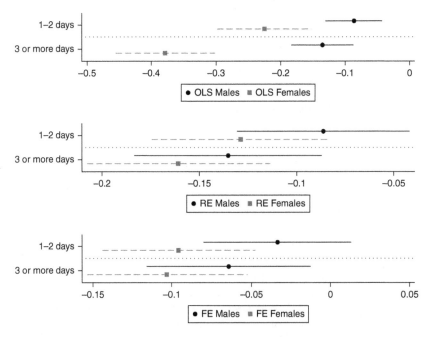

Figure 10.6 *Depression: parameter estimates and 95% confidence interval intervals*

significantly higher energy and optimism scores for both men (0.156) and women (0.183). It is important to underline that the magnitude of the effect of stressful events and negative occurrences such as personal conflicts, termination of a close relationship or unemployment on the

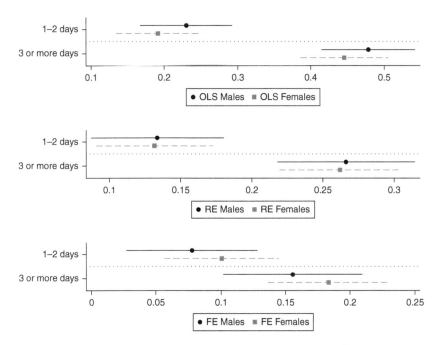

*Figure 10.7   Energy and optimism: parameter estimates and
95% confidence intervals*

different components of subjective well-being in the FE models is generally wider.

Table 10.4 presents the results of OLS, RE and FE models, adjusted for more covariates including health status variables. Compared to the findings reported in Table 10.2, the magnitude of the effects of physical activity on the three main components of subjective well-being further reduced. Once again, for males higher physical activity levels significantly affected life satisfaction and energy and optimism scores; however, for females the dose–response mechanism for physical activity levels was statistically significant only for energy and optimism ratings (Table 10.5).

10.5   CONCLUSION

This study drew on 13 waves (2004–16) of the Swiss Household Panel and examined the causal effect of physical activity on the three main components of subjective well-being (i.e. life satisfaction, positive affect and negative affect) while controlling for a wide set of potential socio-economic,

Table 10.4 Parameter estimates of physical activity on subjective well-being indicators, by gender: OLS, RE and FE specifications (including health status indicators)

	OLS		RE		FE	
	Male	Female	Male	Female	Male	Female
	b/se	b/se	b/se	b/se	b/se	b/se
Life satisfaction						
0 days per week (ref. cat.)						
1–2 days per week	0.142***	0.148***	0.081***	0.094***	0.041*	0.058***
	(0.02)	(0.02)	(0.02)	(0.02)	(0.02)	(0.02)
3 or more days per week	0.233***	0.198***	0.140***	0.111***	0.085***	0.062***
	(0.02)	(0.02)	(0.02)	(0.02)	(0.02)	(0.02)
Unemployed						
Energy and optimism						
0 days per week (ref. cat.)						
1–2 days per week	0.120***	0.080**	0.091***	0.087***	0.057*	0.079***
	(0.03)	(0.03)	(0.02)	(0.02)	(0.03)	(0.02)
3 or more days per week	0.358***	0.306***	0.223***	0.213***	0.133***	0.158***
	(0.03)	(0.03)	(0.02)	(0.02)	(0.03)	(0.02)
Depression						
0 days per week (ref. cat.)						
1–2 days per week	-0.067*	-0.067*	-0.040	-0.069**	-0.006	-0.055*
	(0.03)	(0.03)	(0.02)	(0.02)	(0.02)	(0.02)
3 or more days per week	-0.161***	-0.190***	-0.091***	-0.097***	-0.041	-0.060*
	(0.03)	(0.04)	(0.02)	(0.02)	(0.03)	(0.03)

Notes: * $p < .05$ ** $p < .01$ *** $p < .001$. Adjusted for: age, age^2, household size, number of children, marital status, education, employment status, household equivalent income (quartiles), death of closely related person, termination of a close relationship, conflict with or among related persons, back problems, headaches, chronic illness, health impediment, body mass index, nationality, region of residence, wave.

Table 10.5   *Test of the difference of estimated parameters across physical activity frequency levels (1–2 days per week vs 3 or more days per week) (health status variables included)*

	Life satisfaction		Energy and optimism		Depression	
	F	Prob. > F	F	Prob. > F	F	Prob. > F
OLS Males	24.08	0.0000	99.28	0.0000	12.63	0.0004
OLS Females	8.32	0.0039	109.41	0.0000	21.65	0.0000
RE Males	20.21	0.0000	51.15	0.0000	8.28	0.004
RE Females	1.92	0.1659	57.36	0.0000	2.33	0.1272
FE Males	9.59	0.002	13.89	0.0002	3.38	0.0659
FE Females	0.11	0.7415	19.15	0.0000	0.06	0.8022

demographic, health, relational and environmental confounders. Based on the available literature, which suggests that the relationships under scrutiny could be gender-specific, analyses were run separately for men and women. As expected, the results indicated that physical activity positively affects the main components of subjective well-being, for both men and women. Furthermore, to extend the current literature in the field, this longitudinal study assessed the effect of increasing exercise levels, measured in terms of the number of days the activity was performed per week, on subjective well-being. The findings showed that the prevalence of physical activity influences the various components of subjective well-being differently and confirmed gender-specific patterns (e.g. Dolan et al., 2014). In general, for both men and women being physically active was conducive to higher subjective well-being, and an incremental increase in exercise led to even better ratings on most measures of subjective well-being. In more detail, compared to inactive persons women who engaged in physical activity on 1–2 days per week reported significantly better life satisfaction, energy and optimism, and depression scores, but further changes in the activity level brought about additional smaller benefits, which were statistically significant only on energy and optimism scores. Men who engaged in moderate-intensity physical activity reported higher subjective well-being scores; moreover, the effect of physical activity on life satisfaction and energy and optimism significantly increased as the frequency moved from 1–2 days per week to 3 or more days per week.

Even though the effect of physical activity on subjective well-being was found to be comparatively weak (for instance, the effect of unemployment and other covariates on the components of subjective well-being were larger), the results have practical implications. The collective burden of sedentary behaviour in both economic and social terms is quite high. Therefore, the evidence provided in this chapter strongly supports individuals' engagement in exercise, even at a moderate-intensity level for very few days a week. Accordingly, due to the high overall cost-effectiveness of interventions in this field, the promotion of physical activity, also through the reduction or removal of personal and environmental barriers to physical activity participation (such as time constraints, lack of parks or facilities), could be higher on the agenda of policymakers (and business managers) worldwide (see also Warburton and Bredin, 2016).

Despite several strengths, this study has a few limitations that need to be acknowledged. Two relate to the possible inaccuracy in the measurement of physical activity. In this respect, the Swiss Household Panel provides a self-reported single-item measure of total physical activity that encompasses leisure-time activity, physical activities of daily living and sports. Hence, future research could benefit from the availability of more appropriate (e.g. objectively defined) and detailed measures of frequency, duration and intensity of physical activity, which could avoid biases and allow the calculation of the actual amount of energy expended in exercise as well as information on subdomains of total physical activity, which could capture more accurately the heterogeneity of the effects of distinct activities (Samitz et al., 2011). Another limitation concerns the small size of the subpopulation reporting higher prevalence (three days or more per week) of moderate physical activity, which is not surprising considering that very few people worldwide meet the most recent physical activity recommendations specified by public health agencies (see, e.g. Colley et al., 2011). This limitation prevented us from assessing the exact shape of the dose–response pattern, which is an issue requiring further investigation.

REFERENCES

Bernard, P., I. Dorè, A. J. Romain, G. Hains-Monfette, C. Kingsbury and C. Sabiston (2018), Dose response association of objective physical activity with mental health in a representative national sample of adults: a cross-sectional study. *PLoS ONE*, 13(10), e0204682.

Biddle, S. J., K. R. Fox and S. H. Boutcher (2000), *Physical Activity and Psychological Well-being*. London: Routledge.

Blair, S. N., M. J. LaMonte and M. Z. Nichaman (2004), The evolution of physical activity recommendations: how much is enough? *The American Journal of Clinical Nutrition*, 79(5), 913–20.

Bouchard, C. and T. Rankinen (2001), Individual differences in response to regular physical activity. *Medicine & Science in Sports & Exercise*, 33, 446–51.

Brown, D. W., D. R. Brown, G. W. Heath, L. Balluz, W. H. Giles, E. S. Ford and A. H. Mokdad (2004), Associations between physical activity dose and health-related quality of life. *Medicine & Science in Sports & Exercise*, 36(5), 890–96.

Colley, R. C., D. Garriguet, I. Janssen, C. L. Craig, J. Clarke and M. S. Tremblay (2011), Physical activity of Canadian adults: accelerometer results from the 2007 to 2009 Canadian Health Measures Survey. *Health Reports*, 22(1), 7–14.

De Mello, L. and E. Tiongson (2009), What is the value of (my and my family's) good health? *Kyklos*, 62, 594–610.

Diener, E. (2006), Guidelines for national indicators of subjective well-being and ill-being. *Journal of Happiness Studies*, 7(4), 397–404.

Diener, E. and M. E. Seligman (2004), Beyond money: toward an economy of well-being. *Psychological Science in the Public Interest*, 5(1), 1–31.

Diener, E., R. J. Larsen, S. Levine and R. A. Emmons (1985), Intensity and frequency: dimensions underlying positive and negative affect. *Journal of Personality and Social Psychology*, 48(5), 1253–65.

Diener, E., E. M. Suh, R. E. Lucas and H. L. Smith (1999), Subjective well-being: three decades of progress. *Psychological Review*, 5(1), 1–31.

Dolan, P., G. Kavetsos and I. Vlaev (2014), The happiness workout. *Social Indicators Research*, 119(3), 1363–77.

Dolan, P., T. Peasgood and M. White (2008), Do we really know what makes us happy? A review of the economic literature on the factors associated with subjective well-being. *Journal of Economic Psychology*, 29, 94–122.

Downward, P. and S. Rasciute (2011), Does sport make you happy? An analysis of the well-being derived from sports participation. *International Review of Applied Economics*, 25, 331–48.

Fox, K. R. (1999), The influence of physical activity on mental well-being. *Public Health Nutrition*, 2(3a), 411–18.

Hootman, J. M., C. A. Macera, B. A. Ainsworth, C. L. Addy, M. Martin and S. N. Blair (2002), Epidemiology of musculoskeletal injuries among sedentary and physically active adults. *Medicine and Science in Sports and Exercise*, 34(5), 838–44.

Huang, H. and B. R. Humphreys (2012), Sports participation and happiness: evidence from US microdata. *Journal of Economic Psychology*, 33, 776–93.

Kesaniemi, Y. A., E. Danforth, M. D. Jensen, P. G. Kopelman, P. Lefebvre and B. A. Reeder (2001), Dose-response issues concerning physical activity and health: an evidence-based symposium. *Medicine & Science in Sports & Exercise*, 33, 351–8.

Kessler, R. C., K. A. McGonagle, M. Swartz, D. G. Blazer and C. B. Nelson (1993), Sex and depression in the National Comorbidity Survey I: Lifetime prevalence, chronicity and recurrence.

Kohl, H. W. 3rd (2001), Physical activity and cardiovascular disease: evidence for a dose response. *Medicine & Science in Sports & Exercise*, 33, 472–83; discussion pp. 493–4.

Lathia, N., G. M. Sandstrom, C. Mascolo and P. J. Rentfrow (2017), Happier people live more active lives: using smartphones to link happiness and physical activity. *PLoS ONE*, 12(1), e0160589.

Lee, I. (2007), Dose–response relation between physical activity and fitness: even a little is good; more is better. *JAMA*, 297(19), 2137–9.

Mack, M. G., S. Huddleston, K. E. Dutler and W. Bian (2000), Mood state changes of students enrolled in physical activity classes. *Perceptual and Motor Skills*, 90(3), 911–14.

Maher, J. P., A. L. Pincus, N. Ram and D. E. Conroy (2015), Daily physical activity and life satisfaction across adulthood. *Developmental Psychology*, 51(10), 1407–19.

Mammen, G. and G. Faulkner (2013), Physical activity and the prevention of depression: a systematic review of prospective studies. *American Journal of Preventive Medicine*, 45(5), 649–57.

McDaid, D. and C. L. Cooper (2014), *The Economics of Wellbeing*. Chichester: John Wiley & Sons Ltd.

Morgan, K. and P. A. Bath (1998), Customary physical activity and psychological wellbeing: a longitudinal study. *Age and Ageing*, 27(S3), 35–40.

Rasciute, S. and P. Downward (2010), Health or happiness? What is the impact of physical activity on the individual? *Kyklos*, 63(2), 256–70.

Richards, J., X. Jiang, P. Kelly, J. Chau, A. Bauman and D. Ding (2015), Don't worry, be happy: cross-sectional associations between physical activity and happiness in 15 European countries. *BMC Public Health*, 15, 53–60.

Rodriguez, P., S. Kesenne and B. R. Humphreys (2011), *The Economics of Sport, Health and Happiness*. Cheltenham, UK and Northampton, MA, USA: Edward Elgar Publishing.

Rothon, C., P. Edwards, K. Bhui, R. M. Viner, S. Taylor and S. A. Stansfeld (2010), Physical activity and depressive symptoms in adolescents: a prospective study. *BMC Medicine*, 8(1), 32.

Samitz, G., M. Egger and M. Zwahlen (2011), Domains of physical activity and all-cause mortality: systematic review and dose–response meta-analysis of cohort studies. *International Journal of Epidemiology*, 40, 1382–400.

Van de Velde, S., P. Bracke and K. Levecque (2010), Gender differences in depression in 23 European countries. Cross-national variation in the gender gap in depression. *Social Science & Medicine*, 71(2), 305–13.

Wang, F., H. M. Orpana, H. Morrison, M. De Groh, S. Dai and W. Luo (2012), Long-term association between leisure-time physical activity and changes in happiness: analysis of the Prospective National Population Health Survey. *American Journal of Epidemiology*, 176(12), 1095–1100.

Warburton, D. E. R. and S. S. D. Bredin (2016), Reflections on physical activity and health: what should we recommend? *Canadian Journal of Cardiology*, 32, 495–504.

Warburton, D. E., C. Nicol and S. S. Bredin (2006), Health benefits of physical activity: the evidence. *CMAJ*, 174, 801–9.

Woodcock, J., O. H. Franco, N. Orsini and I. Roberts (2011), Non-vigorous physical activity and all-cause mortality: systematic review and meta-analysis of cohort studies. *International Journal of Epidemiology*, 40(1), 121–38.

World Health Organization (2018), *Global Action Plan on Physical Activity 2018–2030: More Active People for a Healthier World*. Geneva: World Health Organization.

Yook, Y. S., S. J. Kang and I. Park (2017), Effects of physical activity intervention combining a new sport and mindfulness yoga on psychological characteristics in adolescents. *International Journal of Sport and Exercise Psychology*, 15(2), 109–17.

Zhang, Z. and W. J. Chen (2019), A systematic review of the relationship between physical activity and happiness. *Journal of Happiness Studies*, 20(4), 1305–22.

APPENDIX

Table 10.1A *Bivariate statistics, conditional mean values (mean) and standard deviations (male sample N = 8633; female sample N = 9763)*

	Life satisfaction				Energy and optimism				Depression			
	M		F		M		F		M		F	
	mean	SD	mean	SD	mean	SD	mean	SD	mean	SD	mean	SD
Physical activity												
0 days a week	7.93	1.66	8.00	1.75	7.28	2.05	7.11	2.08	1.90	2.25	2.53	2.50
1–2 days	8.24	1.30	8.27	1.35	7.45	1.72	7.25	1.77	1.59	1.81	2.23	2.09
3 days or more	8.36	1.33	8.38	1.35	7.59	1.79	7.47	1.76	1.55	1.87	2.12	2.08
Age												
14/25	8.38	1.26	8.44	1.21	7.46	1.79	7.26	1.82	1.69	1.80	2.23	2.09
26/35	8.1	1.39	8.13	1.41	7.46	1.69	7.33	1.74	1.64	1.88	2.24	2.13
36/45	8.02	1.4	8.07	1.49	7.55	1.77	7.43	1.71	1.67	2.00	2.28	2.18
46/55	8.02	1.48	8.04	1.62	7.44	1.91	7.31	1.94	1.71	2.1	2.39	2.32
56/65	8.11	1.61	8.22	1.66	7.46	1.95	7.27	1.95	1.66	2.05	2.32	2.35
66/75	8.54	1.38	8.40	1.59	7.59	1.95	7.24	2.00	1.39	1.95	2.25	2.36
76 >	8.43	1.64	8.44	1.64	7.01	2.09	6.9	2.17	1.87	2.28	2.13	2.27
Size of household												
1	7.64	1.74	7.86	1.78	7.12	2.00	7.02	2.05	2.08	2.29	2.55	2.45
2	8.31	1.42	8.27	1.51	7.5	1.87	7.28	1.88	1.57	1.96	2.24	2.25
3	8.17	1.35	8.15	1.54	7.46	1.85	7.34	1.79	1.69	2.01	2.38	2.25
4	8.26	1.35	8.34	1.29	7.5	1.76	7.38	1.80	1.60	1.84	2.19	2.13
5 or more	8.33	1.31	8.43	1.29	7.57	1.79	7.38	1.82	1.62	1.86	2.09	2.00

Table 10.1A (continued)

	Life satisfaction				Energy and optimism				Depression			
	M		F		M		F		M		F	
	mean	SD	mean	SD	mean	SD	mean	SD	mean	SD	mean	SD
N. of children aged 0–17												
0	8.15	1.48	8.19	1.56	7.42	1.88	7.24	1.9	1.71	2.04	2.31	2.28
1	8.17	1.41	8.14	1.47	7.50	1.80	7.32	1.82	1.66	1.96	2.34	2.22
2	8.31	1.34	8.32	1.36	7.51	1.81	7.34	1.85	1.54	1.81	2.22	2.14
3	8.33	1.23	8.42	1.32	7.60	1.70	7.44	1.80	1.63	1.83	2.06	1.98
4 or more	8.52	1.27	8.53	1.28	7.42	2.21	7.43	1.86	1.50	1.68	2.08	2.07
Civil status												
Single, never married	8.23	1.34	8.26	1.36	7.38	1.79	7.21	1.82	1.72	1.85	2.30	2.13
Married	8.26	1.39	8.36	1.42	7.54	1.85	7.42	1.84	1.57	1.98	2.16	2.19
Separated	7.17	1.70	7.23	2.11	7.11	2.14	7.09	2.07	2.47	2.58	3.16	2.75
Divorced	7.81	1.86	7.72	1.71	7.46	2.00	7.18	1.95	1.82	2.28	2.61	2.39
Widower/widow	8.06	1.89	7.98	1.94	7.32	2.1	6.99	2.14	1.59	2.23	2.34	2.50
Education												
Compulsory	8.31	1.48	8.25	1.60	7.37	1.97	7.11	2.09	1.76	2.04	2.45	2.39
Apprenticeship	8.11	1.50	8.20	1.50	7.51	1.92	7.42	1.80	1.61	2.03	2.17	2.20
University entrance diploma	8.12	1.33	8.25	1.34	7.37	1.74	7.31	1.65	1.87	2.05	2.24	2.05
Post-apprenticeship diploma	8.23	1.36	8.21	1.40	7.60	1.78	7.42	1.75	1.50	1.83	2.08	2.03
University degree	8.24	1.31	8.25	1.38	7.37	1.58	7.27	1.68	1.68	1.83	2.31	2.06
Employment status												
Employed	8.22	1.34	8.25	1.38	7.52	1.77	7.36	1.77	1.6	1.86	2.20	2.09

Unemployed	6.64	2.37	7.02	2.09	6.7	2.5	6.69	2.04	3.11	2.92	3.27	2.59
Not in labour force	8.29	1.65	8.24	1.69	7.27	2.08	7.15	2.07	1.79	2.3	2.41	2.47

Income quartiles

q1	7.99	1.65	7.98	1.73	7.35	2.06	7.17	2.08	1.87	2.19	2.49	2.45
q2	8.20	1.41	8.24	1.41	7.52	1.75	7.28	1.83	1.66	1.98	2.32	2.2
q3	8.26	1.33	8.34	1.33	7.45	1.82	7.35	1.7	1.6	1.87	2.17	2.08
q4	8.4	1.23	8.52	1.23	7.54	1.71	7.44	1.67	1.46	1.75	1.97	1.94

Death of a closely related person

No	8.20	1.44	8.24	1.48	7.47	1.85	7.27	1.86	1.62	1.95	2.25	2.19
Yes	8.22	1.41	8.20	1.54	7.45	1.84	7.34	1.89	1.78	2.04	2.37	2.33

Termination of a close relationship

No	8.23	1.41	8.27	1.47	7.48	1.84	7.31	1.87	1.61	1.93	2.20	2.19
Yes	7.82	1.60	7.84	1.61	7.28	1.88	7.07	1.85	2.29	2.30	2.96	2.43

Serious conflicts with or among persons closely related to the respondent

No	8.25	1.39	8.30	1.45	7.50	1.84	7.34	1.86	1.57	1.90	2.14	2.15
Yes	7.67	1.70	7.73	1.66	7.05	1.92	6.92	1.90	2.61	2.40	3.20	2.46

Back problems

Not at all	8.33	1.33	8.39	1.36	7.57	1.81	7.52	1.80	1.46	1.82	1.93	2.01
Somewhat	8.12	1.42	8.18	1.51	7.39	1.80	7.13	1.87	1.80	1.95	2.39	2.20
Very much	7.59	1.88	7.73	1.80	6.93	2.16	6.79	2.01	2.56	2.65	3.34	2.66

Headaches

Not at all	8.29	1.39	8.36	1.44	7.56	1.83	7.45	1.85	1.51	1.87	2.03	2.11
Somewhat	8.03	1.43	8.14	1.43	7.29	1.81	7.18	1.79	1.88	2.02	2.35	2.12
Very much	7.75	1.79	7.76	1.80	6.77	2.17	6.7	2.05	2.86	2.65	3.38	2.67

Chronic illness or long-term health problem

No	8.30	1.34	8.37	1.37	7.63	1.77	7.47	1.78	1.42	1.76	1.97	2.00
Yes	7.99	1.58	7.94	1.67	7.09	1.95	6.91	1.98	2.19	2.29	2.91	2.50

Table 10.1A (continued)

	Life satisfaction				Energy and optimism				Depression			
	M		F		M		F		M		F	
	mean	SD	mean	SD	mean	SD	mean	SD	mean	SD	mean	SD
Health impediment in daily activities quartiles												
q1	8.42	1.29	8.48	1.35	7.80	1.70	7.71	1.74	1.26	1.64	1.74	1.91
q2	8.24	1.16	8.40	1.24	7.37	1.69	7.43	1.66	1.41	1.40	1.80	1.75
q3	8.07	1.25	8.11	1.38	7.21	1.66	7.03	1.69	1.89	1.78	2.37	1.99
q4	7.66	1.82	7.77	1.73	6.68	2.17	6.59	2.02	2.77	2.63	3.39	2.59
Body mass index												
<25	8.22	1.41	8.25	1.47	7.49	1.82	7.32	1.84	1.65	1.95	2.26	2.20
25–29.9	8.10	1.62	7.98	1.77	7.35	1.96	7.13	2.05	1.71	2.19	2.40	2.46
>29.9	7.66	1.75	7.97	1.81	7.06	2.39	6.83	2.29	1.76	2.35	2.75	2.71
Nationality												
Foreign	7.93	1.74	7.89	1.78	7.54	2.02	7.07	2.14	1.92	2.35	2.72	2.61
Swiss	8.24	1.37	8.27	1.45	7.45	1.82	7.32	1.83	1.62	1.90	2.22	2.16
Region of residence												
Lake Geneva	8.12	1.57	8.06	1.60	7.52	1.99	7.37	1.99	1.85	2.23	2.57	2.47
Middleland	8.20	1.43	8.22	1.49	7.47	1.80	7.27	1.88	1.65	1.98	2.29	2.19
NW Switzerland	8.19	1.29	8.20	1.49	7.45	1.73	7.24	1.84	1.62	1.81	2.22	2.15
Zurich	8.18	1.36	8.29	1.39	7.36	1.74	7.24	1.72	1.63	1.87	2.19	2.08
East Switzerland	8.37	1.36	8.34	1.44	7.47	1.93	7.27	1.89	1.42	1.80	1.99	2.10
Central Switzerland	8.27	1.51	8.44	1.34	7.52	1.81	7.41	1.75	1.64	1.89	1.94	1.89
Ticino	8.07	1.51	8.03	1.81	7.44	2.15	7.16	2.10	1.94	2.27	3.14	2.74

11. Standing together: is family a resilience factor for subjective wellbeing?

Dalila De Rosa and Matteo Rizzolli

11.1 INTRODUCTION

The term social support, as reported by Barrera and colleagues (1981, p. 435), 'has been popularized to connote the various forms of aid and assistance supplied by family members, friends, neighbors, and others'. The definition underlines either the sphere of social support related to the immediate family or the broader nature of sociality as referred to social interactions. Both aspects were found to be positively associated with subjective wellbeing and human flourishing and many studies on quality of life emphasized social support as a crucial determinant of wellbeing (Abbey and Andrews 1985). On one side married people were found to be happier and more satisfied, with higher levels of purpose in life, optimism and energy and displaying better wage premiums and financial resources than all the other groups (Cohen 1988; House et al. 1988; Case et al. 1992; Gove et al. 1990; Inglehart 1990; Stutzer and Frey 2006; Blanchflower and Oswald 2004; Bierman et al. 2006). On the other hand, people with more satisfying social relations, larger amounts of friends and a higher consumption of relational goods were found to be better off in terms of health, life satisfaction and happiness (Colón et al. 1991; Cacioppo and Cacioppo 2014; Luo et al. 2012; Becchetti et al. 2008; Bruni and Stanca 2008). Furthermore, both family and social relationships were considered as key factors to overcome stressful events (Myers 2003), playing a supportive and protective role against shocks. Individuals receiving higher social support were found to cope better with a variety of life crises including bereavement, rape, job loss, and illness (House 1981; Abbey and Andrews 1985). According to Becker (1981) marriage can be considered as a basic insurance against adverse life events and provides important protective barriers against the stressful consequences of external threats (Liu et al. 2013; Gove et al. 1983; Umberson 1992; Ross 1995). Moreover, it provides economic advantages and it is

215

considered a safety net with married people affording better housing, food and services (Stack and Eshleman 1998) and married men displaying a wage premium and job advantages (Korenman and Neumark 1991).

This chapter investigates the role of different family types as both a driver factor and a buffer for subjective wellbeing. The work relies on the recent economic crisis as an external source of individual stress in order to challenge the protective role of family. The hypothesis tests whether close family relations constitute a buffer against unforeseen economic uncertainty: Which types of families are happier? Did people surrounded by stronger family ties experience lower drops in wellbeing during the recent recession?

The chapter is structured as follows. The next section is a literature review on the application of marriage, family and wellbeing. In sections three and four the data and the method are reported. In section five the results are commented upon.

11.2   LITERATURE REVIEW ON MARRIAGE, FAMILY AND WELLBEING

The link between marriage and wellbeing has been explored from different perspectives: researchers exploited the effects of marriage on health, income, wages, happiness, social wellbeing and psychological health.

Evidence strongly supports the link between health and social/family ties: indeed, compared with those having few social ties, people are less likely to die prematurely if supported by close relationships with friends, family or members of other support groups (Cohen 1988; House et al. 1988). Similarly, broken social ties (becoming widowed, fired or divorced) were found to correlate with increased vulnerability to disease (Dohrenwend et al. 1982). Furthermore, among heart attack patients the rate of a recurring attack within six months was found doubled among those living alone (Case et al. 1992), while among leukaemia patients preparing to undergo bone marrow transplants those who said they had strong social support from their family or friends were found to live longer (Colón et al. 1991).

When looking at happiness the story looks similar: the happiest university students were the ones displaying higher satisfaction with their love life (Emmons and Diener 1985) and those enjoying close relationships were found to cope better with various stresses (Abbey and Andrews 1985; Perlman and Rook 1987). In particular, with regard to marriage, a number of studies support the idea that married people are happier and more satisfied with life compared to those who are single or widowed, and especially those who are divorced or separated (Gove et al. 1990; Inglehart 1990).

Stack and Eshleman (1998) tested the relationship between marital status and happiness, marital status and financial satisfaction and marital status and perceived health in 17 nations and found that, in 16 nations, married people were significantly happier both than single and than cohabiters and they were significantly better off in terms of financial and health satisfaction compared to all the other categories. Blanchflower and Oswald (2004) found that in the US and the UK reported wellbeing (happiness and life satisfaction) was greatest among women, married people, the highly educated and those whose parents did not divorce. They also reported that subsequent marriages are less happy while long-lasting marriages are worth US$100 000 per annum. Moreover, some researchers (Stutzer and Frey 2006) investigated on the possibility of selection bias in the marriage, finding that those who married younger (before 30) were on average singles with above average life satisfaction even before marriage.

On the psychological side of wellbeing, most studies examining marital status and psychological distress found that married men and women have a mental health advantage and present lower distress outcomes compared to their unmarried counterparts (Pearlin and Johnson 1977; Gore and Mangione 1983; Gove et al. 1990; Ross and Mirowsky 1989). Moreover, when looking at the different dimensions that are supposed to capture the functioning and the realization of a person's potential (e.g. competence, emotional stability, engagement, meaning and purpose in life, optimism, accomplishment, social relationships, self-esteem and vitality) the relation between marriage and wellbeing still holds. Bierman et al. (2006) found that the consistently married had significantly higher purpose in life than all other groups once age, race and the presence of children were controlled for. Differently, Shapiro and Keyes (2008) registered only a modest wellbeing advantage for married persons against single persons, while there was more consistent evidence that cohabitants had lower wellbeing than married people. The weaker effect of cohabitations on wellbeing is also confirmed in other studies (Stack and Eshleman 1998), and the phenomenon is known as the 'cohabitation gap' (Soons and Kalmijn 2009). Despite this evidence, Pirani and Vignoli (2016) tested the cohabitation gap hypothesis over time in Italy, finding that even though over the second half of the 1990s cohabiters were running a significantly higher risk of being dissatisfied with their family life, from the first decade of the 2000s the association between union type and family life satisfaction weakened, and data from the second decade of the 2000s was no longer significant, suggesting that cohabiters are no longer less satisfied than spouses. Always with reference to the positive effect of marital status on psychological wellbeing a contrasting position is proposed by Marks and Lambert (1998): the authors found that even though transition to separation/divorce or widowhood was constantly associated with negative effects across a number of dimensions of wellbeing, marriage did not always have a positive robust influence on all dimensions of psychological wellbeing. In fact, there were also cases where unmarried people reported better wellbeing than the married (e.g. in autonomy and personal growth dimensions), suggesting that marriage is not always a universal beneficial determinant of all dimensions of psychological wellbeing.

Moving on to the relation between parenthood and wellbeing, mixed results arise. Some researchers discovered a positive relationship between parenthood and subjective wellbeing, with parents reporting higher levels of happiness, life satisfaction, self-esteem, positive emotions and meaning in life (Stutzer and Frey 2006; Haller and Hadler 2006; Hansen et al. 2009; Angeles 2010; Nelson et al. 2013; Aassve et al. 2012). Kholer et al. (2005) highlighted a large and positive effect on happiness only for the first child, while Herbst and Ifcher (2016), using US data, indicated that parents become happier than non-parents only over a longer time span. However, other researchers reported that having children is negatively related to subjective wellbeing and that the negative relation is mostly explained by the negative impact on financial satisfaction (Stanca 2012; Colombo et al. 2018; Beja 2015; Bhargava et al. 2014).

To this picture it worth adding what has been called family resilience theory. The concept arises from psychology and with the aim of family therapy. The National Network for Family Resiliency defines resilience as 'the family's ability to cultivate strengths to positively meet the challenges of life'. Atkinson et al. (2009) define individual resilience as 'the ability to bounce back and have better physical and mental health outcomes'. Beyond seeing individual family members as potential resources for individual resilience, the concept of family resilience focuses on risk and resilience in the family as a functional unit (Walsh, 1996, 2003; Walsh and Rolland, 2006). The idea is that serious crises and persistent adversity have an impact on the whole family, and in turn key family processes, characteristics, dimensions and properties mediate the adaptation of all members and their relationships. Without deepening the analysis with the psychological and behavioural process able to make families more resilient, in applied economics some researchers focused on the protective role of marriage. Becker (1981) offered the first theoretical framework, which considers marriage as a basic insurance against adverse life events. Thanks to household specialization, each of the spouses has advantageous conditions for human capital accumulation and this is reflected in married people earning higher incomes than single people. In particular, Korenman and Neumark (1991) collected data from a company personnel file to investigate marital pay differences. They found that married workers had a marital pay premium, persisting even within a single firm for a relatively homogeneous group of occupations (managers and professionals) and that married workers in this company received higher performance ratings from their supervisor, displaying higher productivity. Liu et al. (2013) focused on the link between life satisfaction and marital status/marital quality in China. They found that marriage still serves as an important protection against the stressful consequences of external threats.

11.3   DATA

The empirical application is based on a harmonized dataset derived from the Italian National Survey 'Aspects of Daily Life' carried out each year from 1993 by the Italian National Statistical Institute. The survey collects information on citizens' habits and the daily problems they cope with. The thematic areas mainly investigated wide arrays of information from the economic situation to social life, health, lifestyle, leisure and work time, as well as individual personal satisfaction on different life dimensions and on the quality of public services. The dataset provides objective and subjective measures with the aim of depicting a general understanding of the national quality of life.

The dependent variable is derived from the general life satisfaction question: 'All things considered, how satisfied are you with your life as a whole, on a scale between 0 and 10?' This variable has only been available since 2010, thus the analysis considers only the period 2010–15. Yet, using different specifications other individual subjective information is considered as dependent variables: satisfaction with health, job, family/friends relations and household's economic condition, all measured on a scale between 1 and 5. The variables of satisfaction were dichotomized for modelling purpose.

The interest variable of family structure is shaped on the concept of family nucleus and the word family refers exclusively to the primary family's members. Still, given the complexity involved in the definition of family it deserves a bit of discussion. In the mid-1940s the functionalist sociologist George Peter Murdock provided one of the classic definitions of family as 'a social group characterised by common residence, economic co-operation and reproduction. It includes adults of both sexes, at least two of whom maintain a socially-approved sexual relationship, and one or more children, own or adopted, of the sexually cohabiting adults' (Murdock 1949). Yet the last decades have seen the traditional concept of marriage and family quickly changing. Marriage rates are decreasing, cohabitation is becoming a consolidated status and non-traditional families are more common. In this context, if on one side the peculiarities of living together, sharing economic resources and possibly having children remain valid, on the other side a redefinition of family structure is required (Sharma 2013). The redefinition has to cover either the traditional family as composed by married parents with children, or the modern concept of family where cohabiting parents or cohabiting couples appear and married couples are voluntarily childless. Similarly, recent decades have seen the increase of single-parent families where one parent raises one or more children on their own, and numerous studies have focused on the effects of growing up in a single-parent family in terms of children wellbeing (Gennetian 2005; Krein and Beller 1988). Moreover, according to Johnson et al.'s (1999) commitment framework three types of marital commitment can be defined: personal, moral or structural commitment. The first two types of commitment are experienced as internal to the individual and depend on a person's own attitudes and values: personal commitment refers to the extent to which an individual wishes to stay in the relationship, whereas moral commitment refers to the extent an individual believes they ought to stay in the relationship. Contrarily, structural commitment is experienced as external to the individual and refers to the perceptions of constraints that make it costly for the individual to leave the relationship. There are many motivations for individuals to feel personally, morally or structurally committed to a relationship. Among them the presence of children is generally associated with higher commitment and represents a stabilizing factor in cohabiting relationships (Brown and Booth 1996), similarly the religious component enhances the extent of moral commitment in such a way that religious marriage results in more stable unions than civil marriage (ISTAT 2016; Stanley et al. 2004). Furthermore, legal constraints as well as social pressure represent few of the exit costs married couples may experience. This theoretical framework of consent reflects, on the one hand, the strengths of keeping a relationship, and on the other, the costs of letting it go. With these considerations in mind, the variable of family structure is modelled to address such complexity and to meet our assumption: that the higher the strength of family ties the higher the probability of family being a resilience factor for subjective wellbeing. Accordingly, the strength of family ties is modelled on moral commitment factors, namely the presence of children and religiosity, and structural constraints, namely legal marital status. It is worth remarking that these are not the only types of moral or structural commitment but the ones matching data availability. Therefore, religious married couples and married couples with children are assumed to display stronger family ties than cohabiters without or with children, respectively. Conversely, single parents and single individuals are assumed to rely on lower/absent family ties. Therefore the variable of family structure is shaped as follows: (1) *married couples* (with or without children; religious and not religious) as a representation of the traditional nuclear family; (2) *cohabiting couples* (with or without children; religious and not religious) as a representation of the modern quasi-nuclear family; (3) *single father and single mother*; and (4) *single individuals* (adults living alone or with other relatives such as two sisters or with friends) as a representation of the non-family.

The set of individual characteristics is represented by age, gender, divorced/widowed status, education, working condition and working position, leisure activities and social interactions.

The set of regional characteristics come from the Italian Statistical Institute territorial accounts data source, and reports those regional aggregates supposed to capture the local belief system related to the family's values. It includes the regional divorce rate, the ratio between religious marriage and civil marriage, and an indicator capturing the degree of institutionalization of cohabitation as a percentage of cohabiting couples over the total number of couples. Descriptive statistics presented in Appendix 1 (Table 11.1A).

MODEL SPECIFICATION

The first four model specifications consider life satisfaction (and separately all the subjective domains) as a probabilistic function of family structure and individual and local characteristics, with region and time fixed effects. Life satisfaction is the proxy of individual wellbeing, while family structure is our independent variable that consists in a set of dummies as modelled in section three. Individual characteristics represent individual objective factors such as age, gender, education, working position, working conditions and religiosity. Here the aim is to highlight the average effect of different family types on subjective wellbeing.

In particular:

$$LifeSatisfaction_{irt} = \alpha + \beta_1 \, couples_{irt} + \delta IC + \zeta RC + \mu_r + \lambda_t + \varepsilon_{irt}$$
$$(11.1)$$

This baseline specification considers standard nuclear or quasi-nuclear family as married couples and cohabiting couples to be compared with the benchmark of the non-standard family, namely single parents and single individuals. The term *IC* represents the vector of individual characteristics, the term *RC* the set of regional characteristics, while the terms μ_r *and* λ_t represent respectively region and time fixed effects. The assumption is that the stronger the family ties the higher the probability of being satisfied. According to this specification, couples are assumed to have stronger family ties and higher than expected Odd Ratio (OR).

$$LifeSatisfaction_{irt} = \alpha + \beta_1\ married\ couples_{irt} + \beta_2\ cohabiters_{irt} + \delta IC + \zeta RC + \mu_r + \lambda_t + \varepsilon_{irt} \quad (11.2)$$

The second specification investigates the strength of the structural and personal commitment. It compares being married and cohabiting with respect to the categories of single individuals. The hypothesis is the higher the level of commitment the higher the probability of being well. Hence, married couples are expected to report higher OR either with respect to single or to cohabiters.

$$LifeSatisfaction_{irt} = \alpha + \beta_1\ married\ with\ children_{irt} + \beta_2\ cohabiters\ with\ children_{irt} + \beta_3\ married\ without\ children_{irt} + \beta_4\ cohabiters\ without\ children_{irt} + \beta_3\ single\ parents_{irt} + \delta IC + \zeta RC + \mu_r + \lambda_t + \varepsilon_{irt} \quad (11.3)$$

The third specification investigates the strength of the moral commitment with respect to children. It differentiates family structure according to the presence of children (below age 24) in the nucleus. Therefore, married couples with children and cohabiters with children are compared respectively to married couples and cohabiters without children, whereas single parents are compared to single persons. Here the assumption is that familiar ties strengthen with the presence of children so that couples with children are expected to display higher OR. However, it is worth noting that empirical findings show contrasting results on the relation between presence of children and subjective wellbeing, as highlighted in section two.

$$LifeSatisfaction_{irt} = \alpha + \beta_1\ religious\ married_{irt} + \beta_2\ non\text{-}religious\ married_{irt} + \beta_3\ religious\ cohabiters_{irt} + \beta_4\ non\text{-}religious\ cohabiters_{irt} + \delta IC + \zeta RC + \mu_r + \lambda_t + \varepsilon_{irt} \quad (11.4)$$

Similarly, the fourth specification investigates the strength of the moral commitment with respect to religiosity. It differentiates family structure as according to religiosity. Hence, religious married couples are compared to non-religious married couples, religious cohabiters to non-religious. In this case, the assumption is that religious couples display higher levels of moral commitment than non-religious couples reflected in higher satisfaction. It means that the OR of religious couples is expected to be higher than for other family configurations.

$$LifeSatisfaction_{irt} = \alpha + \beta_1 \, couples_{irt} + \beta_2 \, couples_{irt}{}^* \, crisis + \beta_3 \, crisis + \delta IC$$
$$+ \zeta RC + \mu_r + \lambda_t + \varepsilon_{irt} \qquad (11.5)$$

Finally, in order to proxy the effect of the crisis, the fifth specification assesses the effect of being in a family during the crisis on subjective wellbeing. In particular, we considered 2012–14 as the years of the crisis since these represent the years the unemployment rate skyrocketed (Figure 11.3). Here the assumption is that family constitutes a buffer against an exogenous shock, which has affected the whole population at the same time. If the hypothesis is verified, we should observe consistently higher OR for couples over the crisis (coefficient β_2).

It is worth noting that, in absence of longitudinal data or appropriate instrumental variables, the possible unobservable heterogeneity was controlled through time and spatial fixed effects and the set of individual characteristics. Still it was not possible to tackle individuals within heterogeneity and the model specifications just look at the average effects.

RESULTS

The first specification aims at testing the individual effect of being part of a family on subjective wellbeing. From a descriptive point of view, Figure 11.1 shows the Kernel distribution of the four different familiar categories. For values of satisfaction lower than 7 the curves of single persons and single parents lie above the curve of the couples, whereas for

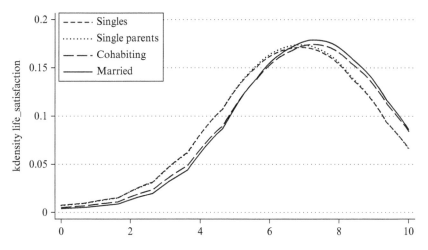

Figure 11.1   Kernel distribution of life satisfaction by four family types

values higher than 7 the shift is evident: couples display higher satisfaction than single persons and single parents and precisely married couples report the highest figures.

Table 11.1 reports logistic estimates for Equation 11.1.

The first row displays the probability of being satisfied experienced by those belonging to a family (both married or cohabiters) with respect to the reference category of single. Couples display a statistically higher probability of achieving life satisfaction with an odds ratio of 1.60. The latter result is consistent with health satisfaction (1.35) and family and friends satisfaction (2.18, 1.31). By contrast, couples report a lower probability of being satisfied with leisure than single individuals (0.918). Almost all the individual covariates display significant estimates and it is worth mentioning two figures: first, marriage length is not a significant predictor of life satisfaction as a whole but longer marriages increase the probability of being satisfied with economic resources, family, leisure and also labour; second, having children is good for life satisfaction as a whole (1.24) but bad for economic and leisure time.

Table 11.2 reports logistic estimates for Equation 11.2.

Married couples show an higher probability of achieving life satisfaction than single individuals with an odds ratio of 1.70, followed by cohabiters that report an odds ratio of 1.49. Yet the coefficients of married and cohabiters are not statically different to one another, therefore the two types of union are not directly comparable as far as life satisfaction is concerned. By contrast, the probability of married couples is found to be significantly higher both than single and than cohabiters with respect to health, family and friends satisfaction (test on coefficient equality significant). The latter results confirm the presence of a cohabitation gap.

The third specification aims at testing moral commitment in the form of children present in the nucleus. Here the assumption is that family ties strengthen with the presence of children so that couples with children are expected to display a higher odds ratio than couples without. Table 11.3 reports estimates from Equation 11.3.

The results clearly highlight that couples with or without children and also single parents report a higher probability of being satisfied with life than single individuals. Yet the test on coefficient for life satisfaction is not statistically significant, meaning that the categories married with and without children as well as cohabiters with and without children cannot be compared. By contrast, with respect to health the test on coefficient is significant for cohabiters, suggesting that cohabiters with children report a higher probability of being satisfied with health (1.46) than cohabiters without children (1.10). Similarly, with respect to leisure those who are

Table 11.1 Couples and life satisfaction

VARIABLES	(1) life_satisfaction	(2) eco_sat	(3) health_sat	(4) family_sat	(5) friend_sat	(6) leisure_sat	(7) work_sat
couple	1.605***	0.984	1.351***	2.185***	1.311***	0.918***	0.966
	(0.180)	(0.023)	(0.046)	(0.086)	(0.044)	(0.021)	(0.030)
age	1.075***	1.046***	0.830***	0.984***	0.953***	0.958***	0.994
	(0.018)	(0.004)	(0.004)	(0.006)	(0.005)	(0.003)	(0.005)
female	0.948	1.074***	0.819***	1.016	0.950***	0.767***	1.017
	(0.057)	(0.013)	(0.013)	(0.022)	(0.016)	(0.009)	(0.019)
divorced	0.739***	0.806***	0.998	0.649***	1.019	0.960*	1.049
	(0.077)	(0.020)	(0.033)	(0.022)	(0.034)	(0.023)	(0.035)
widowed	0.809*	1.170***	0.831***	1.429***	0.906***	1.095***	1.258***
	(0.097)	(0.035)	(0.027)	(0.067)	(0.033)	(0.031)	(0.076)
marriage_length	0.996	1.004***	0.994***	1.006***	0.999	1.004***	1.003***
	(0.003)	(0.001)	(0.001)	(0.001)	(0.001)	(0.001)	(0.001)
working_position	0.901***	0.848***	0.967***	0.960***	0.977**	0.942***	0.842***
	(0.034)	(0.006)	(0.009)	(0.012)	(0.010)	(0.007)	(0.009)
employment_status	1.350***	1.059***	1.314***	1.091***	1.129***	0.677***	1.218***
	(0.054)	(0.009)	(0.014)	(0.017)	(0.013)	(0.006)	(0.019)
education	1.160**	1.209***	1.233***	1.005	1.044**	0.989	1.015
	(0.074)	(0.016)	(0.019)	(0.023)	(0.018)	(0.013)	(0.021)
economic_condition	3.491***	6.945***	1.817***	1.713***	1.480***	1.586***	2.512***
	(0.228)	(0.086)	(0.027)	(0.036)	(0.024)	(0.019)	(0.043)
religiosity	1.330***	1.114***	1.154***	1.164***	1.151***	1.073***	1.108***
	(0.038)	(0.005)	(0.007)	(0.011)	(0.008)	(0.005)	(0.009)
children	1.246***	0.959***	1.070***	1.062**	1.000	0.796***	1.049**
	(0.104)	(0.015)	(0.025)	(0.030)	(0.022)	(0.012)	(0.021)

Table 11.1 (continued)

VARIABLES	(1) life_satisfaction	(2) eco_sat	(3) health_sat	(4) family_sat	(5) friend_sat	(6) leisure_sat	(7) work_sat
friends	1.939***	1.121***	1.486***	1.396***	4.433***	2.073***	1.204***
	(0.111)	(0.014)	(0.022)	(0.030)	(0.073)	(0.025)	(0.022)
social_interaction	2.503***	1.239***	1.437***	1.155***	1.434***	1.349***	1.045**
	(0.217)	(0.017)	(0.027)	(0.028)	(0.028)	(0.018)	(0.019)
coabh_rat1	2.616	0.621	1.019	0.913	1.343	2.332	0.953
	(8.088)	(0.402)	(0.823)	(1.027)	(1.158)	(1.461)	(0.883)
divorce_rate	1.140	1.514	1.540	0.256***	0.480**	0.750	1.611
	(1.463)	(0.415)	(0.515)	(0.119)	(0.172)	(0.196)	(0.615)
unemployment_rate	1.049*	1.010*	1.003	0.985	0.997	1.009	0.990
	(0.026)	(0.006)	(0.007)	(0.010)	(0.007)	(0.005)	(0.008)
Constant	2.818**	0.113***	8.845***	4.895***	2.210***	4.313***	1.270
	(1.376)	(0.012)	(1.223)	(0.908)	(0.319)	(0.439)	(0.194)
Observations	152230	152757	152631	152480	152505	152390	88770
Wald chi^2 (40)	1401	32191	16749	4581	12879	12132	5123
Prob > chi^2	0	0	0	0	0	0	0
Pseudo R-squared	0.102	0.192	0.153	0.0590	0.123	0.0691	0.0591

Note: Robust seeform in parentheses *** p<0.01, ** p<0.05, * p<0.1.

Table 11.2 Marriage and life satisfaction

VARIABLES	(1) life_satisfaction	(2) eco_sat	(3) health_sat	(4) family_sat	(5) friend_sat	(6) leisure_sat	(7) work_sat
married	1.700***	1.029	1.455***	2.353***	1.427***	0.882***	0.988
	(0.225)	(0.028)	(0.058)	(0.111)	(0.055)	(0.023)	(0.035)
cohabiters	1.491***	0.920***	1.204***	1.983***	1.166***	0.973	0.938*
	(0.215)	(0.029)	(0.054)	(0.101)	(0.049)	(0.029)	(0.036)
age	1.075***	1.046***	0.830***	0.984**	0.953***	0.958***	0.995
	(0.018)	(0.004)	(0.004)	(0.006)	(0.005)	(0.003)	(0.005)
female	0.948	1.074***	0.819***	1.016	0.950***	0.767***	1.018
	(0.056)	(0.013)	(0.013)	(0.022)	(0.016)	(0.009)	(0.019)
divorced	0.752***	0.821***	1.027	0.662***	1.054	0.945**	1.058*
	(0.079)	(0.021)	(0.034)	(0.023)	(0.036)	(0.023)	(0.036)
widowed	0.813*	1.174***	0.838***	1.434***	0.914***	1.091***	1.264***
	(0.097)	(0.035)	(0.028)	(0.067)	(0.033)	(0.031)	(0.077)
marriage_length	0.995	1.003***	0.992***	1.004***	0.997***	1.005***	1.003***
	(0.003)	(0.001)	(0.001)	(0.001)	(0.001)	(0.001)	(0.001)
working_position	0.901***	0.848***	0.967***	0.960***	0.978***	0.941***	0.843***
	(0.034)	(0.006)	(0.009)	(0.012)	(0.010)	(0.007)	(0.009)
employment_status	1.349***	1.057***	1.313***	1.089***	1.127***	0.678***	1.218***
	(0.054)	(0.009)	(0.014)	(0.017)	(0.013)	(0.006)	(0.019)
education	1.157**	1.206***	1.229***	1.002	1.040**	0.991	1.014
	(0.074)	(0.016)	(0.019)	(0.023)	(0.018)	(0.013)	(0.021)
economic_condition	3.489***	6.942***	1.816***	1.712***	1.478***	1.587***	2.511***
	(0.228)	(0.086)	(0.027)	(0.036)	(0.024)	(0.019)	(0.043)
religiosity	1.329***	1.113***	1.152***	1.163***	1.149***	1.074***	1.107***
	(0.038)	(0.006)	(0.007)	(0.011)	(0.008)	(0.005)	(0.009)

Table 11.2 (continued)

VARIABLES	(1) life_satisfaction	(2) eco_sat	(3) health_sat	(4) family_sat	(5) friend_sat	(6) leisure_sat	(7) work_sat
children	1.226**	0.946***	1.049**	1.040	0.976	0.806***	1.042**
	(0.106)	(0.015)	(0.025)	(0.031)	(0.023)	(0.012)	(0.021)
friends	1.939***	1.122***	1.486***	1.397***	4.437***	2.072***	1.204***
	(0.111)	(0.015)	(0.022)	(0.030)	(0.073)	(0.025)	(0.022)
social_interaction	2.507***	1.240***	1.438***	1.157***	1.436***	1.347***	1.046**
	(0.218)	(0.017)	(0.027)	(0.028)	(0.029)	(0.018)	(0.019)
coabh_rat1	2.742	0.651	1.078	0.976	1.477	2.233	0.983
	(8.481)	(0.422)	(0.871)	(1.099)	(1.274)	(1.399)	(0.910)
divorce_rate	1.132	1.510	1.531	0.254***	0.475**	0.753	1.610
	(1.453)	(0.414)	(0.512)	(0.119)	(0.170)	(0.197)	(0.614)
unemployment_rate	1.049*	1.010*	1.003	0.985	0.997	1.009	0.990
	(0.026)	(0.006)	(0.007)	(0.010)	(0.007)	(0.005)	(0.008)
Constant	2.806**	0.112***	8.711***	4.891***	2.183***	4.321***	1.265
	(1.369)	(0.012)	(1.204)	(0.907)	(0.315)	(0.440)	(0.194)
Observations	152230	152757	152631	152480	152505	152390	88770
Wald chi² (41)	1402	32189	16775	4565	12897	12143	5124
Prob > chi²	0	0	0	0	0	0	0
Pseudo R-squared	0.102	0.192	0.153	0.0591	0.123	0.0692	0.0591
chi-square	0.614	10.94***	13.76***	8.056***	18.81***	9.154***	1.532
test:married=cohab							

Note: Robust seeform in parentheses *** p<0.01, ** p<0.05, * p<0.1.

Table 11.3 Children and life satisfaction

VARIABLES	(1) life_satisfaction	(2) eco_sat	(3) health_sat	(4) family_sat	(5) friend_sat	(6) leisure_sat	(7) work_sat
married_with_children	2.126***	0.953**	1.537***	2.457***	1.395***	0.706***	1.020
	(0.255)	(0.023)	(0.055)	(0.101)	(0.049)	(0.017)	(0.032)
married_without_children	1.852***	0.977	1.510***	2.415***	1.444***	0.860***	0.972
	(0.300)	(0.029)	(0.068)	(0.137)	(0.063)	(0.025)	(0.039)
cohabiters_with_children	1.851***	0.900**	1.461***	2.125***	1.186***	0.764***	1.043
	(0.396)	(0.040)	(0.104)	(0.157)	(0.070)	(0.031)	(0.055)
cohabiters_without_children	1.534**	0.857***	1.107*	1.950***	1.126**	0.981	0.859***
	(0.281)	(0.034)	(0.060)	(0.127)	(0.061)	(0.038)	(0.043)
single_parents	1.435**	0.791***	1.082	1.065	0.977	0.765***	0.948
	(0.228)	(0.030)	(0.056)	(0.052)	(0.047)	(0.026)	(0.043)
age	1.077***	1.044***	0.831***	0.984**	0.953***	0.957***	0.994
	(0.018)	(0.004)	(0.004)	(0.006)	(0.005)	(0.003)	(0.005)
female	0.942	1.079***	0.818***	1.015	0.950***	0.768***	1.023
	(0.056)	(0.014)	(0.013)	(0.022)	(0.016)	(0.009)	(0.019)
divorced	0.739***	0.842***	1.028	0.660***	1.056	0.951***	1.079**
	(0.078)	(0.022)	(0.035)	(0.023)	(0.037)	(0.024)	(0.037)
widowed	0.816*	1.172***	0.842***	1.436***	0.916***	1.089***	1.280***
	(0.097)	(0.035)	(0.028)	(0.067)	(0.033)	(0.031)	(0.078)
marriage_length	0.993*	1.004***	0.992***	1.003**	0.997***	1.005***	1.003***
	(0.004)	(0.001)	(0.001)	(0.001)	(0.001)	(0.001)	(0.001)
working_position	0.902***	0.848***	0.967***	0.961***	0.978**	0.941***	0.842***
	(0.034)	(0.006)	(0.009)	(0.012)	(0.010)	(0.007)	(0.009)
employment_status	1.349***	1.057***	1.313***	1.089***	1.128***	0.678***	1.220***
	(0.054)	(0.009)	(0.014)	(0.017)	(0.013)	(0.006)	(0.020)
education	1.156**	1.207***	1.229***	1.002	1.040**	0.991	1.014
	(0.073)	(0.016)	(0.019)	(0.023)	(0.018)	(0.013)	(0.021)

Table 11.3 (continued)

VARIABLES	(1) life_satisfaction	(2) eco_sat	(3) health_sat	(4) family_sat	(5) friend_sat	(6) leisure_sat	(7) work_sat
economic_condition	3.490***	6.942***	1.816***	1.712***	1.478***	1.587***	2.510***
	(0.228)	(0.086)	(0.027)	(0.036)	(0.024)	(0.019)	(0.043)
religiosity	1.329***	1.112***	1.152***	1.163***	1.149***	1.074***	1.107***
	(0.038)	(0.006)	(0.007)	(0.011)	(0.008)	(0.005)	(0.009)
friends	1.942***	1.121***	1.486***	1.397***	4.437***	2.072***	1.203***
	(0.111)	(0.014)	(0.022)	(0.030)	(0.073)	(0.025)	(0.022)
social_interaction	2.507***	1.241***	1.440***	1.157***	1.436***	1.347***	1.047**
	(0.218)	(0.017)	(0.027)	(0.028)	(0.029)	(0.018)	(0.019)
coabh_rat1	2.776	0.648	1.070	0.974	1.471	2.240	0.964
	(8.585)	(0.420)	(0.865)	(1.097)	(1.269)	(1.404)	(0.894)
divorce_rate	1.130	1.521	1.536	0.254***	0.476**	0.753	1.626
	(1.450)	(0.417)	(0.514)	(0.119)	(0.170)	(0.197)	(0.621)
unemployment_rate	1.049*	1.010*	1.003	0.985	0.997	1.009	0.990
	(0.026)	(0.006)	(0.007)	(0.010)	(0.007)	(0.005)	(0.008)
Constant	2.708**	0.116***	8.610***	4.857***	2.179***	4.371***	1.285
	(1.324)	(0.012)	(1.191)	(0.901)	(0.315)	(0.446)	(0.197)
Observations	152230	152757	152631	152480	152505	152390	88770
Wald chi^2 (43)	1407	32183	16784	4569	12902	12147	5133
Prob > chi^2	0	0	0	0	0	0	0
Pseudo R-squared	0.102	0.192	0.153	0.0591	0.123	0.0692	0.0592
married_with_child= married_no_child	1.493	1.738	0.383	0.195	1.563	123.8***	3.966**
cohab_with_child=cohab_ no_child	0.495	0.786	10.50***	0.830	0.472	22.46***	8.412***

Note: Robust seeform in parentheses.

married with children report around a 30 per cent lower probability of being satisfied compared to those who are single, whereas those who are married without children report a 20 per cent lower probability, with a significant test on coefficient: it means, as expected, that those who are married and have children are less satisfied with leisure than their childless counterparts.

The fourth specification aims at testing moral commitment in the form of religiosity. In this case, the assumption is that religious couples display stronger family commitment than non-religious couples and accordingly present a higher probability of being well. Couples are assumed to be religious if they declare that they attend religious church at least a couple of times per year. Therefore, non-religious couples are those who never attend church.[1] Estimates confirm the hypothesis for married couples (see Table 11.4): religious married couples show the largest probability of being satisfied (2.00), whereas non-religious couples report a slightly lower probability (1.21) and the test on coefficient is significant, meaning that religious married are more satisfied. When turning to cohabiters the figure is reversed, with non-religious cohabiters reporting a slightly higher probability (1.5) than religious cohabiters (1.4), yet the test on coefficient is not significant. Similar results are reported for health, family and friends satisfaction with religious married couples reporting significantly higher OR than non-religious married couples. For cohabiters the differences in the ORs are not significant. Results suggest that, although in the case of married couples religious commitment operates as a family tie and this is reflected in the higher probability of being well, in the case of cohabiters religious commitment is not a significant determinant.

The fifth specification challenges the strength of family during the years of the crisis. From a descriptive point of view, life satisfaction has decreased over the period 2010–15 and the reduction has similarly affected married, cohabiters, single parents and single individuals (Figure 11.2). At the same time unemployment sharply increased at the national level by more than four percentage points between 2012 and 2014 (Figure 11.3).

Indeed, the variable *crisis* is a dummy-year variable, which assumes value 1 during the worst years of the crisis (2012–14) and value zero otherwise. The hypothesis is that family constitutes a buffer against economic uncertainty and the stronger the family ties the bigger the protective role of family.

The results improve the baseline specification where the standard nuclear or quasi-nuclear family (married couples and cohabiting couples) are compared to the non-(standard) family, (namely single parents and single individuals). In Table 11.5 couples report a significant 5 per cent

Table 11.4 *Marital religiosity and life satisfaction*

VARIABLES	(1) life_ satisfaction	(2) eco_sat	(3) health_sat	(4) family_sat	(5) friend_sat	(6) leisure_sat	(7) work_sat
married_religious	2.004***	1.020	1.510***	2.492***	1.504***	0.877***	1.010
	(0.275)	(0.028)	(0.061)	(0.120)	(0.059)	(0.023)	(0.037)
married_not_religious	1.218	1.063*	1.281***	2.002***	1.210***	0.901***	0.930*
	(0.170)	(0.034)	(0.057)	(0.108)	(0.053)	(0.028)	(0.039)
cohabiters_religious	1.404*	0.906***	1.203***	2.080***	1.174***	0.967	0.961
	(0.254)	(0.034)	(0.065)	(0.134)	(0.060)	(0.034)	(0.045)
cohabiters_not_religious	1.549**	0.950	1.178**	1.808***	1.120*	0.988	0.893*
	(0.337)	(0.047)	(0.083)	(0.138)	(0.072)	(0.046)	(0.052)
age	1.075***	1.046***	0.831***	0.984**	0.954***	0.958***	0.995
	(0.018)	(0.004)	(0.004)	(0.006)	(0.005)	(0.003)	(0.005)
female	0.942	1.074***	0.818***	1.015	0.948***	0.767***	1.017
	(0.056)	(0.013)	(0.013)	(0.022)	(0.016)	(0.009)	(0.019)
divorced	0.757***	0.821***	1.025	0.663***	1.054	0.945**	1.059*
	(0.080)	(0.021)	(0.034)	(0.023)	(0.036)	(0.023)	(0.036)
widowed	0.839	1.171***	0.847***	1.450***	0.926**	1.089***	1.277***
	(0.099)	(0.035)	(0.028)	(0.067)	(0.033)	(0.031)	(0.078)
marriage_length	0.995	1.003***	0.992***	1.004***	0.998***	1.005***	1.003***
	(0.003)	(0.001)	(0.001)	(0.001)	(0.001)	(0.001)	(0.001)
working_position	0.901***	0.848***	0.967***	0.960***	0.977***	0.941***	0.843***
	(0.034)	(0.006)	(0.009)	(0.012)	(0.010)	(0.007)	(0.009)
employment_sta	1.346***	1.058***	1.312***	1.087***	1.125***	0.678***	1.217***
	(0.054)	(0.009)	(0.014)	(0.017)	(0.013)	(0.006)	(0.019)
education	1.159**	1.205***	1.231***	1.004	1.042**	0.991	1.016
	(0.073)	(0.016)	(0.019)	(0.023)	(0.018)	(0.013)	(0.021)

economic_cond	3.477***	6.944***	1.815***	1.709***	1.476***	1.588***	2.509***
	(0.227)	(0.086)	(0.027)	(0.036)	(0.024)	(0.019)	(0.043)
religiosity	1.236***	1.119***	1.129***	1.133***	1.115***	1.078***	1.092***
	(0.039)	(0.006)	(0.008)	(0.012)	(0.009)	(0.006)	(0.010)
children	1.216**	0.947***	1.046*	1.036	0.973	0.806***	1.041**
	(0.105)	(0.015)	(0.025)	(0.030)	(0.023)	(0.012)	(0.021)
friends	1.938***	1.122***	1.486***	1.397***	4.440***	2.072***	1.205***
	(0.111)	(0.014)	(0.022)	(0.030)	(0.073)	(0.025)	(0.022)
social_interaction	2.498***	1.240***	1.437***	1.155***	1.434***	1.348***	1.045**
	(0.217)	(0.017)	(0.027)	(0.028)	(0.029)	(0.018)	(0.019)
coabh_rat1	2.748	0.654	1.058	0.951	1.446	2.239	0.972
	(8.487)	(0.424)	(0.855)	(1.069)	(1.247)	(1.403)	(0.900)
divorce_rate	1.158	1.508	1.536	0.255***	0.477**	0.752	1.624
	(1.488)	(0.414)	(0.514)	(0.119)	(0.170)	(0.197)	(0.620)
unemployment_r	1.049*	1.010*	1.003	0.985	0.997	1.009	0.990
	(0.026)	(0.006)	(0.007)	(0.010)	(0.007)	(0.005)	(0.008)
Constant	3.302**	0.111***	9.125***	5.193***	2.338***	4.282***	1.300*
	(1.613)	(0.012)	(1.262)	(0.962)	(0.338)	(0.437)	(0.199)
Observations	152230	152757	152631	152480	152505	152390	88770
Wald chi^2 (43)	1419	32189	16799	4545	12938	12143	5133
Prob > chi^2	0	0	0	0	0	0	0
Pseudo R-squared	0.104	0.192	0.154	0.0596	0.123	0.0692	0.0592
married_rel=married_no_rel	28.65***	3.437*	39.44***	32.63***	61.78***	1.722	7.336***
cohab_rel=cohab_no_rel	0.131	0.656	0.0644	2.151	0.369	0.155	1.130

Note: Robust seeform in parentheses.

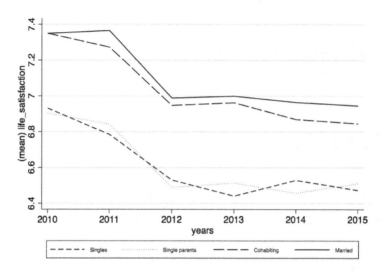

Figure 11.2   Decrease of life satisfaction over the years by four family types

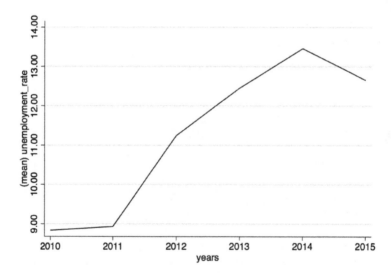

Figure 11.3   Unemployment rate

lower probability of being satisfied with economic resources and with friends' relationships during the years of the crisis. Nonetheless, when looking at overall wellbeing couples report a 24 per cent higher probability of being satisfied with their life as a whole.

Table 11.5 Couples, crisis and life satisfaction

VARIABLES	(1) life_satisfaction	(2) eco_sat	(3) health_sat	(4) family_sat	(5) friend_sat	(6) leisure_sat	(7) work_sat
1.couples	1.436***	1.005	1.381***	2.192***	1.345***	0.930***	0.974
	(0.179)	(0.026)	(0.051)	(0.095)	(0.049)	(0.023)	(0.034)
1.crisis	0.470***	0.833***	0.749***	1.094	1.047	1.008	1.020
	(0.079)	(0.032)	(0.034)	(0.066)	(0.052)	(0.037)	(0.056)
1.couple#1.crisis	1.249**	0.953*	0.953	0.993	0.944*	0.972	0.983
	(0.139)	(0.025)	(0.030)	(0.041)	(0.032)	(0.025)	(0.038)
age	1.075***	1.046***	0.830***	0.984***	0.953***	0.958***	0.994
	(0.018)	(0.004)	(0.004)	(0.006)	(0.005)	(0.003)	(0.005)
female	0.948	1.074***	0.819***	1.016	0.950***	0.767***	1.017
	(0.057)	(0.013)	(0.013)	(0.022)	(0.016)	(0.009)	(0.019)
divorced	0.740***	0.806***	0.998	0.649***	1.019	0.960*	1.049
	(0.077)	(0.020)	(0.033)	(0.022)	(0.034)	(0.023)	(0.035)
widowed	0.808*	1.170***	0.831***	1.429***	0.907***	1.095***	1.258***
	(0.096)	(0.035)	(0.027)	(0.067)	(0.033)	(0.031)	(0.076)
marriage_length	0.996	1.004***	0.994***	1.006***	0.999	1.004***	1.003***
	(0.003)	(0.001)	(0.001)	(0.001)	(0.001)	(0.001)	(0.001)
working_position	0.901***	0.848***	0.967***	0.960***	0.977**	0.942***	0.842***
	(0.034)	(0.006)	(0.009)	(0.012)	(0.010)	(0.007)	(0.009)
employment_stat	1.350***	1.059***	1.314***	1.091***	1.130***	0.677***	1.217***
	(0.054)	(0.009)	(0.014)	(0.017)	(0.013)	(0.006)	(0.019)
education	1.161**	1.209***	1.233***	1.005	1.044**	0.989	1.015
	(0.074)	(0.016)	(0.019)	(0.023)	(0.018)	(0.013)	(0.021)
economic_cond	3.496***	6.945***	1.817***	1.713***	1.479***	1.586***	2.512***
	(0.228)	(0.086)	(0.027)	(0.036)	(0.024)	(0.019)	(0.043)

Table 11.5 (continued)

VARIABLES	(1) life_satisfaction	(2) eco_sat	(3) health_sat	(4) family_sat	(5) friend_sat	(6) leisure_sat	(7) work_sat
religiosity	1.330***	1.114***	1.154***	1.164***	1.151***	1.073***	1.108***
	(0.038)	(0.005)	(0.007)	(0.011)	(0.008)	(0.005)	(0.009)
children	1.249***	0.959***	1.070***	1.061**	1.000	0.796***	1.049**
	(0.104)	(0.015)	(0.025)	(0.030)	(0.022)	(0.012)	(0.021)
friends	1.941***	1.121***	1.486***	1.396***	4.433***	2.073***	1.204***
	(0.111)	(0.014)	(0.022)	(0.030)	(0.073)	(0.025)	(0.022)
social_interaction	2.504***	1.238***	1.437***	1.155***	1.434***	1.349***	1.045**
	(0.217)	(0.017)	(0.027)	(0.028)	(0.028)	(0.018)	(0.019)
coabh_rat1	2.430	0.632	1.031	0.916	1.374	2.361	0.960
	(7.525)	(0.410)	(0.833)	(1.031)	(1.185)	(1.480)	(0.889)
divorce_rate	1.221	1.499	1.525	0.255***	0.474**	0.746	1.604
	(1.570)	(0.411)	(0.510)	(0.119)	(0.170)	(0.195)	(0.612)
unemployment_rat	1.049*	1.010*	1.003	0.985	0.997	1.009*	0.990
	(0.026)	(0.006)	(0.007)	(0.010)	(0.007)	(0.005)	(0.008)
Constant	2.989**	0.111***	8.713***	4.886***	2.170***	4.274***	1.263
	(1.466)	(0.012)	(1.209)	(0.908)	(0.314)	(0.436)	(0.194)
Observations	152230	152757	152631	152480	152505	152390	88770
Wald chi² (41)	1408	32188	16750	4581	12881	12132	5123
Prob > chi²	0	0	0	0	0	0	0
Pseudo R-squared	0.103	0.192	0.153	0.0590	0.123	0.0691	0.0591

Note: Robust seeform in parentheses.

236

CONCLUSION

This chapter investigated the role of family as both a driver factor and a buffer for subjective wellbeing, with special attention to the relationship between different types of family and wellbeing. Indeed, if on the one hand, in the literature, married couples were found to be better off than their unmarried counterparts or than cohabiters, the contribution of this chapter is to extensively disentangle such a relationship by comparing the outcomes of different types of family according to the strength of family ties. Moreover, the chapter aimed to test whether stronger family types constitute a buffer against unforeseen uncertainty.

The results confirmed that married couples display the largest probability of being satisfied with their life, also confirming the existence of a 'cohabitation gap' with respect to health, family and friends satisfaction. In addition, when considering different life domains, couples (married and cohabiters) were found more likely to achieve better outcomes in terms of economic satisfaction, health satisfaction and relationships satisfaction, whereas single persons were found to be more satisfied with leisure time and work.

Once the type of family ties by religiosity were included the results became even stronger. In particular, religious commitment operates as a family tie for married couples and this is reflected in the higher probability of being well for those who are religious and married. Conversely, in the case of cohabiters, religious commitment represents a factor that slightly reduces the probability of being well, mostly because individuals who are religious and cohabiting may feel that their familiar status is incomplete or in transition and therefore they exhibit a lower satisfaction. With regard to the presence of children in the family, the results confirm mixed evidence. Cohabiters with children report a higher probability of being satisfied with health than cohabiters without children, whereas those who are married with children are less satisfied with leisure than their childless counterparts.

Finally, when looking at the effect of uncertainty on the subjective wellbeing of different types of family, the results partially confirm the hypothesis. Couples (both married or cohabiters) report a significant 5 per cent lower probability of being satisfied with economic resources and with friends' relationships during the years of the crisis. Nonetheless, when looking at overall wellbeing couples report a 24 per cent higher probability of being satisfied with their life as a whole.

In conclusion, the chapter challenges the role of the family as a protective factor for wellbeing and models this issue by designing a theoretical framework of family types according to different family commitments. The results partially confirm the hypothesis and further investigation is desirable at least in two ways. First, from a conceptual point of view it would be useful to further disentangle the type of family not only as according to the presence of young children in the nucleus but also by looking at those couples whose sons/daughters are already out of the family. Second, from a technical point of view it would be worthy to test the hypothesis in a panel setting in order to fix possible sources of endogeneity.

NOTE

1. It is worth noting that church means every type of religious place, according to the type of religion the respondent practises.

REFERENCES

Aassve, A., A. Goisis and M. Sironi (2012), Happiness and childbearing across Europe. *Social Indicators Research*, 108(1), 65–86.

Abbey, A. and F. M. Andrews (1985), Modeling the psychological determinants of life quality. *Social Indicators Research*, 16(1), 1–34.

Angeles, L. (2010), Children and life satisfaction. *Journal of Happiness Studies*, 11(4), 523–38.

Atkinson, P. A., C. R. Martin and J. Rankin (2009), Resilience revisited. *Journal of Psychiatric and Mental Health Nursing*, 16(2), 137–45.

Barrera, M., I. N. Sandler and T. B. Ramsay (1981), Preliminary development of a scale of social support: studies on college students. *American Journal of Community Psychology*, 9(4), 435–47.

Becchetti, L., A. Pelloni and F. Rossetti (2008), Relational goods, sociability, and happiness. *Kyklos*, 61(3), 343–63.

Becker, G. (1981), *A Treatise on the Family*. Cambridge, MA: Harvard University Press.

Beja, E. L. (2015), Direct and indirect impacts of parenthood on happiness. *International Review of Economics*, 62(4), 307–18.

Bhargava, S., K. S. Kassam and G. Loewenstein (2014), A reassessment of the defense of parenthood. *Psychological Science*, 25(1), 299–302.

Bierman, A., E. M. Fazio and M. A. Milkie (2006), A multifaceted approach to the mental health advantage of the married: assessing how explanations vary by outcome measure and unmarried group. *Journal of Family Issues*, 27(4), 554–82.

Blanchflower, D. G. and A. J. Oswald (2004), Well-being over time in Britain and the USA. *Journal of Public Economics*, 88(7), 1359–86.

Brown, S. L. and A. Booth (1996), Cohabitation versus marriage: a comparison of relationship quality. *Journal of Marriage and the Family*, 58(3), 668–78.

Bruni, L. and L. Stanca (2008), Watching alone: relational goods, television and happiness. *Journal of Economic Behavior & Organization*, 65(3), 506–28.

Cacioppo, J. T. and S. Cacioppo (2014), Social relationships and health: the toxic effects of perceived social isolation. *Social and Personality Psychology Compass*, 8(2), 58–72.

Case, R. B., A. J. Moss, N. Case, M. McDermott and S. Eberly (1992), Living alone after myocardial infarction: impact on prognosis. *JAMA*, 267(4), 515–19.

Cohen, S. (1988), Psychosocial models of the role of social support in the etiology of physical disease. *Health Psychology*, 7(3), 269–97.

Colombo, E., V. Rotondi and L. Stanca (2018), Macroeconomic conditions and well-being: do social interactions matter? *Applied Economics*, 50(28), 3029–38.

Colón, E. A., A. L. Callies, M. K. Popkin and P. B. McGlave (1991), Depressed mood and other variables related to bone marrow transplantation survival in acute leukemia. *Psychosomatics*, 32(4), 420–25.

Dohrenwend, B., L. Pearlin, P. Clayton, B. Hamburg, B. P. Dohrenwend, M. Riley and R. Rose (1982), Report on stress and life events. In G. R. Elliott and C. Eisdorfer (eds), *Stress and Human Health: Analysis and Implications of Research* (pp. 55–80). New York: Springer.

Emmons, R. A. and E. Diener (1985), Factors predicting satisfaction judgments: a comparative examination. *Social Indicators Research*, 16(2), 157–67.

Gennetian, L. A. (2005), One or two parents? Half or step siblings? The effect of family structure on young children's achievement. *Journal of Population Economics*, 18(3), 415–36.

Gore, S. and T. W. Mangione (1983), Social roles, sex roles and psychological distress: additive and interactive models of sex differences. *Journal of Health and Social Behavior*, 24(4), 300–12.

Gove, W. R., M. Hughes and C. B. Style (1983), Does marriage have positive effects on the psychological well-being of the individual? *Journal of Health and Social Behavior*, 24(2), 122–31.

Gove, W. R., C. B. Style and M. Hughes (1990), The effect of marriage on the wellbeing of adults: a theoretical analysis. *Journal of Family Issues*, 11(1), 4–35.

Haller, M. and M. Hadler (2006), How social relations and structures can produce happiness and unhappiness: an international comparative analysis. *Social Indicators Research*, 75(2), 169–216.

Hansen, T., B. Slagsvold and T. Moum (2009), Childlessness and psychological well-being in midlife and old age: an examination of parental status effects across a range of outcomes. *Social Indicators Research*, 94(2), 343–62.

Herbst, C. M. and J. Ifcher (2016), The increasing happiness of US parents. *Review of Economics of the Household*, 14(3), 529–51.

House, J. S. (1981), *Work Stress and Social Support*. Reading, MA: Addison-Wesley.

House, J. S., K. R. Landis and D. Umberson (1988), Social relationships and health. *Science*, 241(4865), 540–45.

Inglehart, R. (1990), *Culture Shift in Advanced Industrial Society*. Princeton: Princeton University Press.

ISTAT (2016), Statistiche report: Matrimoni, separazioni e divorzi, anno 2015. Technical report, Istituto Nazionale di Statistica.

Johnson, M. P., J. P. Caughlin and T. L. Huston (1999), The tripartite nature of marital commitment: personal, moral, and structural reasons to stay married. *Journal of Marriage and the Family*, 61(1), 160–77.

Kholer, H. P., J. R. Behrman and A. Skytthe (2005), Partner + children = happiness? The effects of partnerships and fertility on well-being. *Population and Development Review*, 31(3), 407–45.

Korenman, S. and D. Neumark (1991), Does marriage really make men more productive? *Journal of Human Resources*, 26(2), 282–307.

Krein, S. F. and A. H. Beller (1988), Educational attainment of children from single-parent families: differences by exposure, gender, and race. *Demography*, 25(2), 221–34.

Liu, H., S. Li and M. W. Feldman (2013), Gender in marriage and life satisfaction under gender imbalance in China: the role of intergenerational support and SES. *Social Indicators Research*, 114(3), 915–33.

Luo, Y., L. C. Hawkley, L. J. Waite and J. T. Cacioppo (2012), Loneliness, health, and mortality in old age: a national longitudinal study. *Social Science & Medicine*, 74(6), 907–14.

Marks, N. F. and J. D. Lambert (1998), Marital status continuity and change among young and midlife adults: longitudinal effects on psychological well-being. *Journal of Family Issues*, 19(6), 652–86.

Murdock, G. P. (1949), *Social Structure*. New York: Macmillan.

Myers, D. G. (2003), Close relationships and quality of life. In D. Kahneman, E. Diener and N. Schwarz (eds), *Well-being: Foundations of Hedonic Psychology* (pp. 374–91). New York: Russell Sage Foundation.

Nelson, S. K., K. Kushlev, T. English, E. W. Dunn and S. Lyubomirsky (2013), In defense of parenthood: children are associated with more joy than misery. *Psychological Science*, 24(1), 3–10.

Ogburn, W. F. and D. S. Thomas (1922), The influence of the business cycle on certain social conditions. *Journal of the American Statistical Association*, 18(139), 324–40.

Pearlin, L. I. and J. S. Johnson (1977), Marital status, life-strains and depression. *American Sociological Review*, 61(2), 704–15.

Perlman, D. and K. S. Rook (1987), Social support, social deficits, and the family: toward the enhancement of well-being. *Applied Social Psychology Annual*, 7, 17–44.

Pirani, E. and D. Vignoli (2016), Changes in the satisfaction of cohabitors relative to spouses over time. *Journal of Marriage and Family*, 78(3), 598–609.

Ross, C. E. (1995), Reconceptualizing marital status as a continuum of social attachment. *Journal of Marriage and the Family*, 57, 129–40.

Ross, C. E. and J. Mirowsky (1989), Explaining the social patterns of depression: control and problem solving – or support and talking? *Journal of Health and Social Behavior*, 30(2), 206–19.

Shapiro, A. and C. L. M. Keyes (2008), Marital status and social well-being: are the married always better off? *Social Indicators Research*, 88(2), 329–46.

Sharma, R. (2013), The family and family structure classification redefined for the current times. *Journal of Family Medicine and Primary Care*, 2(4), 306–10.

Soons, J. P. and M. Kalmijn (2009), Is marriage more than cohabitation? Well-being differences in 30 European countries. *Journal of Marriage and Family*, 71(5), 1141–57.

Stack, S. and J. R. Eshleman (1998), Marital status and happiness: a 17-nation study. *Journal of Marriage and the Family*, 60(2), 527–36.

Stanca, L. (2012), Suffer the little children: measuring the effects of parenthood on well-being worldwide. *Journal of Economic Behavior & Organization*, 81(3), 742–50.

Stanley, S. M., S. W. Whitton and H. J. Markman (2004), Maybe I do: interpersonal commitment and premarital or nonmarital cohabitation. *Journal of Family Issues*, 25(4), 496–519.

Stutzer, A. and B. S. Frey (2006), Does marriage make people happy, or do happy people get married? *The Journal of Socio-Economics*, 35(2), 326–47.

Umberson, D. (1992), Gender, marital status and the social control of health behavior. *Social Science & Medicine*, 34(8), 907–17.

Walsh, F. (1996), The concept of family resilience: crisis and challenge. *Family Process*, 35(3), 261–81.

Walsh, F. (2003), Family resilience: a framework for clinical practice. *Family Process*, 42(1), 1–18.

Walsh, F. and J. S. Rolland (2006), Facilitating family resilience with childhood illness and disability. *Current Opinion in Pediatrics*, 18(5), 527–38.

APPENDIX

Table 11.1A　Descriptive statistics

Variable	Obs	Mean	Std.	Min	Max
life_sat	179 588	0.40	0.490	0	1
econ_sat	180 198	0.46	0.499	0	1
health-sat	180 122	0.82	0.376	0	1
family_sat	179 908	0.92	0.265	0	1
friends_sat	179 937	0.85	0.352	0	1
leisure_sat	179 774	0.66	0.472	0	1
work_sat	93 351	0.76	0.426	0	1
married	213 674	0.68	0.465	0	1
cohabiters	213 674	0.04	0.196	0	1
single parents	213 674	0.10	0.310	0	1
single persons	213 674	0.16	0.374	0	1
age	213 674	10.16	4.22	1	18
gender	213 674	0.51	0.499	0	1
professional_pos	138 086	2.64	0.884	1	4
working_cond	181 692	1.98	0.943	1	3
education	201 526	1.85	0.593	1	3
good_economic cond	212 371	0.55	0.497	0	1
religious	197 307	0.79	0.400	0	1
1child	213 674	0.30	0.461	0	1
2children	213 674	0.33	0.470	0	1
3children	213 674	0.08	0.281	0	1
4children	213 674	0.013	0.117	0	1
5+children	213 674	0.0015	0.039	0	1
friends	199 920	0.70	0.455	0	1
social_inter	213 674	0.42	0.493	0	1

12. Cooperatives and happiness: cross-country evidence on the role of relational capital[1]

Luigino Bruni, Dalila De Rosa and Giovanni Ferri

12.1 INTRODUCTION

Easterlin's paradox – income doesn't always buy happiness (Easterlin, 1974) – is consistent with the finding that happiness differs significantly among comparable countries.For instance, across pairs of analogously affluent neighboring countries unhappy people by 2009 were 8 percent in Australia[2] vis-à-vis New Zealand's 3 percent; 21.5 percent in Greece against 7.5 percent in Spain; 17 percent in Slovenia against 9 percent in Poland. We argue that different endowments of relational capital may help explain that paradox. Specifically, we take the diffusion of cooperatives in a country as a proxy for its relational capital endowment for three reasons. First, theory suggests that, vis-à-vis private limited companies, cooperatives rely more on long-term and informal/implicit (rather than short-term/formal) contracts and interactions. Hence we may expect that cooperatives tend to flourish in countries with larger relational capital endowments. Second, from a strictly measurement perspective, cooperative firms represent a macro-level indicator of relational capital able to complement the micro-level measures, commonly assessed at the individual level. Third, empirical cross-country data reveal a positive correlation between the extent of relational capital and the presence of cooperatives.

However, we have to deal with the paucity of data on the dimension of the cooperative sector. This is somehow surprising since cooperatives play a significant role in almost every country. Possibly, the lack of official data on cooperatives descends from the debatable mainstream tenet that they represent an anomaly with respect to shareholder-owned and profit-seeking entities. So, finding detailed cross-country data on the extent of the cooperative sector wasn't easy as most sources are ad hoc, hardly comparable studies. We complemented the study by Coopseurope (2010), covering 36 European countries, relying on the International Co-operative Alliance (ICA, 2011), which provides details on the 300 largest global cooperatives. Combining the two data sources we use a joint rank ordering to reduce the probability of measuring errors. So, our sample reaches 48 countries. This represents in itself a first contribution.

Next, we test whether more cooperativeness in a country associates with a lower share of unhappy people. We control for the level of socio-economic development by introducing the Human Development Index (HDI) as a regressor alongside our cooperative variable and other control variables. Furthermore, we tackle the expected endogeneity coming from the fact that the extent of cooperativeness might be caused, rather than cause, the degree of happiness by implementing an instrumental variables approach. We find that cooperativeness significantly promotes happiness.

In the rest of the chapter, Section 12.2 draws a review of the main contributions on happiness and relational capital, casting the debate on the background of civil economic thought. Section 12.3 presents the theoretical and empirical foundations justifying why the extent of the cooperative sector may be held as a good proxy of the endowment of relational capital a country has. Section 12.4 describes the data we use in the empirical analysis. In Section 12.5 we introduce our econometric methodology and present our main findings. Section 12.6 concludes by drawing policy implications and making suggestions for future research.

12.2   LITERATURE REVIEW ON SOCIAL CAPITAL, RELATIONAL CAPITAL AND ITS THEORETICAL ROOTS

Social capital has gained attention in the economics profession. Yet the term 'social capital' has been applied to explore rather different phenomena and used with very different meanings and implications. To mention just few of the most popular definitions, Putnam highlights the *micro* dimension of social capital as the 'connections among individuals – social networks, and the norms of reciprocity and trustworthiness that arise from them' (2000, p. 19), where the relations among individuals, households and networks represent social gain. On the contrary, Coleman depicts the *meso* dimension of social capital as 'a variety of different entities [which] all consist of some aspect of social structure, and [which] facilitate certain actions of actors – whether personal or corporate actors – within the structure' (Coleman, 1990, p. 302). The Organisation for Economic Co-operation and Development (OECD) synthetizes the *micro* and *meso* dimensions, saying that 'Social capital includes networks together with shared norms, values and understanding that facilitate co-operation within or among groups' (OECD, 2001, p.41). In turn, Paldam (2000) highlights the fact that three different definitions of social capital coexist – one related to trust, one to ease of cooperation and one to network intensity – and that they only partly overlap. Finally, the World Bank defines the *macro* dimension of social capital as 'the institutions, relationships, and norms that shape the quality and quantity of a society's social interactions', where institutions include 'the most formalized institutional relationships and structures, such as government, the political regime, the rule of law, the court system, and civil and political liberties' (Grootaert and Van Bastelaer, 2002). This suggests that, though the role of social capital is vastly recognized, we have no single unitary concept of social capital and there is still little agreement on the best way to define and measure it (Scrivens and Smith, 2013). In economics, a growing body of literature has focused on the one hand on the determinants of social capital, and on the other on the impacts on development, well-being and happiness. Glaeser et al. (2002) use a standard optimal investment model to analyze an individual's decision to accumulate social capital and fail to find robust evidence that social capital investments fall with the value of time or that geographic/religious groups generate social capital complementarities. Instead, while also stressing the problems of reception, definition and operationalization of social capital, Adam and Rončević (2003) underline the need to build an interdisciplinary and transdisciplinary collaboration of sociology and economics that seems at odds with the approach of Glaeser et al. (2002). In addition, various scholars hold that there is a need to move beyond social capital (Knorringa and Van Staveren, 2007; Nooteboom, 2007). Yet in recent decades, empirical and theoretical literature showed (at least from Putnam, 1993) the strong correlation between different forms of social capital and well-being: as a matter of fact, civil virtues and growth are positively correlated (Fukuyama, 2001) and civically engaged people tend to be happier (Morrow-Howell et al., 2003), report better health status (Borgonovi, 2008) and have a greater sense of purpose in life (Greenfield and Marks, 2004). Moreover, individuals located in places with higher levels of trust report higher levels of subjective well-being (Helliwell and Putnam, 2004; Helliwell and Wang, 2010; Bartolini et al., 2011) and higher levels of institutional trust determine better outcomes in subjective well-being (Hudson, 2006). Likewise, a larger endowment of social capital – in the form of social interactions, relational activities and volunteering – was found to significantly increase happiness and life satisfaction (Helliwell and Putnam, 2004; Becchetti, 2008; Becchetti et al., 2011; Bartolini and Sarracino, 2014; Colombo et al., 2018). In particular, a strong positive link emerges between relational capital and happiness, where relational capital, more than social capital, emphasizes identity and motivation in personalized (face-to-face) interactions (Bruni and Stanca, 2008). In that sense, the concept of relational capital, proposed by Carole Uhlaner (1989) as active political participation, was developed by other authors as consumption and accumulation of 'relational goods' (Bruni, 2008; Pugno, 2009; Sacco and Zamagni, 2006). In particular, Gui (1987, 1996, 2005) referred to the latter as 'encounters', namely productive interpersonal events that deliver relational outputs. In view of this framework, our research question is the following: how does the cooperative culture interplay with those previous results?

Trying to answer this question, some background on the history of economic thought is useful in order to frame the theoretical and philosophical roots of relational capital. For economists the big picture of market mechanism has traditionally featured the invisible hand – the common good as the unintended consequences of private self-interest – mediated by the market.[3]

The concept of 'civil economy' offers a promising alternative approach. The founder of this tradition is Antonio Genovesi (1713–69), a Neapolitan philosopher contemporary to Smith (Bruni and Sugden, 2008, 2013). His vision of civil economy and public happiness claims that the aim of the market or the 'economic principle' is not individual self-interest but *mutual assistance* ('mutua assistenza'):

> Not just any society of man with man be our case, not in the way as even beasts are to some extent sociable, but in a way founded upon reason, for which the members know their reciprocal rights and not only do they not think of violating them, but they even study ways to be benevolent and helpful to each other. (Genovesi, [1765] (2013), II, X, § 11)

The idea that the rationale of the market is mutual advantage is not new, because most of the funders of the discipline shared this vision – think of Ricardo's relative advantages theorem or of Edgeworth's box. However, the civil economy idea of the market explicitly defined as 'mutual assistance' makes the understanding of the market easier, without the need to learn too much regarding the metaphor of the 'invisible hand'. Anyone who had the experience of teaching economic theory knows how surprised students typically are as they find themselves confronted with the logic of market exchange. In people's minds a sort of mercantile fallacy seems to exist, which is very pervasive. Such a fallacy has various manifestations that lie in the background of common sense in the understanding of economic matters. The Smithian idea of the market can be well expressed through the category of 'mutual advantage', the core principle in modern economics, considered in strictly individual terms (nothing in Smith's thought suggests the existence of a collective subject, of a 'we'). Genovesi's view, however, aligned with the classic Aristotle–Aquinas tradition of the common good, is instead characterized by the concept of 'mutual assistance'. We must observe, however, that the difference, small as it may appear, is in fact crucial. In an exchange motivated by 'mutual advantage' each party benefits from the transaction, a transaction that is only possible as long as it is also beneficial to the other party. Hence, trading is *objectively* mutually advantageous, as any economist (and merchant) knows: each party acts in a way that is advantageous to the other. Yet neither of the two parties has any concern for the interests and well-being of the other, no 'we' is required. Market exchange, intended à la Genovesi, as 'mutual assistance', requires instead something more and different from the notion of mutual advantage. The concept of 'assistance' entails an intention, on the part of the person who 'assists', to benefit the person 'assisted'. Assistance supposes an action that is intentionally directed towards another person for the purpose of helping her with her needs, an intention to be helpful to each other. If assistance is mutual – as Genovesi intends it – then these intentions are reciprocal. But mutual assistance is not played entirely in the field of contracts (despite not excluding it); in this perspective it stretches beyond the idea of mutual interest: a good society must be based on something deeper and different than just a sum of individual interests. The needs of some that do not always correspond to the interest of others, but that still ought to be satisfied in a decent society. Not by chance, in the civil economy tradition the most important political and social program was 'Pubblica Felicità' (public happiness). Whereas in the US Declaration of Independence the individual 'pursuit of happiness' was a cornerstone, in Naples the priority was put on public happiness: 'It is a universal law that we cannot make ourselves happy without making others happy as well' (Genovesi, 1979, p. 449).

In the civil economy tradition, cooperation is the nature of the market, its deepest aim, which allows the economy to reach both individual and public happiness (Bruni and Sugden, 2013). Therefore, we interpret our empirical results on cooperation within this cultural tradition and theoretical framework.

12.3 WHY IS THE EXTENT OF THE COOPERATIVE SECTOR A GOOD PROXY OF RELATIONAL CAPITAL'S ENDOWMENT?

The use of this proxy seems justified on three levels. First, theory suggests that, with respect to private limited companies, cooperative firms tend to rely more on long-term and informal/implicit (rather than short-term and formal) contracts (Arrighetti et al., 1997; Campbell and Harris, 1993; Grillo, 2013; Lui et al., 2009; Scott, 1987). Hence, one may expect that cooperatives will flourish in countries with more relational capital. Second, from a strictly measurement perspective cooperative firms represent a macro-level indicator of relational capital able to complement the micro-level measures, commonly assessed at the individual level. Third, empirical cross-country data reveal a positive correlation between the extent of relational capital and the presence of cooperatives.

12.3.1 Some Theoretical Arguments

Here we provide a synthetic description of the idea that goes beyond the possible role of cooperation as a building block of social capital (Paldam, 2000). It has been shown that individuals' happiness depends on their own perception of security (Wills-Herrera et al., 2011), personal involvement (Probst, 2000) and satisfaction with the market economy (Dolan et al., 2008). Hence individuals' participation and their feeling part of the economic game (relational capital) could then be an important determinant of the extent of happiness.

We show that the presence of cooperatives, taken as a proxy of how much a society is inclined to foster individuals' direct and face-to-face participation in the economy, is positively associated with the degree of happiness. Incidentally, this seems to confirm that, in order to account for the happiness/cooperative culture/market economy connection, we need a more socialized idea of the market, that is, the so-called civil economy approach.

Let's try to be more specific about the concept of cooperation. In the mainstream view of the market in neoclassical economics, cooperation comes as a sum of individual self-interested actions, without any 'joint action', let alone any 'mutuality' where the 'common good' is intentional in both parties of the contract. The civil economy tradition, as mentioned, offers a different narrative of the market, where 'mutuality' or the 'common good' of the parties is part of the *intentions* of the agents. Relational capital is taken into account as both 'consumption goods' (working together and sharing positive feelings increases individual happiness) and 'assets' (relational capital facilitates joint production). Thus, in that sense, even though a larger endowment of trust may favor more cooperation (Jones and Kalmi, 2009), when cooperation becomes more widespread it can, in turn, reinforce trust and mutuality. As a matter of fact, although different people display different degrees of intrinsic motivation and experience different forms of reciprocity, once the cooperation dynamic is activated the cost of cooperation tends to reduce while the value of intrinsic motivation tends to increase and the society generates cooperative outcomes (Bruni, 2008). Therefore, reciprocity and cooperation represent the pillars of the civil economy approach.

12.3.2 Some Measurement Arguments

As mentioned, there is still little agreement on the best way to define and measure social capital. According to Scrivens and Smith (2013) there is no *one* social capital but *many*, where *many* stands for different levels: micro level (relations between individuals, family, friends), meso level (relations between organizations or entities) and macro level (regional, national, international networks); and different types: structural (objective and externally observable construct) and cognitive (subjective and intangible concept). These forms of social capital can be, but are not necessarily, complementary (Grootaert and Van Bastelaer, 2002). In recent decades a wide set of measures have attempted to capture the different aspects of social capital. Figure 12.1 reports some of the best known measures belonging to the black box of social capital.

In this context, relational capital is the part of social capital that refers to relationships. In the empirical literature relational capital was mostly measured as the extent of individuals' encounters, which produce relational outputs. The latter can be qualified either in their flow dimension

Macro	Meso	Micro	
Ethno-linguistic fractionalization	**Political participation**		Structural
Contract enforcement	**Individual social support**	Relational capital	
Quality of government/bureaucracy	**Kinship connections**		
Corruption and rule of law	**Friendship connections**		
Political Stability and Liberty	**Associational activity**		
Cooperative culture	**Volunteering and Reciprocity**		
Cross-country measures of Trust (generalized trust, trust in institutions) Social norms Beliefs	Quality of social/family relations Trust in community/neighbors		Cognitive

Figure 12.1   The black box of Social Capital

as 'relational consumption goods' (company, recognition, entertainment) or in their stock dimension as the accumulation of 'relational capital goods' (Gui and Stanca, 2010). Yet, if on one side it is true that more associational activities and a higher rate of reciprocity and volunteering may influence the actual presence of cooperatives, it is also true that an institutionalized cooperative culture may foster the extent of face-to-face interactions. Therefore our aim is to complement the measurement of relational capital by providing an objective stock indicator of relational capital, assessable at the macro level. Besides, from a policy perspective if 'personal relationships are a private matter, and it may seem inappropriate to think of policies aiming to influence the way people build and maintain their intimate connections' (Scrivens and Smith, 2013, p. 24), the presence, size and importance of the cooperative sector in a society seems a much more relevant policy target.

12.3.3   Some Empirical Evidence

As proxies of the endowment of social and relational capital in a country we take three variables reported by the World Values Survey (WVS) and the European Value Survey (EVS): (1) the country level of individuals' generalized trust; (2) the country average of individuals' trust in institutions; and (3) the extent of active membership in voluntary organizations.

We test whether there is a positive correlation between each of these three proxies and the extent of cooperatives across European countries, where this latter variable is measured more precisely by Coopseurope (2010). Specifically, we measure the extent of cooperatives as the percentage share of population employed by cooperatives. The average cooperative employment share so defined is 0.61 percent with a median value at 0.43 percent, a maximum of 1.91 percent (in Italy) and a minimum of 0.02 percent (in Latvia) (Table 12.1). Regarding the level of generalized trust, we find an average of 30.47 percent with a median value at 25.09 percent, a maximum of 76.12 percent (in Denmark) and a minimum of 4.84 percent (in Turkey). As to trust in institutions, we find an average of 42.14 percent with a median value at 41.51 percent, a maximum of 62.71 percent (in Denmark) and a minimum of 19.27 percent (in Croatia). Finally, concerning active membership in voluntary organizations, we find an average of 21.58 percent with a median value of 17.49 percent, a maximum of 59.25 percent (in the UK) and a minimum of 4.26 percent (in Romania).

Table 12.1 also reports the correlation coefficients. It turns out that both generalized trust and active membership in voluntary organizations are positively correlated with the extent of cooperative employment. The first has a correlation of 0.483, statistically significant at the 10 percent

Table 12.1   Cooperative employees vs. generalized trust, voluntary activities and trust in institutions

Country	Cooperative employees (A)	Generalized trust (B)	Voluntary activities (C)	Trust in institutions (D)
Austria	1.27	36.36	16.95	36.27
Belarus	1.03	35.94	5.6	60.97
Belgium	0.13	45.4	18.08	42.48
Bulgaria	0.35	19.59	5.35	36.9
Croatia	0.09	20.17	14.65	19.27
Cyprus	0.64	9.71	26.23	49.02
Czech Republic	0.69	30.61	55.63	30.61
Denmark	1.28	76.12	13.56	62.71
Estonia	0.36	32.34	8.83	41.47
Finland	1.31	58.04	38.53	62.62
France	1.4	18.7	24.95	38.52
Germany	1.01	33.79	18.01	33.79
Greece	0.11	21.65	13.34	37.41
Hungary	0.85	20.97	6.15	24.79
Ireland	0.42	38.48	27.64	49.13
Italy	1.91	27.47	32.98	33.06
Latvia	0.02	25.6	8.5	45.73
Lithuania	0.27	29	22.35	44
Luxembourg	0.1	33	19.7	55.01
Malta	0.06	22.53	4.97	49.2
Moldova	0.26	17.59	26.58	29.83
Netherlands	1.12	42.57	34.32	36.89
Norway	0.89	73.66	49.04	62.34
Poland	1.05	18.14	19.08	33.31
Portugal	0.44	19.7	8.92	44.64
Romania	0.16	19.26	4.26	29.78
Russia	0.2	24.58	13.07	38.32
Serbia	0.09	13.61	14.75	21
Slovakia	0.49	12.7	20.67	44
Slovenia	0.17	24.3	7.27	47.26
Spain	0.84	19.78	16.98	41.56
Sweden	1.52	65.21	45.19	54.95
Switzerland	1.09	51.18	56.1	51.15
Turkey	0.06	4.84	5.57	61.42
Ukraine	0.14	24.48	13.65	34.04
United Kingdom	0.21	29.99	59.25	33.73
Mean	0.61	30.47	21.58	42.14
Median	0.43	25.09	17.495	41.515
Max	1.91	76.12	59.25	62.71

Table 12.1   (continued)

Country	Cooperative employees (A)	Generalized trust (B)	Voluntary activities (C)	Trust in institutions (D)
Min	0.02	4.84	4.26	19.27
Correlation (A B)		0.4835*		
Correlation (A C)			0.4057*	
Correlation (A D)				0.1953

Note: *   indicates statistical significance at the 10% level.

level of confidence. The second has a correlation of 0.405, also statistically significant at the 10 percent level of confidence. On the other hand, the correlation with trust in institutions was found to not be statistically significant. Yet there is some evidence that the extent of cooperativeness across countries is correlated with the degree of relational capital in the same countries.

12.4   THE DATA USED IN OUR EMPIRICAL ANALYSIS

The degree of happiness is recovered from the WVS and the EVS. Specifically, given that our major constraint is the availability of data on cooperatives that are obtainable, as explained below, only for 2008 (ICA, 2011) and 2009 (Coopseurope, 2010) do we take the data point closest to those years from WVS and EVS for each country. The overall list considered includes 48 developed, emerging and developing countries.[4]

For the cross-country extent of cooperativeness we rely on two different data sources: Coopseurope (2010) and ICA (2011). We take data for 36 European countries[5] from Coopseurope (2010), which refer to 2009 and report for each country the number of cooperative enterprises, as well as the number of attached employees and members. Our preferred measure of cooperativeness in a country is the number of employees at national cooperative enterprises taken as a ratio to the countries' overall population. A descriptive snapshot suggests the presence of some two-way correlation between the extent of cooperativeness and that of happiness in Europe.

As shown in Figures 12.2, 12.3 and 12.4 – respectively, in terms of number of employees, members and enterprises, all taken as a ratio to the national population – the presence of cooperativeness is somewhat correlated with happiness.

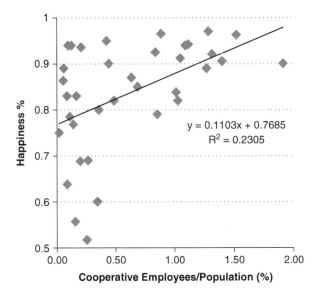

Figure 12.2   Happiness and cooperation in Europe: employees

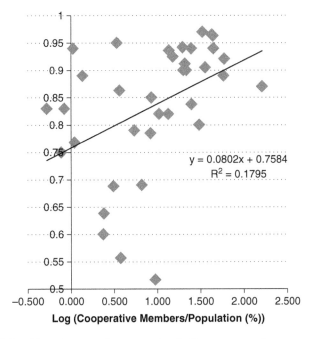

Figure 12.3   Happiness and cooperation in Europe: members

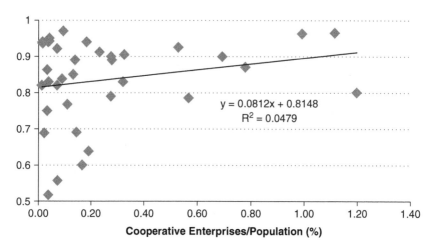

$$y = 0.0812x + 0.8148$$
$$R^2 = 0.0479$$

Cooperative Enterprises/Population (%)

Source: Coopseurope (2010); 36 countries included: Austria, Belarus, Belgium, Bulgaria, Croatia, Cyprus, Czech Republic, Denmark, Estonia, Finland, France, Germany, Greece, Hungary, Ireland, Italy, Latvia, Lithuania, Luxembourg, Malta, Moldova, the Netherlands, Norway, Poland, Portugal, Romania, Russia, Serbia, Slovakia, Slovenia, Spain, Sweden, Switzerland, Turkey, Ukraine, the United Kingdom.

Figure 12.4   Happiness and cooperation in Europe: enterprises

The second data source on cooperatives is ICA (2011) reporting data for 2008 on total revenues of the largest 300 global cooperatives compiled by country of establishment. There are 26 countries involved.[6] Here our measure of cooperativeness in a country is the (logarithm of) total revenues of cooperatives from that country in the Global 300 list scaled by population. Descriptive statistics from ICA (2011) reach world level results (Figure 12.4) that are qualitatively analogous to those above for Europe only. Namely, there is a positive correlation between happiness and cooperativeness.

ICA data seem to offer the only opportunity to enlarge the number of countries in our sample. But we have reservations on the reliability of the ICA-based measure. For instance, a country populated by small cooperatives will be underrepresented since only the 300 largest cooperatives are recorded. Thus, to reduce the bias due to measuring errors, rather than raw data we use the rank order. Specifically, we take two ranks – one, among the European countries only from Coopseurope (2010), and the other from ICA (2011) – and compute a mean adjusted rank (MAR).[7] The MAR plotted against countries' happiness ranking confirms a positive, albeit weaker, correlation (Figure 12.5 and Figure 12.6).

Table 12.2 reports the basic descriptive statistics of all the variables employed in our econometric analysis.

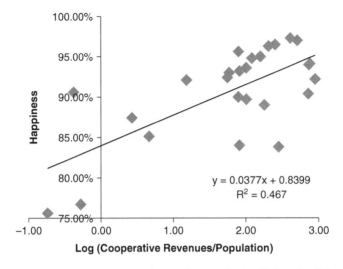

Source: From ICA (2011); 21 countries included: Australia, Brazil, Canada, China, Finland, France, Germany, India, Italy, Japan, Korea, Malaysia, Netherlands, New Zealand, Norway, Spain, Sweden, Switzerland, Taiwan, UK, US. Our calculations based on the adjusted rankings from Coopseurope (2010) and ICA (2011).

Figure 12.5   Happiness and cooperation from the Global 300

Depending on the specification, the dependent variable will be *Happy* – that is, the extent of happiness given by the sum of two percentage values: that of the people who report themselves as 'very happy' and that of those who report being 'quite happy' – or its cross-country rank (*Happyrank*). *Happy* has a mean value of 83.515 ranging from the minimum of 51.700 (Moldova) to the maximum of 97.400 (New Zealand). As to regressors, we have seven cooperative variables. The first three come from Coopseurope (2010) on the said 36 European countries. *Coop_empl* is the ratio of cooperative employees to total population: its average value is 0.612 percent ranging from the minimum of 0.02 percent (Latvia) to the maximum of 1.91 percent (Italy). *Coop_ent* is the ratio of the number of cooperative enterprises (multiplied by 1000) to total population with an average value of 0.261, a minimum of 0.010 (Belarus) and a maximum of 1.200 (Estonia). *Coop_mem* is the ratio of the number of cooperative members to total population: its mean value is 21.017 percent spanning the minimum of 0.520 percent (Croatia) to the maximum of 160.120 percent (Cyprus). In turn, *Coop_rev* is derived from ICA (2011) as the total revenues of the cooperatives in the list of the Global 300 multiplied by 1000 and scaled by the country's total population. Next, *Coopr* is the MAR, as described above.

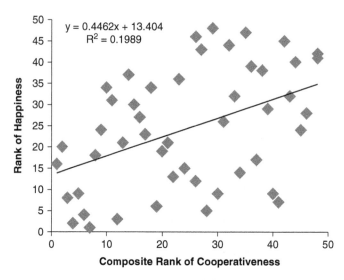

Source: From ICA (2011); 48 countries included: Australia, Austria, Belarus, Belgium, Brazil, Bulgaria, Canada, China, Croatia, Cyprus, Czech Republic, Denmark, Estonia, Finland, France, Germany, Greece, Hungary, India, Ireland, Italy, Japan, South Korea, Latvia, Lithuania, Luxembourg, Malaysia, Malta, Moldova, the Netherlands, New Zealand, Norway, Poland, Portugal, Romania, Russia, Serbia, Singapore, Slovakia, Slovenia, Spain, Sweden, Switzerland, Taiwan, Turkey, Ukraine, the UK, USA.

Figure 12.6   Rank of happiness vs. rank of cooperativeness

Regarding the controls we include a variable designed to capture the degree of economic affluence of the country. The most important control variable is to us the Human Development Index (*Hdi*) promoted by the United Nations (United Nations Development Programme, 1998). In 2010 in our sample, *Hdi* has a mean of 0.814, with a minimum of 0.519 (India) and a maximum of 0.938 (Norway). Some scholars (e.g. Vemuri and Costanza, 2006) find that *Hdi* – together with an index of the value of ecosystem services per km² (as a proxy for natural capital) – can explain 72 percent of the cross-country variation in life satisfaction. In theory, using *Hdi* as a control in our regression rules out entering also per capita gross domestic product (GDP) (*Gdp_pc*) since *Hdi* has *Gdp_pc* as one of its sub-components. However, as some scholars are skeptical of whether other welfare measures actually outperform *Gdp_pc* in their relationship to happiness (e.g. Delhey and Kroll, 2012), in some specifications we replace *Hdi* with *Gdp_pc*. In 2010 in our sample, *Gdp_pc* has a mean of US$26 422 varying between a minimum of US$2953 (India) and a maximum of US$81 683 (Luxembourg). Conforming to our

Table 12.2 Summary statistics

Variables	Number of observations	Mean	Standard deviation	Min.	Max
Dependent variables					
Happy (people very or quite happy, %)[a]	48	85.006	11.095	51.700	97.400
Happyrank (happiness rank of the country)[a]	48	24.438	14.032	1	48
Cooperativeness variables					
Coop_empl (coop employees/population, %)[b]	36	0.612	0.517	0.020	1.910
Coop_ent (coop enterpr./population, *1000)[b]	36	0.261	0.321	.010	1.200
Coop_mem (coop members/population, %)[b]	36	21.017	29.149	0.520	160.120
Coop_rev (coop revenues/population, *1000)[c]	26	2370.181	3116.893	1.800	12427.800
Coopr (cooperativeness rank of the country)[b c]	48	24.541	14.036	1	48
Control variables					
Hdi (2010 HDI)[d]	48	0.814	0.086	0.519	0.938
Hdir (rank of the country for 2010 HDI)[d]	48	24.479	13.982	1	48
Gdp_pc (2010 per capita GDP)[c]	48	26422.460	14501.990	2953	81683
Gdpr (rank of the country for 2010 Gdp_pc)[c]	48	24.500	14.000	1	48
Days_bus (No. days to start a business)[d]	48	16.979	18.834	0.5	122
Pop_density (per km²)[d]	48	320.854	1093.897	3	7589
Urban_pop (percentage on total population)[d]	47	73.149	14.357	32	100
GovDebt_GDP (percentage)[d]	48	54.708	33.643	9	175
Unemp_rate (unemployment rate, %)[d]	48	8.842	4.618	1.000	19.800
Inflation (%)[d]	48	2.938	2.698	−1.094	11.992
Religion_fractionalization[f]	47	0.459	0.221	0.005	0.824
Gini index[g]	48	31.505	5.550	22.260	47.260

257

Table 12.2 (continued)

Variables	Number of observations	Mean	Standard deviation	Min.	Max
Legor_uk^ (legal origin UK)[h]	48	0.208	0.410	0	1
Legor_fr^ (legal origin France)[h]	48	0.354	0.483	0	1
Legor_ge^ (legal origin Germany)[h]	48	0.354	0.483	0	1
Legor_sc^ (legal origin Scandinavia)[h]	48	0.083	0.279	0	1
Gentrust (generalized trust)	48	30.962	16.116	4.84	76.12
Mdvolunt (mean of voluntary activities)	48	27.633	21.269	4.26	92.4
Instrumental variables					
Population (millions)[d]	48	87.093	259.344	0.410	1349.590
Ethnic_fractionalization[f]	47	0.278	0.192	0.002	0.712
Language_fractionalization[f]	47	0.275	0.211	0.002	0.807
Coop_empl_oth[b]	36	0.673	0.031	0.572	0.775

Note: ^ denotes a (0, 1) dummy variable; sources of the data: [a] = WVS, EVS; [b] = Coopseurope (2010); [c] = ICA (2011); [d] = World Bank; [e] = WPT (2010); [f] = Alesina et al. (2003); [g] = SWIID database (Solt, 2009); [h] = La Porta et al. (1998).

approach, *Coopr*, both *Hdir* and *Gdpr* are calculated as the respective rank variables.

Other control variables include the number of days to start a business in a country (*Days_bus*) meant as proxying the ease of doing business and, thus, the extent of the formal market economy.[8] *Days_bus* has a mean of 17 days, a minimum of half a day (New Zealand) and a maximum of 122 days (Brazil). Then, two explanatory variables relate to population: *Pop_density* (population density per km[2]) and *Urban_pop* (the percentage of urban population on the total). These demographic variables capture the depth of the domestic market that may favor trade and growth. That will be the case of increasing urban agglomeration (*Urban_pop*) and growing *Pop_density* if agglomeration benefits outweigh congestion costs (Krugman, 1995). *Pop_density* has a mean of 321 escalating from a minimum of three (Australia) to a maximum of 7589 (Singapore). The average of 73 percent for *Urban_pop* lies between the minimum of 32 percent (India) and the maximum of 100 percent (Singapore).

In turn, three other variables aim to encapsulate how macroeconomic fundamentals might affect a country's happiness. Government debt to GDP ratio (*Govdebt_GDP*) could imply either higher taxes or toil and, thus, likely depress happiness. This variable has a mean of 54.7 percent ranging from a minimum of 9 percent (Estonia) to a maximum of 175 percent (Japan). Unemployment (*Unemp_rate*) can also dampen happiness. In our sample, *Unemp_rate* varies from a minimum of 1 percent (Belarus) to a maximum of 19.8 percent (Spain) and is 8.8 percent at the mean. Finally, *Inflation* can also depress happiness by imposing an opaque and regressive tax on the people at large. In our data, *Inflation* is 2.9 percent at the mean, varying between a minimum of −1.1 percent (Latvia) and a maximum of 12.0 percent (India).

We have six more control variables. First, religion can affect happiness. Specifically, more religious fractionalization (*Relig_fract*) has been shown to impinge negatively on happiness (Mookerjee and Beron, 2005; Okulicz-Kozaryn, 2011). In our countries, the mean value of *Relig_fract* is 0.459 spanning from a minimum of 0.005 (Turkey) to a maximum of 0.824 (USA). Also inequality can arguably affect happiness. Various authors have found a negative relationship between the two variables (e.g. Alesina et al., 2004; Oishi et al., 2011; Ferrer-i-Carbonell and Ramos, 2014). Following the literature, we measure inequality by the Gini index which, in our sample, averages 31.5 moving from a minimum of 22.3 (Sweden) to a maximum of 47.3 (Brazil). The other four are dummy variables capturing a country's legal origin, where one might conjecture that more efficient legal systems make people happier. Drawing on La Porta et al. (1998), countries' legal systems are classified as derived from English origin

(*Legor_uk*; 20.8 percent of the countries), French origin (*Legor_fr*; 35.4 percent), German origin (*Legor_ge*; 35.4 percent) or Scandinavian origin (*Legor_sc*; 8.3 percent).

Finally, two more controls for social capital are considered. The choice to use these two variables is grounded in the literature on social capital presented earlier and on data availability. Generalized trust defined as the percentage of individuals considering most people trustworthy, and voluntary activities as the average percentage of those individuals declaring themselves to be active members of different associations (religious, sport, union, parties, professionals, environmental or artistic). In our countries, on average, 30.9 percent of individuals declare that most people can be trusted, with Turkey ranking at the bottom (4.84 percent) and Denmark at the top (76.12 percent). Similarly, about 27.6 percent of individuals, on average, report being an active member of some associations, with Romania ranking at the bottom (4.26 percent) and India ranking to the top (92.4 percent). Table 12.2 also reports descriptive statistics for four instruments that are justified in more detail later. *Population* captures a country's mass that, on its own, alters the size of its domestic market. It ranges from a minimum of 0.41 million (Malta) to a maximum of 1349 (China) with a mean of 87 million. *Ethnic_fractionalization* (*Ethnic_fract*) has a mean of 0.278, a minimum of 0.002 (South Korea) and a maximum of 0.712 (Canada). *Language_fractionalization* (*Lang_fract*) is 0.275 at the mean varying between a minimum of 0.002 (South Korea) and a maximum of 0.807 (India). Last, following the strategy proposed by Caprio et al. (2007) and Laeven and Levine (2009), we consider an additional instrument, *Coop_empl_oth*, built in a way to eliminate the idiosyncratic component of cooperativeness in a country.

12.5   EMPIRICAL ANALYSIS

The econometric analysis explores whether the bilateral correlation between happiness and cooperativeness highlighted by the descriptive evidence stands up to the inclusion of control variables. In addition, we have to deal with two further issues – reverse causality and potential endogeneity – as well as checking whether the results pass a few robustness checks.

12.5.1   Basic OLS Regression

The basic regression that we estimate focuses on the best quality data for the 36 countries whose cooperativeness is measured by Coopseurope (2010) and takes the following shape:

$Happy_i = \alpha + \beta_1 Hdi_i + \beta_2 Coop\_empl_i + \beta_3 Pop\_density_i + \beta_4 Urban\_pop_i$
$+ \beta_5 Relig\_fract_i + \beta_6 Days\_bus_i + \beta_7 Govdebt\_gdp_i + \beta_8 Unemp\_rat_i +$
$\beta_9 Inflation_i + \beta_{10} Gini_i + \beta_{11} Legor\_fr_i + \beta_{12} Legor\_ge_i + \beta_{13} Legor\_sc_i + \beta_{14}$
$Gen\_trust_i + \beta_{15} Mdvolunt_i + \varepsilon_i$ (12.1)

where, for any country *i*, regressors are as described and justified above.

We estimate equation (12.1) by ordinary least squares (OLS) with robust standard errors to rule out any bias coming from heteroskedasticity.

Table 12.3 reports the initial specification (column 1) and the preferred specification after discarding insignificant regressors (column 2). From the results we notice that: (1) both specifications are good statistical models as *F tests* strongly reject the null hypothesis that all regressors' coefficients are jointly zero; (2) regressions achieve good fit being able to account for above 70 percent of the variability in *Happy*; (3) *Hdi* is confirmed to be positively linked to happiness though not statistically significant; (4) *Coop_empl* is positively and significantly related to *Happy*, so that more cooperativeness associates with more happiness.

The signs of the other independent variables are generally as expected. *Urban_pop* associates with more happiness, possibly owing to its pro-growth effect. On the contrary, *Relig_fract* systematically worsens happiness as does *Gini*. None of the macro fundamental variables achieves significant effects on *Happy*, except the unemployment rate in some specifications. While *Legor_uk* is the omitted legal origin variable, all the other three turn out significant and positive. So, English-origin legal systems associate with higher happiness.

12.5.2 Instrumental Variable Regression

Now we tackle reverse causality and endogeneity. Reverse causality refers to the possibility that it is not cooperativeness to 'cause' happiness but that the reverse is true. That is, people are not happier since they cooperate more but cooperate more since they are happier. And, obviously, this would raise the question of why some people are happier than others to start with. The issue of potential endogeneity enters exactly at this point, and thus solving it means also discarding reverse causality.

There would be endogeneity if our regressions were to include happiness (our dependent variable) and cooperativeness (the explanatory variable in which we are most interested) but a third variable, omitted in the regression, were the 'true' cause of both happiness and cooperativeness. Following the mainstream method to deal with endogeneity (Wooldridge, 2002), we use an instrumental variables approach. Good candidate instruments are variables affecting cooperativeness but not happiness. Then, including those

Table 12.3 Estimations on European countries (with robust standard errors)

Variables	(1) OLS happy	(2) OLS happy	(3) OLS Happy (with gdp)	(4) 2SLS-IV happy	(5) OLS coop_empl (ancillary)	(6) 2SLS-IV Happy (with gdp)	(7) OLS coop_empl (ancillary with gdp)
hdi	0.158	0.031	—	0.031	−1.728	—	—
	(0.502)	(0.367)		(0.298)	(1.625)		
gdppc	—	—	0.000	—	—	0.000*	−0.000
			(0.000)			(0.000)	(0.000)
coop_empl	0.078**	0.074***	0.073***	0.074***	—	0.073***	—
	(0.032)	(0.023)	(0.017)	(0.019)		(0.014)	
religionfract	−0.256***	−0.248***	−0.212**	−0.248***	−0.084	−0.212***	−0.138
	(0.082)	(0.078)	(0.081)	(0.063)	(0.295)	(0.066)	(0.356)
legor_fr	−0.114**	−0.108**	−0.103***	−0.108***	0.085	−0.103***	0.096
	(0.052)	(0.039)	(0.034)	(0.031)	(0.138)	(0.027)	(0.140)
legor_ge	−0.070	−0.071*	−0.067*	−0.071**	0.339*	−0.067**	0.349*
	(0.050)	(0.038)	(0.037)	(0.031)	(0.175)	(0.030)	(0.174)
legor_sc	−0.222**	−0.217***	−0.186***	−0.217***	0.381	−0.186***	0.506*
	(0.084)	(0.077)	(0.061)	(0.062)	(0.318)	(0.050)	(0.253)
days_bus	−0.000	—	—	—	—	—	—
	(0.001)						
gentrust	0.001	0.001	0.001	0.001	0.010*	0.001	0.006
	(0.002)	(0.001)	(0.001)	(0.001)	(0.005)	(0.001)	(0.005)
mdvolunt	0.002	0.002	0.001	0.002**	0.006	0.001**	0.005
	(0.001)	(0.001)	(0.001)	(0.001)	(0.004)	(0.001)	(0.004)
urban_pop	0.004*	0.004**	0.004***	0.004***	−0.001	0.004***	−0.002
	(0.002)	(0.002)	(0.001)	(0.001)	(0.007)	(0.001)	(0.006)
govdebt_gdp	−0.000	—	—	—	—	—	—
	(0.001)						

	(1)	(2)	(3)	(4)	(5)	(6)	(7)
pop_density	0.000 (0.000)	—	—	—	—	—	—
unemp_rate	0.007 (0.005)	0.005 (0.004)	0.006** (0.003)	0.005* (0.003)	0.004 (0.014)	0.006** (0.002)	−0.005 (0.014)
inflation	0.004 (0.012)	—	—	—	—	—	—
gini	−0.007* (0.003)	−0.007** (0.003)	−0.007** (0.003)	−0.007*** (0.003)	−0.001 (0.013)	−0.007*** (0.002)	0.004 (0.013)
coop_empl_oth	—	—	—	—	−10.479*** (1.298)	—	−9.941*** (1.452)
ethnicfractionalization	—	—	—	—	−1.863*** (0.495)	—	−1.697*** (0.414)
languagefractionalization	—	—	—	—	1.081** (0.413)	—	1.166** (0.442)
population	—	—	—	—	0.006*** (0.002)	—	0.006** (0.002)
Constant	0.600 (0.373)	0.730** (0.268)	0.732*** (0.154)	0.730*** (0.217)	8.629*** (1.515)	0.732*** (0.125)	7.035*** (0.924)
Observations	35	35	35	35	35	35	35
R-squared	0.781	0.779	0.789	0.779	0.845	0.789	0.842
F test	5.7**	7.25***	7.73***	7.25***	43.45***	7.73***	39.56***
J overidentification test	—	—	—	6.206	—	7.582***	—
F test instr. irrelevance	—	—	—	—	23.81***	—	27.58***

Note: The table reports regressions coefficients. The dependent variable and the estimation method are reported at the top of each column. In parentheses are robust standard errors. (*): coefficient significant at 10% confidence level; (**): coefficient significant at 5% confidence level; (***): coefficient significant at less than 1% confidence level. The F test tests whether the hypothesis that all the included regressor coefficients are jointly zero can be rejected (*: at 10%; **: at 5%; ***: at 1% level of significance). The J overidentification test tests whether the hypothesis of independence of the instruments and the disturbance process is called into question (insignificance means acceptance). The F test for instrument irrelevance tests whether, on the basis of the ancillary regression, the hypothesis of irrelevance may be rejected (significance means rejection).

instruments in the regression allows to 'clean' the endogeneity and to truly test whether cooperativeness is really related 'of its own' to happiness.

Following a widespread literature, we considered the fractionalization variables proposed by Alesina et al. (2003) as potential instruments. Among them, as said, since religion had been found to affect both happiness (Mookerjee and Beron, 2005; Okulicz-Kozaryn, 2011) and cooperation (Anderson and Mellor, 2009), *Relig_fract* was not a good candidate instrument and we used it rather as a control variable. Instead the other two (*Ethnic_fract* and *Lang_fract*) are good candidates since they are not expected to influence happiness (Hinks, 2012) but could limit peoples' ability to cooperate.[9] Our next instrument is *Population*,[10] a variable that is not expected to directly impact happiness but might reduce cooperation. For example, several game theoretical-based mathematical models show that increasing population size – at least beyond a certain threshold – makes cooperation less likely to evolve (e.g. Nowak et al., 2004; Ohtsuki et al., 2006; Rand and Nowak, 2012). Finally, our last instrument is rather mechanic by construction. We follow the strategy proposed by Caprio et al. (2007) and Laeven and Levine (2009). To filter out the idiosyncratic component of cooperativeness in country i, we calculate the – population weighted – value of *Coop_empl* that turns out considering all the other countries but excluding country i. Then we assign this to be the value of *Coop_empl_oth* for country i.[11]

The instrumental variable approach can be represented as follows:

$$Happy = \alpha_1 x + z_1 \delta_{11} + u \qquad (12.2)$$

where *Happy* is as before. Considering the interpretation of the instrumental variables given by two stages least squares (2SLS), we first define a vector of instruments z_2 correlated with the endogenous explanatory variable x, but uncorrelated with the stochastic error u in regression (12.2). In our model, as said, the instruments in this vector are: *Ethnic_fract*, *Lang_fract*, *Population*, and *Coop_empl_oth*.

The effect of these instruments is captured by the vector of parameter δ_{22} in the auxiliary regression:

$$x = z_1 \delta_{21} + z_2 \delta_{22} + v, \qquad (12.3)$$

where x is the endogenous explanatory variable in (12.2), z_1 is the vector of control variables in (12.2) and x is the residual. After estimating regression (12.3) at the first stage, x is replaced by its estimated values in regression (12.2). This last equation is then estimated at the second stage.

The results of the 2SLS-IV estimation are reported in column 4 of

Table 12.3. The appropriateness of the statistical model (*F test*) and the goodness of the fit (*R² statistic*) still attain. Analogously, the significance and coefficient value of *Coop_empl* are also unchanged.

The Hansen J statistic (overidentification test of all instruments) tells us that the hypothesis of independence of the instruments and the disturbance process is not called into question given that the J test null hypothesis is not rejected at the usual confidence levels.

Column 5 of Table 12.3 addresses the issue of joint irrelevance of the identified instruments. First, we report the ancillary OLS regressions where *Coop_empl* is regressed on the instruments and on the other independent variables. Then we run the F test of the hypothesis of joint irrelevance of the instruments. The hypothesis is rejected at comfortable levels of significance.

12.5.3 Robustness Checks

To further verify the validity of our results, we now conduct a series of robustness checks, beside the one already accomplished by using the instrumental variables approach. Preliminarily, still working on the European countries' sub-sample, we replace *Hdi* with *Gdp_pc*. Then we move on to the larger sample also including non-European countries to run a battery of additional robustness checks. As announced in Section 12.4, enlarging the sample required us moving from the cardinal domain of *Coop_empl* to the ordinal domain of *Coopr*. First, we run OLS estimates. Second, we verify whether the results for *Coopr* are confirmed as moving to the instrumental variables approach. Third, we test whether the OLS results resist a large number of replications via the bootstrap method. Fourth, we check what happens replacing *Hdir* with *Gdp_pcr*. Fifth, and last, we run ordered probit regressions in lieu of OLS regressions.

12.5.4 GDP Per Capita Instead of HDI on European Country Data

Table 12.3 also reports an OLS estimate where we have replaced *Hdi* with *Gdp_pc* (column 3). Results are virtually unaltered. What is of utmost interest to us is that *Coop_empl* has a stable positive coefficient that is statistically different from zero at the 1 percent level of significance.

Also in this case the results of the instrumental variables estimation are almost unchanged and the Hansen J statistic supports the hypothesis of independence of the instruments from the error term (Table 12.3, column 6). Finally, the ancillary regression allows us to calculate an F test whose value rejects the hypothesis of joint irrelevance of the instruments.

12.5.5   Basic OLS Regression on the World Country Sample

One might argue that the positive relationship going from cooperativeness to happiness is a peculiarity of Europe, which might not generalize to the entire world. To answer this we rely on the world country sample where we complement the data from Coopseurope (2010) with that from ICA (2011) by means of the mean adjusted rank. Here also *Happyrank* and *Hdir* replace *Happy* and *Hdi*. The regression equation is as follows:

$$Happyrank_i = \alpha + \beta_1 Hdir_i + \beta_2 Coopr_i + \beta_3 Pop\_density_i + \beta_4 Urban\_pop_i + \beta_5 Relig\_fract_i + \beta_6 Days\_bus_i + \beta_7 Govdebt\_gdp_i + \beta_8 Unemp\_rat_i + \beta_9 Inflation_i + \beta_{10} Gini_i + \beta_{13} Legor\_fr_i + \beta_{11} Legor\_ge_i + \beta_{12} Legor\_sc_i + \beta_{14} Gen\_trust_i + \beta_{15} Mdvolunt_i + \varepsilon_i \qquad (12.4)$$

where, for any country i, the regressors are as described and justified above.

We start estimating this by OLS. The results are supportive (Table 12.4, columns 1 and 2).

The preferred specification (column 2) shows that *Coopr* has a positive and significant relationship with *Happyrank*. So, countries with less cooperativeness (higher *Coopr*) also tend to have less happiness (higher *Happyrank*). While macro variables show no significant impact (except inflation in some specifications), *Happyrank* is positively associated, as expected, with *Hdir* (less happy is less developed) and with *Relig_fract*, in line with Mookerjee and Beron (2005) and Okulicz-Kozaryn (2011). Instead it's somewhat unexpected to find a negative association of *Happyrank* with *Days_bus*, suggesting that more 'market friendly' countries tend to be less happy. The legal origin variables send the same message as in the European sample.

12.5.6   Instrumental Variables Approach on the World Country Sample

These last results are all confirmed by the 2SLS estimate and the J overidentification test rules out the existence of correlation between the instruments and the disturbance process (Table 12.4, column 3). Next the ancillary regression allows ascertaining that the hypothesis of joint irrelevance of the instruments – here consisting in *Ethnic_fract*, *Lang_fract*, and *Population* – may be rejected (Table 12.4, column 4).

12.5.7   The Bootstrap Robustness Check

A further robustness check we perform is running 500 Montecarlo replications of the OLS estimation via the Bootstrap method. This allows making the standard errors more precise.

Table 12.4 *Estimation on all countries (with robust standard errors)*

Variables	(1) OLS happyrank	(2) OLS happyrank	(3) 2SLS-IV happyrank	(4) OLS Coopr (ancillary)	(5) OLS Happyrank (bootstrap)	(6) Ordered Probit happyrank
hdir	0.105	0.045	0.045	-0.025	0.045	0.008
	(0.189)	(0.167)	(0.144)	(0.290)	(0.188)	(0.021)
coopr	0.215**	0.260***	0.260***	—	0.260**	0.040***
	(0.101)	(0.086)	(0.074)		(0.105)	(0.013)
religionfractionalization	20.680**	22.456***	22.456***	-18.001	22.456***	3.472***
	(8.503)	(6.379)	(5.505)	(10.967)	(7.855)	(1.013)
legor_fr	13.569***	11.825**	11.825***	-9.124	11.825**	2.064***
	(4.710)	(4.589)	(3.960)	(6.385)	(5.333)	(0.582)
legor_ge	16.885***	13.409***	13.409***	-8.651	13.409**	2.124***
	(5.634)	(4.387)	(3.785)	(6.688)	(5.446)	(0.593)
legor_sc	16.839***	13.966**	13.966***	-16.436	13.966*	2.096**
	(5.859)	(6.004)	(5.181)	(12.713)	(7.669)	(1.069)
gentrust	-0.077	-0.074	-0.074	-0.316	-0.074	-0.014
	(0.146)	(0.139)	(0.120)	(0.249)	(0.172)	(0.019)
mdvolunt	-0.088	-0.155**	-0.155**	-0.149	-0.155*	-0.023**
	(0.087)	(0.071)	(0.062)	(0.134)	(0.088)	(0.010)
urban_pop	-0.343**	-0.439***	-0.439***	0.228	-0.439***	-0.070***
	(0.132)	(0.102)	(0.088)	(0.159)	(0.118)	(0.016)
govdebt_gdp	0.065*	0.061*	0.061**	-0.105	0.061	0.010**
	(0.032)	(0.034)	(0.029)	(0.067)	(0.043)	(0.005)

Table 12.4 (continued)

Variables	(1) OLS happyrank	(2) OLS happyrank	(3) 2SLS-IV happyrank	(4) OLS Coopr (ancillary)	(5) OLS Happyrank (bootstrap)	(6) Ordered Probit happyrank
inflation	1.493*	1.280*	1.280**	−0.093	1.280	0.178*
	(0.848)	(0.735)	(0.635)	(0.999)	(0.789)	(0.097)
days_bus	−0.117	—	—	—	—	—
	(0.079)					
pop_density	0.000	—	—	—	—	—
	(0.001)					
unemp_rate	0.438	—	—	—	—	—
	(0.427)					
gini	0.287	—	—	—	—	—
	(0.386)					
ethnicfractionalization	—	—	—	12.266	—	—
				(16.883)		
languagefractionalization	—	—	—	5.852	—	—
				(14.686)		
population	—	—	—	0.024***	—	—
				(0.008)		
Constant	5.900	27.970***	27.970***	36.923**	27.970**	—
	(19.867)	(10.186)	(8.790)	(16.713)	(13.389)	

Observations	47	47	47	47	47
R-squared	0.801	0.775	0.4851	0.485	0.775	–
Adjusted R-squared	–	–	–	–	0.7048	–
Pseudo_R-squared	–	–	–	–	–	0.2034
F-Test	18.42***	23.36***	23.36***	10.24***	–	–
J overidentification test	–	–	3.439	–	–	–
F-Test instr. irrelevance	–	–	–	3.42***	–	–
Wald Chi²	–	–	–	–	151.69***	–

Note: The table reports regressions coefficients. The dependent variable and the estimation method are reported at the top of each column. In parentheses are robust standard errors. (*): coefficient significant at 10% confidence level; (**): coefficient significant at 5% confidence level; (***): coefficient significant at less than 1% confidence level. The F test (the Wald Chi² test in the bootstrap regression) tests whether the hypothesis that all the included regressor coefficients are jointly zero can be rejected (*: at 10%; **: at 5%; ***: at 1% level of significance). The J overidentification test tests whether the hypothesis of independence of the instruments and the disturbance process is called into question (insignificance means acceptance). The F test for instrument irrelevance tests whether, on the basis of the ancillary regression, the hypothesis of irrelevance may be rejected (significance means rejection).

The results of this regression confirm the positive link between *Coopr* and *Happyrank*, though the statistical significance of the relationship is weakened (Table 12.4, column 5). There is little change also for the other regressors.

12.5.8 Replacing *Hdir* with *Gdpr*

As several scholars trust per capita GDP better than HDI, we now replace *Hdir* with *Gdpr*, that is, the rank of per capita GDP. The results of the various estimates are reported in Table 12.5.

The OLS estimation confirms the positive yet not statistically significant nexus of *Coopr* with *Happyrank* (Table 12.5, column 1), while the other regressors stay qualitatively the same as in the OLS regression with *Hdir*.

The 2SLS-IV method further corroborates the existence of the positive relationship between cooperativeness and happiness while the orthogonality of the instruments with respect to the error process is validated (Table 12.5, column 2) and the F test rejects the irrelevance of the instruments (Table 12.5, column 3).

The cooperativeness–happiness link we are studying also resists the test offered by estimating the regression via bootstrap (with 500 replications). The results are virtually unchanged (Table 12.5, column 4).

12.5.9 Ordered Probit Approach

One might argue that our rank variables have a limited number of realizations and this could make the OLS estimate inappropriate. To accommodate this potential criticism we run ordered probit regressions both for the specification with *Hdir* and with *Gdpr*.

In both cases, the main results of our empirical analysis are confirmed (Table 12.4, column 6, and Table 12.5, column 5).

12.5.10 Economic Significance

Though hopefully readers are by now convinced that the positive relationship between cooperativeness and happiness is statistically significant and that it is going from the former to the latter, one might still wonder whether its effect is economically significant.

The effect of cooperativeness on happiness is also economically significant. We can easily see this from the European countries regression. Take the estimation with *Gdp_pc* in column 6 of Table 12.3. Holding *Happy* at its mean and raising *Coop_empl* by twice its standard deviation – that is, +1.035, which would more or less equate to upgrading Latvia from its

Table 12.5 Estimation on all countries with Gdpr replacing Hdir (with robust standard errors)

Variables	(1) OLS happyrank	(2) 2SLS-IV happyrank	(3) OLS (ancillary reg.) Coopr	(4) OLS Happyrank (bootstrap)	(5) Ordered Probit happyrank
rgdppc_rank	0.075	0.075	0.247	0.075	−0.005
	(0.156)	(0.134)	(0.246)	(0.175)	(0.023)
coopr	0.252***	0.252***	—	0.252**	0.042***
	(0.083)	(0.071)		(0.108)	(0.013)
religionfractionalization	21.207***	21.207***	−22.039*	21.207**	3.621***
	(6.403)	(5.526)	(12.154)	(8.647)	(1.017)
legor_fr	11.291**	11.291***	−10.530	11.291**	2.102***
	(4.842)	(4.179)	(6.901)	(5.351)	(0.632)
legor_ge	12.841**	12.841***	−10.220	12.841**	2.178***
	(4.862)	(4.196)	(6.676)	(5.577)	(0.684)
legor_sc	12.862**	12.862**	−21.453	12.862	2.281**
	(6.184)	(5.337)	(13.520)	(8.086)	(1.115)
urban_pop	−0.427***	−0.427***	0.281*	−0.427***	−0.073***
	(0.103)	(0.088)	(0.163)	(0.120)	(0.016)
govdebt_gdp	0.060*	0.060**	−0.096	0.060	0.010**
	(0.034)	(0.030)	(0.064)	(0.049)	(0.005)
inflation	1.246*	1.246**	−0.478	1.246	0.203**
	(0.681)	(0.588)	(0.933)	(0.786)	(0.095)
gentrust	−0.060	−0.060	−0.188	−0.060	−0.019
	(0.143)	(0.123)	(0.244)	(0.171)	(0.019)
mdvolunt	−0.157**	−0.157***	−0.110	−0.157*	−0.025***
	(0.063)	(0.055)	(0.138)	(0.081)	(0.009)

Table 12.5 (continued)

Variables	(1) OLS happyrank	(2) 2SLS-IV happyrank	(3) OLS Coopr (ancillary reg.)	(4) OLS Happyrank (bootstrap)	(5) Ordered Probit happyrank
ethnicfractionalization	–	–	7.871 (17.159)	–	–
languagefractionalization	–	–	8.838 (15.001)	–	–
population	–	–	0.020** (0.007)	–	–
Constant	27.407*** (9.838)	27.407*** (8.490)	26.099 (16.506)	27.407** (12.103)	–
Observations	47	47	47	47	47
R-squared	0.776	0.776	0.499	0.776	–
Adjusted R-squared	–	–	–	0.7061	–
Pseudo_R-squared	–	–	–	–	0.203
F-Test	24.36***	24.36***	9.3***	–	–
J overidentification test	–	3.376	–	–	–
F-Test instrument irrelevance	–	–	2.85**	–	–
Wald Chi²	–	–	–	148.6***	–

Note: The table reports regressions coefficients. The dependent variable and the estimation method are reported at the top of each column. In parentheses are robust standard errors. (*): coefficient significant at 10% confidence level; (**): coefficient significant at 5% confidence level; (***): coefficient significant at less than 1% confidence level. The F test (the Wald Chi² test in the bootstrap regression) tests whether the hypothesis that all the included regressor coefficients are jointly zero can be rejected (*: at 10%; **: at 5%; ***: at 1% level of significance). The J overidentification test tests whether the hypothesis of independence of the instruments and the disturbance process is called into question (insignificance means acceptance). The F test for instrument irrelevance tests whether, on the basis of the ancillary regression, the hypothesis of irrelevance may be rejected (significance means rejection).

minimum of 0.02 to the value of 1.05 observed for Poland – would determine an increase in *Happy* from 0.84 to 0.92 or by 9.0 percent. In order to obtain the same effect via income, one would need to raise *Gdp_pc* from US$26 764 to US$89 756 or by 135.4 percent.

To conclude, there seems to be a genuine positive cross-country effect of the extent of cooperativeness on the degree of happiness and that effect is also sizable.

12.6 CONCLUSIONS

Focusing on relational capital, we hypothesized that there might be a positive link between the extent to which people cooperate in their economic dimension and the degree to which people feel happy. Our conjecture is that when a country hosts more economic cooperation its people will be able to build a larger relational capital. In turn, beside fostering trust, that larger relational capital will likely enhance happiness.

Our hypothesis is consistent with the tradition of civil economy developed by Antonio Genovesi ([1765] 2013) and recently revived by a growing strand of literature (Bruni and Zamagni, 2007, 2015, 2017; Bruni, 2008).

We searched for validation of our hypothesis by testing whether there is a positive cross-country link between the extent of cooperativeness and the degree of happiness. To accomplish this task we had to scout for data difficult to come up with on the presence of cooperative enterprises. First, we used relatively detailed data for European countries published by Coopseurope (2010) and ran various econometric estimations on it. Then, to reach a sample of almost 50 countries on which to conduct the regression analysis as a robustness check, we had to put together information coming from different sources and obtained with different methods. In order to limit the potential distortion due to measurement errors, we refrained from using the raw data and opted for focusing on the econometric analysis of rank variables.

Though the evidence of a positive cross-country link between cooperativeness and happiness was relatively clear in the descriptive analysis and in the OLS regression, we had to find some valid instrumental variables to address the issue of potential endogeneity between cooperativeness and happiness. The two-stage instrumental variables approach provided qualitative confirmation of the results obtained in the OLS estimations. We also showed that the estimated impact of cooperativeness on happiness is economically sizable. To conclude, even though additional refinements and robustness checks could strengthen our test, we can claim that there seems to be a positive link between cooperativeness and happiness.

Further work is needed. Besides providing confirmation of our results in wider databases, it would be particularly desirable to investigate whether the nexus between cooperativeness and happiness is direct or whether it is conveyed through some transmission channels like trust. On the one hand, a normative prescription is that national and supranational statistical agencies should strive harder to collect data on the presence of cooperative enterprises. On the other hand, on positive grounds we can doubt that significant progress in that respect will be achieved shortly. Hence, given that the paucity of data available to this task might be persistent, the research agenda on how cooperativeness and happiness interact could benefit from the experimental approach.

NOTES

1. This chapter is derived in part from an article published in *Applied Economics*, 7 February 2019, copyright Taylor & Francis, available online: https://doi.org/10.1080/00 036846.2019.1575944.
2. For Australia, see also the specific debate that emerged about this country (e.g. Blanchflower and Oswald, 2005; Leigh and Wolfers, 2006).
3. The classic texts are from Adam Smith: 'By directing that industry in such a manner as may be of the greatest value, [the merchant] intends only his own gain, and he is in this, as in many other cases, led by an invisible hand to promote an end which was no part of his intention. Nor is it always the worse for society that is was no part of it' (Adam Smith, [1776] 1976, p. 456).
4. When not otherwise specified by a year in parenthesis next to the country name, data refer to WVS (2009): Australia, Austria (EVS, 2008), Belarus (EVS, 2008), Belgium (EVS, 2008), Brazil, Bulgaria, Canada, China, Croatia (EVS, 2008), Cyprus, Czech Republic (EVS, 2008), Denmark (EVS, 2008), Estonia (EVS, 2008), Finland, France, Germany (EVS, 2008), Greece, Hungary (EVS, 2008), India, Ireland (EVS, 2008), Italy, Japan, South Korea, Latvia (EVS, 2008), Lithuania (EVS, 2008), Luxembourg (EVS, 2008), Malaysia, Malta (EVS, 2008), Moldova, Netherlands, New Zealand, Norway, Poland, Portugal (EVS, 2008), Romania, Russia, Serbia, Singapore (WVS, 2010), Slovakia (EVS, 2008), Slovenia (EVS, 2008), Spain, Sweden, Switzerland, Taiwan, Turkey, Ukraine, United Kingdom, USA.
5. Austria, Belarus, Belgium, Bulgaria, Croatia, Cyprus, Czech Republic, Denmark, Estonia, Finland, France, Germany, Greece, Hungary, Ireland, Italy, Latvia, Lithuania, Luxembourg, Malta, Moldova, Netherlands, Norway, Poland, Portugal, Romania, Russia, Serbia, Slovakia, Slovenia, Spain, Sweden, Switzerland, Turkey, Ukraine, United Kingdom.
6. Australia, Austria, Belgium, Brazil, Canada, China, Denmark, Finland, France, Germany, India, Ireland, Italy, Japan, South Korea, Malaysia, Netherlands, New Zealand, Norway, Singapore, Spain, Sweden, Switzerland, Taiwan, UK, USA.
7. To make the ICA rank (based on 26 countries) comparable to the Coopseurope rank (based on 36 countries) we need to adjust it. We rescale the ICA rank multiplying it by $0.7222 = 26/36$. Then the MAR is the mean of the adjusted-ICA rank for the 14 European countries which are observed both from ICA and Coopseurope. Alternatively, the MAR is either simply the adjusted-ICA rank for the 12 non-European countries observed in ICA or simply the Coopseurope rank for the 22 European countries for which we have no observations from ICA.

8. Following an influential paper by Djankov et al. (2002), the World Bank compiles data on the various factors of the ease of doing business. Unfortunately the composite index is only available from 2013 onwards and we had to rely on its sub-components. We chose the two most prominent indicators: 'days to start up a business' and 'number of procedures to start up a business'. As expected, the two are strongly correlated (their pairwise correlation is 0.626, significant at the 1 percent confidence level) and, noticing that the latter turned out to be insignificant in our regressions, we selected the former.
9. See La Ferrara (2002, 2003) for the negative effect of ethnic fragmentation on cooperation. See Clark and Bonggeun (2012) and Cox (2010) for the negative effects of language fractionalization on trust and cooperation.
10. A recent paper using population as an instrument is Rose (2013).
11. Since *Coopr* is a rank we couldn't calculate the same instrument for it. Instead we use the first three instruments only.

REFERENCES

Adam, F. and B. Rončević (2003), Social capital: recent debates and research trends, *Social Science Information*, 42(2): 155–83.

Alesina, A., A. Devleeschauwer, W. Easterly, S. Kurlat and R. Wacziarg (2003), Fractionalization, *Journal of Economic Growth*, 8: 155–94.

Alesina, A., R. Di Tella and R. MacCulloch (2004), Inequality and happiness: are Europeans and Americans different?, *Journal of Public Economics*, 88(9): 2009–42.

Anderson, L. R. and J. M. Mellor (2009), Religion and cooperation in a public goods experiment, *Economics Letters*, 105(1): 58–60.

Arrighetti, A., R. Bachmann and S. Deakin (1997), Contract law, social norms and inter-firm cooperation, *Cambridge Journal of Economics*, 21(2): 171–95.

Bartolini, S., E. Bilancini and M. Pugno (2011), Did the decline in social connections depress Americans' happiness?, *Social Indicators Research*, http://doi:10.1007/s11205-011-9971-x.

Bartolini, S. and F. Sarracino (2014), Happy for how long? How social capital and economic growth relate to happiness over time, *Ecological Economics*, 108: 242–56.

Becchetti, L. (2008), Relational goods, sociability, and happiness, *Kyklos*, 61: 343–63.

Becchetti, L., G. Trovato and D. A. Londono Bedoya (2011), Income, relational goods and happiness, *Applied Economics*, 43(3): 273–90.

Blanchflower, D. G. and A. J. Oswald (2005), Happiness and the human development index: the paradox of Australia, IZA Discussion Papers, No. 1601.

Borgonovi, F. (2008), Doing well by doing good: the relationship between formal volunteering and self-reported health and happiness, *Social Science & Medicine*, 66(11): 2321–34.

Bruni, L. (2008), *Reciprocity, Altruism and the Civil Society: In Praise of Heterogeneity*, London: Taylor & Francis.

Bruni, L. and L. Stanca (2008), Watching alone: happiness, relational goods and television, *Journal of Economic Behavior & Organization*, 65: 506–28.

Bruni, L. and R. Sugden (2008), Fraternity: why the market need not be a morally free zone, *Economics & Philosophy*, 24: 35–64.

Bruni, L. and R. Sugden (2013), Reclaiming virtue ethics for economics, *Journal of Economic Perspectives*, 27: 141–64.

Bruni, L. and S. Zamagni (2007), *Civil Economy*, Oxford: Peter Lang.

Bruni, L. and S. Zamagni (2015), *The Civil Economy*, London: Agenda.

Bruni, L. and S. Zamagni (2017), *Civil Economy. Another Idea of the Market*, Newcastle upon Tyne: Agenda Publishing.

Campbell, D. and D. Harris (1993), Flexibility in long-term contractual relationships: the role of co-operation, *Journal of Law and Society*, 20(2): 166–91.

Caprio, G., L. Laeven and R. Levine (2007), Bank valuation and corporate governance, *Journal of Financial Intermediation*, 1(4): 584–617.

Clark, J. and K. Bonggeun (2012), The effect of neighborhood diversity on volunteering: evidence from New Zealand, *The BE Journal of Economic Analysis & Policy*, 12(1): 1–49.

Coleman, J. S. (1990), *The Foundations of Social Theory*, Cambridge, MA: Harvard University Press.

Colombo, E., V. Rotondi and L. Stanca (2018), Macroeconomic conditions and well-being: do social interactions matter?, *Applied Economics*, 50(28): 3029–38.

Coopseurope (2010), European Cooperatives. Key Statistics, www.coopseurope.coop.

Cox, M. D. (2010), Silencing the call to action: a bird's eye view of minority language media and political participation in Eurasia, *Transition Studies Review*, 17(1): 181–93.

Delhey, J. and C. Kroll (2012), A 'happiness test' for the new measures of national well-being: how much better than GDP are they?, WZB Discussion Paper, No. SP I 2012–201.

Djankov, S., R. La Porta, F. Lopez-de-Silanes and A. Shleifer (2002), The regulation of entry, *The Quarterly Journal of Economics*, 117(1): 1–37.

Dolan, P., T. Peasgood and M. White (2008), Do we really know what makes us happy? A review of the economic literature on the factors associated with subjective well-being, *Journal of Economic Psychology*, 29(1): 94–122.

Easterlin, R. (1974), Does economic growth improve the human lot? Some empirical evidence, in P. A. David and M. W. Reder (eds), *Nations and Households in Economic Growth: Essays in Honor of Moses Abramovitz* (pp. 89–125), New York: Academic Press.

EVS – European Values Survey (2008), http://www.atlasofeuropeanvalues.eu/new/europesekaarten.php.

Ferrer-i-Carbonell, A. and X. Ramos (2014), Inequality and happiness, *Journal of Economic Surveys*, 28(5): 1016–27.

Fukuyama, F. (2001), Social capital, civil society and development, *Third World Quarterly*, 22(1): 7–20.

Genovesi, A. [1765] (2013), *Lezioni di economia civile*, Milan: Vita e Pensiero.

Genovesi, A. (1979), *Scritti*, Milan: Feltrinelli.

Glaeser, E. L., D. Laibson and B. Sacerdote (2002), An economic approach to social capital, *The Economic Journal*, 112: F437–F458.

Greenfield, E. A. and N. F. Marks (2004), Formal volunteering as a protective factor for older adults' psychological well-being, *The Journals of Gerontology Series B: Psychological Sciences and Social Sciences*, 59(5): S258–S264.

Grillo, M. (2013), Competition rules and the cooperative firm, *Journal of Entrepreneurial and Organizational Diversity*, 2(1): 36–53.

Grootaert, C. and T. Van Bastelaer (2002), Understanding and measuring social capital: a synthesis of findings and recommendation from the social capital initiative, World Bank, Social Capital Initiative Working Paper No. 24.

Gui, B. (1987), Éléments pour une definition d'"économie communautaire, Notes et Documents de l'Institut International Jacques Maritain, no. 19/20.

Gui, B. (1996), On relational goods: strategic implications of investment in relationships, *International Journal of Social Economics*, 23(10/11): 260–78.

Gui, B. (2005), From transactions to encounters: the joint generation of relational goods and conventional values, in B. Gui and R. Sugden (eds), *Economics and Social Interactions* (pp. 23–51), Cambridge: Cambridge University Press.

Gui, B. and L. Stanca (2010), Happiness and relational goods: well-being and interpersonal relations in the economic sphere, *International Review of Economics*, 57(2): 105–18.

Helliwell, J. and R. Putnam (2004), The social context of well-being, *Philosophical Transactions – Royal Society of London Series B Biological Sciences*, 359(1449): 1435–46.

Helliwell, J. and S. Wang (2010), Trust and well-being, NBER Working Paper Series No. 15911.

Hinks, T. (2012), Fractionalization and well-being: evidence from a new South African data set, *New Zealand Economic Papers*, 46(3): 253–71.

Hudson, J. (2006), Institutional trust and subjective well-being across the EU, *Kyklos*, 59(1): 43–62.

ICA – International Co-operative Alliance (2011), *Global300 Report 2010*, https://www.ica.coop/en/global300.

Jones, D. C. and P. Kalmi (2009), Trust, inequality and the size of the co-operative sector: cross-country evidence, *Annals of Public and Cooperative Economics*, 80(2): 165–95.

Knorringa, P. and I. Van Staveren (2007), Beyond social capital: a critical approach, *Review of Social Economy*, 65(1): 1–9.

Krugman, P. (1995), Growing world trade: causes and consequences, *Brookings Papers on Economic Activity*, 1: 327–77.

La Ferrara, E. (2002), Self-help groups and income generation in the informal settlements of Nairobi, *Journal of African Economies*, 11(1): 61–89.

La Ferrara, E. (2003), Kin groups and reciprocity: a model of credit transactions in Ghana, *American Economic Review*, 93(5): 1730–51.

La Porta, R., F. Lopez-de-Silanes, A. Shleifer and R. W. Vishny (1998), Law and finance, *Journal of Political Economy*, 106: 1113–55.

Laeven, L. and R. Levine (2009), Bank governance, regulation, and risk-taking, *Journal of Financial Economics*, 93(2): 259–75.

Leigh, A. and J. Wolfers (2006), Happiness and the human development index: Australia is not a paradox, IZA Discussion Papers, No. 1916.

Lui, S. S., Y. Y. Wong and W. Liu (2009), Asset specificity roles in interfirm cooperation: reducing opportunistic behavior or increasing cooperative behavior?, *Journal of Business Research*, 62(11): 1214–19.

Mookerjee, R. and K. Beron (2005), Gender, religion and happiness, *The Journal of Socio-Economics*, 34(5): 674–85.

Morrow-Howell, N., J. Hinterlong, P. Rozario and F. Tang (2003), Effects of volunteering on the well-being of older adults, *Journals of Gerontology: Series B: Psychological Sciences and Social Sciences*, 58(3): S137–S145.

Nooteboom, B. (2007), Social capital, institutions and trust, *Review of Social Economy*, 65(1): 29–53.

Nowak, M. A., A. Sasaki, C. Taylor and D. Fudenberg (2004), Emergence of cooperation and evolutionary stability infinite populations, *Nature*, 428: 646–50.

OECD (2001), *The Well-Being Of Nations: The Role Of Human And Social Capital*, Paris: OECD Publishing.

Ohtsuki, H., C. Hauert, E. Lieberman and M. A. Nowak (2006), A simple rule for the evolution of cooperation on graphs and social networks, *Nature*, 441(7092): 502–5.

Oishi, S., S. Kesebir and E. Diener (2011), Income inequality and happiness, *Psychological Science*, 22(9): 1095–100.

Okulicz-Kozaryn, A. (2011), Does religious diversity make us unhappy?, *Mental Health, Religion & Culture*, 14(10): 1063–76.

Paldam, M. (2000), Social capital: one or many? Definition and measurement, *Journal of Economic Surveys*, 14(5): 629–53.

Probst, T. M. (2000), Wedded to the job: moderating effects of job involvement on the consequences of job insecurity, *Journal of Occupational Health Psychology*, 5(1): 63–73.

Pugno, M. (2009), The Easterlin paradox and the decline of social capital: an integrated explanation, *The Journal of Socio-Economics*, 38(4): 590–600.

Putnam, R. D. (1993), *Making Democracy Work: Civic Traditions in Modern Italy*, Princeton: Princeton University Press.

Putnam, R. (2000), *Bowling Alone: The Collapse and Revival of American Community*, New York: Simon and Schuster.

Rand, D. G. and M. A. Nowak (2012), Evolutionary dynamics in finite populations can explain the full range of cooperative behaviors observed in the centipede game, *Journal of Theoretical Biology*, 300: 212–21.

Rose, A. K. (2013), Surprising similarities: recent monetary regimes of small economies, NBER Working Paper No. 19632, November.

Sacco, P. L. and S. Zamagni (eds) (2006), *Teoria economica e relazioni interpersonali. Il mulino*, Bologna. ISBN 8815114327.

Scott, R. E. (1987), Conflict and cooperation in long-term contracts, *California Law Review*, 75: 2005–54.

Scrivens, K. and C. Smith (2013), Four interpretations of social capital: an agenda for measurement, OECD Statistics Working Papers, 2013/06.

Smith, A. [1776] (1976), *Wealth of Nations*, Oxford: Oxford University Press.

Solt, F. (2009), Standardizing the World Income Inequality Database, *Social Science Quarterly*, 90: 231–42.

Uhlaner, C. (1989), Relational goods and participation: incorporating sociability into a theory of rational action, *Public Choice*, 62: 253–85.

United Nations Development Programme (1998), *Human Development Report 1998*, New York: Oxford University Press.

Vemuri, A. W. and R. Costanza (2006), The role of human, social, built, and natural capital in explaining life satisfaction at the country level: toward a national well-being index (NWI), *Ecological Economics*, 58: 119–33.

Wills-Herrera, E., L. E. Orozco, C. Forero-Pineda, O. Pardo and V. Andonova (2011), The relationship between perceptions of insecurity, social capital and subjective well-being: empirical evidences from areas of rural conflict in Colombia, *The Journal of Socio-Economics*, 40(1): 88–96.

Wooldridge, J. M. (2002), *Econometric Analysis of Cross Section and Panel Data*, Cambridge, MA: MIT Press.

WPT – World Penn Tables (2010), https://pwt.sas.upenn.edu.

WVS – World Values Survey (various years), http://www.worldvaluessurvey.org/wvs.jsp.

13. The relationship between migrant acceptance and wellbeing: evidence from the Gallup Migrant Acceptance Index

Neli Esipova, Julie Ray and Anita Pugliese

13.1 INTRODUCTION

In the aftermath of the migrant crisis that peaked in Europe in 2015 and the negative reaction toward migrants that accompanied it, a team of Gallup researchers[1] developed a Migrant Acceptance Index (MAI) with the hope of being able to scientifically gauge people's personal acceptance of migrants not just in Europe, but also throughout the rest of the world.

The results from Gallup's inaugural global study of adults in 140 countries in 2016 and 2017 – which is being repeated in 2019 – confirmed some of the researchers' hypotheses based on previous Gallup analysis. For example, given their belief that their countries should not accept Syrian refugees and their long-held opinions that their countries should decrease immigration,[2] we expected that populations in Eastern Europe would be among the least accepting of migrants in the world. But the analysis also led the researchers to several exciting and interesting discoveries.

For example, one of the key findings from the inaugural index was the role that personal interaction with migrants can potentially play in countering stereotypes against migrants and in easing their integration in their adopted countries. The researchers expected to see some evidence of social contact effect, but they were surprised by how robust the relationship was across almost all countries surveyed. In all but five countries that Gallup surveyed, people scored higher on Gallup's Migrant Acceptance Index if they personally knew at least one migrant.

And, because of the vast size of Gallup's global sample, the researchers were also able to discover that people's acceptance of migrants – or lack thereof – is related to how the self-identified migrants in the sample evaluated their own lives. The findings revealed that migrants living in countries scoring lowest on Gallup's Migrant Acceptance Index evaluate their lives less positively than those who live in countries that are the most accepting of migrants.

In this chapter we delve into the background of the development of the index and discuss some of the more pivotal findings from the initial study, including the relationship that emerged between migrant acceptance and migrants' emotional health and overall wellbeing.[3]

13.2 GALLUP'S INAUGURAL MIGRANT ACCEPTANCE INDEX

Gallup created the Migrant Acceptance Index using three questions that it first asked of adults in in 140 countries in 2016 and 2017 through its World Poll survey instrument.[4] The questions measure acceptance by increasing degrees of proximity, asking whether people think immigrants living in their country, becoming their neighbor and marrying into their families are good things or bad things.

Migrant Acceptance Index Questions

Now, I would like to ask you some questions about foreign immigrants – people who have come to live and work in this country from another country. Please tell me whether you, personally, think each of the following is a good thing or a bad thing.

Immigrants living in this country	A good thing
An immigrant becoming your neighbor	A bad thing
An immigrant marrying one of your close relatives	(It depends)*
	(Don't know/Refused)*

* = Volunteered response

Source: Gallup World Poll.

The index is a sum of the points across the three questions, with a maximum possible score of 9.0 (all three are good things) and a minimum possible score of zero (all three are bad things). The higher the score, the more accepting the population is of migrants. 'A good thing' response is worth three points in the calculation, a volunteered response of 'it depends' or 'don't know' is worth one point, and a 'bad thing' is worth zero points.

The total sample included more than 147 000 adults aged 15 and older, and among them more than 8000 self-identified first-generation migrants. In all, 29 countries' index scores fall more than one standard deviation below the country-level mean score and 23 countries' index scores fall more than one standard deviation above the country-level mean score. The bulk of the rest of the world falls in the middle.

Scores on Gallup's Migrant Acceptance Index ranged widely across the 140 countries where the questions were asked in the field period, from a high of 8.26 in Iceland to a low of 1.47 in North Macedonia (Table 13.1).[5]

Many countries on the front lines of the recent migrant crisis in Europe are among the least accepting countries in the world for migrants, which Gallup defined as those with index scores that fall one standard deviation below the country-level mean score. Most of the least accepting countries are located along the Balkan route that once channeled asylum seekers from Greece to Germany. They are geographically and culturally clustered.

The most accepting countries for migrants hail from all over the globe – Oceania, Western Europe, sub-Saharan Africa and North America. However, the common thread tying many of the most accepting countries together is their long traditions as migrant-receiving countries – the US, Australia, Canada and New Zealand, for example.

Interestingly, with a few exceptions the countries with the lowest scores are a list of the ones that did not adopt the Global Compact for Safe, Orderly

Table 13.1   Least and most accepting countries for migrants

Least accepting of migrants		Most accepting of migrants	
North Macedonia	1.47	Iceland	8.26
Montenegro	1.63	New Zealand	8.25
Hungary	1.69	Rwanda	8.16
Serbia	1.80	Canada	8.14
Slovakia	1.83	Sierra Leone	8.05
Israel	1.87	Mali	8.03
Latvia	2.04	Australia	7.98
Czech Republic	2.26	Sweden	7.92
Estonia	2.37	United States	7.86
Croatia	2.39	Nigeria	7.76

Note: Based on 138 countries surveyed in 2016; US and Canada surveyed in 2017; top possible score is 9.0.

Source: Gallup World Poll 2016–17.

and Regular Migration that was signed in late 2018. In fact, six of the ten countries that score a 2.39 or lower (out of a possible 9.0) on the index either rejected the legally nonbinding agreement outright or delayed their decisions.

However, two of the most accepting countries in the world for migrants, according to the index, also did not sign on: Australia and the US both rejected the pact.

Commonwealth of Independent States Least Accepting; Oceania Most Accepting

Many of the 20 least accepting countries are located in this region, so it is not surprising that the Commonwealth of Independent States (CIS) is the least accepting region in the world for migrants.

The region's Migrant Acceptance Index score is 3.26 out of a possible 9.0 (Table 13.2). Russia's score of 2.60 on the index is chiefly responsible for the region's low overall score, but just two countries – Turkmenistan and Armenia – score slightly higher than the global average of 5.34.

The Middle East, excluding the Gulf Cooperation Council (GCC) countries, is the next lowest region, with a score of 3.70. South Asia, Southeast

Table 13.2   Migrant Acceptance Index, by region

	Migrant Acceptance Index
Oceania	8.02
Northern America	7.89*
Sub-Saharan Africa	6.47
Gulf Cooperation Council	6.11
European Union	5.92
Latin America and the Caribbean	5.89
East Asia	5.29
Non-EU Europe	4.89
South Asia	4.88
Northern Africa	4.59
Southeast Asia	4.48
Middle East	3.70
Commonwealth of Independent States	3.26

Note: Based on 138 countries surveyed in 2016; US and Canada surveyed in 2017; top possible score is 9.0. * Revised from initial estimates released in August 2017 to reflect the inclusion of Canada and a later survey in the US.

Source: Gallup World Poll 2016–17.

Asia, East Asia, Northern Africa and non-EU countries in Europe all post scores lower than the global average.

The regions with the highest index scores are Oceania (Australia and New Zealand) at 8.02 and North America at 7.89 (revised upward from the initial estimate of 7.26 with the inclusion of Canada and a US survey conducted later in 2017).

Most Educated, Youngest Generations More Accepting

Worldwide, adults in certain demographic groups are more accepting of migrants than those in other demographics (Table 13.3). For example,

Table 13.3   Migrant Acceptance Index, by demographics

	Migrant Acceptance Index
Education	
Primary education or less	4.93*
Secondary education	5.55*
Completed four years of education after high school and/or earned college degree	6.13*
Generation	
Gen. Zers (1997 or later)	5.71
Millennials (1980–96)	5.46*
Gen. Xers (1965–79)	5.23*
Baby boomers (1946–64)	5.07*
Traditionalists (before 1946)	5.34*
Rural/urban	
Rural	5.16*
Urban	5.70*
Income group	
Poorest 20%	5.04
Second 20%	5.07*
Middle 20%	5.22
Fourth 20%	5.14
Richest 20%	5.53

Note: Based on 138 countries surveyed in 2016; US and Canada surveyed in 2017; top possible score is 9.0. * Revised from initial estimates released in August 2017 to reflect the inclusion of Canada and a later survey in the US.

Source: Gallup World Poll 2016–17.

acceptance increases linearly with education. With an index score of 6.13, those with at least four years of education after high school or with college degrees are the most likely of all educational groups to be accepting.

Those within the wealthiest 20 percent of a population in a country[6] – who are also more likely to have higher education – are also more likely to be accepting of migrants compared with respondents in all lower income groups, as are residents of urban areas as opposed to those living in rural areas.

At the global level, younger generations are the most accepting of migrants, while older people are less so. Those in the postmillennial generation are the most accepting of all age cohorts. However, traditionalists – the oldest generation – are more accepting than Generation Xers and baby boomers.

The CIS region is the only region worldwide that does not follow these global patterns – acceptance of migrants is low regardless of people's education, generation or income level, or whether residents live in urban or rural areas. However, in the CIS those with less education tend to be slightly more accepting.

Case Study: EU Most Divided in World on Acceptance of Migrants

With a Migrant Acceptance Index score of 5.92 (out of a possible 9.0), the European Union (as a single entity) scores just above the global average (5.34) (Table 13.4). But the scores largely follow an east–west divide inside the region. Along with Hungary, other Eastern European countries such as Slovakia, Latvia, Czech Republic, Estonia and Croatia are among the ten least accepting countries in the world. Sweden and Ireland are the two EU member countries among the ten most accepting countries.

No other region of the world is more divided on Gallup's new Migrant Acceptance Index than the EU, where scores range from a high of 7.92 in Sweden to a low of 1.69 in Hungary.

Looking at the 20 most accepting and 20 least accepting countries, Luxembourg, the Netherlands and Spain would end up on the most accepting list, while Bulgaria, Lithuania and Romania would join the least accepting list. Top EU destination countries, including Germany, the United Kingdom, France and Italy all fall lower in the rankings, but they have index scores higher than the average for the EU.

The divide between EU countries in Central and Eastern Europe and those in Western Europe underscores the challenges that the EU faces as it tries to create a cohesive policy on migration: The index score for EU countries in Western Europe is 6.73, compared with 2.77 for EU countries in Central and Eastern Europe.

Table 13.4   Migrant Acceptance Index scores vary across the European Union

Sweden	7.92	Cyprus	5.41
Ireland	7.74	Malta	4.95
Luxembourg	7.54	Slovenia	4.42
Netherlands	7.46	Greece	3.34
Spain	7.44	Poland	3.31
Denmark	7.09	Romania	2.93
Germany	7.09	Lithuania	2.72
Portugal	6.65	Bulgaria	2.42
United Kingdom	6.61	Croatia	2.39
Finland	6.58	Estonia	2.37
Italy	6.49	Czech Republic	2.26
France	6.46	Latvia	2.04
Belgium	6.16	Slovakia	1.83
Austria	6.06	Hungary	1.69

Note: Maximum possible score on the index is 9.0.

Source: Gallup World Poll 2016–17.

Youngest, Most Educated Are Most Accepting

Although Migrant Acceptance Index scores vary widely across the European Union, the demographic patterns of support are in line with what Gallup finds in most global regions. Acceptance generally rises with education, and those in the highest 20 percent income group (within countries) are more likely to be accepting of migrants than those in lower income groups.

Younger generations in the EU are the most accepting of migrants, while older people are the least accepting (Table 13.5). Those in the post-millennial generation are the most accepting of all. Traditionalists – the oldest generation – are the least accepting of all.

Despite the huge gap in index scores between EU countries in Western Europe and those in Central and Eastern Europe, within these regions migrant acceptance tends to be higher among these same demographic groups – the youngest generation, those with more education and those with the highest income.

However, scores among even the most accepting EU populations in Eastern Europe are about half as high as scores among the least accepting EU populations in Western Europe.

Table 13.5   Migration acceptance divides EU

	Western European EU Index score	Central/Eastern European EU Index score
Generation		
Gen. Z (1997 and later)	7.16	3.13
Millennials (1980–96)	6.98	2.94
Gen. X (1965–79)	6.87	2.85
Baby boomers (1946–64)	6.63	2.72
Traditionalists (pre-1946)	5.91	2.09
Income group		
Poorest 20%	6.22	2.56
Second 20%	6.54	2.65
Middle 20%	6.93	2.75
Fourth 20%	6.83	2.76
Richest 20%	7.12	3.12
Education		
Primary education or less	6.10	2.48
Secondary	6.76	2.70
Four-year college degree	7.39	3.38

Note: Maximum possible score on index is 9.0.

Source: Gallup World Poll 2016–17.

Case Study: Migrant Acceptance in North Macedonia and Albania

Over the past several years the European Union has repeatedly attempted to start accession negotiation talks with North Macedonia and Albania – two Balkan neighbors whose views toward migrants are worlds apart. North Macedonia's score of 1.47 on Gallup's Migrant Acceptance Index is the lowest in the world, while Albania, with a score of 7.22, is one of the most accepting countries (Table 13.6).

Scores in the EU with its current makeup range from a high of 7.92 in Sweden to a low of 1.69 in Hungary. Northern Macedonia's score is lower than the one for Hungary, while Albania's score ranks it just after Spain.

Albania's higher score on the index may reflect the hospitality that is ingrained within the country's culture. As an old Albanian saying goes, 'Before the house belongs to the owner, it first belongs to God and the guest'. North Macedonia, on the other hand, sealed its border with Greece during the recent migrant crisis.

Table 13.6   Migrant Acceptance Index scores across EU, Macedonia and Albania

Sweden	7.92	Cyprus	5.41
Ireland	7.74	Malta	4.95
Luxembourg	7.54	Slovenia	4.42
Netherlands	7.46	Greece	3.34
Spain	7.44	Poland	3.31
Albania*	7.22	Romania	2.93
Denmark	7.09	Lithuania	2.72
Germany	7.09	Bulgaria	2.42
Portugal	6.65	Croatia	2.39
United Kingdom	6.61	Estonia	2.37
Finland	6.58	Czech Republic	2.26
Italy	6.49	Latvia	2.04
France	6.46	Slovakia	1.83
Belgium	6.16	Hungary	1.69
Austria	6.06	North Macedonia*	1.47

Notes: The maximum possible score on the index is 9.0.
*   Albania and North Macedonia are candidate countries.

Source: Gallup World Poll 2016–17.

Desire to Migrate in Both Countries on the Higher Side Compared with EU

Relatively high percentages in each country would also personally like to migrate permanently to other countries. Sixty-two percent of Albanians and 33 percent of Macedonians in 2017 said they would like to migrate permanently to another country if they could, which is higher than the wishes in almost all existing EU member states (Table 13.7). Germany is a top desired destination for potential migrants in both countries.

Case Study: Migrant Acceptance in Canada and the US

Canada and the US are among the top 10 most accepting countries in the world for migrants, but Canadians are somewhat more accepting than Americans are of migrants. Canada scores an 8.14 (out of a possible 9.0) on Gallup's Migrant Acceptance Index, ranking it fourth out of 140 countries, while the US ranks ninth, with a score of 7.86 (Table 13.8).[7]

The future of the reputation of both Canada and the US as receiving countries remains in question. Under Prime Minister Justin Trudeau, Canada's government has opened its doors wider to migrants and refugees,

Table 13.7   Desire to migrate permanently across EU, Macedonia and Albania

Albania*	62%	Spain	17%
Italy	36%	Germany	16%
North Macedonia*	33%	Hungary	16%
Cyprus	30%	Poland	16%
Belgium	27%	Bulgaria	15%
United Kingdom	26%	Portugal	15%
Lithuania	25%	Croatia	14%
Slovenia	25%	Slovakia	14%
Romania	24%	Denmark	13%
France	21%	Luxembourg	13%
Greece	21%	Ireland	12%
Latvia	20%	Sweden	12%
Malta	18%	Austria	10%
Netherlands	18%	Czech Republic	10%
Estonia	17%	Finland	10%

Note: *Albania and North Macedonia are candidate countries.

Source: Gallup World Poll 2016–17.

Table 13.8   Top ten most accepting countries for migrants

	Migrant Acceptance Index
Iceland	8.26
New Zealand	8.25
Rwanda	8.16
Canada	8.14
Sierra Leone	8.05
Mali	8.03
Australia	7.98
Sweden	7.92
United States	7.86
Nigeria	7.76

Source: Gallup World Poll 2016–17.

and the US government under President Donald Trump has been shutting its doors.

Although partisan identification is not asked in the World Poll, the political nature of the issue is apparent in who in the population approves

Table 13.9   Migrant acceptance and the political divide

	Migrant Acceptance Index
Americans	
Approve of Trump	7.08
Disapprove of Trump	8.54
Confident in national government	7.57
Not confident in national government	8.09
Approve of country's leadership	7.32
Disapprove of country's leadership	8.36
Canadians	
Approve of Trudeau	8.64
Disapprove of Trudeau	7.84
Confident in national government	8.51
Not confident in national government	7.46
Approve of country's leadership	8.65
Disapprove of country's leadership	7.76

Source: Gallup World Poll 2016–17.

of each leader. In the US, those who approve of Trump's job performance score a 7.08 out of a possible 9.0 on the Migrant Acceptance Index, while those who disapprove score nearly 1.5 points higher – 8.54. In Canada, those who approve of Trudeau's job performance score an 8.64, while the score is 7.84 among those who disapprove (Table 13.9).

Religious People in Each Country Are Less Accepting

Americans who are highly religious are more likely to identify as Republicans – the party of the president – and as conservatives. In the more secular Canada, similar to the pattern in the US, Canadians who are more religious tend to affiliate with the Conservative Party rather than Trudeau's Labor Party.

Consistent with this relationship, in both the US and Canada people who say religion is an important part of their daily lives are less accepting of migrants than are people for whom religion is not that important (Table 13.10).

In the US, people who say religion is not an important part of their daily lives *and* who say they are not confident in the national government are the most accepting of migrants (8.46), while the index score is 7.28 for those who say religion is an important part of their daily lives and are confident in the national government. The pattern is the same in Canada.

Table 13.10   Migrant acceptance lower among religious in US and Canada

	Migrant Acceptance Index
Americans	
Religion important in daily life	7.81
Religion not important in daily life	8.27
Canadians	
Religion important in daily life	8.00
Religion not important in daily life	8.49

Source: Gallup World Poll 2016–17.

The divide in migrant acceptance grows even larger among those who approve of Trump and are religious. The index score for Americans who approve of Trump and say religion is important in their daily lives is 6.97, while the score is 8.61 among those who are not religious and do not approve of Trump.

13.3   CULTURAL NORMS, TRADITIONS AND MIGRANT ACCEPTANCE

At the global level, the closer the degree of personal proximity, the less likely people are to say it is a good thing. A majority worldwide (54 percent) say migrants living in their countries is a good thing. Slightly fewer – but still half, at 50 percent – say a migrant becoming their neighbor is a good thing, and 44 percent say a migrant marrying a close relative is a good thing.

Unique factors – such as cultural norms and traditions – are also at work. Countries in which the gap between the percentages who say migrants living in a country and marrying into their families are good things is particularly wide – at least 19 percentage points or more – largely cluster in Gulf Cooperation Countries, Central Asia, South Asia and North Africa (Table 13.11).

The largest difference among countries is in Turkmenistan, where 67 points separate the percentage who see migrants in their country as a good thing (83 percent) and the percentage who say the same about migrants marrying into their families (16 percent). This largely reflects the favorable attitudes toward foreigners who bring jobs into the country versus the cultural taboo associated with marrying outside of one's ethnic group.

In the United Arab Emirates (UAE), where the gap is second-largest

Table 13.11   Gap in attitudes toward migrants

	Migrants in country a good thing (%)	Migrants marrying relatives a good thing (%)	Difference (pct. pts.)
Turkmenistan	83	16	67
United Arab Emirates	79	31	48
Saudi Arabia	75	38	37
Libya	68	38	30
Senegal	87	57	30
Nepal	77	48	29
Tajikistan	52	24	28
Mauritania	55	27	28
Tunisia	77	51	26
Myanmar	39	14	25
Pakistan	37	12	25
Afghanistan	33	8	25
Egypt	45	21	24
Singapore	54	31	23
Somalia	56	33	23
Kosovo	46	24	22
Uzbekistan	54	32	22
Palestinian Territories	42	20	22
Kuwait	46	25	21
Yemen	38	18	20
Niger	76	57	19
India	53	34	19
Kazakhstan	43	24	19
South Africa	59	40	19

Source: Gallup World Poll 2016–17.

at 48 points, the government encourages Emirati men to marry Emirati women. UAE residents from other Gulf Cooperation Countries and other Islamic countries often must go through the additional step of obtaining the approval of their respective countries to marry.

Smaller Differences Among Countries at Opposite Ends

At the same time, in some of the most accepting and least accepting countries for migrants there is little difference between the percentages who say migrants living in the country and marrying into families are good things. For example, in the most accepting country, Iceland, and in

Table 13.12   Gap in attitudes toward migrants among least and most accepting countries

Gap among least accepting		Gap among most accepting	
North Macedonia	2	Iceland	2
Montenegro	8	New Zealand	2
Hungary	6	Rwanda	6
Serbia	5	Canada	2
Slovakia	0	Sierra Leone	2
Israel	10	Mali	7
Latvia	3	Australia	2
Czech Republic	8	Sweden	2
Estonia	7	United States	2
Croatia	4	Nigeria	10

Note: Difference in the percentage who say migrants in country are a good thing minus percentage who say migrants marrying into their families is a good thing.

Source: Gallup World Poll 2016–17.

the least accepting country, North Macedonia, just two percentage points separate people's attitudes on these two measures. Interestingly, this is also true in the US (Table 13.12).

13.4   MIGRANT ACCEPTANCE RELATED TO SOCIAL CONTACT

Allport's interpersonal contact theory[8] states that direct interpersonal contact with members of minority and other social groups is one of the most effective ways to reduce stereotyping, prejudice and intergroup conflict. By inference, direct interpersonal contact with migrants ought to reduce stereotyping and prejudice against them and ease their transition and integration into the social fabric of their adopted countries.

With immigration taking such a high-profile position around the world, understanding which countries are predisposed to accept or reject migrants can help shed light on where immigration issues are likely to arise. More important, however, is the possibility that simple interpersonal contact with migrants can help moderate potential prejudice and discrimination across national boundaries, cultures and languages.

Testing this relationship in our data, Gallup researchers[9] found that in 134 out of the 139 countries analyzed people scored higher on Gallup's Migrant Acceptance Index if they personally knew at least one migrant.

Worldwide, the index score among people who know a migrant is 6.78 (out of a possible 9.0), while among those who don't personally know a migrant, it is 4.80 (Figure 13.1).

Scores in almost all countries were higher if there was interpersonal contact – which was established by asking people if they personally know a migrant. Just five countries – Afghanistan, Benin, Congo (Brazzaville), Malawi and the United Arab Emirates – did not show evidence of the contact effect.

This effect emerged on six continents, across myriad language groups, and within samples made up of men and women, young and old, rich and poor, and educated and uneducated alike. Although these data do not allow us to determine the causal direction of the observed effects, it is likely that the effect works in both directions, as other researchers have demonstrated, but with the stronger effect moving from contact to attitudes.

Acceptance of Migrants Rises the More People Interact with Each Other

People's acceptance of migrants also depends on the way they live their lives. For example, the more social people are, the higher their scores are on Gallup's Migrant Acceptance Index. At the global level, the index score for people who interact with their friends more than ten times in a typical week is 5.82 (out of a possible 9.0), while the score for those who interact with their friends once or not at all is 4.82 (Table 13.13).

The tendency for more social people to be more accepting of migrants holds in all regions of the world where Gallup asks these questions, but in some regions the gap is even wider. In the European Union, for example, the index score for those who typically interact with friends more than ten times in a given week is 6.72, while it is 3.66 among those who interact once or not at all.

At the global level, younger generations are the most accepting of migrants, while older people are less accepting. But within each age group index scores typically rise with the number of social interactions people have. In fact, among the traditionalists the number of social interactions has even more of a positive effect than it does among younger cohorts.

13.5   ACCEPTING MIGRANTS AND LINKS TO EMOTIONAL EXPERIENCES

Gallup's data measure multiple dimensions of wellbeing, capturing people's day-to-day emotional states – such as enjoyment, stress or anger – as well

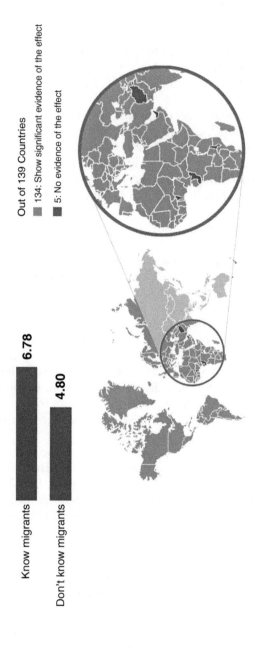

Migrant Acceptance Index Is Higher Among Those Who Know Migrants

Do you, personally, know any immigrants living in your country?

Know migrants **6.78**

Don't know migrants **4.80**

Out of 139 Countries

134: Show significant evidence of the effect

5: No evidence of the effect

Source: Gallup World Poll.

Figure 13.1 Migrant Acceptance Index

Table 13.13   Migrant Acceptance Index increases with social interaction

	World Index score	EU countries Index score
0–1 interactions	4.82	3.66
2–5 interactions	4.99	5.33
6–10 interactions	5.41	6.33
11+ interactions	5.82	6.72

Note: Number of interactions with friends in a typical week. Based on surveys conducted in 138 countries in 2016; question about social interaction not asked in US.

Source: Gallup World Poll 2016–17.

as their satisfaction with their lives. People's Migrant Acceptance Index scores are related to both.

People's Migrant Acceptance Index scores are related to their positive and negative daily experiences – their experiential wellbeing. Gallup asks people if they felt a lot of enjoyment, smiled or laughed a lot, felt well rested, felt treated with respect, or learned or did something interesting the day before the survey. The more positive daily experiences people have, the more accepting they are of migrants.

Negative experiences have the opposite effect. Migrant Acceptance Index scores decrease with each negative experience – worry, stress, anger, physical pain, sadness – that people say they felt the previous day. However, the differences are less dramatic than they are with positive experiences.

These relationships hold in nearly every part of the world, but the emotional gaps vary by region. Gaps between those experiencing no positive emotions and five positive emotions are widest in regions that have been most affected during the recent migrant crisis (including the European Union), in other regions grappling with migration-related issues (such as the Gulf Cooperation Council countries) and in Oceania (Table 13.14).

Whether People Accept Migrants Relates to How They Rate Their Own Lives

People's acceptance of migrants also depends on how they see their own lives in general. People's life evaluations are highly related to income, which is also related to Migrant Acceptance Index scores, so it is not that surprising that those who see their lives at the top – thriving – are more likely to accept migrants.

Table 13.14   Migrant Acceptance Index, by daily experiences

	World Index score	EU countries Index score
Number of positive daily experiences		
0	4.02	3.49
1	4.31	4.46
2	4.65	5.33
3	4.94	5.53
4	5.38	6.13
5	5.75	6.67
Number of negative daily experiences		
0	5.27	6.11
1	5.38	6.40
2	5.13	5.74
3	4.90	5.30
4	4.91	4.83
5	4.94	4.66

Note: Based on surveys conducted in 138 countries in 2016; questions about experiences not asked in US.

Source: Gallup World Poll 2016–17.

For the past decade, Gallup has asked adults worldwide to evaluate their lives on the Cantril Self-Anchoring Striving Scale, where '0' represents the worst possible life and '10' represents the best possible life. Gallup classifies people as 'thriving' if they rate their current lives a 7 or higher and their lives in five years an 8 or higher, and 'suffering' if they rate both their current and future life situations a 4 or lower. Those in the middle are 'struggling'.

Globally, the Migrant Acceptance Index score for those who rate their current and future lives positively enough to be considered 'thriving' is 5.78. The score for those who rate their current and future lives poorly enough to be considered 'suffering' is 4.67 (Table 13.15). However, the gap in the scores between those who are thriving and suffering varies from region to region. The biggest gaps are in many of the regions that have been most affected in the recent migrant crisis.

In the CIS, the region with the lowest Migrant Acceptance Index scores in the world, people's acceptance of migrants does not change regardless of education or income – which does not follow the global trend. However, in the CIS the relationship between people's life evaluations and migrant acceptance is the same as it is in the rest of the world.

Table 13.15   Migrant Acceptance Index, by life evaluation

	World Index score	EU countries Index score
Thriving	5.78	6.74
Struggling	5.23	5.83
Suffering	4.67	3.98

Note: Based on surveys conducted in 138 countries in 2016; questions about life evaluations not asked in US.

Source: Gallup World Poll 2016–17.

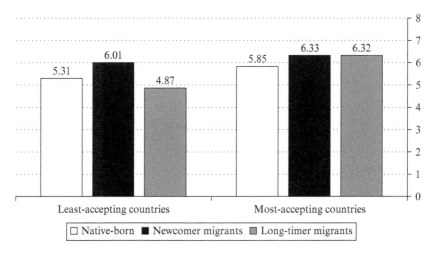

Source: Gallup World Poll 2016–17.

Figure 13.2   Current life evaluations by Migrant Acceptance Index

Migrants' Happiness Tied to Whether They Are Accepted

People's acceptance of migrants – or the lack thereof – is linked to how migrants themselves rate their own life satisfaction. The findings show that migrants living in countries scoring lowest on Gallup's Migrant Acceptance Index evaluate their lives less positively than those who live in countries that are the most accepting of migrants (Figure 13.2).

In the least accepting countries, migrants who have been in their new countries for less than five years – newcomers – rate their current lives more positively than the native-born. But this positivity fades the longer migrants stay in countries where the population is not receptive to them. The life evaluations of those who have been in the country five years or more – long-timers – are statistically much lower than the scores for newcomers, but their life evaluations also drop lower than the scores for the native-born.

In the most accepting countries the story changes. Newcomer migrants and long-time migrants both rate their lives higher than the native-born do. Further, migrants do not lose their positive outlook the longer they stay: the life evaluations of newcomers and long-timers are statistically the same.

Life in the Future

Migrants and the native-born in the least accepting countries rate their future lives *in five years* better than their present situations, but they still lag far behind their counterparts in the most accepting countries. Newcomers in the least accepting countries have a more positive outlook for their lives than the native-born do, but long-timers again are more pessimistic than either group (Figure 13.3).

In the most accepting countries, the native-born and newcomer migrants share the same level of optimism about their lives in five years, but long-timers give their future lives higher ratings than the native-born or newcomers do.

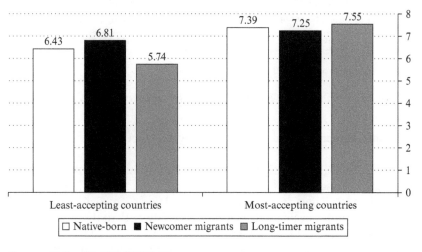

Source: Gallup World Poll 2016–17.

Figure 13.3   Future life evaluations by Migrant Acceptance Index

13.6   MIGRANT EMPLOYMENT AND MIGRANT ACCEPTANCE

Gallup classifies respondents based on their answers to several questions about employment. Among those in the workforce, Gallup's employment metrics allow for a calculation of the percentage of migrants and the native-born[10] working full time for an employer, the percentage who are unemployed, and the percentage who are underemployed.

Employed Full Time By an Employer

The Gallup Employed Full Time for an Employer Index measures the percentage of the workforce that is employed full time by an employer. A person is classified as employed by an employer if he or she works at least 30 hours per week for an employer.

Unemployment

The Gallup Unemployment Rate is the percentage of unemployed adults who actively looked for work within the preceding four weeks and could have begun to work in that time frame. Gallup's unemployment measure is comparable to the Bureau of Labor Statistics and the International Labour Organization unemployment calculations.

Underemployment

The Gallup Underemployment Index measures the percentage of adults in the workforce who are working at less than the desired capacity. People are classified as 'underemployed' if they are employed part time but want to work full time or if they are unemployed but want to be working.

In our previous research on migrant wellbeing in 2013[11] we found that migrants in high-income countries were more likely to be unemployed and underemployed than their counterparts among the native-born population in their countries. The present analysis focuses on employment status using the most recent data available.

In general, based on the analysis of data collected between 2016 and 2018, Gallup finds that the majority of migrants worldwide are part of the labor force in their adopted countries, but they tend to be more likely than the native-born to be underemployed or unemployed – but this is really only true because of patterns in high-income countries.[12] In low-income to middle-income countries migrants tend to be just as likely as the native-born to be underemployed or unemployed.

In low- to middle-income countries there are few statistically significant differences between migrants and the native-born when we looked through the lens of migrant acceptance.

However, in the least accepting high-income countries, migrants were less likely than the native-born to be employed full time for an employer and more likely to be underemployed and unemployed than the native-born. Further, in the most accepting high-income countries, these differences between the native-born and migrants shrink considerably (Table 13.16).

This suggests that migrants in the least accepting high-income countries are not reaping the employment bonuses that migrants in the most accepting high-income countries are. In fact, they have an employment deficit.

Table 13.16   Employment among migrants and the native-born, by development and Migrant Acceptance Index

	Native-born (%)	Migrants (%)
Low- to middle-income countries		
Least accepting countries		
Labor Force Participation Index*	58	56
Employed Full Time for an Employer Index	46	52
Underemployment Index	17	19
Unemployment Index	8	11
Most accepting countries		
Labor Force Participation Index*	63	66
Employed Full Time for an Employer Index	25	24
Underemployment Index	28	33
Unemployment Index	11	11
High-income countries		
Least accepting countries		
Labor Force Participation Index*	59	68
Employed Full Time for an Employer Index	75	61
Underemployment Index	10	26
Unemployment Index	6	16
Most accepting countries		
Labor Force Participation Index*	66	67
Employed Full Time for an Employer Index	62	54
Underemployment Index	15	24
Unemployment Index	6	9

Note: * Based on total population. All other employment metrics are based on workforce.

Source: Gallup World Poll 2016–17.

At the same time it is important to acknowledge that gaps remain between the native-born and migrants even in the most accepting countries, so the employment situation is better in these countries, but it is still worse than that of the native-born.

These patterns are important because they probably have a bearing on the wellbeing of these migrants that warrants further investigation. For nearly a decade Gallup's global surveys have consistently shown that people with 'good jobs' (defined as those who are formally employed full time by an employer) tend to have the highest wellbeing of those in the workforce.

13.7   SUMMARY

Gallup's analysis of the results from its inaugural Migrant Acceptance Index offers a glimpse into how different migrants' lives are – and how different they could be – when the people around them accept them. But in addition to that, the analysis suggests that life is better for *everyone* in countries where acceptance is high – regardless of development – and worse in countries where it is low.

While making no inferences about causality, we do see that migrants, as well as the native-born living in countries that are the least accepting of migrants, evaluate their lives less positively than those who live in countries that are the most accepting. And the more positive daily experiences people have, the more accepting they are of migrants. Although the differences are less dramatic, the opposite is also true. Migrant acceptance decreases with each negative experience that people have.

If countries want to maximize the positive contributions that migrants can make to sustainable development, and foster inclusive societies, they need to understand the emotional component as well as the economic one. This is because other Gallup research shows that improving and sustaining high wellbeing is vital to any population's overall health and to its economy.

High wellbeing closely relates to key health outcomes such as lower rates of healthcare utilization, workplace absenteeism, workplace performance and the new occurrence of chronic diseases. It's also a predictor of employee engagement, customer engagement, turnover and workplace safety – all factors that can affect a country's ability to reach its economic potential.

13.8   METHODOLOGY

These results are based on telephone and face-to-face interviews with approximately 1000 adults, aged 15 and older, conducted throughout

2016 in 138 countries and in 2017 in the US. In some countries, such as India, Russia and China, the sample sizes are much larger, between 2000 and 4000 adults. For results based on the total sample of national adults, the margin of sampling error ranges from ±2.1 percentage points to ±5.6 percentage points at the 95 percent confidence level. All reported margins of sampling error include computed design effects for weighting.

Employment results are based on Gallup World Poll data collected from 2016 to 2018, which included responses from a total of 392 922 native-born residents and 23 675 migrants.

NOTES

1. Neli Esipova, Dr. Anita Pugliese, Dr. John Fleming and Julie Ray.
2. Esipova and Ray (2017).
3. Some of the data and analysis included in this chapter have been previously released via Gallup's website. Those instances are noted throughout the chapter.
4. Gallup's World Poll continually surveys residents in more than 150 countries, representing more than 99 percent of the world's adult population, using randomly selected, nationally representative samples. Gallup typically surveys 1000 individuals in each country, using a standard set of core questions that has been translated into the major languages of the respective country. In some regions, supplemental questions are asked in addition to core questions. Face-to-face interviews take approximately one hour, while telephone interviews take about 30 minutes. In many countries the survey is conducted once per year, and fieldwork is generally completed in two to four weeks.
5. Esipova et al. (2018b).
6. Gallup collects self-reported annual per capita income figures from each respondent and assigns each respondent to one of the five income categories, based on the respondent's position in the income distribution of the country. Gallup divides each country sample into quintiles by annual per capita income. This measure of income indicates how well a person is doing financially in comparison with other people in the country where he or she currently lives.
7. Esipova et al. (2018a).
8. Allport (1954).
9. Fleming et al. (2018).
10. Data are adjusted with regard to age, sex and education to allow for fairer comparisons between migrants' situations with those of other populations, such as the native-born.
11. International Organization for Migration (2013).
12. High-income and low- and middle-income groups are based on World Bank country classifications.

REFERENCES

Allport, G. W. (1954), *The Nature of Prejudice*. Cambridge, MA: Perseus Books.
Esipova, N., A. Pugliese and J. Ray (2018a), Migrant acceptance in Canada, U.S. follows political lines. Gallup, April. Retrieved from: https://news.gallup.com/poll/233147/migrant-acceptance-canada-follows-political-lines.aspx.
Esipova, N., A. Pugliese and J. Ray (2018b), Revisiting the most- and least-accepting

countries for migrants. Gallup, December. Retrieved from: https://news.gallup.com/opinion/gallup/245528/revisiting-least-accepting-countries-migrants.aspx.

Esipova, N. and J. Ray (2017), Syrian refugees not welcome in Eastern Europe. Gallup, May. Retrieved from: https://news.gallup.com/poll/209828/syrian-refugees-not-welcome-eastern-europe.aspx.

Fleming, J., N. Esipova, A. Pugliese, J. Ray and R. Srinivasan (2018), DATA-SURVEY: Migrant Acceptance Index: a global examination of the relationship between interpersonal contact and attitudes toward migrants. *Border Crossings*, 8(1). Retrieved from: https://journal.tplondon.com/index.php/bc/article/view/1107.

International Organization for Migration (2013), *World Migration Report 2013: Migrant Well-Being and Development*. Paris: IOM.

Index

absolute income 95
activity(ies)
  defined 49
  virtuous 49–50
adaptation 6, 18, 56, 119, 150, 218
addiction, concept of 31
  manifestation of heightened craving
    and weakened goal orientation
    36
  -related research 35
addiction disorder 37
adult-onset depression 37
adult psychopathologies 41
Alaimo, Leonardo Salvatore 11,
    113–27
Alberti, Leon Battista 69–70, 79
amoral familism 70, 83
anticipation of reward 35
anxiety 37, 40–41, 134, 155, 190,
    193–4
Aquinas, Thomas 6, 11, 79
  beatitude for 98
  characterizes virtue as good quality
    of mind 100
  commercial transaction 105
  contribution to common good 105
  fellowship of friends 99
  friendship, notion of 98–9, 106–7
    types of 103
  goods, categories of 103
  human inclinations 103
  John Duns Scotus intellectual rivalry
    with 106
  love as the principle of movement
    98–9
  love, classification of
    love of concupiscence 108
    love of friendship 108
  mutual assistance 100–104, 106
  natural and artificial wealth,
    distinction between 104

notion of happiness 96–9, 106
  types of 101
rational choice model of economics
  104
seller and buyer, relationship
  between 105
subvenio term employed by 104
Summa Theologiae 100, 102, 104
  on virtues 100–103, 105
  on wage market 105–6
  on wealth 96, 98, 103–6
Aristotelian–Tomistic tradition 70
Aristotle 35–6, 60, 96–7, 99, 102–3, 115
  acceptance of habit 100
  approach to happiness 5–6
  behavior guided by irrational or
    rational desires 32–3
  category of actions guided by
    epithumia 33
  desire (orexis), types of
    for eudaimonia 31
    led by anger or threat 31
    for pleasure 31
  divided psyche 37
  emphasis on moderation 30
  on human nature 58–9
  human souls both sensitive and
    rational faculty 31
  judgement on man 30
  new synthesis of 40–44
  Nicomachean Ethics 47, 51
  observance on presence of
    instrumentality 50
  observation on appetitive pleasures
    37
  on passion 31
  on phronesis 30–32
  on pleasures 31
  rational desires 34
  rational faculty 36
  rejects life of asceticism 31